# Second Workshop on Computational Approaches to Discourse (CODI 2021)



Punta Cana, Dominican Republic and Online
10-11 November 2021

ISBN: 978-1-7138-9184-0

**Printed from e-media with permission by:**

Curran Associates, Inc.
57 Morehouse Lane
Red Hook, NY 12571

**Some format issues inherent in the e-media version may also appear in this print version.**



Printed with permission by Curran Associates, Inc. (2024)



Association for Computational Linguistics
209 N. Eighth Street
Stroudsburg, Pennsylvania 18360

Phone: 1-570-476-8006
Fax: 1-570-476-0860

acl@aclweb.org

**Additional copies of this publication are available from:**

Curran Associates, Inc.
57 Morehouse Lane
Red Hook, NY 12571 USA
Phone: 845-758-0400
Fax: 845-758-2633
Email: curran@proceedings.com
Web: www.proceedings.com

EMNLP 2021

# The Second Workshop on Computational Approaches to Discourse

## Proceedings of the Workshop

November 10 - 11, 2021

**Acknowledgements**

Christian Hardmeier was supported by the Swedish Research Council under grant 2017-930.

# Preface

Welcome to the 2nd Workshop on Computational Approaches to Discourse, CODI 2021! CODI is intended to provide a venue for researchers working on all aspects of discourse. Our aim is to provide a venue for the entire discourse processing community where we can present and exchange our theories, algorithms, software, datasets, and tools.

The workshop consists of invited talks, contributed paper and demo presentations, and discussion sessions. We received paper submissions that span a wide range of topics, addressing issues related to discourse representation and parsing, anaphora and coreference resolution, dialogue, applications, and more. As the workshop is hybrid this year, papers are presented live either in person or remotely and discussed during live Q&A sessions. There will also be prerecorded videos available.

We are happy that CODI 2021 features two shared tasks. The CODI-CRAC 2021 shared task on anaphora, bridging, and discourse deixis resolution in dialogue is a joint shared task between the CODI and CRAC workshops at EMNLP. This shared task goes beyond previous ones as its input is transcribed spoken dialogue, and in that it includes anaphoric relations beyond coreference. This effort is spearheaded by Carolyn Rosé. The DISRPT 2021 shared task continues a series of successful DISRPT shared tasks on discourse segmentation, relation classification and connective detection. The organization team is led by Amir Zeldes. As we hope that the next CODI workshops will also feature shared tasks and other special events, the workshop also includes a discussion on future shared tasks, special sessions on discourse representation and parsing, coreference resolution, and multilingual discourse processing.

We thank our invited speakers, **Jackie Chi Kit Cheung**, McGill University, who works on language understanding and question answering in context, and **Vera Demberg**, Saarland University, who works on computational and cognitive models of text generation and understanding. We would also like to thank our reviewers for their thoughtful and instructive comments. They helped us to prepare an inclusive workshop program. Finally we would like to thank the EMNLP 2021 workshop chairs Parisa Kordjamshidi and Minlie Huang who organized the EMNLP workshop program under very challenging circumstances.

The CODI Organizers,

Chloé Braud, Christian Hardmeier, Junyi Jessy Li, Annie Louis, Michael Strube, and Amir Zeldes

**Organizers:**

Chloé Braud, CNRS - IRIT
Christian Hardmeier, University of Edinburgh and Uppsala University
Junyi Jessy Li, The University of Texas at Austin
Annie Louis, Google
Michael Strube, Heidelberg Institute for Theoretical Studies
Amir Zeldes, Georgetown University

**Program Committee:**

Carenini, Guiseppe, University of British Columbia, Canada
Cheung, Jackie Chi Kit, McGill University, Canada
Demberg, Vera, Saarland University, Germany
Denis, Pascal, INRIA, France
Dipper, Stefanie, University of Bochum, Germany
Gong, Zhengxian, Soochow University, China
Ferracane, Elisa, University of Texas at Austin, US
Grishina, Yulia, Amazon (Berlin), Germany
Inui, Kentaro, Tohuku University, Japan
Ji, Yangfeng, University of Virginia, US
Kurfalı, Murathan, Stockholm University, Sweden
Kurohashi, Sadao, Kyoto University, Japan
Lapshinova-Koltunski, Ekaterina, Saarland University, Germany
Loáiciga, Sharid, University of Potsdam, Germany
Liu, Qun, Huawei, China
Muller, Philippe, Université Paul Sabatier, France
Müller, Mark-Christoph, HITS gGmbH, Germany
Ng, Vincent, University of Texas at Dallas, US
Ogrodniczuk, Maciej, Warsaw University, Poland
Poesio, Massimo, Queen Mary University of London, UK
Rutherford, Attapol Te, Chulalongkorn University, Thailand
Webber, Bonnie, University of Edinburgh, UK
Xiong, Deyi, Tianjin University, China
Zinsmeister, Heike, Hamburg University, Germany

**Invited Speakers:**

Jackie Chi Kit Cheung, McGill University, Canada
Vera Demberg, Saarland University, Germany

# Table of Contents

# Conference Program

**Nov. 10, 2021**

**09:00–12:00 CODI-CRAC Shared Task**

**09:05–09:30 *Welcome***

09:05–09:30 *The CODI-CRAC 2021 Shared Task on Anaphora, Bridging, and Discourse Deixis in Dialogue*
Sopan Khosla, Juntao Yu, Ramesh Manuvinakurike, Vincent Ng, Massimo Poesio, Michael Strube and Carolyn Rosé

09:30–09:45 *Neural Anaphora Resolution in Dialogues*
Hideo Kobayashi, Shengjie Li and Vincent Ng

09:45–10:00 *Anaphora Resolution in Dialogue: Description of the DFKI-TalkingRobots System for the CODI-CRAC 2021 Shared-Task*
Tatiana Anikina, Cennet Oguz, Natalia Skachkova, Siyu Tao, Sharmila Upadhyaya and Ivana Kruijff-Korbayova

10:00–10:15 *The Pipeline Model for Resolution of Anaphoric Reference and Resolution of Entity Reference*
Hongjin Kim, Damrin Kim and Harksoo Kim

10:15–10:30 *An End-to-End Approach for Full Bridging Resolution*
Joseph Renner, Priyansh Trivedi, Gaurav Maheshwari, Rémi Gilleron and Pascal Denis

**10:30–11:00 *Coffee Break***

11:00–11:15 *Adapted End-to-End Coreference Resolution System for Anaphoric Identities in Dialogues*
Liyan Xu and Jinho D. D. Choi

11:15–11:30 *Anaphora Resolution in Dialogue: Cross-Team Analysis of the DFKI-TalkingRobots Team Submissions for the CODI-CRAC 2021 Shared-Task*
Natalia Skachkova, Cennet Oguz, Tatiana Anikina, Siyu Tao, Sharmila Upadhyaya and Ivana Kruijff-Korbayova

11:30–11:45 *The CODI-CRAC 2021 Shared Task on Anaphora, Bridging, and Discourse Deixis Resolution in Dialogue: A Cross-Team Analysis*
Shengjie Li, Hideo Kobayashi, and Vincent Ng

**Nov. 10, 2021 (continued)**

**11:45–12:00** ***Visioning Discussion and Next Steps***

**12:00–13:30** ***Lunch Break***

**13:30–14:30** **Invited Talk**
*Keeping Track of Entities Over Time, Minds, and Knowledge Sources*
Jackie Chi Kit Cheung

**14:30–14:45** ***Mini Break***

**14:45–15:45** **Pragmatics and Applications**

14:45–15:00 *"I'll be there for you": The One with Understanding Indirect Answers*
Cathrine Damgaard, Paulina Toborek, Trine Eriksen and Barbara Plank

15:00–15:10 *Improving Text Generation via Neural Discourse Planning*
Alexander Chernyavskiy and Dmitry Ilvovsky

15:10–15:25 *Developing Conversational Data and Detection of Conversational Humor in Telugu*
Vaishnavi Pamulapati and Radhika Mamidi

15:25–15:35 *Investigating non lexical markers of the language of schizophrenia in spontaneous conversations*
Chuyuan Li, Maxime Amblard, Chloé Braud, Caroline Demily, Nicolas Franck and Michel Musiol

15:35–15:45 *Discourse-Driven Integrated Dialogue Development Environment for Open-Domain Dialogue Systems*
Denis Kuznetsov, Dmitry Evseev, Lidia Ostyakova, Oleg Serikov, Daniel Kornev and Mikhail Burtsev

**Nov. 10, 2021 (continued)**

**15:50–16:15 Anaphora and Coreference**

15:50–16:00 *Coreference Chains Categorization by Sequence Clustering*
Silvia Federzoni, Lydia-Mai Ho-Dac and Cécile Fabre

16:00–16:15 *Resolving Implicit References in Instructional Texts*
Talita Anthonio and Michael Roth

**16:15–16:45 *Coffee Break***

**16:45–18:15 Discourse Relations**

16:45–17:00 *A practical perspective on connective generation*
Frances Yung, Merel Scholman and Vera Demberg

17:00–17:15 *Semi-automatic discourse annotation in a low-resource language: Developing a connective lexicon for Nigerian Pidgin*
Marian Marchal, Merel Scholman and Vera Demberg

17:15–17:30 *Comparison of methods for explicit discourse connective identification across various domains*
Merel Scholman, Tianai Dong, Frances Yung and Vera Demberg

17:30–17:40 *A Novel Corpus of Discourse Structure in Humans and Computers*
Babak Hemmatian, Sheridan Feucht, Rachel Avram, Alexander Wey, Muskaan Garg, Kate Spitalnic, Carsten Eickhoff, Ellie Pavlick, Bjorn Sandstede and Steven A. Sloman

17:40–17:55 *Revisiting Shallow Discourse Parsing in the PDTB-3: Handling Intra-sentential Implicits*
Zheng Zhao and Bonnie Webber

17:55–18:05 *Improving Multi-Party Dialogue Discourse Parsing via Domain Integration*
Zhengyuan Liu and Nancy Chen

18:05–18:15 *discopy: A Neural System for Shallow Discourse Parsing*
René Knaebel

**Nov. 11, 2021**

09:00–10:00 **Invited Talk**
*Inter annotator agreement in discourse annotation – the role of domain knowledge and individual differences*
Vera Demberg

**10:25–11:15 Discourse and Multilinguality**

10:25–10:35 *Tracing variation in discourse connectives in translation and interpreting through neural semantic spaces*
Ekaterina Lapshinova-Koltunski, Heike Przybyl and Yuri Bizzoni

10:35–10:50 *Capturing document context inside sentence-level neural machine translation models with self-training*
Elman Mansimov, Gábor Melis and Lei Yu

10:50–11:05 *DMRST: A Joint Framework for Document-Level Multilingual RST Discourse Segmentation and Parsing*
Zhengyuan Liu, Ke Shi and Nancy Chen

11:05–11:15 *Visualizing Cross-Lingual Discourse Relations in Multilingual TED Corpora*
Zae Myung Kim, Vassilina Nikoulina, Dongyeop Kang, Didier Schwab and Laurent Besacier

**11:15–12:00 Discussion and Closing of Main CODI Workshop**

**12:00–13:30** ***Lunch Break***

**Nov. 11, 2021 (continued)**

**13:30–15:30 DISRPT 2021 Shared Task Session 1**

13:30–13:45 *The DISRPT 2021 Shared Task on Elementary Discourse Unit Segmentation, Connective Detection, and Relation Classification*
Amir Zeldes, Yang Janet Liu, Mikel Iruskieta, Philippe Muller, Chloé Braud and Sonia Badene

13:50–14:20 *A Transformer Based Approach towards Identification of Discourse Unit Segments and Connectives*
Sahil Bakshi and Dipti Misra Sharma

14:20–14:50 *Multi-lingual Discourse Segmentation and Connective Identification: MELODI at DISRPT2021*
Morteza Ezzabady, Philippe Muller, and Chloé Braud

14:50–15:20 *Delexicalised Multilingual Discourse Segmentation for DISRPT 2021 and Tense, Mood, Voice and Modality Tagging for 11 Languages*
Tillmann D́onicke

**15:30–16:00 *Coffee Break***

**16:00–17:30 DISRPT 2021 Shared Task Session 2**

16:00–16:30 *A Unified Approach to Discourse Relation Classification in nine Languages*
Hanna Varachkina and Franziska Pannach

16:30–17:00 *DisCoDisCo at the DISRPT2021 Shared Task: A System for Discourse Segmentation, Classification, and Connective Detection*
Luke Gessler, Shabnam Behzad, Yang Janet Liu, Siyao Peng, Yilun Zhu, Amir Zeldes

**17:00–17:15 *Closing Remarks***

# "I'll be there for you": The One with Understanding Indirect Answers

**Cathrine Damgaard,**♡ **Paulina Toborek,**♡ **Trine Eriksen**♡ and **Barbara Plank**
Department of Computer Science
IT University of Copenhagen
{catd, pato, trer, bapl}@itu.dk

## Abstract

Indirect answers are replies to polar questions without the direct use of word cues such as 'yes' and 'no'. Humans are very good at understanding indirect answers, such as 'I gotta go home sometime', when asked 'You wanna crash on the couch?'. Understanding indirect answers is a challenging problem for dialogue systems. In this paper, we introduce a new English corpus to study the problem of understanding indirect answers. Instead of crowdsourcing both polar questions and answers, we collect questions and indirect answers from transcripts of a prominent TV series and manually annotate them for answer type. The resulting dataset contains 5,930 question-answer pairs. We release both aggregated and raw human annotations. We present a set of experiments in which we evaluate Convolutional Neural Networks (CNNs) for this task, including a cross-dataset evaluation and experiments with learning from disagreements in annotation. Our results show that the task of interpreting indirect answers remains challenging, yet we obtain encouraging improvements when explicitly modeling human disagreement.

## 1 Introduction

Humans are very good at interpreting indirect answers to polar questions. In conversations, even if direct answers are possible, humans often prefer indirect answers due to cooperativeness and to advance the dialogue (Stenström, 1984). For dialogue systems and Natural Language Processing (NLP) more generally, however, interpreting indirect answers remains a challenge (Clark et al., 2019). Recent seminal work introduced CIRCA, a new large-scale dataset containing pairs of polar questions and indirect answers in English (Louis et al., 2020). This allows for data-driven experiments in this question-answering domain.

♡The authors contributed equally to this work.

| |
|---|
| **Q:** Hey. Everything ok?<br>**A:** I'm just mad at my agent.<br>**L:** NO, NO, YES |
| **Q:** Are you back from Minsk?<br>**A:** Well, just for a couple of days.<br>**L:** YES, NO, YES, SUBJECT TO SOME CONDITIONS |

Table 1: Examples from the dataset with polar question (Q), indirect answer (A) and annotator labels (L).

Understanding indirect answers is a pragmatic problem, and even though humans typically have little difficulty in interpreting indirect answers, they may not all agree on a possible interpretation. Work on learning from human disagreement has shown that incorporating disagreement from human annotation is not only noise, but can provide valuable information (Plank et al., 2014; Aroyo and Welty, 2015; Rodrigues and Pereira, 2018).

Motivated by these two lines of research, we propose a new dataset for studying indirect answers. We provide both aggregated (ground truth/gold) annotations and the raw annotations. This allows us to study the effect of learning to integrate human disagreement into understanding indirect answers. Our dataset, called FRIENDS-QIA, was created by collecting question and answer pairs from transcripts of a popular TV series. The data collection differs in comparison to the recently introduced CIRCA corpus. In their study, a set of 10 dialogue prompts were defined, and both questions and answers were collected by crowdsourcing (Louis et al., 2020). Following this step, the annotation was crowdsourced again, resulting in a set of labels which was later conflated into a relaxed set of six classes. Instead, we opted to collect the data from transcripts and manually annotate the question-answer pairs in house (by three of the authors of this paper, all highly proficient in English). Examples from our dataset are provided in Table 1. A data statement is provided in Appendix A.



*Proceedings of the 2nd Workshop on Computational Approaches to Discourse*, pages 1–11
November 10–11, 2021. 

**Contributions** In this paper, we a) introduce a new dataset, FRIENDS-QIA, with 5,930 polar question-indirect answer pairs in English;[1] b) study the effectiveness of neural classifiers based on Convolutional Neural Networks, both with traditional pre-trained word embeddings and contextualized BERT embeddings; c) provide results on cross-dataset evaluation, for which we train a model on both CIRCA and FRIENDS-QIA; and d) show that modeling human disagreement via deep learning from crowds is beneficial for this task.

## 2 Related Work

The task of understanding indirect answers in Natural Language Processing is relatively new and has not been attempted by many yet. To enable progress on the task, Louis et al. (2020) created and released the first large-scale English language corpus, CIRCA, consisting of 34,268 polar questions and their corresponding indirect answers. The difficulty of interpreting indirect answers is, however, widely studied in some early papers, (e.g. Green and Carberry, 1992, 1999). Following this work, de Marneffe et al. (2009) propose a logical inference model with probabilistic methods. They realize the influence of discourse conditions as well as the difference between the literal meaning of the answer and the interpretation by the two speakers. Hockey et al. (1997) further underline the complexity of interpreting indirect answers to polar questions. They explore the existing Edinburgh map task corpus (Thompson et al., 1993) which consists of two-person dialogues already coded for dialogue structure. Clark et al. (2019) recently also explore the understanding of indirect answers and report on the difficulty of the task. They create a new dataset, BOOLQ, by combining search queries from the Google search engine as questions and passages on Wikipedia pages as answers. They attempt to classify such indirect answers by training BERT-based neural models. Louis et al. (2020) further experiment with training BERT models from scratch and by transfer learning from BOOLQ, building on top of Clark et al. (2019). Their newly created dataset, CIRCA, includes 10 question prompt types, spanning a wide variety of communication situations. Their study shows promising results, and inspired our work.

Preparing a dataset for classification tasks often requires collecting labels from multiple annotators. A unanimous gold standard label cannot always be clearly achieved (e.g. Aroyo and Welty, 2015; Rodrigues et al., 2013; Palomaki et al., 2018; Pavlick and Kwiatkowski, 2019). The problem of learning from multiple annotators has become more important and several attempts have been made to deal with biases present in such data. Yan et al. (2014) look into different levels of expertise among annotators and how a model can learn from this, taking into consideration the biases present while labeling the dataset. By measuring the inter-annotator agreement and incorporating the annotator uncertainty in model training, Plank et al. (2014) show that modelling annotator disagreement can be useful even in cases of seemingly more objective annotation tasks, like part-of-speech tagging. An interesting and similar approach was suggested by Rodrigues and Pereira (2018). Their method, deep learning from crowds (DLFC), adds a crowd layer on top of a neural network which takes advantage of the reliability and bias from different annotators. It assumes access to the raw annotations from the training data. This is in contrast to the weighting approach proposed by Plank et al. (2014), who integrate aggregated disagreement from a sample. As we have the full data available with multiple annotations in FRIENDS-QIA, we here experiment with the deep learning from crowds (DLFC) approach proposed by Rodrigues and Pereira (2018). The key idea is to train a model directly from the noisy annotator-specific annotations modeled as additional per-annotator auxiliary tasks on top of the gold distribution. By using backpropagation and creating annotator-specific weights in the crowd layer, it allows us to include the label bias in the model's learning. There is emerging interest in learning from disagreement, and we refer the reader to a recent survey on this topic (Uma et al., 2021).

## 3 FRIENDS-QIA Corpus

We introduce a new corpus called FRIENDS-QIA for studying indirect answers. The three steps involved in corpus construction are: data collection, data preprocessing and data annotation.

Instead of crowdsourcing the data collection as done by Louis et al. (2020), we attempt to exploit already existing data by simply looking for useful question-answer (QA) pairs in dialogues. We use the existing transcriptions of the American televi-

[1] FRIENDS-QIA is available at: `https://github.com/friendsQIA/Friends_QIA`.

| 1: Yes | 2: No | 3: Yes, subject to some conditions |
|---|---|---|
| **Monica:** You still work at the multiplex? **Chip:** Oh, like I'd give up that job! Free popcorn and candy, anytime I want. I can get you free posters for your room. | **Monica:** He is right, isn't he? **Chandler:** Y'know what, I think this might be one of the times he's wrong. | **Joey:** Now if a cow should die of natural causes, I can have one of those right? **Phoebe:** Not if I get there first. |
| 4: Neither yes nor no | 5: Other | 6: N/A |
| **Phoebe:** Okay—ooh, but are you going to have time to read it? **Rachel:** Oh, I read that in high school. | **Monica:** I need more swordfish. Can you get me some more swordfish? **Kitchen Worker:** I don't speak English. | **Joey:** You know more than one Fun Bobby? **Chandler:** I happen to know a Fun Bob. |

Table 2: Examples of QA pairs from FRIENDS-QIA for each of the 6 labels.

sion sitcom "Friends".[2] This data provides rich dialogues from conversations covering regular, everyday topics. FRIENDS-QIA includes 10 seasons consisting of 17–25 episodes each. This sums to a total of 228 episodes of the TV series. The full dataset, including metadata, is described in Appendix C.

### 3.1 Data Collection

To collect the QA pairs we manually scan all episodes of "Friends" for polar questions and retrieve both the question and the answer as well as which character said each of the two. A few examples are listed below.

**Example 3.1**
***Joey:*** *Hey Pheebs, you wanna help?*
***Phoebe:*** *Oh, I wish I could, but I don't want to.*

**Example 3.2**
***Rachel:*** *Hey! So, did you quit?*
***Chandler:*** *No, I almost did, couldn't leave Ross there without a spotter!*

**Example 3.3**
***Joey:*** *(intrigued) Really?*
***Mr. Treeger:*** *Yeah, you could dance real good with her, she's the same size as me.*

As the examples show, some answers directly give away cues (e.g., Example 3.2 starts with a "No,"). We preprocess the data manually, to obfuscate direct cues and enrich short questions with information from the context, to keep the setup similar to prior work and model single question-answer pairs. The data preprocessing motivation and details are outlined next.

[2]The transcriptions are available at `https://fangj.github.io/friends/`

### 3.2 Data Preprocessing

To prepare the QA pairs in a useful format for the task at hand, we assign each collected pair to one of four categories. The categories are included in the final FRIENDS-QIA dataset and describe if, and in what way, the question or answer had to be modified. Modifications include removing direct cues to the answers 'yes' or 'no', such as 'yeah' or 'nope' (a full list is provided in Appendix B), adding context to the question in case we deem it insufficient, as well as removing metadata and irrelevant parts of the question or answer. The four categories are listed below along with their respective description.

1. Able to use question and answer, exactly as they are
2. Have to only remove yes/no/nope/yeah (etc.) in the answer
3. Clarifying/adding context to the question (or rarely the answer)
4. Questions with an answer only containing a yes/no/nope/yeah (etc.)

Example 3.1 is a QA pair which is useful for our task exactly as it is. It has a polar question and a perfectly indirect answer with no direct mappers or cues, so we assign this QA pair to category 1.

However, in Example 3.2 we remove a bit of irrelevant context, namely the "Hey!" in the question. Furthermore, the answer contains an actual "No", which should not be present in an indirect answer, so this is also removed. These modifications cause the QA pair to be assigned to category 2. The modified example is shown below.

**Example 3.4**
***Rachel:*** *So, did you quit?*

*Chandler: I almost did, couldn't leave Ross there without a spotter!*

Example 3.3 is from category 3, where we need to do a larger modification to make the QA pair useful. This modification could for example be to add context, which is usually found in the transcript lines immediately above the question. The modified example is shown below.

**Example 3.5**
*Joey: Really? Marge has a girlfriend?*
*Mr. Treeger: You could dance real good with her, she's the same size as me.*

Category 4 contains QA pairs where the answer consists of only a direct mapper or cue alone, so it cannot easily be modified into an indirect answer. Therefore, this category is ultimately excluded from the final FRIENDS-QIA dataset.

### 3.3 Data Annotation

We adopt the RELAXED label set as introduced by Louis et al. (2020). It consists of six classes: YES, NO, YES SUBJECT TO SOME CONDITIONS, NEITHER YES NOR NO, OTHER and N/A. A description of each class as used in FRIENDS-QIA is as follows:

1. YES: The answer is either a definite yes, a probably yes or a sometimes yes
2. NO: The answer is either a definite no or a probably no
3. YES, SUBJECT TO SOME CONDITIONS: The answer is only yes/no, if a certain condition is satisfied
4. NEITHER YES NOR NO: The answer does not imply yes nor no
5. OTHER: The answer is not related to the question
6. N/A: Lack of majority agreement

The label distribution of FRIENDS-QIA is shown in Figure 1.

#### 3.3.1 Annotator Agreement and Aggregation

We measure the agreement and thereby the reliability of the annotations in FRIENDS-QIA. The three annotators independently labeled all QA pairs in the dataset. The raw agreement distribution of the annotations is listed in Table 3, which includes the agreement for each of the final three categories

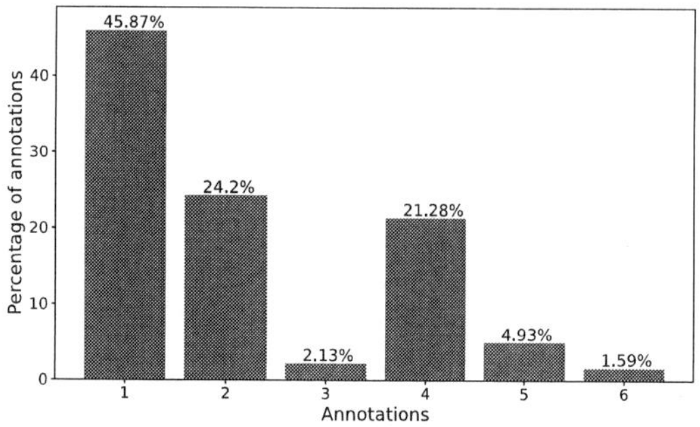


Figure 1: Gold label distribution.
1: YES, 2: NO, 3: YES, SUBJECT TO SOME CONDITIONS, 4: NEITHER YES NOR NO, 5: OTHER, 6: N/A.

described in Section 3.2 as well as for the entire FRIENDS-QIA (all three categories). The resulting Fleiss Kappa score of the full dataset is 0.8833.

| | **All agree** | **Two agree** | **All disagree** |
|---|---|---|---|
| Full dataset | 75.02% | 23.39% | 1.59% |
| Category 1 | 72.79% | 25.48% | 1.73% |
| Category 2 | 77.80% | 20.70% | 1.50% |
| Category 3 | 77.17% | 21.54% | 1.29% |

Table 3: Annotator agreement.

We use majority voting to aggregate the gold standard from the three annotations. In few cases (1.59%), all three annotators disagreed on the label, and we map these to N/A. Examples from FRIENDS-QIA are provided in Table 2, where the QA pairs with label 1–5 were given the same label by at least two annotators, whereas the example with label 6 is a case of full annotator disagreement.

For compatibility with CIRCA, we exclude OTHER (as we found it annotated when the question was not polar in CIRCA) and N/A, which is very infrequent in FRIENDS-QIA (only 1.59% of the labels). We note here that OTHER is used in FRIENDS-QIA in cases where the answer is not related to the question —which is possible due to the dialogue context on which FRIENDS-QIA is based.

| **Dataset** | **FRIENDS-QIA** | **CIRCA** |
|---|---|---|
| All | 5,930 | 32,993 |
| Train | 4,744 | 26,394 |
| Dev | 593 | 3,300 |
| Test | 593 | 3,299 |

Table 4: Data split and dataset sizes using labels 1–4.

The resulting dataset used in the experiments contains 5,930 question-answer pairs over four labels. The dataset sizes after splitting it are listed in Table 4, including a comparison to the CIRCA dataset (Louis et al., 2020). The splits for both datasets are stratified to ensure similar label distribution across all three sets.

Table 5 provides additional insights into the two datasets, by providing measures on vocabulary size, length of the instance as well as type-token ratio (TTR). We observe that FRIENDS-QIA is richer in terms of vocabulary, has higher lexical variety and contains on average longer utterances, despite the smaller overall size compared to CIRCA.

| Statistic | Q | A | Q + A |
|---|---|---|---|
| **FRIENDS-QIA** | | | |
| Vocabulary size | 4,207 | 4,843 | 6, 373 |
| Maximum length | 80 | 188 | 195 |
| Average length | 11 | 13 | 24 |
| Type-token ratio | 0.06 | 0.06 | 0.04 |
| **CIRCA** | | | |
| Vocabulary size | 2,003 | 7,317 | 7,499 |
| Maximum length | 25 | 27 | 38 |
| Average length | 7 | 6 | 14 |
| Type-token ratio | 0.01 | 0.03 | 0.02 |

Table 5: Vocabulary statistics (in number of tokens).

## 4 Experiments

We experiment with different variants of a Convolutional Neural Network (CNN). In particular, we explore the use of BERT embeddings, a crowd layer and combining datasets to obtain higher performance on FRIENDS-QIA.

**Base CNN** Our CNNs are implemented with inspiration from Kim (2014), who uses 1-dimensional convolutions in parallel. As shown in Figure 2, our implementation of the parallel convolutions consists of a convolutional 1d, a max pooling, a flatten and a dropout layer, after which they are concatenated and fed to the final output layer which uses softmax as activation function. The convolutional layer applies the ReLU activation function after which the maximum of each filter is selected. The dropout layer applies a dropout rate of 0.5 which is the same rate we use on the final layer when we apply regularization with a constraint of the L2-norm on the weights. The models either take English BERT embeddings (Devlin et al., 2019) as input or use GloVe embeddings (Pennington et al., 2014). The models are

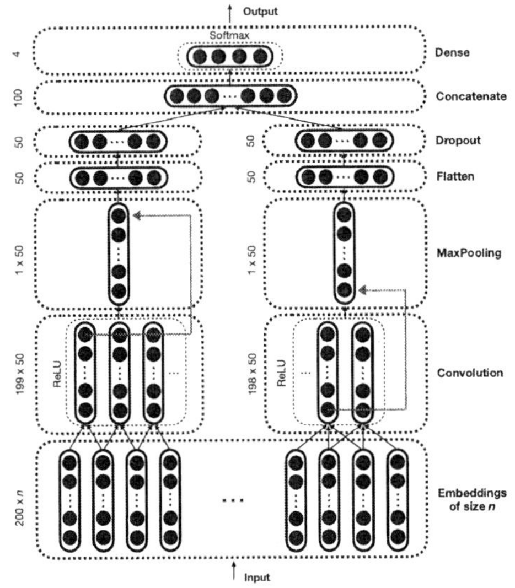


Figure 2: CNN architecture.

optimized using the Adam optimizer (Kingma and Ba, 2015). This general architecture is what all of our CNN variants are built upon. In preliminary experiments we took a portion of the training data as hyperparameter tuning set. We performed a grid search on the base CNN to find the optimal hyperparameters. For the CNN with BERT no further hyperparameter tuning was done.

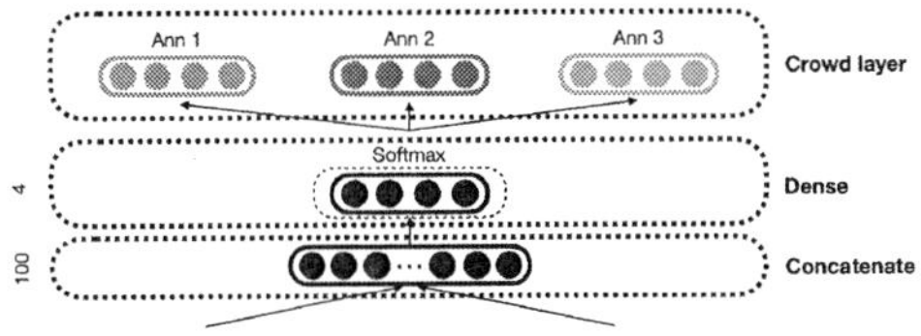


Figure 3: Illustration of deep learning from crowds proposed by Rodrigues and Pereira (2018).

**Crowd Layer** Figure 3 illustrates the key idea of the DLFC approach we adopt on top of our CNN. Training the models with a crowd layer is closely based on the paper and code by Rodrigues and Pereira (2018). Following their implementation, our crowd layer is applied on top of the existing network. It takes as input the output of the dense layer and uses the annotator-specific labels, each modeled as a separate task, to propagate errors through the network and adjust the gradients. The layer is applied on the already trained and saved base model with an annotator-specific weight matrix ($\mathbf{W}^r$), and further training is performed with the crowd layer. We found this setup to perform best. For the CNN+crowd layer model we use the same parameters as when training the base model. After training, the crowd layer is removed to allow for the final classification using the original dense layer with a softmax activation function.

**Evaluation** Accuracy and macro-average F1-score are the evaluation metrics. We first report results on the development set, and report the performance of the best models on the test portion. As baselines, we provide results of a majority baseline and a Naive Bayes model with word trigrams.

## 5 Results

The main results on the development set are given in Table 6. It provides results of a majority baseline, the CNN with GloVe and BERT embeddings, and the CNN trained with the crowd layer. We first discuss results for models trained on FRIENDS-QIA, followed by results on training with FRIENDS-QIA *and* CIRCA.

| | Accuracy | F1-score |
|---|---|---|
| Majority baseline | 49.07 | 16.46 |
| Train on FRIENDS-QIA: | | |
| Naive Bayes | 52.45 | 37.08 |
| CNN | 54.86 | 33.02 |
| CNN (Q only) | 49.92 | 23.46 |
| CNN (A only) | 55.09 | 35.32 |
| CNN, multi-input | 53.91 | 35.61 |
| CNN + crowd layer | **55.71** | **39.38** |
| CNN with BERT | **64.08** | 49.16 |
| CNN with BERT (Q only) | 43.79 | 26.96 |
| CNN with BERT (A only) | 52.22 | 29.96 |
| CNN with BERT, multi-input | 61.27 | 50.31 |
| CNN with BERT + crowd layer | 63.46 | **55.00** |
| Train on FRIENDS-QIA + CIRCA: | | |
| Naive Bayes | 52.11 | 45.67 |
| CNN | 53.51 | 43.16 |
| CNN with BERT | 61.27 | 48.65 |

Table 6: Results on the FRIENDS-QIA development data.

**Take-aways** There are four take-aways. First, we observe the difficulty of the task. This can be seen from the low baseline results: The majority baseline reaches an accuracy of 49.07 and F1-score of 16.46. The Naive Bayes model reaches an accuracy of 52.45 and F1-score of 37.08.

Second, we test several variants of the base CNN with GloVe embeddings: one which takes the concatenation of question and answer as input (CNN), one that models question and answer separately (CNN, multi-input), and a CNN using only the answer or the question. The latter provides information on how much signal is represented in the answer (or question) alone. As the results in Table 6 show, multi-input modeling is not consistently the best model (on both metrics). Training the CNN on answers alone is highly predictive and performs substantially better than the question alone. This corroborates findings by Louis et al. (2020): the answer alone is highly predictive for the task (yet not sufficient). Overall, the best models are obtained when considering both question and answer, reaching an accuracy of 54.86 and F1-score of 33.02 on the development set with base CNN.

Third, we observe that modeling the annotator uncertainty is beneficial. When we add the crowd layer to the base CNN (CNN + crowd layer), we observe both improved accuracy and F1-score, reaching 55.71 and 39.38, respectively. This is encouraging, as it shows that the disagreement in human annotations is informative for this task.

Finally, we observe that using BERT embeddings as input representations consistently and remarkably improves the performance of the model. The CNN model with BERT reaches an accuracy of 64.08 and F1-score of 49.16, which is an absolute improvement of over 9% in accuracy and over 16% in F1-score. What is, however, striking, is that this trend does not hold for the BERT-based model trained on answer or question alone; we attribute this to the limited context, but this result warrants further investigation. Especially the F1-score is not even better than the base CNN model with GloVe embeddings on answers alone. Nevertheless, BERT representations overall improve the best models that take question-answer pairs as input, which are necessary for the overall best performance on the task.

We observe that the crowd layer for the CNN taking the concatenation of question and answer as input (CNN) further improves upon BERT representations, for which we obtain an F1-score of 55 and the overall best performance with the CNN with BERT *and* crowd layer. The accuracy with the crowd layer does not improve considerably, which shows that the crowd layer is not equally helpful for all classes. We hypothesize that the crowd layer is particularly helpful for infrequent classes, which are the most difficult for this task and which we observed the highest annotator disagreement on. This is in fact the case, as we will discuss in Section 6.

**Training on FRIENDS-QIA and CIRCA** We investigated whether we could improve the model further by using also the CIRCA data as additional training data. The bottom rows of Table 6 show that this is not the case; taking the union of the two datasets is generally not beneficial. The limited added vocabulary of CIRCA does not yield better generalization within FRIENDS-QIA.

| | Accuracy | F1-score |
|---|---|---|
| Majority baseline | 49.07 | 16.46 |
| Train on FRIENDS-QIA: | | |
| CNN with BERT | **61.33** | 45.65 |
| CNN with BERT, multi-input | 61.10 | 45.53 |
| CNN with BERT + crowd layer | 60.32 | **47.89** |
| Train on FRIENDS-QIA + CIRCA: | | |
| CNN with BERT | 58.52 | 41.82 |

Table 7: Results on the FRIENDS-QIA test data.

**Test Set Results** Table 7 shows the results of evaluating the best models and baselines on the test set. The results corroborate our findings from the development set. Training with the crowd layer is beneficial, and improves F1-score from 45.65 to 47.89. Similarly as on the development set, overall accuracy slightly drops with the crowd layer (it is within a 1% range). Training on the union of the two datasets does not outperform a model trained on FRIENDS-QIA alone.

## 6 Discussion

In the following section, we provide additional insights on the task.

**Crowd Layer Analysis** We observe a consistent improvement of overall macro F1-score, at a cost of a slight drop in accuracy. Therefore we analyze the per-class F1-score for the BERT-based model trained with and without the crowd layer. Moreover, we analyze the resulting estimated annotator bias matrices obtained from the crowd layer.

| | 1 | 2 | 3 | 4 |
|---|---|---|---|---|
| CNN with BERT | 73.42 | 51.93 | 14.23 | 57.06 |
| CNN with BERT + crowd layer | 72.28 | 53.98 | 38.72 | 55.05 |

Table 8: Per-class results on the development set.
1: YES, 2: NO, 3: YES, SUBJECT TO SOME CONDITIONS, 4: NEITHER YES NOR NO.

The results are presented in Table 8. The results confirm that the crowd layer is particularly useful for more easily confused (in this task low frequency) classes, namely 3 (YES, SUBJECT TO SOME CONDITIONS). It helps on 2 (NO) as well. The crowd layer hurts the most frequent class, which aligns well with the overall gain in macro F1-score at a slight cost in accuracy.

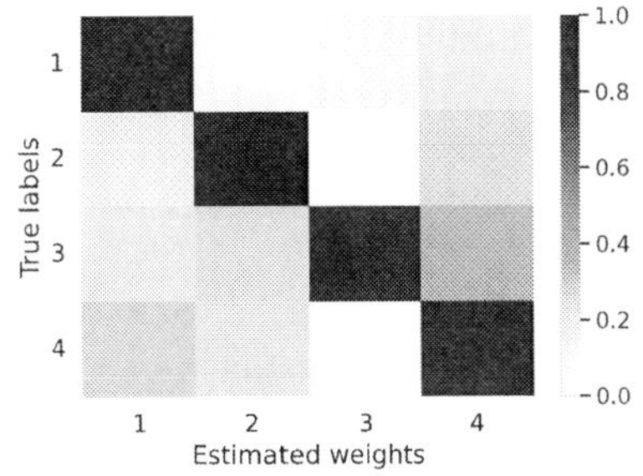


(a) Annotator 1

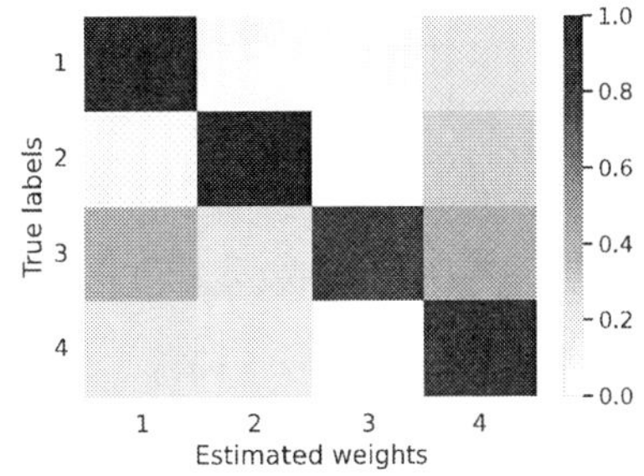


(b) Annotator 2

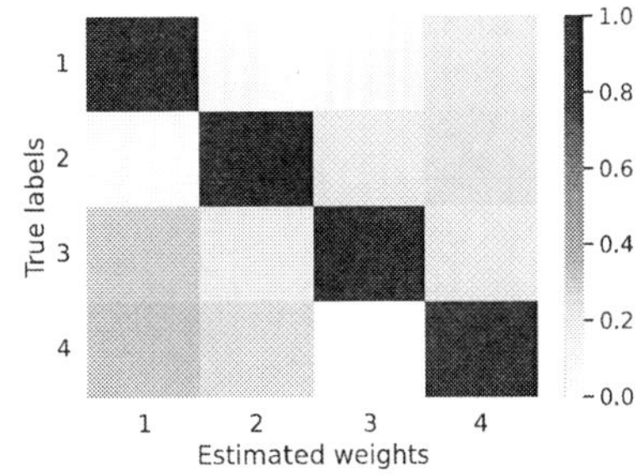


(c) Annotator 3

Figure 4: Normalized weight matrices from the crowd layer for each annotator.
1: YES, 2: NO, 3: YES, SUBJECT TO SOME CONDITIONS, 4: NEITHER YES NOR NO.

Figure 4 shows the three annotator-specific weight matrices extracted from the crowd layer. Overall, the weight matrices show several patterns. The dark diagonals mean that the estimated weights are high and the annotators agree with the gold standard. This is also reflected in the raw agreement as shown in Table 3. The crowd layer generally models each annotator similarly with a few exceptions. One of them is a clear uncertainty of label 3 (YES, SUBJECT TO SOME CONDITIONS). This fits exactly with the label distribution in the FRIENDS-QIA, where class 3 is heavily underrepresented. For annotator 2, the estimated weights are visibly lower for the gold standard 3 (YES, SUBJECT TO SOME CONDITIONS). That means that this annotator tends to give other labels, mostly 1 (YES) and 4 (NEITHER YES NOR NO), when the actual gold standard is 3 (YES, SUBJECT TO SOME CONDITIONS). The annotators 1 and 2 assign label 4 (NEITHER YES NOR NO) more often, in cases where the gold standard was actually one of the other labels. This pattern is not as apparent for annotator 3, which means that this annotator agreed slightly more with the gold labels than the other two annotators.

**Incorrect Predictions** Figure 5 shows the annotator agreement for correct and incorrect predictions of CNN with BERT (using FRIENDS-QIA on the test set). It is clear that the model is more likely to predict the wrong label, when the annotators are also in disagreement with each other.

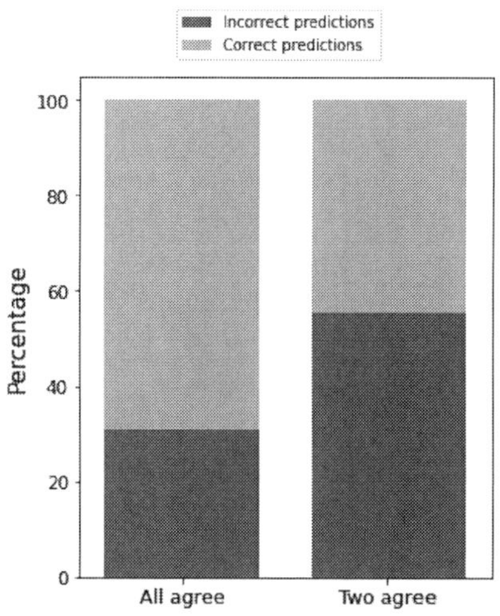


Figure 5: Correct and incorrect predictions of CNN with BERT vs. annotator agreement.

Furthermore, we show the amount of correct and incorrect predictions of CNN with BERT for each category (which were described in Section 3.2) in Figure 6. The amounts are generally similar, but category 3, which required the largest modifications such as adding context to the question, is slightly harder to classify than category 1 and 2, which required either no modification or removing direct cues in the answer, respectively.

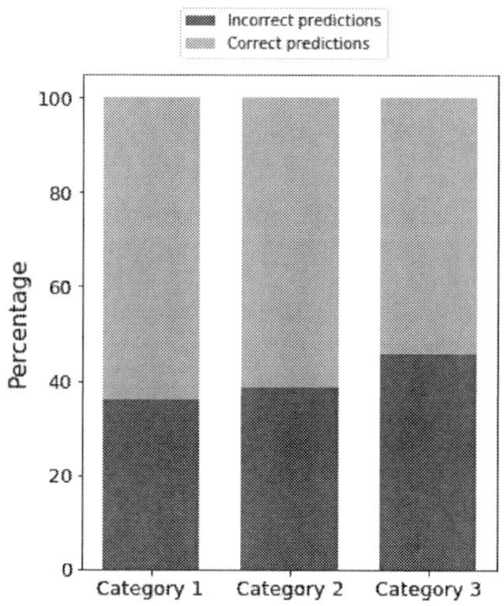


Figure 6: Correct and incorrect predictions of CNN with BERT vs. category.

**FRIENDS-QIA versus CIRCA** In general, we see a lower performance when we train and evaluate on FRIENDS-QIA, compared to using the CIRCA data for training and evaluation (we also trained models on CIRCA alone and evaluate on FRIENDS-QIA but leave them out for space reasons). The difference in performance is largely due to the general differences between the two datasets, and we describe a few of those differences as well as the reasons for them in the following paragraphs.

First of all, the data is collected in a different way, which greatly affects the content of the questions and answers. CIRCA is created specifically for the task at hand by Louis et al. (2020), namely understanding indirect answers, and was created under specific, topic-restricted settings, consisting of 10 different dialogue prompts. FRIENDS-QIA is obtained from a more open domain (yet, confined to typical TV series dialogues) and includes a broader context (also reflected in the vocabulary size differences). For example, it includes cases of both sarcasm and irony as well as additional information in the utterances, which might not be related to the actual question or answer.

Secondly, FRIENDS-QIA includes multi-sentence responses. Given the dialogue context, we observe cases where the speaker might change their mind in-between the sentences, further complicating the task of interpreting the questions and answers. This is very different from CIRCA due to the restricted and written setup, resulting in the CIRCA data being much more concise in meaning and structure than FRIENDS-QIA.

Third of all, a major difference between CIRCA and FRIENDS-QIA is the data size. FRIENDS-QIA contains much fewer QA pairs than CIRCA, which makes it considerably more difficult for the CNNs to learn well from. Additionally, FRIENDS-QIA has fewer annotations contributing to the gold standard (three versus five annotations in CIRCA), yet each of the three corresponds to a single annotator for FRIENDS-QIA, which is not the case in CIRCA.

## 7 Conclusions and Future Work

In this paper, we present FRIENDS-QIA, a corpus for studying indirect answers in English dialogues. We propose to mine TV series transcripts of a well-known TV series. Recent work proposed this challenging answer-understanding task, and collected CIRCA, a dataset on question-answer pairs from 10 dialogue prompts constructed instead using crowdsourcing (Louis et al., 2020). Motivated by their work, we propose FRIENDS-QIA. It contains a total of 5,930 question-answer pairs, and is released both with a majority label and the raw annotations.

Our results with CNNs show that a model trained with BERT embeddings outperforms a CNN trained with GloVe word representations. Most interestingly, this is, however, only the case for a model that considers both question and answer. Training on the answers alone provides reasonable signal for the task, but is not sufficient to resolve the indirect answer.

Understanding indirect answers is a challenging pragmatic task, and even human annotators might not agree on a single gold label. We experiment with a way to leverage disagreement in labeling, which proves encouraging: the macro F1-score of the two best CNN models further improves, when fine-tuning with a crowd layer that encodes individual annotator preferences. This is encouraging, as — to the best of our knowledge — human disagreement has not yet been leveraged in modeling for understanding indirect answers; our dataset can be considered a starting point for further research in learning from disagreement.

Overall, the data in FRIENDS-QIA was originally written in a manuscript for the TV series, then uttered in a spoken dialogue context on the show and ultimately transcribed again. Our results show that understanding indirect answers remains a challenging task. We are missing out on influential factors such as intonation, body language and discourse relations from this dialogue context, when we only process the QA pairs in written form. Modeling such factors is interesting and challenging future work.

## Acknowledgements

We would like to thank the anonymous reviewers for their thorough feedback, as well as ITU's High-performance Computing Cluster team for providing computational resources used in this work. This research is in part supported by the Independent Research Fund Denmark (DFF) grant 9063-00077B.

## References

Lora Aroyo and Chris Welty. 2015. Truth is a lie: Crowd truth and the seven myths of human annotation. *AI Magazine*, 36(1):15–24.

Emily M. Bender and Batya Friedman. 2018. Data statements for natural language processing: Toward mitigating system bias and enabling better science. *Transactions of the Association for Computational Linguistics*, 6:587–604.

Christopher Clark, Kenton Lee, Ming-Wei Chang, Tom Kwiatkowski, Michael Collins, and Kristina Toutanova. 2019. BoolQ: Exploring the surprising difficulty of natural yes/no questions. In *Proceedings of the 2019 Conference of the North American Chapter of the Association for Computational Linguistics: Human Language Technologies, Volume 1 (Long and Short Papers)*, pages 2924–2936, Minneapolis, Minnesota. Association for Computational Linguistics.

Marie-Catherine de Marneffe, Scott Grimm, and Christopher Potts. 2009. Not a simple yes or no: Uncertainty in indirect answers. In *Proceedings of the SIGDIAL 2009 Conference*, pages 136–143, London, UK. Association for Computational Linguistics.

Jacob Devlin, Ming-Wei Chang, Kenton Lee, and Kristina Toutanova. 2019. BERT: Pre-training of deep bidirectional transformers for language understanding. In *Proceedings of the 2019 Conference of the North American Chapter of the Association for Computational Linguistics: Human Language Technologies, Volume 1 (Long and Short Papers)*, pages 4171–4186, Minneapolis, Minnesota. Association for Computational Linguistics.

Nancy Green and Sandra Carberry. 1992. Conversational implicatures in indirect replies. In *30th Annual Meeting of the Association for Computational Linguistics*, pages 64–71, Newark, Delaware, USA. Association for Computational Linguistics.

Nancy Green and Sandra Carberry. 1999. Interpreting and generating indirect answers. *Computational Linguistics*, 25(3):389–435.

Beth Ann Hockey, Deborah Rossen-Knill, Beverly Spejewski, Matthew Stone, and Stephen Isard. 1997. Can you predict responses to yes/no questions? yes, no, and stuff. In *Fifth European Conference on Speech Communication and Technology*.

Yoon Kim. 2014. Convolutional neural networks for sentence classification. In *Proceedings of the 2014 Conference on Empirical Methods in Natural Language Processing (EMNLP)*, pages 1746–1751, Doha, Qatar. Association for Computational Linguistics.

Diederik P. Kingma and Jimmy Ba. 2015. Adam: A method for stochastic optimization. volume abs/1412.6980.

Annie Louis, Dan Roth, and Filip Radlinski. 2020. "I'd rather just go to bed": Understanding indirect answers. In *Proceedings of the 2020 Conference on Empirical Methods in Natural Language Processing (EMNLP)*, pages 7411–7425, Online. Association for Computational Linguistics.

Jennimaria Palomaki, Olivia Rhinehart, and Michael Tseng. 2018. A case for a range of acceptable annotations. In *SAD/CrowdBias@ HCOMP*, pages 19–31.

Ellie Pavlick and Tom Kwiatkowski. 2019. Inherent disagreements in human textual inferences. *Transactions of the Association for Computational Linguistics*, 7:677–694.

Jeffrey Pennington, Richard Socher, and Christopher Manning. 2014. Glove: Global vectors for word representation. In *Proceedings of the 2014 Conference on Empirical Methods in Natural Language Processing (EMNLP)*, page 1532–1543, Doha, Qatar. Association for Computational Linguistics.

Barbara Plank, Dirk Hovy, and Anders Søgaard. 2014. Learning part-of-speech taggers with inter-annotator agreement loss. In *Proceedings of the 14th Conference of the European Chapter of the Association for Computational Linguistics*, pages 742–751, Gothenburg, Sweden. Association for Computational Linguistics.

Filipe Rodrigues, Francisco Pereira, and Bernardete Ribeiro. 2013. Learning from multiple annotators: Distinguishing good from random labelers. *Pattern Recognition Letters*, 34(12):1428–1436.

Filipe Rodrigues and Francisco C. Pereira. 2018. Deep learning from crowds. In *Thirty-Second AAAI Conference on Artificial Intelligence (AAAI-18)*. Association for the Advancement of Artificial Intelligence.

Anna-Brita Stenström. 1984. *Questions and responses in English conversation*. Krieger Pub Co.

Henry S. Thompson, Anne H. Anderson, Ellen Gurman Bard, Gwyneth Doherty-sneddon, Alison Newlands, and Cathy Sotillo. 1993. The HCRC map task corpus: natural dialogue for speech recognition. In *Human Language Technology: Proceedings of a Workshop Held at Plainsboro, New Jersey, March 21-24, 1993*.

Alexandra N. Uma, Tommaso Fornaciari, Dirk Hovy, Silviu Paun, Barbara Plank, and Massimo Poesio. 2021. Learning from disagreement: A survey. *The Journal of Artificial Intelligence Research*, Forthcoming.

Yan Yan, Rómer Rosales, Glenn Fung, Ramanathan Subramanian, and Jennifer Dy. 2014. Learning from multiple annotators with varying expertise. *Machine Learning*, page 291–327.

## A FRIENDS-QIA Data Statement

Following (Bender and Friedman, 2018), the following outlines the data statement for FRIENDS-QIA:

A. CURATION RATIONALE: Collection of examples of polar questions and curated answers for identification of indirect answer types.

B. LANGUAGE VARIETY: US (en-US) mainstream English.

C. SPEAKER DEMOGRAPHIC: Characters in a TV series.

D. ANNOTATOR DEMOGRAPHIC: All annotators are female, highly proficient in English. Native languages include Danish and Polish. Socioeconomic status: higher-education student.

D. SPEECH SITUATION: Both standard and colloquial US English, i.e., spontaneous speech.

D. TEXT CHARACTERISTICS: Sentences from transcripts of a TV series.

PROVENANCE APPENDIX: The data originates from `https://fangj.github.io/friends/`.

## B FRIENDS-QIA Direct Mappers

### B.1 Direct mappers which are removed

To avoid having direct mappers or cues in the answers, we remove all occurrences of the words listed below, if they "stand alone".

- Yes / yeah / yup / yep / yeah-eah / yah
- No / nope / nah / na / noo(...) / na-ah

### B.2 Direct mappers which are *not* removed

We had to draw a line somewhere, between what to keep and what to remove. We ultimately decided to only remove variants of "yes" and "no" listed in the previous section. This results in keeping terms such as the ones listed below, which otherwise in certain cases might also act as a direct mapper or cue to the answer meaning "yes" or "no".

- Of course (not) / absolutely (not) / totally (not) / definitely (not) / certainly (not) / obviously (not) / apparently (not) / I guess (not)
- Alright / all right / affirmative / that's right / right / that's correct / sure / exactly / fine / please / okay / OK / 'kay / exclusively
- No way / no can do
- Thank you / thanks / no thanks / I don't know / maybe / kind of / (not) really (not)
- Uhuh / a-huh / mm-hm / mm-mh

## C FRIENDS-QIA Variables

Here we list the variables which FRIENDS-QIA contains as well as a description of them.

- SEASON is the season of the TV series from which the QA pair was extracted.
- EPISODE is the episode (of the season) of the TV series from which the QA pair was extracted.
- CATEGORY tells the category which the QA pair was assigned to during data collection in order to know which preprocessing had to be performed.
- Q_PERSON is the name of the character of "Friends" who asked the question.
- A_PERSON is the name of the character of "Friends" who said the answer.
- Q_ORIGINAL is the original, non-modified question taken directly from the transcription.
- A_ORIGINAL is the original, non-modified answer taken directly from the transcription.
- Q_MODIFIED is the modified question (might be exactly the same as Q_ORIGINAL, if no modification was needed).
- A_MODIFIED is the modified answer (might be exactly the same as A_ORIGINAL, if no modification was needed).
- ANNOTATION_1 is the annotation given by annotator 1.
- ANNOTATION_2 is the annotation given by annotator 2.
- ANNOTATION_3 is the annotation given by annotator 3.
- GOLDSTANDARD is the aggregated gold label from the three annotators.

# Developing Conversational Data and Detection of Conversational Humor in Telugu

**Vaishnavi Pamulapati** and **Radhika Mamidi**
Language Technologies Research Center
International Institute of Information Technology, Hyderabad
vaishnavi.p@research.iiit.ac.in, radhika.mamidi@iiit.ac.in

## Abstract

In the field of humor research, there has been a recent surge of interest in the sub-domain of Conversational Humor (CH). This study has two main objectives. (a) develop a conversational (humorous and non-humorous) dataset in Telugu. (b) detect CH in the compiled dataset. In this paper, the challenges faced while collecting the data and experiments carried out are elucidated. Transfer learning and non-transfer learning techniques are implemented by utilizing pre-trained models such as FastText word embeddings, BERT language models and Text GCN, which learns the word and document embeddings simultaneously of the corpus given. State-of-the-art results are observed with a 99.3% accuracy and a 98.5% f1 score achieved by BERT.

## 1 Introduction

Humor as a phenomenon has interested scholars from diverse fields since time immemorial (Morreall, 2012). The abundance of research studies dedicated to humor is not only due to the fascinating nature of the domain but also due to its impact in everyday life (Martin and Lefcourt, 1983)(McGee and Shevlin, 2009).

In a conversational discourse between interlocutors, their attitude, present state of mind, psychological distance between the topic of humor and the individual (McGraw and Warren, 2010) determine whether what is intended to be humorous is perceived so. Conversational Humor (CH) is a subset of verbal humor. Verbal humor exists in the verbality of what is being spoken. Canned jokes (such as light-bulb jokes, knock-knock jokes) are a part of verbal humor, where they are not context-dependent, i.e., they can be removed from a conversation and still perceived as humorous. On the other hand, CH is heavily dependent on various factors including speakers' personalities, the relevant culture that is referenced, and current events. Numerous studies that focus on the detection of humor in short jokes/tweets rely on the contrastive discourse relation present in humorous instances (Liu et al., 2018). However, in conversations, participants' personalities, their sense of humor, and the relationship between the participants, add unique complexities to the task of detection of CH. The following example (translated) from a Telugu stage play, *Kanyasulkam.*

Puta: *Where is he?*
Madhu: *You don't listen to me, I have already told you that the person you're looking for is not here!*

**Context:**

Giri and Rama are hiding under Madhu's bed. Puta is looking for Giri and the latter is hiding because he is scared of Puta. The audience, Giri and Rama know that Madhu is lying about Giri's whereabouts. This irony is recognized by the audience and causes Dramatic Irony (Dempster, 1932)(Pamulapati et al., 2020). This depicts how the participants contribute to CH.

There have been attempts at formulating a typology for CH. Dynel (2009) defined CH and enlisted the different types of verbal discourses that cause CH. Similarly, Pamulapati et. al (2020) developed a hierarchical framework that considers whether it is a monologue/dialogue, the benignity of the utterance, the type, and techniques used to cause CH. Despite the recent interest in CH, there is a need for more computational work in this field as researchers are striving to make virtual assistants like Siri and Alexa produce more human-like discourses. This paper aims to further the research in this direction by working on the task of detection of CH. For low resource languages such as Telugu, finding conversations for the purposes of this study proved to be a challenge. To the best of our knowledge, this work is the first attempt to compile conversational data in Telugu. To compensate for the paucity of data, pre-trained neural



*Proceedings of the 2nd Workshop on Computational Approaches to Discourse*, pages 12–19
November 10–11, 2021. 

network models such as FastText and BERT and the state-of-the-art Text GCN model are used for the task of detection of CH.

## 2 Related Work

Chaudhary, et. al (Chaudhary et al., 2021) used features at several levels such as morpho-syntactic, lexico-semantic and pragmatic level and architectures including Logistic Regression, Gaussian Näive Bayes, and SVM to detect and generate CH. They utilized an existing dataset on Kaggle that comprises 200k+ Reddit jokes in English.

Weller and Seppi (Weller and Seppi, 2019) employ a Transformer architecture for humor detection and explain the advantages over traditional classifiers such as CNN and compare their results with human annotated data. Existing datasets such as Short Jokes dataset on Kaggle and Pun of the Day were used. Apart from these they had mined Reddit jokes and used the number of upvotes to demarcate the humorous jokes from the non-humorous jokes.

Annamoradnejad and Zoghi (2020) use BERT to generate embeddings for their combined dataset of several existing humorous datasets, including the dataset provided by Khandelwal et. al (2018). Different classifiers such as SVM and XLNet are compared with their proposed model, the latter giving an F1 score of 98.2 percent.

Yao et. al (2019) proposed a Graphical Convolutional Networks architecture (GCN) for text classification. The framework builds a text graph based on word co-occurrence using the dataset's text. These aforementioned studies provided motivation to incorporate BERT, FastText and TextGCN architectures in the experiments for detecting Conversational Humor.

## 3 Data and Preparation

To compile humorous data for the task of humor recognition, jokes from various sources were scraped including jokes section of news websites like Times of India (Samayam)[1], and other miscellaneous sources such as Blogspot websites[2]. As the area of focus is Conversational Humorous data, the dataset was filtered to assemble jokes that followed a conversational format.

Though extensive attempts to obtain conversational data from movies or TV shows were made, due to reasons such as unavailability of transcripts, manual transcription needed, and unavailability of multilingual OCRs[3], this direction proved to be unfeasible. Despite jokes being used, in the final dataset several conversational features are intact. All instances of the final humorous data used are of the same format as

Speaker 1: *utterance 1*
Speaker 2: *utterance 2*
...
Speaker n: *utterance n.*

Therefore, features such as turn taking and sequence organization are present. Turn-taking organization is where participants alternate their utterances, minimizing the noise arising from clashing of utterances to have a smooth or effective communication (Sacks et al., 1978). Sequence organization is the organization of these turns. If the conversational goal is to seek information, the first turn is the question, and the second turn is the answer (Schegloff et al., 1977).

### 3.1 Humorous Data

After filtering, a total of 2,047 conversational jokes were compiled. These jokes did not follow a standard structural format. Therefore, manual intervention was applied to make a homogeneous conversational humorous dataset (translated example given below) as the model could distinguish humorous and non-humorous data based on structural features, rather than semantic.

**Original Conversational Joke:**

"*Hey! Your dog is exactly like a tiger!*", said Suresh. "*That is (emphasis) a tiger. It has been going around talking and thinking about love and has turned into a dog!*", replied Mahesh.

**Manually Converted to:**

Suresh: *Hey! Your dog is exactly like a tiger!*
Mahesh: *That is (emphasis) a tiger. It has been going around talking and thinking about love and has turned into a dog!*

### 3.2 Non-Humorous Data

To assemble non-humorous conversations, tweets and their replies were scraped to form conversations. A reply to a tweet engages with the original tweet's user and their audience. Any subsequent

[1] https://telugu.samayam.com/telugu-jokes/funny-jokes/articlelist/49228696.cms

[2] https://bit.ly/3yL2HuX

[3] As the Telugu script was abundantly mixed with Roman script in the movie dialogues

replies are either directed at the original tweet's user or at the other replies' users.

Every tweet is assigned several attributes such as tweet ID, user ID, timestamp, etc. Using a tweet's ID, conversation ID and timestamp, tweets and their replies were compiled to form a conversation. A combination of Twint[4], an advanced Twitter scraping tool, and Twitter's API v2 endpoint[5] were used to assemble the data.

To avoid the non-canonical forms of words obtained from scraping Telugu tweets written in roman script, 'lang: te' (aiming to fetch tweets written in Telugu script) was used as a filter when scraping tweets. In addition, in order to build a multidomain non-humorous dataset (Mihalcea and Strapparava, 2005), hashtags such as '#cinema', '#politics', '#cooking', etc. were used as filters when collecting tweets.

Usernames were not used as speakers in the conversation for two reasons. Firstly, for the sake of anonymity, and secondly, usernames and names contain numbers and special characters. Consequently, to generate a natural conversation, the usernames were replaced by common Telugu names. Using the tweet's author ID, speaker identity was preserved. For instance,

User123: *Hello, how is today's weather?*
User456: *It seems to be very sunny.*
User123: *Oh, wonderful!*

In both instances, 'User123' is replaced by the same common Telugu name. This resulted in a corpus of 10,156 conversations. Tweets that contained hashtags such as '#funny', '#joke', '#hahaha', or smiling/laughing emojis were removed to improve the dataset. After checking the corpus, conversations that contained profanity were removed to avoid ambiguity whether the conversation was humorous (Fägersten, 2012), finally resulting in 6,202 non-humorous conversations.

### 3.3 Attempts at Homogenizing Entire Dataset

To make the non-humorous data and humorous data as similar as possible in structure, several changes were made to the collected jokes and non-humorous conversations (statistics in Table 1)

- Preprocessing steps such as removal of URLS, hashtags, and emojis were performed. In the case of a tweet, if emojis comprised the entirety of an utterance, the predecessor utterance was demarcated the end of the conversation, as removing that utterance is essentially changing the conversation.

- The average number of utterances of all the conversational jokes was calculated to be approximately 3. Hence, the non-humorous conversations were trimmed to result in an average of 3 utterances to prevent the model learning patterns based on structural features.

- As previously mentioned, only those conversational jokes and tweets in Telugu script were included in the data. For the tweets, the filter 'lang: te' was used for this purpose. This filter is applied on an average to the characters of a tweet. Therefore, if most characters are in the Telugu script, then it is considered 'lang: te'. Due to this, a tweet may not entirely be in Telugu script but may contain words written in roman script. These words can belong to either English or Telugu languages. For example, the words underlined are written in Roman script, some are English words while others are Telugu. These words written in Roman script were detected using the Python package Langdetect[6]. Subsequently, a Python API, Google Transliteration[7], was used.

- In Telugu culture, it is common that the name of the target/butt of the jokes is named *Subbarao*, or *Apparao* and so on. These are similar in theme to *Sardarji* jokes[8]. These names, found abundantly in the humorous dataset, replaced speaker's names in the non-humorous dataset. This was to prevent the model learning that conversations involving speakers having these names implied humor, which is not the case.

## 4 Outline of Methodology

There are two approaches that are chosen as part of our proposed methodology (Fig. 1) . The first is the use of pre-trained models, which is then further used for our downstream task of Conversational

[4]https://github.com/twintproject/twint

[5]https://developer.twitter.com/en/docs/twitter-api/early-access

[6]`https://github.com/shuyo/language-detection`

[7]`https://pypi.org/project/google-transliteration-api/`

[8]`https://en.wikipedia.org/wiki/Sardarji_joke`

| | Humorous Data | Non-Humorous Data |
|---|---|---|
| **Collected Data** | 6,107 | 10,156 |
| **Post Filtration** | 2,047 | 6,202 |

Table 1: Statistics of Conversational Dataset

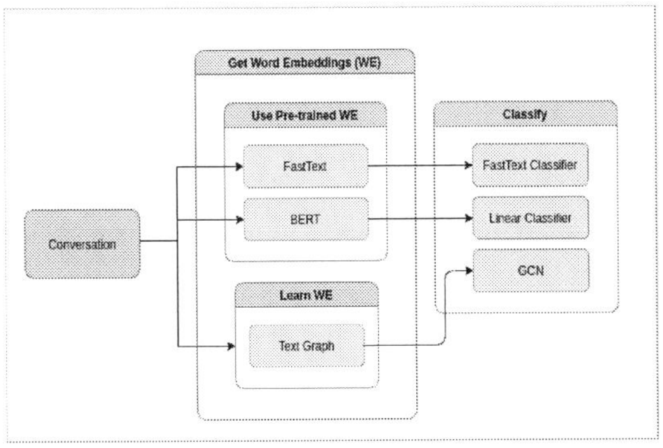


Figure 1: Outline of Methodology

Humor detection. The second is by learning the word embeddings of the conversations using a heterogeneous text graph over which a convolutional neural network is optimized to classify the text. For the first approach we use FastText and BERT's pre-trained models (non-English or dedicated to Indian languages such as Multilingual-BERT or MuRIL) as they have been trained on a large quantity of data. Subsequently, for the second approach, the Text Graphical Convolutional Network (GCN) framework proposed by Yao et. al (2019) is implemented and fine-tuned.

## 5 Text GCN

### 5.1 Heterogeneous Graph

There have been several attempts at learning word representations by mapping words and the documents they are a part of to a graph and learning the word-word and word-document relations using different features. In the paper by Yao et. al (2019), using unsupervised learning, they build a heterogenous graph of words and documents. First, this graph is built using word co-occurrence and document-word relations, after which a Text Graphical Convolutional Network is learnt on the corpus.

Using term frequency-inverse document frequency (TF-IDF), edges are constructed between words and documents. Similarly, based on word co-occurrence, edges are constructed between words to make word-word relations. Instead of focusing on word co-occurrence in a single document (in our case, a conversation), a fixed sliding window on all the documents of the corpus is used to calculate global co-occurrence information.

Using PMI (point-wise mutual information), word associations are calculated. These word associations help us capture the relation between word nodes. A positive PMI implies a high association between words. Whereas a negative PMI implies little or no relation between words x and y. Yao et. al (2019) considered only positive values, and only these edges were considered for the heterogenous text graph.

### 5.2 GCN for Text Classification

A two layered GCN is applied on the built heterogenous graph. A single layer GCN captures information about a node's immediate neighbors, further stacking of such layers integrates a larger neighborhood in its understanding. (2019) experimented with 2 layers of GCN and observed that further stacking of layers did not improve performance. After experimenting, the first layer's embedding size was limited to 200, whereas the window size was set to 20, along with learning rate as 0.02 and dropout rate as 0.5. The training and test data were split into 80:20 ratio and the number of training epochs was stopped early if after 10 successive epochs the validation loss did not decrease.

## 6 FastText

### 6.1 Word Embeddings

FastText uses sub-word information to capture a word's representation (Bojanowski et al., 2017). A word is split into character n-grams, and these collectively make up the embedding for a word. FastText is highly advantageous for an agglutinative language such as Telugu (Srinivasu and Manivannan, 2018). In an agglutinative language, a lexeme is attached with suffixes which carry information such as gender, number (singular/plural) or tense. For instance, the word below is made up of smaller morphemes.

*intikochindhannamaata*

**Morphemes that make up the word:**

*illu + ki + ochuta + i + anamata + emphasis*

**Translation:**

*house + to + come + past tense marker + apparently + emphasis*

Facebook has released its pre-trained FastText word embeddings for 157 languages[9] including Indian languages like Telugu. For the purposes of this study, Telugu pre-trained word embeddings are used.

### 6.2 FastText Classifier

The classifier considers a text given as a bag of n-grams. These n-grams are hashed so that their lookup is easier and faster. After fetching the n-grams' embeddings, they are averaged to form the hidden variable of the linear classifier. FastText fetches the pre-trained word vectors of the bag of n-grams and averages it to result in the text's representation. The model was trained for 15 epochs, with the dimension of word embeddings set to 300, the number of word n-grams set to 2 (bigrams), learning rate set to 1.0, and loss set to hierarchical softmax. As it is an imbalanced dataset, class weights are also considered for classification.

## 7 BERT

### 7.1 Language Modeling

An important distinction must be made between FastText and BERT. FastText is a Facebook library that offers a word embedding algorithm. However, BERT is a language model. Given a corpus of text, a word embedding algorithm learns a distributed representation of a word based on a window of context. On the contrary, a language model learns the likelihood of a word's appearance in a sequence based on its context (unidirectionally or bidirectionally). BERT can be summed up as a pre-trained model on massive unstructured data using bidirectional encoder representations from Transformers.

BERT considers the complete context surrounding a word and is trained on unlabeled data. BERT contains a stack of encoders such as the Vanilla Transformer that has multi-headed attention layers. It is layered by a feedforward neural network and softmax layer for the purpose of downstream tasks. However, Vanilla Transformers are modeled to look at a word's context unidirectionally. Therefore, to mitigate this disadvantage, BERT uses masking of words/tokens at random so the model can learn the probability of the word appearing in its entire surrounding context over iterations (Devlin et al., 2018).

This pre-trained model can be plugged in for many downstream tasks by taking the pooled output of BERT and passing it to a neural network suitable for the task at hand. An important feature of BERT to be noted is that it does not consider whole words like Word2Vec but rather 'word pieces', and hence is useful for agglutinative languages such as Telugu and can handle unknown or erroneous spelled words.

Numerous pre-trained models are available on HuggingFace. Instead of restricting to using BERT pre-trained models, BERT's cousins AlBERT and DistilBERT are also experimented with. AlBERT and DistilBERT strive to reduce the computational complexity. Specified below are the pre-trained models used for the purposes of this study:

- BERT: Multilingual base model (cased, trained on top 104 languages with the largest Wikipedia), MuRIL (Multilingual Representations for Indian Languages, trained on 17 Indian languages),
- AlBERT: Indic-BERT (ALBERT model pre-trained only on 12 major Indian languages),
- DistilBERT: A distilled version of Multilingual base model (cased)

### 7.2 Linear Classifier

The pooled output of the BERT (or AlBERT or DistilBERT) encoders is directly sent to a classifier and, after that to a softmax layer. Class weights are considered here, too, due to the imbalanced dataset (2,047 humorous conversations, whereas 6,202 non-humorous conversations). A Pytorch classifier that applies a linear transformation to the given data is used. Subsequently, Cross Entropy loss function is chosen.

## 8 Results and Discussion

After collecting and pre-processing the tweets and their replies to form non-humorous conversations, experiments were run with Text GCN, FastText and various BERT models (refer to Table 3). The respective model is trained on 80% of the data and is tested on 20% of unseen data. As there are 2,047 instances of humorous conversations whereas 6,202 total instances of non-humorous conversations, this makes it an unbalanced dataset. The weights of the

[9] https://fasttext.cc/docs/en/crawl-vectors.html

| Nearest Neighbors | Translation |
|---|---|
| iMxulO | in this |
| vAtilO | in those |
| xInilO | in this |
| xAnilO | in that |
| axi | that |
| vItilO | in these |

Table 2: FastText nearest neighbors of word 'aNxulO'

classes are taken into consideration. Accuracy and F1 score are used as evaluation metrics.

Highest accuracy results are obtained by Multilingual BERT by Google. Multilingual BERT is trained on 104 languages using Wikipedia dumps of the respective language. This model is pre-trained with both objectives: Masked Language Modeling (MLM) and Next Sentence Prediction. Additionally, it is observed that FastText and BERT models perform comparatively better than Text GCN. The low F1 score implies a low precision and low recall. This means that the model does not predict that the text is humorous well and sufficiently. In Section 5.1, it is specified that the edges between word-word nodes are given weights based on PMI (point-wise mutual information). The word pair with the highest PMI(12.34) is

*<aMxulO, kaxA>*

**Translation:**

*<in that, right (in the sentence 'you finished your homework, right?'>*

It is evident that both words have no syntactic or semantic relation. Thus, the heterogeneous graph does not capture word relations well. In comparison, FastText's nearest neighbors defined in the pre-trained model for the word 'aNxulO' (translates to 'in that') are shown in Table 2.

By inspecting the nearest neighbors of the queried word, FastText captures syntactic (plural of 'in that' is 'in those') and semantic relations (antonym of 'in that' is 'in this'). This highlights the importance of word embeddings for the model's overall performance for the task to be carried out. Word representations is a key aspect that contributes to the effectiveness and performance of text classification (Shen et al., 2018)(Wang et al., 2018).

As mentioned in Section 3.3, conversational text written in Roman script was transliterated to Telugu script using Google Transliterate API. The API produces an array of most probable transliterations of the input given, after which the first element is considered by default. However, at times, the API does not produce accurate results with a slight margin of error. Thus, potentially producing word(s) that do not exist in the language's vocabulary.

For instance, if the API produces the word *'rANiMcina'*, when it should correctly be *'rAniMcina'* (an error difference of one character) and Text GCN or word embedding algorithms such as Word2Vec encounter this incorrectly transliterated word, it will treat it as an out-of-vocabulary word. Hence, not capturing this unknown word's relation with the correct word *'rAniMcina'*.

FastText and BERT fill this inadequacy by taking sub-word or word-piece information. As the difference between the incorrectly transliterated word and the actual word from the language is one-character, both FastText and BERT will produce word embeddings which will be closer as compared to what TextGCN would produce. For a language such as Telugu, where suffixes are attached to carry semantic and synctactic information, breaking a word into sub-words or word-pieces becomes crucial. Another advantage that transfer learning applications such as FastText and BERT models provide is that they are pre-trained on vast amounts of Wikipedia data and can therefore generalise a word's meaning in a context better (Table 3).

| Architecture | Accuracy | F1 Score |
|---|---|---|
| Text GCN | 0.592 | 0.374 |
| FastText | 0.973 | 0.946 |
| **Multilingual BERT** | **0.993** | **0.985** |
| MuRIL | 0.988 | 0.977 |
| Indic-BERT | 0.992 | 0.982 |
| Multilingual DistilBERT | 0.990 | 0.980 |

Table 3: Performance of architectures implemented for Conversational Humor recognition

## 9 Conclusion and Future Work

In this work, the problem of conversational humor detection in Telugu is addressed. Different word embedding algorithms or language models, coupled with different classifiers are used to solve the work at hand. The performances of the various models are evaluated and analyzed to glean insights regarding the mechanisms employed. For low-resource Indian languages such as Telugu, the hurdles that lack of data pose are avoided as pre-trained models on a substantial amount of Telugu data are used effectively.

The BERT model trained on 104 languages, Multilingual BERT base (cased) by Google, delivered the best performance with an accuracy of 99.3% and an f1 score of 98.5%. Comparatively, FastText comes close with merely a 2% difference in accuracy, 97.3% and an f1 score of 94.6%. State-of-the-art results are thus produced by utilizing transfer learning techniques and methodologies.

Telugu movie scripts could be analyzed to comprehend the trends in the types of humor used in Telugu culture, the influencing factors, and the importance of shared knowledge of culture in the perception of humor (Pamulapati et al., 2020). Instead of using premeditated conversations, real-time conversations transcribed from humorous Telugu interviews would capture the essence of conversational humor better. Detection of humor in conversations could be taken one step further to detect a particular technique(s) or type(s) of Conversational Humor.

## References


Issa Annamoradnejad and Gohar Zoghi. 2020. Colbert: Using bert sentence embedding for humor detection. *arXiv preprint arXiv:2004.12765*.

Piotr Bojanowski, Edouard Grave, Armand Joulin, and Tomas Mikolov. 2017. Enriching word vectors with subword information. *Transactions of the Association for Computational Linguistics*, 5:135–146.

Tanishq Chaudhary, Mayank Goel, and Radhika Mamidi. 2021. Towards conversational humor analysis and design. *arXiv preprint arXiv:2103.00536*.

Germaine Dempster. 1932. *Dramatic irony in Chaucer*, volume 3. Stanford University Press.

Jacob Devlin, Ming-Wei Chang, Kenton Lee, and Kristina Toutanova. 2018. Bert: Pre-training of deep bidirectional transformers for language understanding. *arXiv preprint arXiv:1810.04805*.

Marta Dynel. 2009. Beyond a joke: Types of conversational humour. *Language and Linguistics Compass*, 3(5):1284–1299.

Kristy Beers Fägersten. 2012. *Who's swearing now? The social aspects of conversational swearing*. Cambridge Scholars Publishing.

Ankush Khandelwal, Sahil Swami, Syed S Akhtar, and Manish Shrivastava. 2018. Humor detection in english-hindi code-mixed social media content: Corpus and baseline system. *arXiv preprint arXiv:1806.05513*.

Lizhen Liu, Donghai Zhang, and Wei Song. 2018. Modeling sentiment association in discourse for humor recognition. In *Proceedings of the 56th Annual Meeting of the Association for Computational Linguistics (Volume 2: Short Papers)*, pages 586–591.

Rod A Martin and Herbert M Lefcourt. 1983. Sense of humor as a moderator of the relation between stressors and moods. *Journal of personality and social psychology*, 45(6):1313.

Elizabeth McGee and Mark Shevlin. 2009. Effect of humor on interpersonal attraction and mate selection. *The Journal of psychology*, 143(1):67–77.

A Peter McGraw and Caleb Warren. 2010. Benign violations: Making immoral behavior funny. *Psychological science*, 21(8):1141–1149.

Rada Mihalcea and Carlo Strapparava. 2005. Making computers laugh: Investigations in automatic humor recognition. In *Proceedings of Human Language Technology Conference and Conference on Empirical Methods in Natural Language Processing*, pages 531–538.

John Morreall. 2012. Philosophy of humor.

Vaishnavi Pamulapati, Gayatri Purigilla, and Radhika Mamidi. 2020. A novel annotation schema for conversational humor: Capturing the cultural nuances in kanyasulkam. In *Proceedings of the 14th Linguistic Annotation Workshop*, pages 34–47.

Harvey Sacks, Emanuel A Schegloff, and Gail Jefferson. 1978. A simplest systematics for the organization of turn taking for conversation. In *Studies in the organization of conversational interaction*, pages 7–55. Elsevier.

Emanuel A Schegloff, Gail Jefferson, and Harvey Sacks. 1977. The preference for self-correction in the organization of repair in conversation. *Language*, 53(2):361–382.

Dinghan Shen, Guoyin Wang, Wenlin Wang, Martin Renqiang Min, Qinliang Su, Yizhe Zhang, Chunyuan Li, Ricardo Henao, and Lawrence Carin. 2018. Baseline needs more love: On simple word-embedding-based models and associated pooling mechanisms. *arXiv preprint arXiv:1805.09843*.

B Srinivasu and R Manivannan. 2018. Computational morphology for telugu. *Journal of Computational and Theoretical Nanoscience*, 15(6-7):2373–2378.

Guoyin Wang, Chunyuan Li, Wenlin Wang, Yizhe Zhang, Dinghan Shen, Xinyuan Zhang, Ricardo Henao, and Lawrence Carin. 2018. Joint embedding of words and labels for text classification. *arXiv preprint arXiv:1805.04174*.

Orion Weller and Kevin Seppi. 2019. Humor detection: A transformer gets the last laugh. *arXiv preprint arXiv:1909.00252*.

Liang Yao, Chengsheng Mao, and Yuan Luo. 2019. Graph convolutional networks for text classification. In *Proceedings of the AAAI Conference on Artificial Intelligence*, volume 33, pages 7370–7377.

# Investigating non lexical markers of the language of schizophrenia in spontaneous conversations

**Chuyuan Li[1], Maxime Amblard[1], Chloé Braud[2]**
**Caroline Demily[3], Nicolas Franck[3], Michel Musiol[1,4]**
[1] Université de Lorraine, CNRS, Inria, LORIA, F-54000 Nancy, France
[2] IRIT, Université de Toulouse, CNRS, ANITI, Toulouse, France
[3] Centre Hospitalier le Vinatier & UMR 5229, CNRS - Univeristé Lyon 1, Lyon, France
[4] ATILF, UMR 7118, Université de Lorraine, CNRS, 54000 Nancy, France
[1,4] `{firstname.name}@loria.fr`, [2] `chloe.braud@irit.fr`

## Abstract

We investigate linguistic markers associated with schizophrenia in clinical conversations by detecting predictive features among French-speaking patients. Dealing with human-human dialogues makes for a realistic situation, but it calls for strategies to represent the context and face data sparsity. We compare different approaches for data representation – from individual speech turns to entire conversations –, and data modeling, using lexical, morphological, syntactic, and discourse features, dimensions presumed to be tightly connected to the language of schizophrenia. Previous English models were mostly lexical and reached high performance, here replicated (93.7% acc.). However, our analysis reveals that these models are heavily biased, which probably concerns most datasets on this task. Our new delexicalized models are more general and robust, with the best accuracy score at 77.9%.

## 1 Introduction

Schizophrenia is defined as a severe mental illness (APA, 2015) that comes with varied symptoms, ranging from delirium to hallucinations. Among these symptoms, there are language disorders, especially the so-called *positive thought disorder* (i.e., disorganized language output such as *derailment* and *tangentiality*) [1] and *negative thought disorder*[2] (Kuperberg, 2010). Schizophrenia affects about 1% of the world's adult population, with cognitive troubles for 70-80% of the patients (Potvin et al., 2017). Since the symptoms often affect language skills, several studies proposed using NLP techniques on patients' productions (Section 2) to identify what is affected in language, thus understand better the disease and its symptoms and how language works in general.

In this paper, we explore linguistic markers of schizophrenia through feature exploration within a classification system. We do so on spontaneous dialogues in French where all the previous work was in English and most used social media data or monologues. Replicating state-of-the-art results allows us to confirm some previous findings of specific features of the language of schizophrenia.

Our study focuses on two aspects: carefully exploring data representations and investigating preliminary modeling of dialogues, both with scarce data. Using spontaneous conversations makes for a realistic scenario – the patient is merely talking with her clinician. However, representing dialogues is not easy: we restrict ourselves to patients' speech turns, and test varied context windows to tackle data sparsity. Additionally, we compare several representations and confirm that lexicon is a good indicator, making for high-performing models with at best 93.7% (acc.). Nevertheless, our analysis demonstrates that it probably corresponds to a bias in our data caused by the constraints imposed during the collection process. Most of the datasets are likely biased the same way. This analysis led us to delexicalized models while focusing on dimensions presumed to be affected in schizophrenia: morpho-syntactic, syntactic, dialogue, and discourse information are therefore considered. Our best delexicalized model gets 77.9% (acc.) and shows the importance of morpho-syntactic information and high-level features in dialogue.

When dealing with medical data, ethical questions arise. The diagnosis of schizophrenia is complex and relies on many indices. Automatic systems could provide psychiatrists with further clues, possibly alleviating the need for the patients to go through several cognitive tests, but this is a long-reach goal. It is clear that the systems developed can not substitute for a human expert, as a diagnosis

[1]*Derailment*: spontaneous speech that tends to slip off track. *Tangentiality*: reply to a question in an oblique or irrelevant manner.

[2]Negative thought disorder are those of poverty of speech and language (known as *alogia*) and poverty of content.



*Proceedings of the 2nd Workshop on Computational Approaches to Discourse*, pages 20–28
November 10–11, 2021. 

is a medical act. Moreover, linguistic clues, while crucial, have to be interpreted within the patient's social environment.

**Contributions** This study: (i) is the first in French, replicating English studies with comparable results with less data and resources; (ii) continues seminal work on schizophrenia detection in dialogues but with a focus on modeling and bias - two crucial issues for a task inherently data-scarce; (iii) reveals language features of schizophrenia, confirming psychologists' descriptions on the use of complex structures or the capacity to maintain conversation.[3]

## 2 Related work

Psychiatrists rely on language and speech behavior as one of the main clues in psychiatric diagnosis (Ratana et al., 2019). They found that these patients' speech tends to be less predictable (Salzinger et al., 1964, 1970; Salzinger, 1979), with a poorer vocabulary (Salzinger and Hammer, 1963; Manschreck et al., 1991). It has also been found that their productions tend to be more grammatically deviant (Hoffman and Sledge, 1988) and less syntactically complex than that of controls (Fraser et al., 1986; Morice and Ingram, 1982). At the discourse level, they associate words within a larger context than controls (Maher et al., 2005) with often more diffuse associations (Chaika, 1974; Elvevåg et al., 2007). They also present referential impairments - categorized as vagueness, missing information, or confusing reference (Rochester, 2013; Docherty et al., 1996) -, and specific discontinuities at the discourse level (Musiol and Trognon, 2000; Rebuschi et al., 2014).

On the other hand, many researchers have used NLP methods to help to identify mental disorders, such as depression (Howes et al., 2014; Guntuku et al., 2019; Sekulić and Strube, 2019), post-traumatic stress disorder (Pedersen, 2015; Kleim et al., 2018), suicide risk (Benton et al., 2017), Alzheimer's disease (Orimaye et al., 2014; Fraser et al., 2016), and autism (Goodkind et al., 2018; Sakishita et al., 2019).

For schizophrenia, previous work has mainly focused on lexical information (Mitchell et al., 2015; Hong et al., 2012; Birnbaum et al., 2017; Xu et al., 2019). Unlike ours, these studies rely on Linguistic Inquiry Word Count (LIWC) categories (Pennebaker et al., 2001) - psycho-metrically validated lexicon mapping words to psychological concepts), Latent Dirichlet Allocation (LDA) (Blei et al., 2003) - inferring topics in each document, and Brown clustering (Brown et al., 1992) - grouping contextually similar words into the same cluster. However, most of these resources are only available in English.

More recent approaches considered syntactic, semantic, and sentiment information (Kayi et al., 2017; Allende-Cid et al., 2019). Both studies show good performance with morpho-syntactic features, especially with Part-Of-Speech (POS) tags.[4] They were based on narrative texts (essays and tweets). We here demonstrate that some findings can generalize to spontaneous conversations.

Amblard et al. (2020) proposed the first study on detecting schizophrenia patients from conversations, mostly limited to lexical features. Also, close to our work, Howes et al. (2012a,b, 2013) investigated linguistic features in transcripts of conversations between patients and clinicians. The authors tried to predict patient satisfaction and adherence to treatment on the concatenation of speech turns of the patient. Inspired by the work of Howes et al. (2012b), we also use higher-level features (see Section 3) on real conversations but directly investigating a model of detecting patients with schizophrenia symptoms. Furthermore, we extend previous work by varying the length of dialogues and testing more complex features, including sequences of POS tags, finer tree representations, and dialogical information.

## 3 Approach

**Varying dialogue size:** Our data are composed of 41 dialogues with $2,811$ words, and 268 speech turns on average (when limited to patients/controls). The clinician's speech turns are ignored in all dialogues to reduce their impact on classification, but further studies should also include the interaction. First, we concatenate all the speech turns of a patient/control (**Full** setting), thus making for a large document that contains the whole context. Since the documents are long, it could be hard for the system to find regularities, especially with only a few classification instances (i.e., 41). The opposite

[3]Our code is on: `https://github.com/chuyuanli/non-lexical-markers-scz-conv`.

[4]POS tagging is a process of marking up a word in a text to a particular part of speech. Allende-Cid et al. (2019) tested two types of POS tags: a general one called meta-POS (12 labels) and a precise one POS (160 labels). Both allow performance higher than chance.

| Setting | #Doc. total | #Speech T./doc. min | max | avg | #Word/doc. min | max | avg |
|---|---|---|---|---|---|---|---|
| Indiv. | 10,319 | 1 | 1 | 1 | 1 | 274 | 11 |
| W-128 | 893 | 1 | 34 | 11 | 128 | 317 | 145 |
| W-256 | 443 | 1 | 72 | 20 | 256 | 424 | 271 |
| W-512 | 209 | 2 | 129 | 42 | 512 | 609 | 530 |
| Full | 41 | 76 | 555 | 268 | 703 | 6,778 | 2,811 |

Table 1: Number of documents, speech turns and words per document when varying the window.

option is to classify each speech turn individually (**Indiv.**): this leads to more instances (10,319), but we lose the context of the neighboring speech turns. Moreover, the speech turns are of varied length with an average of 11 words; some of them contain too few words to be informative. The last option is in between: we use a window of at least $n$ words (**W-**$n$), always going until the end of the current speech turn, to assess the possibility of identifying distinctive features already in smaller blocks of conversation. We test $n \in \{128, 256, 512\}$, providing with middle representations (see Table 1). The number of instances is (resp.) 893, 443, and 209, with an average number of speech turns 11, 20, and 42. This configuration allows keeping some context without overwhelming the model.

**Comparing representations:** Existing work on schizophrenia language demonstrated the importance of lexical features. For French, as for many languages, we do not have access to a resource such as LIWC. We thus propose to simply include bag-of-words (bow) and $n$-grams ($n \in \{2, 3\}$) to our models as a proxy for topic identification.

Howes et al. (2012b) showed the importance of features specific to spontaneous dialogues that do involve lexicon but in a more generic way: OCR corresponds to *Open Class Repair* initiators (*pardon?, huh?*); *Backchannel* (BC) responses are phatic expressions (*yeah, hum mm*). To reflect text organization, we also include discourse features by extracting the forms (without disambiguation) corresponding to connectives (*but, because, since*) as identified in LexConn (Roze et al., 2012).

Finally, we test the two following non-lexical features: Part-Of-Speech $n$-grams and treelets. Allende-Cid et al. (2019) demonstrated that POS tags are effective features. We also test for larger patterns with sequences, POS $n$-gram with $n \in \{1, 2, 3\}$. Kayi et al. (2017) only used the dependencies as syntactic features. We extend to *treelet* features (Johannsen et al., 2015) based on the de-

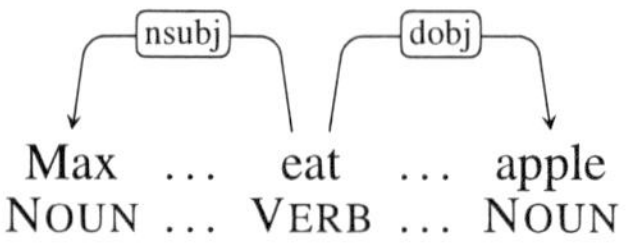


Figure 1: An example of syntactic relation represented as `treelet`.

pendency parse trees: 2-*treelet* corresponds to 2 tokens with a syntactic relation between a head and a dependent, e.g., 'VERB→nsubj→NOUN', and 3-*treelet* corresponds to 3 tokens with 2 syntactic relations: could be 1 head dominates 2 dependents or a chain of dependencies, e.g., 'PRON←poss←NOUN←nsubj←VERB'. See Figure 1 for an illustration.

## 4 Experimental setting

**Data:** Forty-one conversations between patients (18) or controls (23) and a psychologist come from SLAM project (Rebuschi et al., 2014; Amblard et al., 2015). The transcripts are standardized and follow a transcription guide. The groups are balanced with gender, age, intelligence quotient (IQ) score, years of studies, and three cognitive tests' results (WAIS-III, TMT, CVLT)[5]. They are free exchanges carried out in a medical setting where the psychologist is not personally involved - her main action is to maintain the exchange. Preliminary experiments showed that we could distinguish the two groups with relatively high accuracy with the clinician's data. We thus removed clinician's speech turns to reduce this impact and only focused on patients' factors. Further studies are needed to decide how to take into account the entire interaction.

**Classification:** We compare several classification algorithms: Support Vector Machines (SVM) (Cortes and Vapnik, 1995), Logistic Regression (LR), Random Forest (RF), Perceptron (Perc), and Naive Bayes (NB), without and with feature selection based on importance weight, all implemented in Scikit-Learn (Pedregosa et al., 2011). Hyper-parameters are:

- Naive Bayes: smoothing $\alpha \in V = \{0.001, 0.005, 0.01, 0.1, 0.5, 1, 5, 10, 100\}$;

[5]WAIS-III: Wechsler Adult Intelligence Scale (WAIS) is an IQ test designed to measure intelligence and cognitive ability in adults and older adolescents. Trail Making Test (TMT) is a widely used test to assess executive abilities in patients. California Verbal Learning Test (CVLT) measures episodic verbal learning and memory.

| Features | Full | Indiv. | W-512 |
|---|---|---|---|
| bow | **93.66** | **72.43** | - |
| ngram | 85.61 | 69.59 | - |
| OCR | 60.62 | 50.17 | 59.28 |
| BC | 74.48 | 54.79 | 67.86 |
| Connectives | 72.44 | 55.28 | 73.57 |
| POS | 53.66 | 55.80 | 60.09 |
| 2-POS | 67.36 | 56.33 | 71.74 |
| 3-POS | 71.65 | 56.53 | 72.55 |
| 2-treelet | 69.19 | 56.73 | 74.19 |
| 3-treelet | 66.78 | 55.34 | 69.03 |
| 1-2-3-POS | 69.01 | 58.36 | 72.67 |
| POS+2-3-treelet | 66.59 | 57.77 | 72.39 |
| 3-POS+BC | 74.93 | 57.46 | **77.86** |

Table 2: Best averaged accuracy for Full, Individual and W-512 (underlined: best setting for each feature).

- Logistic Regression: $L_2$ and regularization $C \in V$;
- SVM with linear kernel: $L_2$ and regularization $C \in V \cup \{1000\}$;
- Perceptron: $L_2$ and $\alpha \in V$;
- Random Forest: max_depth $\in \{2, None\}$;

Thresholds for feature selection are the range of 10 values equally distributed from $1e-5$ to the weight of the $50^{th}$ most important feature (thus allowing to keep at least 50 features), plus the mean and median of the weights.

Since our dataset is minimal, we use nested cross-validation to assess the performance of our system: tune hyper-parameters on $K-1$ folds and then evaluate on the left-out fold, repeating the whole process $M$ times ($K = M = 5$). We report average accuracy over the $M$ out folds. Best hyper-parameters values and algorithms are given in Appendix A.2.

## 5 Results

**Lexical features:** We compare different representations for Full and Indiv. settings - the most similar to long narrative texts or short Twitter messages. As in previous work, we found that lexical information is very effective (Table 2: *bow* and *n-gram*) with at best 93.66% in accuracy. However, analysis from previous studies suggested a potential issue: Mitchell et al. (2015) reported that health-related lexicon is more represented in the tweets dataset, and Howes et al. (2012b) that the most predictive unigrams are about conditions, treatment and, medication. We investigate our data using Spearman correlation[6] to rank lexical features and find similar results: terms linked to the condition are in top ranks for schizophrenia (*maladie [disease], traitement [treatment], médecin [doctor]*), while terms related to studies (*licence [bachelor], thèse [PhD]*) and social life (*vacances [holidays], monde [world / people]*) are correlated with controls. This finding is due to the nature of our data: patients talk about their disease with a clinician, and controls talk more about their everyday life. These features perform well because they reflect a lexical bias in data collection. However, the models will not be usable in the wild.

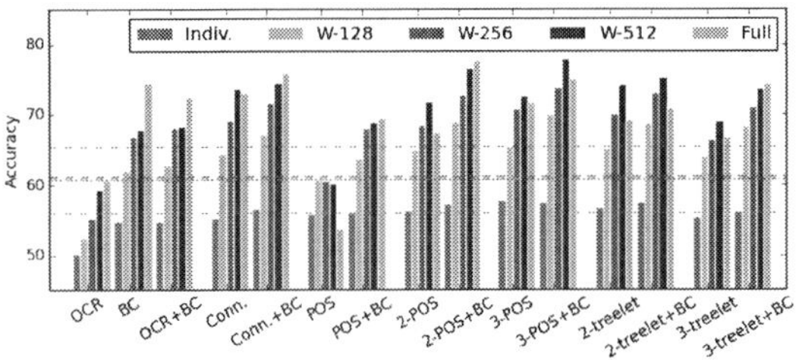


Figure 2: Accuracy for all features and window sizes. OCR: *Open Class Repair*, BC: *Backchannel response*, Conn.: *connectives*. W-$n$: window size.

**Dialogue and discourse:** Figure 2 presents results on selected subsets of non- or less- lexicalized features for the five splits of our data. Horizontal lines correspond to the majority vote baselines.

Concerning dialogue features, OCR gives poor results mostly behind the baseline, while BC is above with 74.48% (Full). Moreover, combining with BC to another feature set almost consistently allows improvements (not the case with OCR). These features are good indicators, contrary to what was reported in (Howes et al., 2012b). Note that we directly use the tokens as features rather than the proportion of BC per word, which allows more refined analysis. The most informative features for controls are phatic expressions (*ah, ok, hum-hum, vraiment [really], c'est ça [that's right / yeah, right]*). At the same time, patients with schizophrenia are correlated with more ambiguous expressions which are also used in non-phatic contexts

[6] $p$-value$< 0.05$, coefficient $|\rho| > 0.3$

(*je comprends [I understand], bien sûr [of course], exactement [exactly]*), i.e., less BC responses: this supports that the patients are less prone to maintain the conversation.

Connectives also give promising results, at best 73.6%. Trend shows that controls use longer connectives (*jusqu'à ce que [until that], au point de [to the point that]*) *vs.* patients (*donc [so], puis [then]*). Connectives linked to the present moment are also highly correlated to schizophrenic group (*maintenant (que) [now (that)], depuis que [ever since]*); this might refer to changes after treatment.

**POS tags and syntax:** Sequences of POS tags (2-POS and 3-POS) and of treelet (2-treelet and 3-treelet) are fully non-lexicalized features. They capture some internal structure of the interaction. We obtain our best scores with the longest sequences (3-POS, 72.55% acc., 74.34% $F_1$). These scores are higher than the ones reported by Kayi et al. (2017) on tweets (69.20% $F_1$) or essays (69.76% $F_1$) with simple POS tags and a lot more documents, and are very close to Allende-Cid et al. (2019) with meta-POS (75.1% in $F_1$): this confirms the predictive power of POS for the task.

We found that patients with schizophrenia used more verbs than controls (e.g., 2-POS such as VERB-ADP[7], 3-POS such as PRON-AUX-VERB), and, as in (Kayi et al., 2017), a higher proportion of adverbs. Precisely, we observe that the usage of adverbs of time (*parfois [sometimes], plus maintenant [not anymore], quasiment jamais [almost never]*), of place (*ici déjà [here already]*) and of frequency and manner (*beaucoup plus [much more], beaucoup mieux [much better]*) is higher than that of controls - this is possibly linked to the exchange about their (current) heath condition. On the other hand, controls employ a higher portion of linking adverbs (*enfin [finally], donc [so], quand même [anyway]*).

Syntactic features confirm these observations, the most predictive being verbal structures, followed by adverbial modifiers (*advmod, advcl*)[8]. This goes along with (Kayi et al., 2017), in which the top parse tag is *advmod*, and confirms clinician's descriptions on the use of less complex syntactic structures for patients with schizophrenia. Controls tend to use more complicated syntactic structures, such as those with SCONJ (subordinating conjunction) and CCONJ (coordinating conjunction), confirmed by our analysis of discourse connectives.

**Context window size:** Our experiments were also designed to test the impact of the context when dealing with dialogues. Figure 2 demonstrates that, in general, the larger the window, the better the scores. Individual speech turns are too small and contain no context. However, using the whole conversation most often leads to a drop in performance compared to our largest window (512 words) due to data sparsity, as we can observe for connective, $n$-POS and $n$-treelet. OCR and Backchannels do not follow this trend, meaning that they are probably less sparse.

These experiments demonstrate that using the block of conversation is relevant – the models find enough information to make accurate classification –, while allowing to increase the number of classification instances artificially.

**Best algorithm:** Among the 5 classifiers, NB generally performs well when dealing with word counts (in Full and Indiv.), while SVM and LR are generally better in other cases. More precisely, SVM performs better when the context window is relatively large, and the data sparsity is more pronounced (Full). At the same time, LR is better at dealing with small to medium-sized contexts (Indiv. and W-n settings). Detailed information is in the supplementary material.

## 6 Conclusion

We used conversations involving patients with schizophrenia in order to learn about language features associated with the disease. We compared various settings to represent dialogues and several representations to deal with data scarcity and lexical bias. Our experiments replicate performances as high as previous studies in English. Further experiments will be designed to take into account the entire interaction, probably with neural networks. We would also like to investigate the effect of adversarial loss in mitigating the bias within a neural model.

We hope that this paper will remind us of the importance of looking for bias in data and exploring higher-level, less language-dependent information to produce robust systems and draw more general conclusions on conversational data.

[7] ADP stands for adposition and it covers preposition and postposition.

[8] *advmod* is a (non-clausal) adverb or adverbial phrase; *advcl* is an adverbial clause modifier. They serve to modify a verb or other predicate.

## Acknowledgements

The authors thank the anonymous reviewers for their insightful comments and suggestions. This work was supported by the PIA project "Lorraine Université d'Excellence", ANR-15-IDEX-04-LUE, as well as the CPER LCHN (Contrat de Plan État-Région - Langues, Connaissances et Humanités Numériques). We would like to thank the Centre Hospitalier Le Vinartier for having contributed decisively to the implementation of the experimentation. Experiments presented in this paper were carried out in secured nodes on the Grid'5000 testbed. We would like to thank the Grid'5000 community (see `https://www.grid5000.fr`).

## References

Hector Allende-Cid, Juan Zamora, Pedro Alfaron-Faccio, and María Alonso. 2019. A machine learning approach for the automatic classification of schizophrenic discourse. *IEEE Access*, pages 45544–45554.

Maxime Amblard, Chloé Braud, Chuyuan Li, Caroline Demily, Nicolas Franck, and Michel Musiol. 2020. Investigation par méthodes d'apprentissage des spécificités langagières propres aux personnes avec schizophrénie (investigating learning methods applied to language specificity of persons with schizophrenia). In *Actes de la 6e conférence conjointe Journées d'Études sur la Parole (JEP, 33e édition), Traitement Automatique des Langues Naturelles (TALN, 27e édition), Rencontre des Étudiants Chercheurs en Informatique pour le Traitement Automatique des Langues (RÉCITAL, 22e édition). Volume 2: Traitement Automatique des Langues Naturelles*, pages 12–26.

Maxime Amblard, Karën Fort, Caroline Demily, Nicolas Franck, and Michel Musiol. 2015. Analyse lexicale outillée de la parole transcrite de patients schizophrènes. *Traitement Automatique des Langues*, 55(3):91 – 115.

American Psychiatric Association APA. 2015. *DSM-5-Manuel diagnostique et statistique des troubles mentaux*. Elsevier Masson.

Adrian Benton, Margaret Mitchell, and Dirk Hovy. 2017. Multitask learning for mental health conditions with limited social media data. In *Proceedings of the 15th Conference of the European Chapter of the Association for Computational Linguistics: Volume 1, Long Papers*, pages 152–162.

Michael L Birnbaum, Sindhu Kiranmai Ernala, Asra F Rizvi, Munmun De Choudhury, and John M Kane. 2017. A collaborative approach to identifying social media markers of schizophrenia by employing machine learning and clinical appraisals. *J Med Internet Res*, 19(8):e289.

David M Blei, Andrew Y Ng, and Michael I Jordan. 2003. Latent dirichlet allocation. *Journal of machine Learning research*, 3(Jan):993–1022.

Peter F Brown, Vincent J Della Pietra, Peter V Desouza, Jennifer C Lai, and Robert L Mercer. 1992. Class-based n-gram models of natural language. *Computational linguistics*, 18(4):467–480.

Elaine Chaika. 1974. A linguist looks at "schizophrenic" language. *Brain and language*, 1(3):257–276.

Corinna Cortes and Vladimir Vapnik. 1995. Support-vector networks. *Machine learning*, 20(3):273–297.

Nancy M Docherty, Maddalena DeRosa, and Nancy C Andreasen. 1996. Communication disturbances in schizophrenia and mania. *Archives of General Psychiatry*, 53(4):358–364.

Brita Elvevåg, Peter W Foltz, Daniel R Weinberger, and Terry E Goldberg. 2007. Quantifying incoherence in speech: an automated methodology and novel application to schizophrenia. *Schizophrenia research*, 93(1-3):304–316.

Kathleen C Fraser, Jed A Meltzer, and Frank Rudzicz. 2016. Linguistic features identify alzheimer's disease in narrative speech. *Journal of Alzheimer's Disease*, 49(2):407–422.

William I Fraser, Kathleen M King, Philip Thomas, and Robert E Kendell. 1986. The diagnosis of schizophrenia by language analysis. *The British Journal of Psychiatry*, 148(3):275–278.

Adam Goodkind, Michelle Lee, Gary E Martin, Molly Losh, and Klinton Bicknell. 2018. Detecting language impairments in autism: A computational analysis of semi-structured conversations with vector semantics. *Proceedings of the Society for Computation in Linguistics*, 1(1):12–22.

Sharath Chandra Guntuku, Daniel Preotiuc-Pietro, Johannes C Eichstaedt, and Lyle H Ungar. 2019. What twitter profile and posted images reveal about depression and anxiety. In *Proceedings of the International AAAI Conference on Web and Social Media*, volume 13, pages 236–246.

Ralph E Hoffman and William Sledge. 1988. An analysis of grammatical deviance occurring in spontaneous schizophrenic speech. *Journal of neurolinguistics*, 3(1):89–101.

Kai Hong, Christian G Kohler, Mary E March, Amber A Parker, and Ani Nenkova. 2012. Lexical differences in autobiographical narratives from schizophrenic patients and healthy controls. In *Proceedings of the 2012 Joint Conference on Empirical Methods in Natural Language Processing and Computational Natural Language Learning*, pages 37–47.

Christine Howes, Matt Purver, Rose McCabe, Patrick GT Healey, and Mary Lavelle. 2012a. Helping the medicine go down: Repair and adherence in patient-clinician dialogues. In *Proceedings of SemDial 2012 (SeineDial): The 16th Workshop on the Semantics and Pragmatics of Dialogue*, page 155.

Christine Howes, Matthew Purver, and Rose McCabe. 2013. Using conversation topics for predicting therapy outcomes in schizophrenia. *Biomedical informatics insights*, 6:BII–S11661.

Christine Howes, Matthew Purver, and Rose McCabe. 2014. Linguistic indicators of severity and progress in online text-based therapy for depression. *ACL 2014*, page 7.

Christine Howes, Matthew Purver, Rose McCabe, Patrick Healey, and Mary Lavelle. 2012b. Predicting adherence to treatment for schizophrenia from dialogue transcripts. In *Proceedings of the 13th Annual Meeting of the Special Interest Group on Discourse and Dialogue*, pages 79–83.

Anders Johannsen, Dirk Hovy, and Anders Søgaard. 2015. Cross-lingual syntactic variation over age and gender. In *Proceedings of the nineteenth conference on computational natural language learning*, pages 103–112.

Efsun Sarioglu Kayi, Mona Diab, Luca Pauselli, Michael Compton, and Glen Coppersmith. 2017. Predictive linguistic features of schizophrenia. In *Proceedings of the 6th Joint Conference on Lexical and Computational Semantics (* SEM 2017)*, pages 241–250.

Birgit Kleim, Andrea B Horn, Rainer Kraehenmann, Matthias R Mehl, and Anke Ehlers. 2018. Early linguistic markers of trauma-specific processing predict post-trauma adjustment. *Frontiers in Psychiatry*, 9:645.

Gina R Kuperberg. 2010. Language in schizophrenia part 1: an introduction. *Language and linguistics compass*, 4(8):576–589.

Brendan A Maher, Theo C Manschreck, Jakob Linnet, and Steven Candela. 2005. Quantitative assessment of the frequency of normal associations in the utterances of schizophrenia patients and healthy controls. *Schizophrenia Research*, 78(2-3):219–224.

Theo C Manschreck, Brendan A Maher, Jill E Rosenthal, and Jonathan Berner. 1991. Reduced primacy and related features in schizophrenia. *Schizophrenia Research*, 5(1):35–41.

Margaret Mitchell, Kristy Hollingshead, and Glen Coppersmith. 2015. Quantifying the language of schizophrenia in social media. In *Proceedings of the 2nd workshop on Computational linguistics and clinical psychology: From linguistic signal to clinical reality*, pages 11–20.

Rodney D Morice and John CL Ingram. 1982. Language analysis in schizophrenia: Diagnostic implications. *Australian and New Zealand Journal of Psychiatry*, 16(2):11–21.

Michel Musiol and Alain Trognon. 2000. *Eléments de psychopathologie cognitive: le discours schizophrène*. A. Colin.

Sylvester Olubolu Orimaye, Jojo Sze-Meng Wong, and Karen Jennifer Golden. 2014. Learning predictive linguistic features for alzheimer's disease and related dementias using verbal utterances. In *Proceedings of the workshop on computational linguistics and clinical psychology: From linguistic signal to clinical reality*, pages 78–87.

Ted Pedersen. 2015. Screening twitter users for depression and ptsd with lexical decision lists. In *Proceedings of the 2nd workshop on computational linguistics and clinical psychology: from linguistic signal to clinical reality*, pages 46–53.

Fabian Pedregosa, Gaël Varoquaux, Alexandre Gramfort, Vincent Michel, Bertrand Thirion, Olivier Grisel, Mathieu Blondel, Peter Prettenhofer, Ron Weiss, Vincent Dubourg, et al. 2011. Scikit-learn: Machine learning in python. *the Journal of machine Learning research*, 12:2825–2830.

James Pennebaker, Martha Francis, and Roger Booth. 2001. *Linguistic inquiry and word count (LIWC)*.

Stéphane Potvin, Ginette Aubin, and Emmanuel Stip. 2017. L'insight neurocognitif dans la schizophrénie. *L'Encéphale*, 43(1):15–20.

Randall Ratana, Hamid Sharifzadeh, Jamuna Krishnan, and Paul Pang. 2019. A comprehensive review of computational methods for automatic prediction of schizophrenia with insight into indigenous populations. *Frontiers in psychiatry*, 10:659.

Manuel Rebuschi, Maxime Amblard, and Michel Musiol. 2014. Using SDRT to analyze pathological conversations. Logicality, rationality and pragmatic deviances. In Manuel Rebuschi, Martine Batt, Gerhard Heinzmann, Franck Lihoreau, Michel Musiol, and Alain Trognon, editors, *Interdisciplinary Works in Logic, Epistemology, Psychology and Linguistics: Dialogue, Rationality, and Formalism*, volume 3 of *Logic, Argumentation & Reasoning*, pages 343 – 368. Springer.

Sherry Rochester. 2013. *Crazy talk: A study of the discourse of schizophrenic speakers*. Springer Science & Business Media.

Charlotte Roze, Laurence Danlos, and Philippe Muller. 2012. Lexconn: a french lexicon of discourse connectives. *Discours. Revue de linguistique, psycholinguistique et informatique. A journal of linguistics, psycholinguistics and computational linguistics*, (10).

Masahito Sakishita, Chihiro Ogawa, Kenji J Tsuchiya, Toshiki Iwabuchi, Taishiro Kishimoto, and Yoshinobu Kano. 2019. Autism spectrum disorder's severity prediction model using utterance features for automatic diagnosis support. In *International Workshop on Health Intelligence*, pages 83–95. Springer.

K Salzinger. 1979. Ecolinguistics: A radical behavior theory approach to language behavior.

Kurt Salzinger and Muriel Hammer. 1963. Some formal characteristics of schizophrenic speech as a measure of social deviance. *Annals of the New York Academy of Sciences*.

Kurt Salzinger, Stephanie Portnoy, and Richard S Feldman. 1964. Verbal behavior of schizophrenic and normal subjects. *Annals of the New York Academy of sciences*, 105(15):845–860.

Kurt Salzinger, Stephanie Portnoy, David B Pisoni, and Richard S Feldman. 1970. The immediacy hypothesis and response-produced stimuli in schizophrenic speech. *Journal of Abnormal Psychology*, 76(2):258.

Ivan Sekulić and Michael Strube. 2019. Adapting deep learning methods for mental health prediction on social media. In *Proceedings of the 5th Workshop on Noisy User-generated Text (W-NUT 2019)*, pages 322–327.

Shihao Xu, Zixu Yang, Debsubhra Chakraborty, Yasir Tahir, Tomasz Maszczyk, Yi Han Victoria Chua, Justin Dauwels, Daniel Thalmann, Nadia Magnenat Thalmann, Bhing-Leet Tan, et al. 2019. Automated lexical analysis of interviews with individuals with schizophrenia. In *Proceedings of the 9th International Workshop on Spoken Dialogue System Technology*, pages 185–197. Springer.

# A Appendices

## A.1 OCR and backchannel word list

In order to improve reproducibility, we give the full list of tokens used for OCR (Table 3) and backchannel (Table 5), as well as their corresponding translation in English (Table 4, Table 6). They were obtained by translating the list given by the authors of we contacted, and by adding a few additional terms specific to French.

| pardon vous disiez | pardon | ah vous parler pardon |
|---|---|---|
| excusez-moi | excuse moi | bon je suis désolée |
| désolé(e) | (ah) ouais ? | ah bon ? |
| c'est vrai ? | c'est euh ? | hum ? |
| de quoi | c'est quoi ? | c'est-à-dire |
| euh ? | dites moi plus | mais encore |

Table 3: Open class repair initiators list (French).

| pardon you said | pardon | ah pardon you were saying |
|---|---|---|
| excuse-me | excuse me | i am sorry |
| sorry | (ah) yes? | ah really? |
| is it true? | it's euh? | huh? |
| of what | what is it? | which means |
| euh? | tell me more | but still |

Table 4: Open class repair initiators list (English translation).

| oui | ouais | ouais voilà |
|---|---|---|
| oui c'est ça | oui bah oui | oui... forcément |
| bah ouais | hum (hum) | muh mmh |
| mmh/mmhh | d'accord | ok |
| voilà | c'est ça | c'est vrai |
| c'est sûr | ça c'est clair | eh bien sûr |
| carrément | bien sûr | super |
| ok... bon | d'accord ça marche | certes |
| mais hein | je comprends | vraiment |
| bien | bon | très bien |
| quand même | tout à fait | certainement |
| exactement | tant mieux | oh |
| ah | ben | alors ben |
| ah d'accord | ah ça euh | eh bah c'est bien |

Table 5: backchannel response list (French).

| yes | yeah | yeah that's it |
|---|---|---|
| yes that's it | yes euh yes | yes... for sure |
| euh yeah | hum (hum) | muh mmh |
| mmh/mmhh | okay | ok |
| that's it | that's it | that's true |
| (yes) (for) sure | that's clear/clearly/definitely | eh of course |
| completely | of course | super |
| ok... then | all right | indeed/yes |
| but hein | i understand | really |
| good | well | very good |
| still | exactly | certainly/sure |
| exactly | all the better/so much the better | oh |
| ah | well | so... well |
| ah okay | ah (this) euh | eh well that's good |

Table 6: backchannel response list (English translation).

## A.2 Best scores and corresp. settings

| | Full | | | | Indiv. | | | | W-512 | | | |
|---|---|---|---|---|---|---|---|---|---|---|---|---|
| Features | Acc. | Algo | Hyper-params. | Thres. | Acc. | Algo | Hyper-params | Thres. | Acc. | Algo | Hyper-params | Thres. |
| bow | 93.66 | NB | $\alpha = 0.001$ | 9 | 72.43 | NB | $\alpha = 0.1$ | $1e-5$ | - | - | - | - |
| ngram | 85.61 | SVM | $C = 5$ | 4 | 69.59 | SVM | $C = 5$ | 2 | - | - | - | - |
| OCR | 60.62 | LR | $C = 0.001$ | $1e-5$ | 50.17 | PERC | $\alpha = 0.001$ | mean | 59.28 | NB | $\alpha = 0.001$ | 2 |
| BC | 74.48 | SVM | $C = 0.1$ | 9 | 54.79 | RF | $max\_depth = 2$ | $1e-5$ | 67.86 | RF | $max\_depth = None$ | 1 |
| Connectives | 72.44 | RF | $max\_depth = 2$ | 2 | 55.28 | LR | $C = 100$ | 5 | 73.57 | RF | $max\_depth = 2$ | median |
| POS | 53.66 | NB | $\alpha = 0.001$ | 5 | 55.80 | LR | $C = 1$ | $1e-5$ | 60.09 | SVM | $C = 100$ | $1e-5$ |
| 2-POS | 67.36 | SVM | $C = 100$ | 3 | 56.33 | LR | $C = 1$ | $1e-5$ | 71.74 | LR | $C = 100$ | mean |
| 3-POS | 71.65 | SVM | $C = 100$ | 2 | 56.53 | SVM | $C = 0.5$ | $1e-5$ | 72.55 | SVM | $C = 100$ | 1 |
| 2-treelet | 69.19 | RF | $max\_depth = 2$ | $1e-5$ | 56.73 | LR | $C = 5$ | $1e-5$ | 74.19 | LR | $C = 100$ | 6 |
| 3-treelet | 66.78 | SVM | $C = 100$ | 8 | 55.34 | LR | - | $1e-5$ | 69.03 | LR | $C = 100$ | 6 |
| 1-2-3-POS | 69.01 | SVM | $C = 1000$ | 1 | 58.36 | LR | $C = 100$ | $1e-5$ | 72.67 | SVM | $C = 100$ | 7 |
| POS+2-3-treelet | 66.59 | SVM | $C = 1000$ | 4 | 57.77 | SVM | $C = 0.5$ | $1e-5$ | 72.39 | LR | $C = 100$ | 4 |
| 3-POS + BC | 74.93 | SVM | $C = 100$ | 8 | 57.46 | LR | $C = 5$ | $1e-5$ | 77.86 | SVM | $C = 100$ | $1e-5$ |

Table 7: Best scores (averaged accuracy Acc.), best algorithms (Algo), corresponding hyper-parameters (Hyper-params.) and threshold (Thres.) for full documents (Full), individual speech turns (Indiv.) and Window size of 512 tokens (W-512).

# Discourse-Driven Integrated Dialogue Development Environment for Open-Domain Dialogue Systems

**Denis Kuznetsov**[◇] **Dmitry Evseev**[◇] **Lidiya Ostyakova**[◇]
**Oleg Serikov**[◇,‡,♡] **Daniel Kornev**[◇] **Mikhail Burtsev**[◇,‡]

[◇]Moscow Institute of Physics and Technology, Moscow
[‡]AIR Institute, Moscow [♡]Higher School of Economics, Moscow
kuznetsov.dp@phystech.edu, dmitrii.evseev@phystech.edu,
l.ostyakova@yandex.ru, oserikov@hse.ru,
danielko@deeppavlov.ai, burtcev.ms@mipt.ru

## Abstract

Development environments for spoken dialogue systems are popular today because they enable rapid creation of the dialogue systems in times when usage of the voice AI Assistants is constantly growing. We describe a graphical Discourse-Driven Integrated Dialogue Development Environment (DD-IDDE) for spoken open-domain dialogue systems. The DD-IDDE allows dialogue architects to interactively define dialogue flows of their skills/chatbots with the aid of the discourse-driven recommendation system, enhance these flows in the Python-based DSL, deploy, and then further improve based on the skills/chatbots usage statistics. We show how these skills/chatbots can be specified through a graphical user interface within the VS Code Extension, and then run on top of the Dialog Flow Framework (DFF). An earlier version of this framework has been adopted in one of the Alexa Prize 4 socialbots while the updated version was specifically designed to power the described DD-IDDE solution.

## 1 Introduction

Conversational AI focused on the development of the dialogue systems is one of the most challenging areas in the artificial intelligence given the subjectivity of the human language interpretation, and is gaining more and more popularity across both academia (Viewer, 2021) and consumer & enterprise markets (Statista, 2020).

Dialogue systems are classified into task-oriented dialogue systems and chat (or non-task-oriented) dialogue systems. Usually they are studied differently, but combining them has been proposed (Lee et al., 2006), and has been found effective in improving user impressions and the relationships with users (Lucas et al., 2018). While task-oriented systems are more widespread and used in different business scenarios (Bocklisch et al., 2017), building systems that can carry multi-turn open-domain conversations is still far from a solved problem (Hu et al., 2021).

While there is a significant effort in using large generative models (Brown et al., 2020), (Roller et al., 2020) in the open-domain dialogue systems, recent tests of GPT-3 (Marcus and Davis, 2020), and Conversational AI challenges like Alexa Prize Socialbot Grand Challenge (Ram et al., 2018) highlight the inherent weaknesses of these models, namely inability to maintain context, avoid contradictions, and control the dialogue strategically in the long dialogues. These fallacies experienced by us and other teams during the Amazon Alexa Prize 3 (Gabriel et al., 2020) led us to the importance of continuing research towards the tightly-controlled open-domain dialogue management frameworks like E-STDM (Finch and Choi, 2020).

During the Amazon Alexa Prize 4 (Hu et al., 2021) competition we developed (Baymurzina et al., 2021) a first iteration of such framework called Dialog Flow Framework (DFF) (Kuznetsov and Evseev, 2021) to aid in rapid development of open-domain "skills" covering various societal topics in our DREAM Socialbot. Usage showed that while users enjoy controlled conversation in their favorite domains, they often interrupt the conversation with the out-of-domain (Konrád et al., 2021) responses leading it into the non-anticipated directions.

Feedback of our Alexa Prize 4 team members who wrote DFF-based open-domain "skills" shows that predictions of the possible user response could significantly cut the time needed by the developer to design and develop these skills.

The key insight into the conversation is that each utterance in the dialogue is also a kind of action being performed by the speaker (Austin, 1962). These actions are called speech or dialog acts (Jurafsky and Martin, 2009). Yet while dialog acts used by some of the Alexa Prize teams e.g., MIDAS (Yu et al., 2019), are quite sophisticated in understand-



*Proceedings of the 2nd Workshop on Computational Approaches to Discourse*, pages 29–51
November 10–11, 2021. ©2021 Association for Computational Linguistics

ing higher level user intents conceptually similar to those used in task-oriented systems (Bocklisch et al., 2017), they are single turn-based and don't support the development of the open-domain conversations that are interactional and sequential (Eggins and Slade, 1996). Indeed, these dialog act taxonomies lack connection to the discourse level of the casual conversation analysis as shown by (Halliday and M., 2004).

In the effort of making it easier for developers to design and develop sequential and interactional multi-turn open-domain dialogue "skills" we propose a new graphical Discourse-Driven Integrated Dialogue Development Environment (DD-IDDE) that combines a novel Discourse-Driven Recommendation System and a DSL for the Dialog Flow Framework, encapsulated together into an extension to the popular IDE Visual Studio Code.

## 2 Related Work

One of the first Development Environments designed for spoken language systems, (Denecke, 2000), was created in 2000. While it supported an entire dialogue system development lifecycle, it lacked the power of the modern NLP components such as NER, Entity Linking, etc. as well as the means for the development of the open-dialogue skills/chatbots. Today, there is a variety of dialogue development frameworks that have emerged to aid in rapid dialogue system creation. Rule-based approaches used e.g. in (Bocklisch et al., 2017) are common in the task-oriented systems broadly used in businesses. Other systems incorporate support for full development lifecycle of the dialogue systems starting with individual NLP ML models and ending with the complete chatbots (Burtsev et al., 2018). Some of these systems are also encapsulated in the form of web-based IDEs e.g. (Lawrence et al., 2021).

Domain-specific languages (DSLs) are typically used in dialogue systems to aid in rapid layout of the dialogue logic. One of the oldest DSLs in this space, AIML (Wallace, 2001) was created as an XML dialect that supports pattern matching of the user utterance and template-based entity extraction and was used in development of the famous open-domain dialogue system "A.L.I.C.E." (Wallace, 2009). RASA DSL (Bocklisch et al., 2017) was designed for the development of the task-oriented systems and includes NLU (intent detection and entity extraction) and stories (actions for intents) components. JAICF (AI, 2021), a JavaScript-based state machine-based DSL, was designed to support both task-oriented systems and chatbots.

A winner of Alexa Prize 2, Gunrock team enhanced their socialbot's (Yu et al., 2019) internal Dialog Flow framework with the MIDAS dialog act scheme to create an adaptive and unique conversation experience with the user. However it does not enable bot developers with the mechanisms to manage dialogue strategically across multiple conversation turns. Slugbot (Bowden et al., 2019), another Alexa Prize team, proposed a DRDM dialogue model to control the coherence of the open-domain dialogue using discourse relations. Their approach introduced a combination of dialog acts and four discourse relations from the PDTB 2.0 (Prasad et al., 2008) as means to model interaction within individual turns and at a higher level. Nonetheless, PDTB 2.0 is based on the 1-million-word Wall Street Journal corpus which is a written language and is not best suited for the spoken casual conversation analysis.

DD-IDDE is powered by the Dialog Flow Framework (DFF) derived from the E-STDM framework which is conceptually similar to both Dialog Flow framework described in (Yu et al., 2019) and the DRDM-dialogue model. It's newly developed DSL was specifically created so that: (1) all conditions, responses and even dialogue flows could be implemented as Python functions, and (2) conditions for state transition could use any of the available annotators like Speech Function Classifier and Predictor and others within the larger DREAM socialbot or derived chatbots and assistants. However, while it is relatively common for dialogue flow frameworks to have a built-in DSL and support pluggable NLU components, DD-IDDE specifically incorporates the support for the novel Discourse-Driven Recommendation System as well as the visual tools aiding in designing open-domain dialogues across multiple conversation steps.

## 3 Concepts

Development of the discourse-driven open-domain dialogue "skills" and chatbots is an ongoing iterative cycle that includes: (1) design of the "skill"/chatbot as the sequence of conditional transitions between states, aided by the discourse moves recommendations, (2) development of the "skill"/chatbot, (3) deployment, ending with the (4) analysis of the running solution, followed by the restart of the cycle.

**Flows, Nodes, Transitions, Conditions and Responses:** We split the dialogue graph into the logically related parts called *Flows* to make it more convenient to work with. Each *Flow* represents a dialogue subgraph. Typically, flows can be organized to cover different topics in the dialogue graph. Like in (Finch and Choi, 2020), we identify the states of the dialogue at a certain moment, such states correspond to the *Nodes* of the dialogue graph. Being in a certain node of the graph, we can go to an another node if the *Condition* that corresponds to this *Transition* is true. After each transition, the *Responses* corresponding to the node are returned.

**Speech Functions and Discourse Moves:** While other solutions often incorporate dialogue/speech acts (DAMSL-SWBD, ISO standard, HCRC etc.) to recognize the higher-level user intentions in a particular context and describe discourse of conversations, they still lack the ability to represent conversational structure and make it impossible to analyze discourse at the dialogue level. In DD-IDDE, we propose implementation of more enhanced intents called Speech Functions that not only represent single turns but also reflect their role in the larger dialogue context.

Eggins and Slade in (Eggins and Slade, 1996) introduced an approach connecting dialogue turns and cross-turn discourse structure patterns specific for casual conversation as the higher-level abstraction. At turn level, they extended Halliday's concept of Speech Functions (Halliday and M., 2004) that express pragmatic goals of speakers and can be used as an enhanced alternative to Dialogue and Speech Acts. Advantages of Speech Functions are in specified grammatical criteria for Speech Function identification and the ability to constrain a comprehensive systematic discourse model of dialogues with the help of them.

These Speech Functions express different discourse purposes and can compound patterns that are expressed by so-called moves. There are three types of Discourse Moves as defined by Eggins and Slade: (i) **Opening** moves are used to start a discussion of a new topic in the dialogue. (ii) **Sustaining** moves develop the current topic of conversation. (iii) **Reacting** moves denote the transfer of the role of the current speaker. The first subtype of reacting moves are **responses** (`React.Response`), which lead dialogues or topics of conversation to completion, the second one is **rejoinders** (`React.Rejoinder`), which, on the contrary, prolong the conversation.

To enable users design dialogue flows with the aid of the Speech Functions and Discourse Moves, we built **Speech Function Classifier** (4.2) and **Speech Function Predictor** (4.3).

**DFF DSL:** DFF DSL is Python-based language for definition of a dialogue graph, conditions of transitions between nodes (e.g. checks for Speech Functions), and functions for processing user or dialogue system utterances (e.g. entity extraction). All the elements in DFF DSL can be callable (functions), including dialogue graphs, which makes the DSL flexible and extensible.

**DFF Extensions:** DFF DSL extensions are modules which can be used in the dialog flow for NLU or NLG. NLU extensions include Speech Function Classifier, Speech Function Predictor and Entity Extraction Module. DFF DSL extensions for NLG are Slot Filling Module (fills the dialogue system's response template with extracted entities), Factoid Response Generation Module (provides content of pages from text databases) and Generic Responses Module (returns short utterances such as "Yes" or "No", which represent appropriate Speech Function responses to user utterance's Speech Function).

## 4 Implementation

### 4.1 Core

We use **Dialog Flow Framework** (DFF) as a core of the DD-IDDE. Creating conversational agents with the support of the open-domain skills is challenging as was shown, for example, in (Kuratov et al., 2019). Currently, there are many ready-made solutions (Finch and Choi, 2020), (Lison and Kennington, 2016), (Ultes et al., 2017), (Bocklisch et al., 2017).

The alpha version of DFF was developed during the Alexa Prize 4 Challenge, based on E-STDM (Finch and Choi, 2020). After the Challenge, all the shortcomings formulated during the competition were taken into account and the DFF DSL was rewritten. DFF (Kuznetsov and Evseev, 2021) is flexible, expressive, minimal, easy to expand through ready-made extensions or own extensions, as well as collect statistics with subsequent analysis.

Having minimal dependencies, DFF is lightweight and stateless. This allows it to be used directly as a service in the case of the microservice architecture applications or as a separate API accessible from outside.

DFF has an expressive Python-based DSL called **DFF DSL** specially designed to be a minimalistic and extensible scripting markup language when compared to other solutions (e.g., AIML, RiveScript, ChatScript, botml), which supports using specific extensions (e.g., discourse-driven integrated dialogue development, a mechanism to extract and use entities based on their Wikidata, generic responses based on the speech functions ontology and etc).

There is a set of community-created extentions that are well documented, and it is straightforward to add own extentions to the framework.

### 4.2 Speech Function Classifier

To aid in the development of the **Speech Function Classifier**, we picked the Santa Barbara Corpus of Spoken American English, which consists of 60 transcriptions of the naturally-occurring spoken conversations. Three face-to-face dialogues were preprocessed and then labeled with the Speech Functions into a small dataset including about 1700 manually annotated utterances. Two annotators reached an inter-annotator agreement of $\kappa = 0.71$ on 1200 utterances which is considered to be a good result. By limiting taxonomy from 45 to 33 classes, using a hierarchical algorithm based on several Logistic Regression models with different parameters, and a rule-based approach, the last version of **Speech Function Classifier** achieved an F1-score varying from 52% to 71% depending on the distribution of the Speech Functions in a particular dialogue. The resulting **Speech Function Classifier** annotator classifies each phrase in the user's utterance as well as each dialogue system's response candidate with Speech Functions. This classification enables the dialogue system to predict the dialogue system's response Speech Functions most expected by the user.

### 4.3 Speech Function Predictor

**Speech Function Predictor** yields probabilities of speech functions that can follow a speech function predicted by Speech Function Classifier. **Speech Function Predictor** is a model based on the statistics of speech function sequences in the manually annotated data. As the collected data is not fully representative, rules were added covering missing cases of speech functions sequences. **Speech Function Predictor** annotation to each last phrase of the user's utterances serves as a recommendation for a dialogue system's next response. It is deployed as the HTTP endpoint available for the VS Code extension as the Recommendation API.

### 4.4 Discourse-Driven Recommendation System

The recommendation system uses Speech Functions used to classify each bot utterance as an input for the Speech Function Predictor to suggest the possible kinds of user responses. The same mechanism is then used to design next bot responses based on the user responses, enabling the rapid design of the sequential discourse-driven open-domain dialogue system.

### 4.5 Graphical User Interface

The DD-IDDE offers a split GUI (Serikov and Babadeev, 2021) that offers both visual design of the current open-domain skill's/chatbot's dialogue flows and a mechanism for working with the code-behind that represents the logic of the aforementioned skill/chatbot. It also provides a mechanism to obtain recommendations for the discourse moves for the selected node(s).

Visual dialogue graph editor allows users to sketch DFF scenarios in form of the dialogue graph. Here, the nodes of the graph are System States, the transitions are allowed by users' utterances (see figure 4). It is powered by the modified Draw.IO (JGraph Ltd, 2021), (Dieterichs and Rouillé, 2021) editor interface.

Code behind editor is a Python editor, and it shows DFF DSL produced from the dialogue flows designed in the visual editor. It can be extended with the standard Pylint-based recommendations and aids user in fixing errors prior to launching the target skill/chatbot.

This GUI is provided in the form of the VS Code Extension.

### 4.6 Conversational Analysis

The DD-IDDE enables users to further improve their skills/chatbots based on the analysis of the user behavior. A DFF Extension was made that allows collecting the particular dialogue flows and individual nodes usage statistics at run-time as well as showing statistics charts in a dashboard.

### 4.7 General Statistical Recommendation System

The aforementioned DFF Extension for Conversation Analysis enables DFF open-domain "skill" developers to use the collected statistics of frequencies of transitions between nodes to focus developer's attention on the user behavior.

## 5 Evaluation

**DFF DSL vs pure Python:** DFF DSL helps to implement scenario skills more easily. For example, Coronavirus skill in DFF DSL format takes about 250 lines, while in pure Python format - about 650 lines. Coronavirus skill in DFF DSL has a clear structure (21 states and 27 transitions), in pure Python the skill has 19 functions and the main function which handles the scenario contains 64 if/else statements, where some of the if/else conditions are nested (making the code harder for maintenance).

**Developing With and Without Discourse-Driven Recommendations:** Development of DFF DSL-based open-domain "skill" is a multi-step cycle that includes initial skill design, development, test, deployment, feedback gathering, until skill quality is improved. The most challenging parts of the skill design are: (1) prediction of the out-of-domain responses that can be not so obvious for developers, and (2) sequential dialogue design. Our initial experiments with the DD-IDDE and its Discourse Moves recommendations showed that time required to address both the out-of-domain responses and to design sequential dialogue was significantly cut compared to the pure DFF DSL skills design.

## Conclusions and Future Directions

In this paper, we introduced a new Discourse-Driven Integrated Dialogue Development Environment (DD-IDDE) focused on aiding users in building open-domain skills/chatbots based on the discourse-driven recommendations. Our DD-IDDE makes it possible for novice users to rapidly design their scenario-driven skills in the visual editor with the discourse move recommendations, and then expand their skills with the custom Python code. In the future versions we plan to further expand the DD-IDDE to enable seamless transitions between the manually edited DFF DSL and its visual graph representation, add deeper integration of the statistics into the main interface of the VS Code extension, as well as add other extentions to the underlying DFF framework.

## Acknowledgements

Authors are deeply grateful to the Alexa Prize organizers for their feedback and advice during the Alexa Prize Grand Challenge 4. Authors also thanks our contributor Dmitry Babadeev who became an owner of the VS Code extension encapsulating the DD-IDDE, and all members of Neural Networks and Deep Learning Lab for their support and advice during the project development. Oleg Serikov is partially supported by the framework of the HSE University Basic Research Program.

## References

Just AI. 2021. Jaicf. `https://github.com/just-ai/jaicf-kotlin/wiki`.

John Langshaw Austin. 1962. *How to do things with words*. William James Lectures. Oxford University Press.

Dilyara Baymurzina, Denis Kuznetsov, Dmitry Evseev, Dmitry Karpov, Alsu Sagirova, Anton Peganov, Fedor Ignatov, Elena Ermakova, Daniil Cherniavskii, Sergey Kumeyko, Oleg Serikov, Yury Kuratov, Lidiya Ostyakova, Daniel Kornev, and Mikhail Burtsev. 2021. Dream technical report for the alexa prize 4. *4th Proceedings of Alexa Prize*.

Tom Bocklisch, Joey Faulkner, Nick Pawlowski, and Alan Nichol. 2017. Rasa: Open source language understanding and dialogue management.

Kevin K. Bowden, JiaQi Wu, Wen Cui, Juraj Juraska, Vrindavan Harrison, Brian Schwarzmann, Nick Santer, and Marilyn A. Walker. 2019. Slugbot: Developing a computational model and framework of a novel dialogue genre. *CoRR*, abs/1907.10658.

Tom B. Brown, Benjamin Mann, Nick Ryder, Melanie Subbiah, Jared Kaplan, Prafulla Dhariwal, Arvind Neelakantan, Pranav Shyam, Girish Sastry, Amanda Askell, Sandhini Agarwal, Ariel Herbert-Voss, Gretchen Krueger, Tom Henighan, Rewon Child, Aditya Ramesh, Daniel M. Ziegler, Jeffrey Wu, Clemens Winter, Christopher Hesse, Mark Chen, Eric Sigler, Mateusz Litwin, Scott Gray, Benjamin Chess, Jack Clark, Christopher Berner, Sam McCandlish, Alec Radford, Ilya Sutskever, and Dario Amodei. 2020. Language models are few-shot learners.

Mikhail Burtsev, Alexander Seliverstov, Rafael Airapetyan, Mikhail Arkhipov, Dilyara Baymurzina, Nickolay Bushkov, Olga Gureenkova, Taras Khakhulin, Yuri Kuratov, Denis Kuznetsov, et al.

2018. Deeppavlov: Open-source library for dialogue systems. In *Proceedings of ACL 2018, System Demonstrations*, pages 122–127.

Matthias Denecke. 2000. An integrated development environment for spoken dialogue systems. In *Proceedings of the COLING-2000 Workshop on Using Toolsets and Architectures To Build NLP Systems*, pages 51–60, Centre Universitaire, Luxembourg. International Committee on Computational Linguistics.

Henning Dieterichs and Vincent Rouillé. 2021. Draw.io vs code integration. https://github.com/hediet/vscode-drawio.

S. Eggins and D. Slade. 1996. Analysing casual conversation.

James D. Finch and Jinho D. Choi. 2020. Emora stdm: A versatile framework for innovative dialogue system development.

Raefer Gabriel, Yang Liu, Anna Gottardi, Mihail Eric, Anju Khatri, Anjali Chadha, Qinlang Chen, Behnam Hedayatnia, Pankaj Rajan, Ali Binici, Shui Hu, Karthik Gopalakrishnan, Seokhwan Kim, Lauren Stubel, Kate Bland, Arindam Mandal, and Dilek Z. Hakkani-Tür. 2020. Further advances in open domain dialog systems in the third alexa prize socialbot grand challenge.

M. A. K. Halliday and Christian Matthiessen M. I. M. 2004. *An introduction to functional grammar / M.A.K. Halliday*, 3rd ed. / rev. by christian m.i.m. matthiessen. edition. Hodder Arnold London.

Shui Hu, Yang Liu, Anna Gottardi, Behnam Hedayatnia, Anju Khatri, Anjali Chadha, Qinlang Chen, Pankaj Rajan, Ali Binici, Varun Somani, Yao Lu, Prerna Dwivedi, Lucy Hu, Hangjie Shi, Sattvik Sahai, Mihail Eric, Karthik Gopalakrishnan, Seokhwan Kim, Spandana Gella, Alexandros Papangelis, Patrick Lange, Di Jin Nicole Chartier, Mahdi Namazifar, Aishwarya Padmakumar, Sarik Ghazarian, Shereen Oraby, Anjali Narayan-Chen, Yuheng Du, Lauren Stubell, Savanna Stiff, Kate Bland, Arindam Mandal, Reza Ghanadan, and Dilek Hakkani-Tur. 2021. Further advances in open domain dialog systems in the fourth alexa prize socialbot grand challenge. https://d7qzviu3xw2xc.cloudfront.net/alexa/alexaprize/docs/sgc4/Alexa-Prize-Technical-Paper-2021_Final.pdf.

JGraph Ltd. 2021. diagrams.net. https://github.com/jgraph/drawio.

Dan Jurafsky and James H. Martin. 2009. *Speech and language processing : an introduction to natural language processing, computational linguistics, and speech recognition*. Pearson Prentice Hall, Upper Saddle River, N.J.

Jakub Konrád, Jan Pichl, Petr Marek, Petr Lorenc, Van Duy Ta, and Ondrej Kobza. 2021. Alquist 4.0: Towards social intelligence using generative models and dialogue personalization. *4th Proceedings of Alexa Prize*.

Yuri Kuratov, Idris Yusupov, Dilyara Baymurzina, Denis Kuznetsov, Daniil Cherniavskii, Alexander Dmitrievskiy, Elena Ermakova, Fedor Ignatov, Dmitry Karpov, Daniel Kornev, et al. 2019. Dream technical report for the alexa prize 2019. *3rd Proceedings of Alexa Prize*.

Denis Kuznetsov and Dmitry Evseev. 2021. Dialog flow framework @ deepmipt github. https://github.com/deepmipt/dialog_flow_framework/.

Andrew Lawrence, Braden Ream, Michael Hood, and Tyler Han. 2021. Visual skill building. https://www.voiceflow.com/.

Cheongjae Lee, Sangkeun Jung, Minwoo Jeong, and Gary Geunbae Lee. 2006. Chat and goal-oriented dialog together: a unified example-based architecture for multi-domain dialog management. In *2006 IEEE Spoken Language Technology Workshop*, pages 194–197.

Pierre Lison and Casey Kennington. 2016. Opendial: A toolkit for developing spoken dialogue systems with probabilistic rules. In *Proceedings of ACL-2016 system demonstrations*, pages 67–72.

Gale M. Lucas, Jill Boberg, David Traum, Ron Artstein, Jonathan Gratch, Alesia Gainer, Emmanuel Johnson, Anton Leuski, and Mikio Nakano. 2018. Getting to know each other: The role of social dialogue in recovery from errors in social robots. In *Proceedings of the 2018 ACM/IEEE International Conference on Human-Robot Interaction*, HRI '18, page 344–351, New York, NY, USA. Association for Computing Machinery.

Gary Marcus and Ernest Davis. 2020. Experiments testing gpt-3's ability at commonsense reasoning: results. https://cs.nyu.edu/~davise/papers/GPT3CompleteTests.html.

Rashmi Prasad, Nikhil Dinesh, Alan Lee, Eleni Miltsakaki, Livio Robaldo, Aravind Joshi, and Bonnie Webber. 2008. The Penn Discourse TreeBank 2.0. In *Proceedings of the Sixth International Conference on Language Resources and Evaluation (LREC'08)*, Marrakech, Morocco. European Language Resources Association (ELRA).

Ashwin Ram, Rohit Prasad, Chandra Khatri, Anu Venkatesh, Raefer Gabriel, Qing Liu, Jeff Nunn, Behnam Hedayatnia, Ming Cheng, Ashish Nagar, Eric King, Kate Bland, Amanda Wartick, Yi Pan, Han Song, Sk Jayadevan, Gene Hwang, and Art Pettigrue. 2018. Conversational ai: The science behind the alexa prize.

Stephen Roller, Emily Dinan, Naman Goyal, Da Ju, Mary Williamson, Yinhan Liu, Jing Xu, Myle Ott, Kurt Shuster, Eric M. Smith, Y-Lan Boureau, and Jason Weston. 2020. Recipes for building an open-domain chatbot.

Oleg Serikov and Dmitry Babadeev. 2021. Dd-idde alpha version 0.2.1. https://github.com/deepmipt/vscode-dff/releases/tag/0.2.1.

Statista. 2020. Number of digital voice assistants in use worldwide from 2019 to 2024 (in billions)*. https://www.statista.com/statistics/973815/worldwide-digital-voice-assistant-in-use/.

Stefan Ultes, Lina M Rojas Barahona, Pei-Hao Su, David Vandyke, Dongho Kim, Inigo Casanueva, Paweł Budzianowski, Nikola Mrkšić, Tsung-Hsien Wen, Milica Gasic, et al. 2017. Pydial: A multi-domain statistical dialogue system toolkit. In *Proceedings of ACL 2017, System Demonstrations*, pages 73–78.

Google Books Ngram Viewer. 2021. Chatbot, natural language processing popularity. https://books.google.com/ngrams/graph?content=chatbot%2C+natural+language+processing&year_start=2000.

Richard Wallace. 2001. Artificial intelligence markup language (aiml). https://web.archive.org/web/20060505035935/http://aitools.org/aiml/spec/.

Richard S. Wallace. 2009. *The Anatomy of A.L.I.C.E.*, pages 181–210. Springer Netherlands, Dordrecht.

Dian Yu, Michelle Cohn, Yi Mang Yang, Chun-Yen Chen, Weiming Wen, Jiaping Zhang, Mingyang Zhou, Kevin Jesse, Austin Chau, Antara Bhowmick, Shreenath Iyer, Giritheja Sreenivasulu, Sam Davidson, Ashwin Bhandare, and Zhou Yu. 2019. Gunrock: A social bot for complex and engaging long conversations.

# A User Interaction

## A.1 Designing

Having installed the DD-IDDE VS Code Extension [1], user creates a new .drawio file in the `common/dff_markup_scenarios` with the name of the target skill scenario, e.g., `pet_scenario.drawio` - see 1.

User then proceeds with defining the Speech Function of the starting node by double-clicking on it - see 2.

Once the first node has been set up, user can use the *Speech Function Recommendations* to pick the next discourse moves by clicking on the "Show Suggestions" menu item - see 3.

User then continues adding nodes based on their scenario, with the aid of the Speech Function recommendations - see 4.

## A.2 Developing

Once the designed skill is sufficiently outlined, user proceeds with the use of the Show Markup functionality that generates the code based on the designed skill - see 5.

With the generated DFF DSL code, user can now add the additional code-behind functionality such as the use of the regular expressions, custom intents, and the like - see 6.

## A.3 Analyzing

In the Conversational Analysis dashboard user can observe the frequency of nodes' visits of the individual dialogue flows, rates of transitions within dialogues, as well as the frequency of the user responses. User can also collect statistics of annotations of user and bot utterances, custom data coming from other DFF extentions, e.g., classification of user utterances with the speech functions, user and bot emotions etc. The dashboard is described in more detail in appendix D. The dashboard allows users to select as many dialogues as one dialog and show user behavior on it. On this dialog graph is shown for one dialog 12 and on this one for many 8.

## A.4 VS Code Extension Graphical User Interface Illustrations

VS Code Extension GUI is shown in figures 1, 2, 3, 4, 5, 6

[1] `https://github.com/deepmipt/vscode-dff/releases/tag/0.2.1`

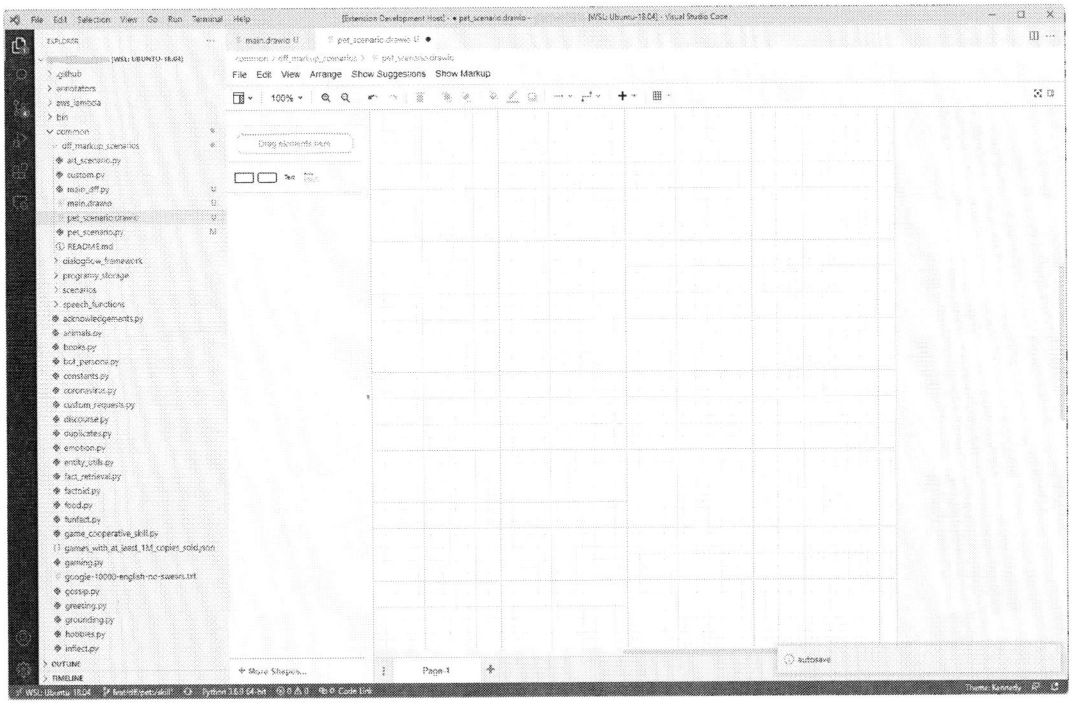


Figure 1: New .drawio file created in VS Code

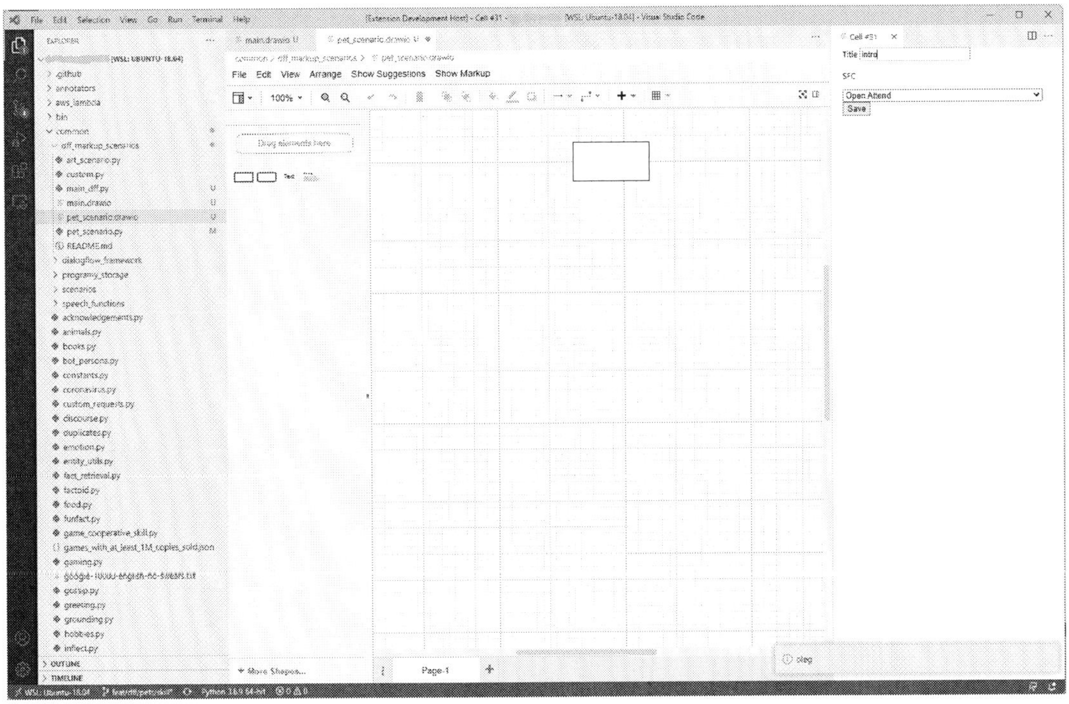


Figure 2: Setting Speech Function for the current node

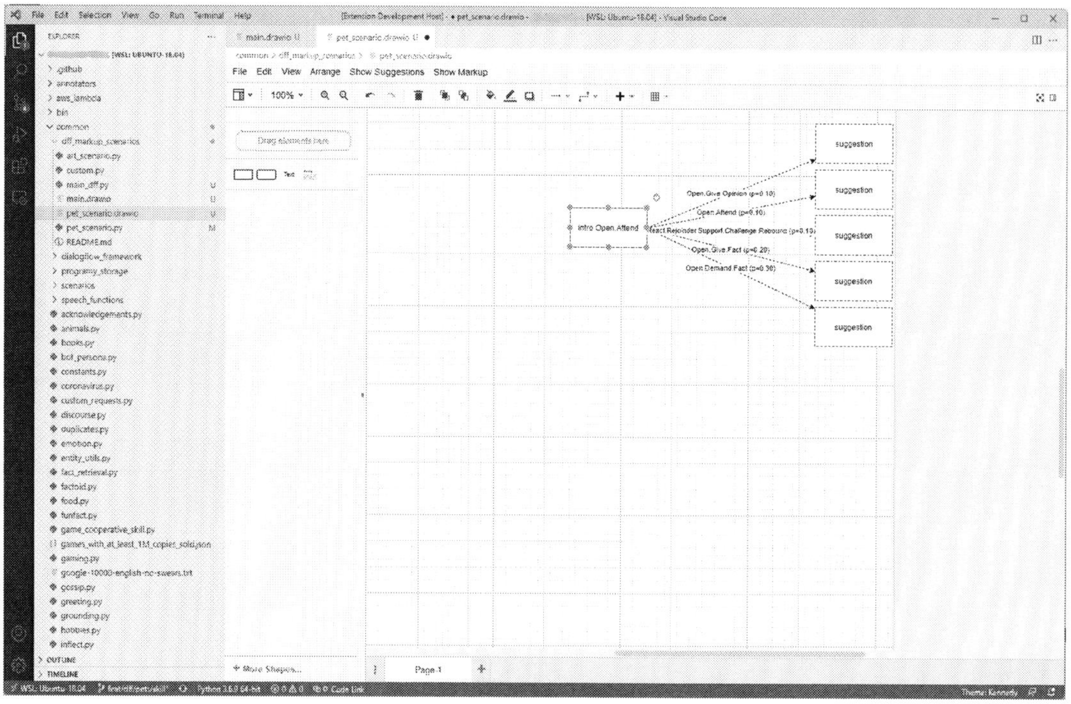


Figure 3: Using the *Speech Function Recommendations*

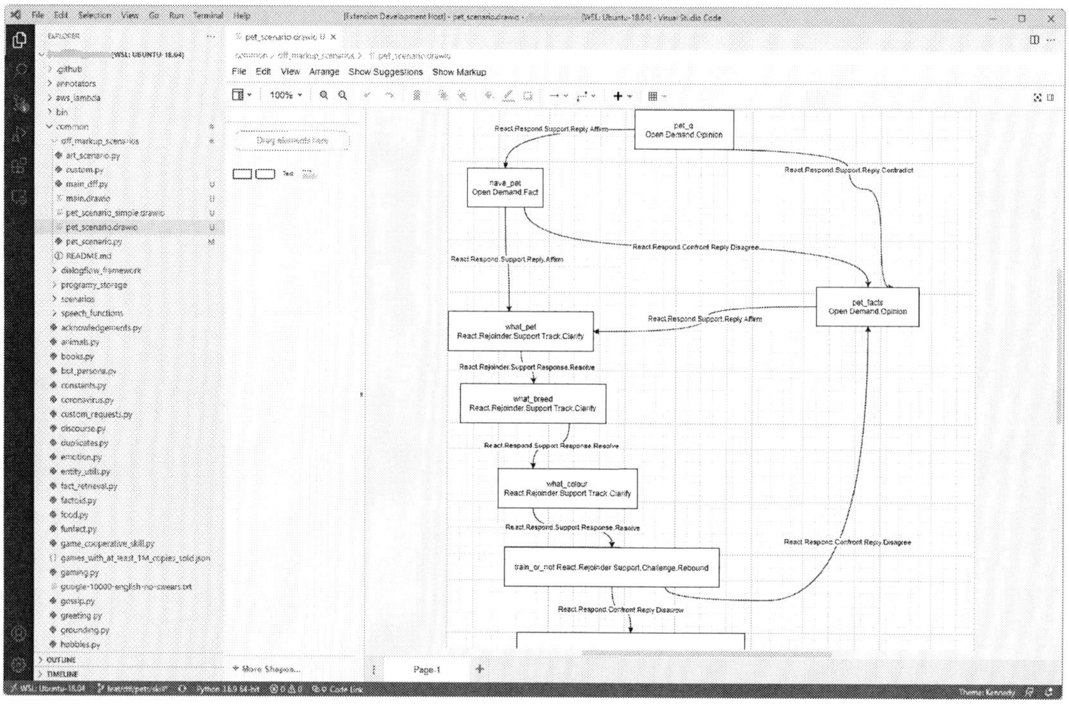


Figure 4: Outlining Scenario In VS Code Extension

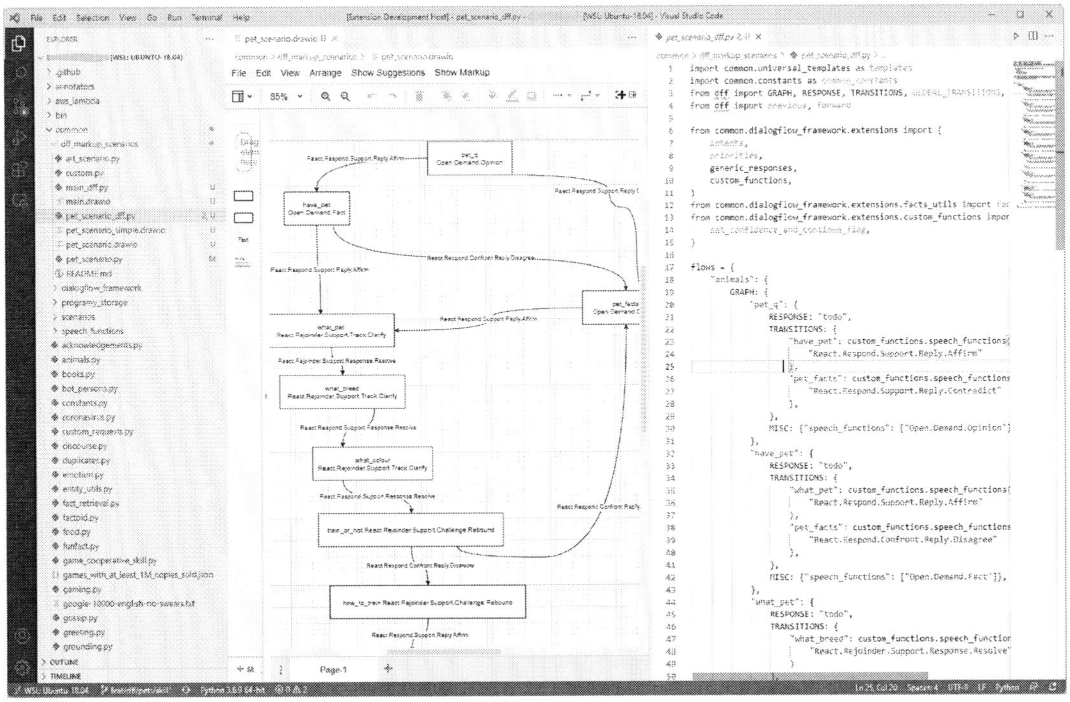

Figure 5: Using the Show Markup functionality to generate DFF Markup Code

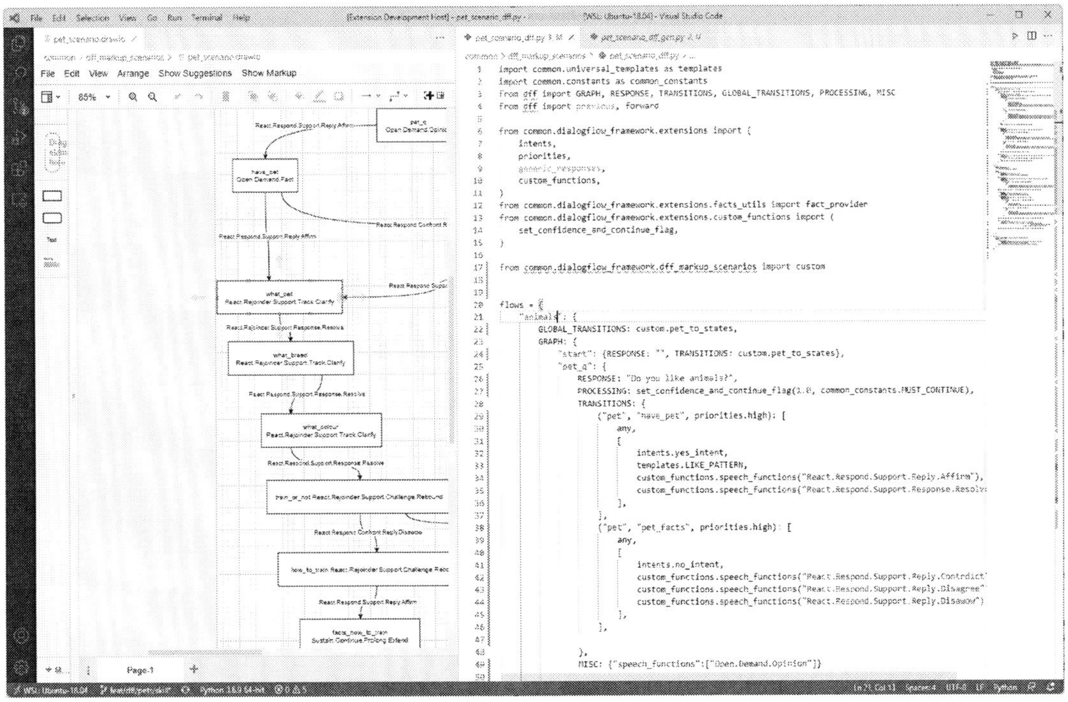

Figure 6: Adding Custom Code to the DFF Markup File

## B DFF: Detailed Overview

### B.1 Description

DFF as well as many extentions for it are distributed with an open source license, like many other frameworks (e.g., Emora STDM, AIML, RiveScript, ChatScript, botml, OpenDial, PyDial). DFF is distributed with Apache 2.0 license.

DFF DSL is a Python-based DSL for designing scenario-driven skills/chatbots. The main element of a skill in DFF DSL format is a dialogflow (a set of nodes and transitions between them, which refers to a particular subtopic). A dialogflow is a Python dictionary where keys are node names and elements describe response in this node and transitions to other nodes in the same dialogflow or in other dialogflows (Fig. 13). The main features of a dialogflow in DFF DSL format:

- a condition for transition between nodes can be one of predefined conditions in DFF DSL (for example, a regular expression or a function which checks the speech function in the user utterance, etc.)
- a response can be a string or a function
- processing of user utterance and response with custom functions (which can be used, for example, for slot extraction and slot filling (Fig. 14))
- extensions for using facts databases (for example, Wikipedia) for response generation (Fig. 16) or generic responses to user utterance speech function

The solution, like many others (e.g., AIML), is based on the state machine. However, unlike others, DFF aids in the development of the open-domain skills/chatbots with the help of the discourse moves recommendation making it easy to design these skills and chatbots. It also incorporates a mechanism to extract and use entities based on their Wikidata types, as well as to provide generic responses based on the speech functions ontology.

DFF was designed to be extensible as a modular system. With the external extentions, DFF can be significantly expanded as in complex frameworks (Finch and Choi, 2020), (Bocklisch et al., 2017). There is a set of community-created extentions that are well documented, and it is straightforward to add own extentions to the framework.

DFF DSL is automatically validated before starting the bot, making it easy to identify issues beforehand..

### B.2 Transitions

The target node for transition can be:

- the node name from the current dialogflow;
- the name of another dialogflow and the node in this dialogflow;
- special keywords (“forward” - to the next node in the current dialogflow, “back” - to the previous node, “repeat” - to make cycle transition, “previous” - to the previous active node).

Transitions between nodes can be local (which can be used only in the dialogflow where they were defined) or global (can be used in any other dialogflow).

## C DFF: Extensions

The approach of dividing DFF into modules allows users to incorporate both lightweight annotators, classifiers, and so on, as well as modules based on neural models that require a large amount of resources in their solutions.

In production ready systems, it is necessary to use keywords and a matching pattern for the agent to work, as well as the selection of entities, the presence of ontologies, the identification of intents, the classification of sentiments, and much more.

### C.1 Generic Responses Module

Generic responses are short utterances, generated by the bot in response to a particular speech function in user utterance. Generic responses can be useful if the user is proactive and responds with long and detailed utterances, the bot in this case will say somewhat like “yes”, “I agree”. Examples of generic responses:

- “No” in response to "React.Respond.Confront.Reply.Contradict" and "React.Respond.Reply.Contradict" speech functions;
- “I don’t know.” to "React.Respond.Confront.Reply.Disawow" and "React.Respond.Reply.Disawow";
- “I don’t agree with you” to "React.Respond.Confront.Reply.Disagree" and "React.Respond.Reply.Disagree";

- “Yes” to "React.Respond.Support.Reply.Affirm", "React.Respond.Support.Reply.Agree" and "React.Respond.Reply.Agree".

Generic responses are implemented as an extention for DFF DSL with one cycled node of dialogflow and a response function which extracts a speech function from the user utterance and generates a suitable generic response.

### C.2 Other Extentions

**Entity Extraction Module** is used to find entities of particular types in the user utterance and store them in shared memory. Entities can be extracted by:

- **Wikidata Entity Type**: user can specify a Wikidata ID for the given entity type to find entities of this type in the given utterance, e.g. to find a city user should specify "wiki:Q515" (which corresponds to “city” in Wikipedia)

- **Entity Tag** from the set of ("PERSON", "LOCATION", "ORGANIZATION", etc.): user can specify one of these tags to find entities of this type, e.g., to find a location user should specify "tag:LOCATION"

**Slot Filling Module** is used to fill extracted entities in the slots of the response.

**Factoid Response Generation Module** provides content of the page from the databases like Wikipedia, wikiHow, etc. mentioned as the argument of the extension function.

**Generic Responses Module** returns short utterances (for example, “Yes”, “No”, “I agree” etc.) that represent selected speech functions as appropriate response to the selected user utterance’s speech functions.

# D DFF: Conversational Analysis Dashboard

The statistics DFF extention [2] comes with a dashboard that displays various statistics. Using them, users can evaluate the user's use of script branches. The dashboard is shown in figures 7, 8, 9, 10, 12

[2] https://github.com/kudep/dff-node-stats/

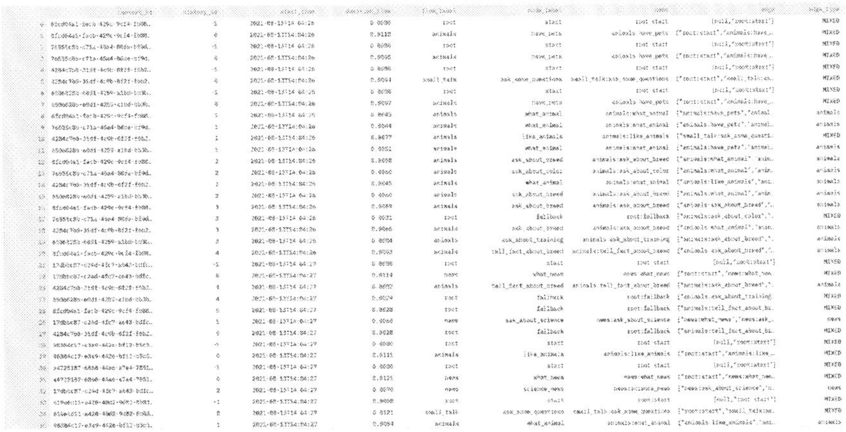

Figure 7: Statistic data frame is shown in the Dashboard

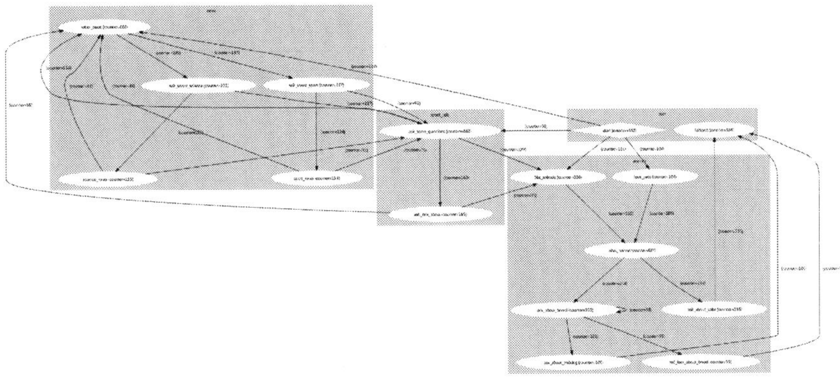

Figure 8: Transition graph with counters is built for all dialogues. Counters show numbers of users hitting these nodes or edges.

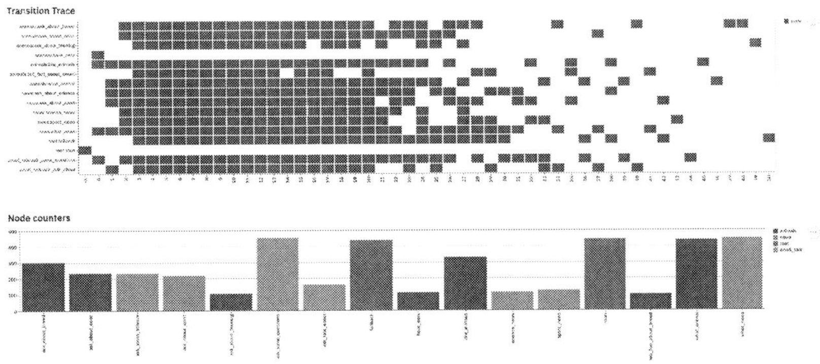


Figure 9: These figures are built in the dashboard. The top figure shows nodes that will be sent by all users at a certain step of the dialogue. The abscissa axis shows the order of a step in the dialog, the ordinate axis shows the node in which the user is located for this step. The bottom figure shows the frequency of users hitting each node, different colors are shown in different flows in which the nodes

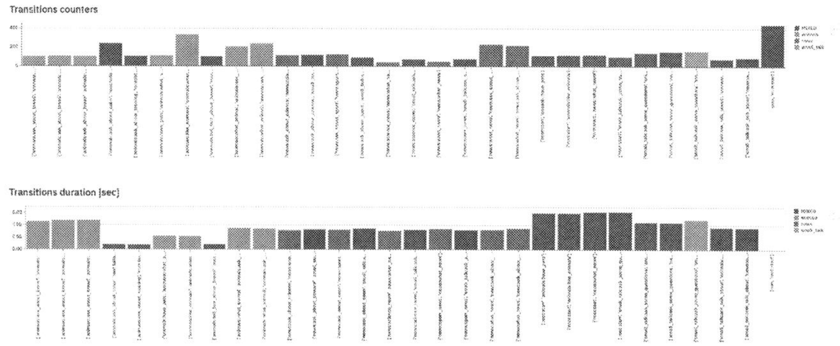


Figure 10: Statistic of transitions in dashboard. The top figure shows the frequency of users hitting each transition between nodes. The bottom figure shows duration of processing time for each transition between nodes. Different colors are shown in different flows in which the nodes.

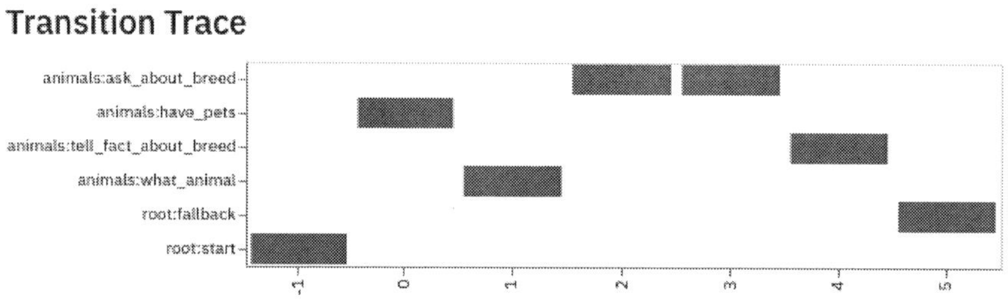


Figure 11: Statistic of transition in dashboard for one dialog. This figure shows the user transitions from node to node. The abscissa axis shows the order of a step in the dialog, the ordinate axis shows the node in which the user is located for this step.

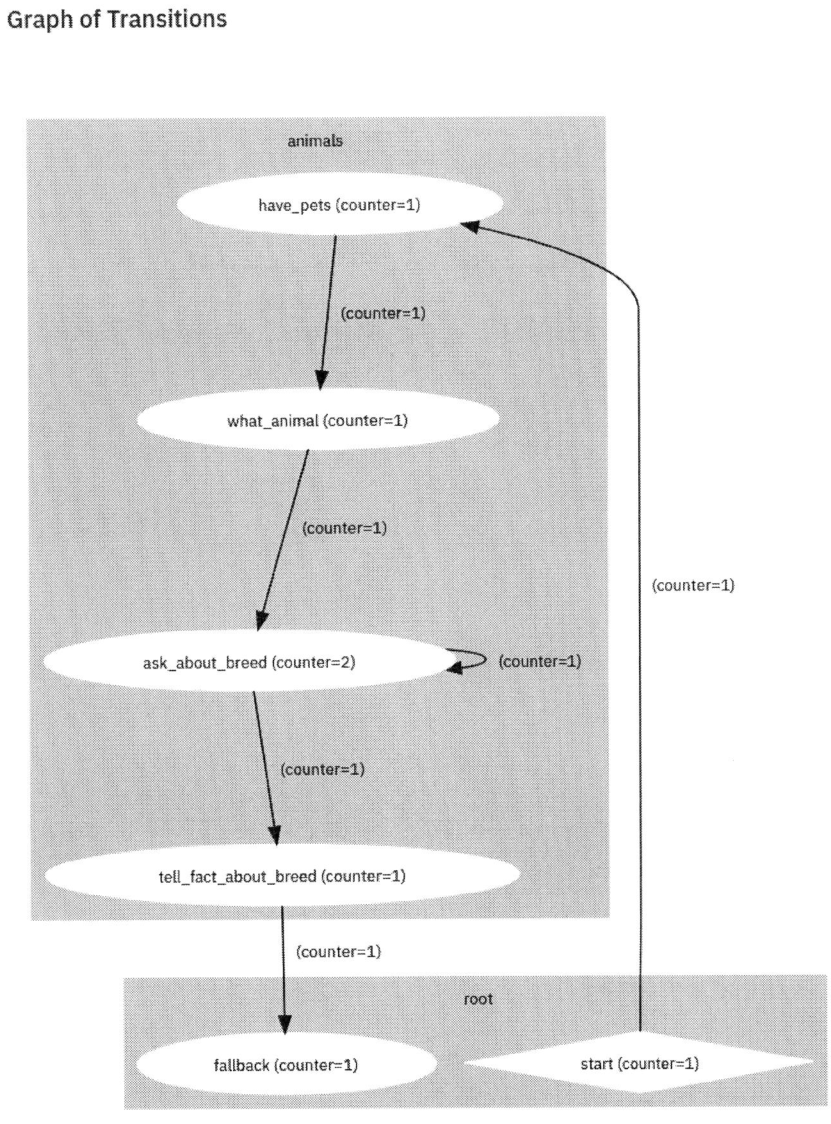


Figure 12: This figure is built in the dashboard. The graph shows user transitions through the script graph using one dialog as an example. Counters show numbers of users hitting these nodes or edges.

## E Additional Code Examples

This section of the appendix contains the code and tables with descriptions

```
"drawing": {
    GLOBAL_TRANSITIONS: {
        "what_painter": custom_functions.drawing_request,
    },
    GRAPH: {
        "what_painter": {
            RESPONSE: "Pictures of what painters do you like?",
            TRANSITIONS: {forward(): intents.always_true}
        },
        "what_paintings": {
            RESPONSE: "I also like pictures of {user_fav_painter}. "
                      "What kind of paintings do you like to draw: "
                      "landscapes, portraits or something else?",
            PROCESSING: [custom_functions.entities(user_fav_painter="wiki:Q1028181"),
                         custom_functions.slot_filling],
            TRANSITIONS: {forward(): intents.always_true}
        },
        "how_to_draw": {
            RESPONSE: custom_functions.how_to_draw_response,
            TRANSITIONS: {
                ("facts", "how_to_draw"): intents.yes_intent
            }
        }
    },
},
```

Figure 13: Example of dialog flow in DFF DSL format

```
"what_paintings": {
    RESPONSE: "I also like pictures of {user_fav_painter}. "
              "What kind of paintings do you like to draw: "
              "landscapes, portraits or something else?",
    PROCESSING: [custom_functions.entities(user_fav_painter="wiki:Q1028181"),
                 custom_functions.slot_filling],
    TRANSITIONS: {forward(): intents.always_true}
},
```

Figure 14: DFF DSL elements for entity extraction from user utterance and slot filling in response

```
PROCESSING: [custom_functions.entities(user_fav_painter="tag:LOCATION"),
             custom_functions.slot_filling],
```

Figure 15: DFF DSL elements for entity extraction using Entity Detection annotator

```
"facts": {
    GLOBAL_TRANSITIONS: {"how_to_draw": intents.facts},
    GRAPH: {"how_to_draw": {
                RESPONSE: fact_provider("wikiHow", "Improve-Your-Drawing-Skills"),
                TRANSITIONS: {"how_to_draw": intents.facts}}
    }
},
```

Figure 16: Dialog Flow with "fact_provider" - a function for response generation using a wikiHow article

```
generic_responses flow = {
    GLOBAL_TRANSITIONS: {
        generic_response_state: sys_response_to_speech_function_request,
    },
    GRAPH: {
        "generic_response": {
            RESPONSE: usr_response_to_speech_function_response,
            TRANSITIONS: {repeat(): sys_response_to_speech_function_request}
        }
    }
}
```

Figure 17: Dialogflow for generic responses generation

```python
if quarantine_end(last_utterance):
    logging.info('Quarantine end detected')
    reply, confidence = QUARANTINE_END_PHRASE, 0.95
elif last_bot_phrase in [WORK_AND_STAY_HOME_PHRASE, CDC_STAY_HOME_RECOMMENDATION]:
    if ' why ' in last_utterance_text or last_utterance_text[:3] == 'why':
        reply, confidence = EXPLAIN_PHRASE, 0.95
elif dontlike(last_utterance):
    reply, confidence = '', 0
elif asked_have(last_utterance):
    reply, confidence = BOT_CORONAVIRUS_PHRASE, 0.95
    reply = improve_phrase(reply)
elif vaccine_safety_request(last_utterance):
    reply, confidence = VACCINE_SAFETY_PHRASE, 0.95
elif emotion_detected(last_utterance, 'fear') or emotion_detected(last_utterance, 'anger'):
    r = random()
    if r < 0.5:
        reply, confidence = FEAR_HATE_REPLY1, 0.95
    else:
        reply, confidence = FEAR_HATE_REPLY2, 0.95
    reply = improve_phrase(reply)
elif get_chance_request(last_utterance):
    reply, confidence = "As I am not your family doctor, " \
                        "my knowledge about your resilience to coronavirus is limited.", 0.95
    reply = f'{reply} Please, check the CDC website for more information.'  # Daniil suggestion
elif 'to learn more' in last_bot_phrase:
    fear_prob = get_emotions(dialog['utterances'][-1], probs=True).get('fear', 0)
    logging.debug(f'Fear prob {fear_prob}')
    if is_no(last_utterance):
        logging.info('Another fact request detected, answer is NO')
        reply = corona_switch_skill_reply()
        confidence = 0.98
        human_attr["coronavirus_skill"]['stop'] = True
    elif fear_prob > 0.9:
        logging.info('Corona fear detected')
        reply = 'Just stay home, wash your hands and you will be fine. We will get over it.'
        confidence = 0.95
    elif is_yes(last_utterance):
        logging.info('Returning a fact')
        reply, confidence = return_fact(self.facts,
                                        human_attr['coronavirus_skill']['used_phrases'],
                                        asked_about_age, met_last), 1
    else:
        reply, confidence = '', 0
```

Figure 18: Coronavirus skill in pure Python

```
GRAPH: {
    "quarantine_end": {
        RESPONSE: "Although most American states are easing the restrictions, "
        "the Coronavirus pandemics in the majority of the states hasn't been reached yet. "
        "If you want to help ending it faster, please continue social distancing as much as you can.",
        PROCESSING: [int_prs.set_confidence(DEFAULT_CONFIDENCE)],
    },
    "uninteresting_topic": {RESPONSE: "", PROCESSING: [int_prs.set_confidence(ZERO_CONFIDENCE)]},
    "bot_has_covid": {
        RESPONSE: "As a socialbot, I don't have coronavirus. I hope you won't have it either.",
        PROCESSING: [int_prs.set_confidence(DEFAULT_CONFIDENCE)]
        # offer_more should be here by original idea, but it's useless due default function arguments
        # in legacy version of code (see coronavirus_skill.scenario: 554 and 375)
    },
    "vaccine_safety": {
        RESPONSE: "All CDC-approved vaccines are safe enough for you - "
        "of course, if your doctor does not mind against using them. "
        "I can't say the same about getting infected, however, "
        "so vaccines are necessary to prevent people from that..",
        PROCESSING: [int_prs.set_confidence(DEFAULT_CONFIDENCE)],
    },
    "user_feel_emotion": {
        RESPONSE: rsp.choice(
            [
                "Please, calm down. We are a strong nation, we are vaccinating people "
                "and we will overcome this disease one day.",
                "Please, chin up. We have already defeated a hell lot of diseases, "
                "and I am sure that coronavirus will be the next one.",
            ]
        ),
        PROCESSING: [int_prs.set_confidence(USER_FEEL_EMOTION_CONFIDENCE)],
    },
    "user_resilience_to_covid": {
        RESPONSE: "As I am not your family doctor, "
        "my knowledge about your resilience to coronavirus is limited. "
        "Please, check the CDC website for more information.",
        PROCESSING: [int_prs.set_confidence(DEFAULT_CONFIDENCE)],
    },
    "covid_symptoms": {
        RESPONSE: "According to the CDC website, "
        "The main warning signs of coronavirus are: "
        "difficulty breathing or shortness of breath, "
        "persistent pain or pressure in the chest, "
        "new confusion or inability to arouse, "
        "bluish lips or face. If you develop any of these signs, "
```

Figure 19: Coronavirus skill DFF DSL format

| **Speaker** | **Utterance** | **Speech Function** |
|---|---|---|
| Bot | Do you like animals? | Open.Demand.Opinion |
| User | yeah | React.Respond.Support.Reply.Affirm |
| Bot | Would you like to have a pet? | Open.Demand.Opinion |
| User | yeah | React.Respond.Support.Reply.Affirm |
| Bot | Cool! What pet is it? | React.Rejoinder.Support.Track.Clarify |
| User | I have a dog. His name is Archie. | React.Respond. Confront.Reply.Resolve |
| Bot | I also would like to have such a friend. What breed is your pet? | React.Rejoinder.Support.Track.Clarify |
| User | He is a golden retriever. | React.Respond. Confront.Reply.Resolve |
| Bot | Alright. And what color is it? | React.Rejoinder.Support.Track.Clarify |
| User | He's golden one with white ears. | React.Respond. Confront.Reply.Resolve |
| Bot | Have you ever tried to train your pet? | React.Rejoinder. Support.Challenge.Rebound |
| User | Yeah, I train him every week in the park. | React.Respond.Support.Reply.Affirm |
| Bot | Would you like to know how dogs are trained? | React.Rejoinder. Support.Challenge.Rebound |
| User | okay | React.Respond.Support.Reply.Affirm |
| Bot | Some breeds are more independent and hard to train than others. | Sustain.Continue.Prolong.Extend |
| User | yeah | React.Respond.Support.Register |

Table 1: Dialog Example

| **Speech Function** | **Discourse purpose** |
|---|---|
| Open.Attend | attention seeking |
| Open.Demand.Fact | demand factual information |
| Open.Demand.Opinion | demand evaluative information |
| Open.Give.Fact | give factual information |
| Open.Give.Opinion | give evaluative information |
| Sustain.Continue.Prolong.Extend | offer additional or contrasting information |
| Sustain.Continue.Prolong.Elaborate | clarify and restate |
| Sustain.Continue.Prolong.Enhance | qualify previous move by giving details |
| Sustain.Continue.Monitor | check that audience is still engaged |
| React.Rejoinder.Confront.Challenge.Counter | dismiss addressee's right to his/her position |
| React.Rejoinder.Confront.Response.Re-challenge | question relevance of a prior move |
| React.Rejoinder.Support.Challenge.Rebound | dismiss addressee's right to his/her position |
| React.Rejoinder.Support.Response.Resolve | provide clarification |
| React.Rejoinder.Support.Track.Check | elicit repetition of a misheard element |
| React.Rejoinder.Support.Track.Clarify | verify information heard |
| React.Rejoinder.Support.Track.Confirm | confirm information heard |
| React.Rejoinder.Support.Track.Probe | volunteer further details |
| React.Respond.Confront.Disengage | show unwillingness to interact |
| React.Respond.Confront.Reply.Contradict | negate prior information |
| React.Respond.Confront.Reply.Disagree | provide negative respond to question |
| React.Respond.Confront.Reply.Disawow | deny acknowledgement of information |
| React.Respond.Support.Develop.Elaborate | clarify and restate a prior move |
| React.Respond.Support.Develop.Enhance | qualify previous move by giving details |
| React.Respond.Support.Develop.Extend | offer additional or contrasting information |
| React.Respond.Support.Engage | show willingness to interact |
| React.Respond.Support.Register | display attention to the speaker |
| React.Respond.Support.Reply.Acknowledge | indicate knowledge of information given |
| React.Respond.Support.Reply.Affirm | provide positive response to the question |
| React.Respond.Support.Develop.Enhance | deny acknowledgement of information |
| React.Respond.Support.Reply.Agree | indicate support of information given |

Table 2: Discourse Purposes of Speech Functions

# Coreference Chains Categorization by Sequence Clustering

**Silvia Federzoni** and **Lydia-Mai Ho-Dac** and **Cécile Fabre**
CLLE, CNRS & University of Toulouse
Toulouse, France
{silvia.federzoni, hodac, cecile.fabre}@univ-tlse2.fr

## Abstract

The diversity of coreference chains is usually tackled by means of global features (length, types and number of referring expressions, distance between them, etc.). In this paper, we propose a novel approach that provides a description of their composition in terms of sequences of expressions. To this end, we apply sequence analysis techniques to bring out the various strategies for introducing a referent and keeping it active throughout discourse. We discuss a first application of this method to a French written corpus annotated with coreference chains. We obtain clusters that are linguistically coherent and interpretable in terms of reference strategies and we demonstrate the influence of text genre and semantic type of the referent on chain composition.

## 1 Introduction

Coreference chains are discourse structures built upon a set of referential expressions (or mentions) denoting a common discourse entity (Corblin, 1995; Poesio et al., 2016a). They provide a fundamental mechanism for text interpretation and contribute to cohesion between clauses (Halliday and Hasan, 1976). Linguistic analysis and automatic detection of coreference chains are still a challenge, due to their complexity and the diversity of their composition (Recasens et al., 2011). In particular, a large diversity of linguistic expressions may be used to mention a discourse entity, such as proper nouns, pronouns, possessives, definite or demonstrative noun phrases, in various syntactic positions. This diversity is usually tackled by studying the global characteristics of the coreference chains (Nedoluzhko and Lapshinova-Koltunski, 2016; Kunz and Lapshinova-Koltunski, 2015), e.g. the number of mentions, their type, the distance between them or by focusing only on the characteristics of the first two mentions.

We propose a method that complements these approaches by considering chains as linear sequences of mentions. This makes it possible to identify categories of coreference chains in terms of chaining, which gives new insights for linguistic characterization and provides knowledge about variational dimensions that can help to improve coreference resolution systems (Lapshinova-Koltunski and Kunz, 2020).

We resort to sequence analysis techniques which are generally used in social sciences to build typologies of "typical sequences" to study life-course trajectories, family histories, professional career paths. In such studies, sequences are used to model the chronology of states or events (Studer and Ritschard, 2014; Brzinsky-Fay et al., 2006). We apply these techniques to coreference chains categorization by considering each mention as a state in the chain chronology, and by characterizing mentions with features traditionally used for studying referring expressions and resolving coreference such as mention types and syntactic functions, relations between mentions, degree of accessibility (Ariel, 2001; Walker, 2000; Poesio et al., 2016b).

This paper presents a first step in which only mention types are considered. We apply sequence analysis to a French written corpus annotated with topical chains. We discuss the results in two steps: first we show that the obtained clusters are linguistically interpretable; then we demonstrate that text genre and semantic nature of the referent influence the coreference chain composition.

## 2 Description of the experiment

### 2.1 Data

We use a written French corpus, the AnnoDis corpus, annotated with topical chains, which correspond to coreference chains that are built upon a prominent or topical element (Asher et al., 2017). It provides 581 chains annotated in full long structured texts and organized in three sub-corpora pertaining to various non-narrative genres : geopoli-



*Proceedings of the 2nd Workshop on Computational Approaches to Discourse*, pages 52–57
November 10–11, 2021. 

tics reports (GEOP), linguistics articles (LING) and encyclopedic texts (WIK2) (Péry-Woodley et al., 2011)[1], see Table 1.

| | Words | Chains | Mentions |
|---|---|---|---|
| GEOP | 266,000 | 234 | 1,125 |
| LING | 169,000 | 87 | 478 |
| WIK2 | 231,000 | 260 | 1,853 |
| **AnnoDis** | 666,000 | 581 | 3,456 |

Table 1: Number of words, coreference chains and mentions in the AnnoDis corpus.

Among the wide range of linguistic features that can be considered for characterizing mentions this first experiment focuses on the grammatical category only, which provides the simplest information on chain typology. Each mention of the coreference chains is labeled by one of the 8 types listed in Table 2 (definite, demonstrative or indefinite NPs, NPs without determiners, proper nouns, possessives, pronouns, other).

| Mention type | GEOP | LING | WIK2 | AnnoDis |
|---|---|---|---|---|
| Def. NP | 499 | 185 | 514 | 1,198 |
| Dem. NP | 115 | 49 | 108 | 272 |
| Ind. NP | 56 | 21 | 49 | 126 |
| NoDet NP | 14 | 6 | 44 | 64 |
| Proper N. | 63 | 41 | 338 | 442 |
| Possessives | 59 | 9 | 114 | 182 |
| Pronouns | 288 | 142 | 596 | 1,026 |
| Other | 31 | 25 | 90 | 146 |
| **Total** | 1,125 | 1,853 | 478 | 3,456 |

Table 2: Distribution of mention types in the AnnoDis corpus and his sub-corpora

### 2.2 Sequence analysis

We carry out the sequence analysis using the `TraMineR` toolbox (Gabadinho et al., 2009, 2011), that brings together various features designed to handle sequential data. This allows us to identify and visualize sequences, but also to implement clustering and statistical methods to identify categories of sequences.

**Sequences length** Length variation may have a strong impact on the clustering. According to the distribution of the data in our corpus, we decided to limit the variation in sequence length by taking into account the first seven mentions only. This means that 21% of the chains have been cut.

**Optimal matching** The similarity between the pairs of sequences is measured by using the optimal matching based on the Levenshtein distance. The optimal matching between two sequences is the minimum cost to transform one into the other by taking into account both the substitution and insertion or deletion operations. We chose this method because it can be applied to sequences of unequal lengths e.g. chains of two or seven mentions (Studer and Ritschard, 2014; Gabadinho et al., 2011). To compute the substitution-cost matrix we used the "TRATE" method, which determines the costs from the estimated transition rates (Lesnard and Saint Pol, 2006; Gabadinho et al., 2011).

**Hierarchical clustering** Since we have no hypothesis regarding the optimal number of clusters, we use hierarchical clustering and apply the Ward's linkage criterion which calculate the variance of clusters. We observed the results with different values, from 2 to 5. In this paper, we discuss in more details the results we obtained with 3 and 5 clusters.

## 3 Results

The first application of the clustering method was experimented on the 581 sequences provided by the AnnoDis corpus. Each sequence was automatically clustered in three and five classes according to the grammatical category of the mentions.

### 3.1 Description of the clusters

**3-way clustering:** The three classes of chains clearly differ according to the type of the first mention. Figure 1 gives a global overview of the three classes. Each color corresponds to a grammatical category of the mentions. Within each graph, the different chains are sorted according to their similarity, by using the multidimentional scaling (Popper and Heymann, 1996; Yeturu, 2020), in order to better visualize the heterogeneity of the classes.

The first cluster (C1-3w[2]) groups together the largest number of sequences (317) among which 89.6% (284) start with a definite NP (in light yellow). Typically, there are other definite NPs as next mentions.

[1]The AnnoDis corpus is available at: `http://redac.univ-tlse2.fr/corpus/annodis/`

[2]We use this notation to indicate the number of the cluster and whether it is part of 3-way clustering (3w) or 5-way clustering (5w).

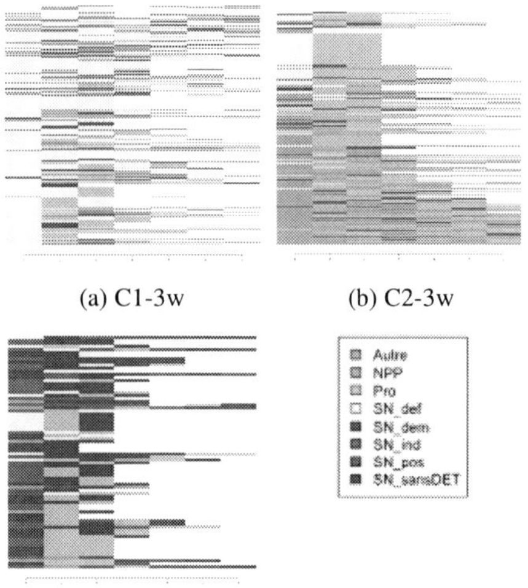


(a) C1-3w (b) C2-3w

(c) C3-3w

Figure 1: 3-way clustering

Example (1) illustrates an excerpt of a C1-3w chain in which all mentions (underlined) are definite NPs (namely: *the Champagne vineyard* [...] *the vineyard* [...] *the vineyard* [...] *the Champagne vineyard*).

**(1)** *le vignoble champenois s'étendait sur quelques [...] le vignoble connaît [...] le vignoble s'est réduit à 12 000 hectares. Aujourd'hui, en 2007, le vignoble champenois s'étend sur 32 341 hectares.*

Cluster C2-3w groups together 201 sequences among which 50.7% (102) start with a proper noun (in light violet) and 28.8% (58) with a definite NP (in light yellow). The next mentions are mainly proper nouns or pronouns (in light orange). In contrast with cluster C1-3w, there are very few definite NPs as next mentions. Example (2) shows a typical C2-3w chain (*F. de Saussure* [...] *he* [...] *him* [...] *he*).

**(2)** *Chez F. de Saussure, l'analogie [...], il pose [...]. Pour lui, cette tendance [...]. Comme H. Paul, il ramène le concept [...]*

Finally, cluster C3-3w gathers 63 sequences, among which 47.6% (30) begin with an indefinite NP (in fuchsia) as first mention and 36.5% (23) with a demonstrative NP (in blue), mostly followed by other demonstrative NPs or pronouns (in light orange). Example (3) illustrates a C3-3w chain which starts with an indefinite NP (*an oppositional connotation*, followed by two demonstratives (*This*, *this dichotomy*).

**(3)** *[...] présente ainsi fréquemment une connotation oppositionnelle (sinon contradictoire) avec le linguistique. Ceci est particulièrement crucial [...] Cette dichotomie pose problème au psychologue [...].*

A preliminary interpretation of these results suggests that these three classes of coreference chains may be pointing at three different strategies for introducing and maintaining the referent. Chains in cluster C2-3w (proper nouns followed by pronouns) seem typically associated to human referents. In addition, the sequence of pronouns may also indicate that the referent is likely to be the topic of discourse. Chains in C3-3w are rather used for presenting ideas or concepts. Demonstratives NPs are likely to encapsulate large portions of text presenting such propositional content under an abstract anaphora (e.g. *this question*).

**5-way clustering:** We give here a quick overview of the results obtained with 5 clusters. Chains with indefinite and demonstrative NPs (C3-3w) are still clustered in a class (C2-5w). The 5-way clustering provides a different distribution of the chains that begin with a definite NP (C1-3w) and a proper noun (C2-3w).

More precisely, we see that a finer categorization is provided for the chains that begin mostly with a definite NP. Chains in C1-5w (45 sequences) are mainly composed by definite NPs with little variation in categories of the next mentions (as previously exemplified in (1)). In contrast, chains in C3-5w (272 sequences) present a greater variety of next mention types, while cluster C4-5w (96 sequences) mainly exhibits pronouns as next mentions. Finally, cluster C5-5w (105 sequences), begins mostly with proper nouns, next mentions being mainly proper nouns or pronouns.

This categorization highlights more clearly the homogeneity of the chains, as suggested by Obry et al. (2017). It also points at a difference within chains that are typically associated to human referents, namely C4-5w and C5-5w. The strong presence of pronouns indicates that the referent is not in competition with other referents, while the alternation between proper nouns and pronouns or possessives suggests that the referent is not sufficiently accessible because of competition between referents or long-distance coreferential relation.

What follows reports a first experiment to back up this qualitative analysis.

### 3.2 Interpretation of the clusters

Chain composition can vary according to language, mode, genre or register (Grishina and Stede, 2015; Kunz et al., 2016), text type (narrative or non-narrative) or the semantic nature of referent (Longo, 2013). In this study, we focus on two parameters: text genre (corresponding to the three sub-corpora) and the semantic nature of referent. The chi-squared test was used to observe correlations between these two parameters and the classes of chains.

#### Text genre

**3-way clustering:** The chi-squared test highlights a significant relationship (df = 4, p-value = 2.575e-06) between classes and text genres of the corpus. The observation of the Pearson's residual highlights a negative correlation between C3-3w and the WIK2 sub-corpus, a positive correlation between C2-3w and the WIK2 sub-corpus and a negative one between C2-3w and the GEOP sub-corpus. There are no other correlations.

Following these first results, we can say that chains composed by proper nouns followed by pronouns are more frequent in encyclopedic texts than in geopolitical reports. In geopolitical texts we find a majority of chains composed by definite noun phrases followed by pronouns.

**5-way clustering:** The chi-squared test highlights a significant relationship (df = 8, p-value = 1.945e-05) between classes and text genres of the corpus. The observation of the Pearson's residual highlights correlations similar to that observed for the 3-way clustering: a negative correlation between C2-5w and the WIK2 sub-corpus, a positive correlation between cluster C5-5w and the WIK2 sub-corpus and a negative one between cluster C5-5w and the GEOP sub-corpus. There are no other correlations. The differences between C4-5w and C5-5w are not dependant on the text genres.

**Semantic nature of referent** A semi-automatic annotation has been carried out to distinguish chains referring to human or non-human in the AnnoDis corpus.

**3-way clustering:** The correlation between the classes and the human or non-human nature of the referent is even clearer. The chi-squared test highlights a significant relationship between classes and referent types (df = 2, p-value < 2.2e-16), with a positive correlation between C2-3w and chains referring to humans and between C1-3w and C3-3w and chains referring to non-humans.

| | Human | Non-human |
|---|---|---|
| GEOP | 136 | 98 |
| LING | 22 | 65 |
| WIK2 | 138 | 122 |
| AnnoDis | 296 | 285 |

Table 3: Number of human and non-human chains

**5-way clustering:** The chi-squared test highlights a significant relationship between classes and referent types (df = 4, p-value < 2.2e-16), with a positive correlation between C4-5w and C5-5w and chains referring to humans. There is also a positive correlation between C2-5w and C3-5w and chains referring to non-humans.

## 4 Discussion and perspectives

This application of sequence analysis to coreference chain description provides clusters that are linguistically coherent and interpretable and that reflect different strategies for introducing and maintaining the referent. This method allows for fine-grained analyses of the mentions chaining and demonstrate that text genres and the semantic nature of referent influence the chain composition.

Next steps will consist in refining the model in several ways. First, we will take into account more fine-grained features, for example by distinguishing the different types of pronouns (personal, demonstratives, indefinite, possessives). This may prove useful to highlight further differences in the composition of chains, potentially also related to the referent types. We will also test other features, such as syntactic functions, relations between mentions, degree of accessibility, coupled with different settings for sequence clustering and a larger variety of referent types (e.g. concrete referent vs abstract referent, generic vs specific, individuals vs collectives, also taking advantage of named entity information); the application of this method to a larger corpus will make it possible to take into account a broader range of text genres and referent types.

Such a description is a complement to more traditional descriptions and may have longer term applications to coreference resolution, since taking into account variation is crucial to improve the systems (Recasens and Hovy, 2010; Uryupina and Poesio, 2012). Soon et al. (2001) show that entity-type information could be a useful feature for coreference resolution. In the same line, (Khosla and Rose, 2020) demonstrate that neural models using contextualised representations like BERT (Peters et al., 2018) improve coreference resolution performances when entity-type features are explicitly taking into account.

## References


Mira Ariel. 2001. Accessibility theory: An overview. *Text representation: Linguistic and psycholinguistic aspects*, 8:29–87.

Nicholas Asher, Philippe Muller, Myriam Bras, Lydia-Mai Ho-Dac, Farah Benamara, Stergos Afantenos, and Laure Vieu. 2017. ANNODIS and related projects: case studies on the annotation of discourse structure. In Nancy Ide and James Pustejovsky, editors, *Handbook of Linguistic Annotation*, pages 1241–1264. Springer Netherlands.

Christian Brzinsky-Fay, Ulrich Kohler, and Magdalena Luniak. 2006. Sequence analysis with Stata. *The Stata Journal*, 6(4):435–460.

Francis Corblin. 1995. *Les formes de reprise dans le discours. Anaphores et chaînes de référence.* Presses Universitaires de Rennes.

Alexis Gabadinho, Gilbert Ritschard, Nicolas Séverin Mueller, and Matthias Studer. 2011. Analyzing and visualizing state sequences in R with TraMineR. *Journal of statistical software*, 40(4):1–37.

Alexis Gabadinho, Gilbert Ritschard, Matthias Studer, and Nicolas S Müller. 2009. Mining sequence data in R with the TraMineR package: A user's guide. *Geneva: Department of Econometrics and Laboratory of Demography, University of Geneva.*

Yulia Grishina and Manfred Stede. 2015. Knowledge-lean projection of coreference chains across languages. In *Proceedings of the Eighth Workshop on Building and Using Comparable Corpora*, Beijing, China.

Michael A. K. Halliday and Ruqaiya Hasan. 1976. *Cohesion in English.* Longman: London.

Sopan Khosla and Carolyn Rose. 2020. Using type information to improve entity coreference resolution. In *Proceedings of the First Workshop on Computational Approaches to Discourse*, pages 20–31. Association for Computational Linguistics.

K. Kunz and Ekaterina Lapshinova-Koltunski. 2015. Cross-linguistic analysis of discourse variation across registers. *Nordic Journal of English Studies*, 14:258–288.

Kerstin Kunz, Ekaterina Lapshinova-Koltunski, and José Manuel Martinez. 2016. Beyond identity coreference: Contrasting indicators of textual coherence in English and German. In *Proceedings of the Workshop on Coreference Resolution Beyond OntoNotes (CORBON 2016)*, pages 23–31.

Ekaterina Lapshinova-Koltunski and Kerstin Kunz. 2020. Exploring coreference features in heterogeneous data. In *Proceedings of the First Workshop on Computational Approaches to Discourse*, pages 53–64. Association for Computational Linguistics.

Laurent Lesnard and Thibaut de Saint Pol. 2006. Introduction aux méthodes d'appariement optimal (optimal matching analysis). *Bulletin de méthodologie sociologique. Bulletin of sociological methodology*, 90:5–25.

Laurence Longo. 2013. *Vers des moteurs de recherche "intelligents" : un outil de détection automatique de thèmes.* Phd thesis, Université de Strasbourg.

Anna Nedoluzhko and Ekaterina Lapshinova-Koltunski. 2016. Contrasting coreference in Czech and German: from different frameworks to joint results. In *Computational Linguistics and Intellectual Technologies: Proceedings of the 22nd International Conference "Dialogue-21"*, Moscow, Russia.

Vanessa Obry, Julie Glikman, Céline Guillot-Barbance, and Bénédicte Pincemin. 2017. Les chaînes de référence dans les récits brefs en français: étude diachronique (xiiie-xvie s.). *Langue française*, 3:91–110.

Matthew E Peters, Mark Neumann, Mohit Iyyer, Matt Gardner, Christopher Clark, Kenton Lee, and Luke Zettlemoyer. 2018. Deep contextualized word representations. *arXiv preprint arXiv:1802.05365.*

Massimo Poesio, Sameer Pradhan, Marta Recasens, Kepa Rodriguez, and Yannick Versley. 2016a. Annotated corpora and annotation tools. In Massimo Poesio, Roland Stuckardt, and Yannick Versley, editors, *Anaphora Resolution: Algorithms, Resources, and Applications*, pages 97–140. Springer Berlin Heidelberg, Berlin, Heidelberg.

Massimo Poesio, Roland Stuckardt, and Yannick Versley, editors. 2016b. *Anaphora Resolution.* Theory and Applications of Natural Language Processing. Springer Berlin Heidelberg.

Richard Popper and Hildegarde Heymann. 1996. Analyzing differences among products and panelists by multidimensional scaling. In Tormod Naes and Einar Risvik, editors, *Multivariate analysis of data in sensory science*, volume 16 of *Data Handling in Science and Technology*, pages 159–184. Elsevier.

Marie-Paule Péry-Woodley, Stergos Afantenos, Lydia-Mai Ho-Dac, and Nicholas Asher. 2011. La ressource ANNODIS, un corpus enrichi d'annotations discursives. *Traitement Automatique des Langues*, 52(3):71–101.

Marta Recasens and Eduard Hovy. 2010. Coreference resolution across corpora: Languages, coding schemes, and preprocessing information. In *Proceedings of the 48th Annual Meeting of the Association for Computational Linguistics*, pages 1423–1432, Uppsala, Sweden. Association for Computational Linguistics.

Marta Recasens, Eduard Hovy, and M. Antònia Martí. 2011. Identity, non-identity, and near-identity: Addressing the complexity of coreference. *Lingua*, 121(6):1138–1152.

Wee Meng Soon, Hwee Tou Ng, and Daniel Chung Yong Lim. 2001. A machine learning approach to coreference resolution of noun phrases. *Computational linguistics*, 27(4):521–544.

Matthias Studer and Gilbert Ritschard. 2014. A comparative review of sequence dissimilarity measures. *LIVES Working Paper No. 33.*, Geneva, Switzerland: Swiss National Centre of Competence in Research.

Olga Uryupina and Massimo Poesio. 2012. Domain-specific vs. uniform modeling for coreference resolution. In *Proceedings of the Eight International Conference on Language Resources and Evaluation (LREC'12)*, Istanbul, Turkey. European Language Resources Association (ELRA).

Marilyn A. Walker. 2000. Vers un modèle de l'interaction du centrage avec la structure globale du discours. *Verbum*, XXII(1):31–58.

Kalidas Yeturu. 2020. Chapter 3 - machine learning algorithms, applications, and practices in data science. In Arni S.R. Srinivasa Rao and C.R. Rao, editors, *Principles and Methods for Data Science*, volume 43 of *Handbook of Statistics*, pages 81–206. Elsevier.

# Resolving Implicit References in Instructional Texts

**Talita Rani Anthonio** **Michael Roth**
University of Stuttgart
Institute for Natural Language Processing
{anthonta,rothml}@ims.uni-stuttgart.de

## Abstract

The usage of (co-)referring expressions in discourse contributes to the coherence of a text. However, text comprehension can be difficult when referring expressions are non-verbalized and have to be resolved in the discourse context. In this paper, we propose a novel dataset of such *implicit references*, which we automatically derive from insertions of references in collaboratively edited how-to guides. Our dataset consists of 6,014 instances, making it one of the largest datasets of implicit references and a useful starting point to investigate misunderstandings caused by underspecified language. We test different methods for resolving implicit references in our dataset based on the Generative Pre-trained Transformer model (GPT) and compare them to heuristic baselines. Our experiments indicate that GPT can accurately resolve the majority of implicit references in our data. Finally, we investigate remaining errors and examine human preferences regarding different resolutions of an implicit reference given the discourse context.

## 1 Introduction

Implicit language phenomena can be challenging for both human and machine processing. For example, references play a crucial role in instructional texts as they provide answers to questions such as *Which objects need to be used?* If such references are not made explicitly, they might be clear to readers who have task-specific knowledge, but for others they might cause problems or misunderstandings. Resolving such *implicit references* could improve clarity and prevent problems in discourse processing when multiple interpretations exist.

In natural language processing, implicit references have been handled as part of existing tasks such as semantic role labeling of implicit arguments (Gerber and Chai, 2012, cf. §3). Implicit arguments are generally hard to model computationally because they do not show up in easy to

| **Defrost Ground Beef** |
|---|
| (1) Place the ground beef in a microwave. |
| (2) Microwave until it finishes thawing. |
| (3) Use ______ within 1 or 2 days. |
| (3') Use the beef within 1 or 2 days. |
| (3") Use the microwave within 1 or 2 days. |

Table 1: Simplified example based on the wikiHow article "Defrost Ground Beef": sentences (1–3) show the original version of a text. Sentence (3') and (3") show revised versions that include a manually inserted or automatically generated reference (see §5), respectively.

learn surface patterns (Ruppenhofer et al., 2009). The use of role-semantic formalisms further complicates progress in this direction because manual annotation requires trained annotators and previous training datasets have been comparatively small. For example, most datasets of implicit arguments consist of just hundreds of instances or only predicate-specific annotations (Moor et al., 2013).

We propose a task and dataset of implicit references which we obtain without manual annotation. Specifically, we create a dataset by extracting insertions of references in the revision history of collaboratively edited how-to guides. Previous work has shown that revisions in instructional texts are typically made to improve a text (Anthonio and Roth, 2020). Based on this observation, we assume that explicit references are inserted when an implicit reference is perceived as problematic in discourse context. A simplified example from our dataset and an illustration of our task are provided in Table 1.

As shown by the example, our data consists of insertions of single references and the task is to predict these inserted references. As a benefit over existing work, the task does not depend on any formalism of role semantics, which means that models can be evaluated in an end-to-end setting.

As a dataset for the proposed task, we provide

6,014 instances of implicit references, which we extracted automatically by comparing different versions of articles in wikiHow[1]. In practice, we make use of an existing resource of wikiHow sentences and revisions called wikiHowToImprove (Anthonio et al., 2020), from which we select specifically those cases in which a *referring expression* was inserted that refers to an *entity* mentioned in the preceding context. Based on this dataset, we set up a cloze task in which we evaluate the ability of computational models to generate references for insertions that occur naturally in publicly available texts. Finally, we analyze predictions of different modeling approaches as well as differences between model-generated and human-inserted references, which provide useful insights regarding potential weaknesses of existing models and potential causes of human misunderstandings.

In sum, we make the following contributions:

- We propose a new task that requires NLP models to generate explicit references to resolve cases of implicit language (§2).
- We provide a dataset of 6,014 texts that involve the insertion of an explicit reference according to the text's revision history (§4).
- We show that methods based on the Generative Pre-trained Transformer model (GPT) present a strong baseline for this task (§5).
- We conduct two analyses that shed light on the strengths of GPT and reveal potential avenues for future research (§6).

## 2 Implicit Reference Resolution

**Task definition.** We formally define the task of resolving implicit references as a generation task that requires the prediction of a reference $S$, given:

1. The original/revised sentence and its preceding context $C_p$, which includes at least one mention that co-refers to the correct reference (for the example shown in Table 1: *Place the ground beef in a microwave. Microwave until it finishes thawing. Use ______*).
2. The number of tokens $L$ of the reference to be generated according to the final version of a sentence (in case of the example: 2).
3. The follow-up context $C_f$, which contains the remaining tokens of the original/revised sentence to ensure that the reference fits into the sentence grammatically (in the example, *within 1 or 2 days* needs to fit after *Use ____*).

Performing this task requires a model to generate the sequence of tokens $s_1 \ldots s_L$ for the reference $S$ conditioned on the context $\langle C_p, C_f \rangle$. In practice, the full task can be approached by first sampling candidate reference tokens $r_1 \ldots r_L$ from a conditional probability distribution $P(r_i | C_p, r_1 \ldots r_{i-1})$ and then re-ranking the highest scoring candidates according to the full sequence probability $P(C_p, r_1 \ldots r_L, C_f)$. Formulating the task in this way enables a direct application of language models and we demonstrate suitable baselines based on an auto-regressive language model in Section 5.

## 3 Related Work

The task of resolving implicit references can be viewed as a modified version of implicit argument labeling. First studies on implicit argument labeling were conducted by Gerber and Chai (2010) and Ruppenhofer et al. (2009). Gerber and Chai (2010) collected a dataset by manually labeling implicit arguments of 10 different nominal predicates in NomBank (Meyers et al., 2004), yielding about 1,000 instances. Ruppenhofer et al. (2009) created a dataset through manual annotation of fictional text. Their dataset contains more different predicates than previous studies, but is smaller in size. More recent studies make use of the two datasets and attempted to create additional training data artificially (Silberer and Frank, 2012; Roth and Frank, 2013; Laparra and Rigau, 2013a,b; Chiarcos and Schenk, 2015). Many of them are based on co-reference and discourse salience, which we also use for our baselines. Schenk and Chiarcos (2016) propose an unsupervised approach by aligning implicit arguments to semantic role labeling annotated data. Cheng and Erk (2019, 2018) generated large amounts of training data automatically using co-reference resolution. They also build a neural model based on argument fillers that occur multiple times in a narrative event chain. Finally, there are also datasets with domain-specific annotations such as geographic-event roles (Ebner et al., 2020) and on recipes (Jiang et al., 2020).

Another closely related task is zero anaphora resolution, which has been extensively studied in pro-drop languages such as Chinese (Yeh and Chen,

[1]http://www.wikihow.org

2003) and Japanese (Taira et al., 2008; Isozaki and Hirao, 2003; Seki et al., 2002; Nakaiwa, 1997; Imamura et al., 2009). A closely related study to ours is Imamura et al. (2009), who used language model probabilities as features.

As a commonality, previous work addresses semantic arguments of predicates that are realized outside a local syntactic scope. Our definition of implicit references subsumes such arguments, with the main difference that our task does not require the type of an argument or its semantic role to be specified. As a consequence, references in our task can fill one, none or multiple roles of different predicates. Once the correct reference has been identified, our task additionally requires the generation of a referring expression. This task has been addressed separately in previous work, for instance, using rule-based approaches (Reiter and Dale, 2000), feature-based machine learning (Nenkova and McKeown, 2003; Greenbacker and McCoy, 2009; Same and van Deemter, 2020; Kibrik et al., 2016), and deep neural networks (Castro Ferreira et al., 2016; Cao and Cheung, 2019).

## 4 Data

The starting point for our data are revision histories from wikiHow, in which we can find insertions of references that were implicit in earlier versions of a sentence. We use wikiHowToImprove (Anthonio et al., 2020), a resource derived from wikiHow that consists of approximately 2.7 million sentences and their revisions. For our purpose, we extract sentences in which a reference was inserted during revision. Most of the sentences in wikiHow are only edited once (about 83%). In other cases, intermediate versions are mostly the result of stylistic refinements or typo corrections. Therefore, we only make use of the final version of a sentence (henceforth *revised sentence*), which includes an inserted reference, and the *original sentence*, in which the reference is assumed to be implicit. As a result, each data point in our collection consists of a pair of two versions of a sentence, henceforth *original-revised sentence pair*. We describe our selection of implicit references in Section 4.1 and present the data statistics in Section 4.2.

### 4.1 Collection

In order to find pairs with an implicit reference in the original sentence that is explicit in the revised sentence, we take the instances where the revised sentence was created by inserting a word or contiguous set of words in the original sentence. In other words, eliminating the insertion from the revised sentence yields the original sentence. This is a logical starting point, as the implicit reference in the original sentence can be verbalized through insertion. We find cases with contiguous insertions in wikiHowToImprove by computing the differences between the original and revised sentence using `difflib`.[2] As a result, we found 336,129 sentence pairs in which the original sentence was only modified by a contiguous insertion.

In the next step, we identify the subset of insertions that are referential and resolvable in context: that is, we identify words and phrases that refer to a discourse entity. Our study focuses on insertions of single references (i.e., referring expressions that refer to exactly one discourse entity), which are usually not verbalized by sequences exceeding three tokens. Therefore, we only consider insertions that consist of one, two or three word tokens (i.e., unigram, bigram and trigram insertion). We identify references by obtaining co-reference chains on the paragraph level using the Stanza[3] coreference parser. More specifically, by using a combination of the revised sentence and the original context, we can identify referring expressions that are explicit in the revised sentence and coreferent with discourse entities in the original context. Therefore, we parse the revised sentence and the preceding sentences from the *original context*, within the same paragraph.

We add the corresponding original-revised sentence pair to our collection if the full span of the insertion (*full insertion*) or parts of it refer to an entity in the discourse context. In other words, the insertion can contain tokens in addition to the referring expression. However, we only keep insertions that include additional tokens if the additional tokens are required grammatically, given their position in the sentence (e.g., *<u>of</u> you*, *<u>of</u> the shoe*). In particular, we keep the insertions that consist of a reference and specific types of function words (determiners, prepositions) or punctuation.[4] We excluded cases with conjunctions and non-function words as these insertions mainly add or extend factual information. Examples of different insertions

[2] `https://docs.python.org/3/library/difflib.html`

[3] `https://stanfordnlp.github.io/stanza/`

[4] We rely on automatic part-of-speech tags for this additional filtering procedure.

| Insertion | Reference | Example |
|---|---|---|
| unigram (*N*=2,599) | unigram | **This treatment** can be performed by a dermatologist but **it** is quite expensive. |
| bigram (*N*=1,837) | unigram (*N*=700) | If **you** are using the mobile app, tap the "More" button and then tap **your** name. Select the photo's of **you** tab. |
| | bigram (*N*=1,137) | It's not pleasant to read **a book** that has been "personalized" by someone else. If it rains or **the book** gets lost, you'll have to pay to replace **it**. |
| trigram (*N*=1,578) | unigram (*N*=118) | Bend your left **knee** and lift it ( as close as you can get **it**). |
| | bigram (*N*=1,370) | 1. Clean canvas **shoes** by spot washing using a mild detergent and soft toothbrush. Test the spray on the tongue of **the shoe** to make sure it won't stain. |
| | trigram (*N*=90) | Check the outer labelling on **the ham shank** to see if **its** fully cooked. If **it** isn't, use the other method instead. Remove the wrapping and place **the ham shank** in a roasting pan. |

Table 2: Examples of from our dataset: underlined tokens mark an insertion, tokens in bold highlight references to the same entity. Tokens that are underlined *and* highlighted are the reference tokens to be predicted in our task. Note that the span of the reference can differ from the insertion because of additional tokens (e.g., punctuation).

and inserted references are shown in Table 2. Note that some sentences contain grammar/spelling related errors, which were not corrected in the shown versions of the wikiHow articles.

## 4.2 Statistics

In total, our collection procedure yields 6,014 instances. More specifically, it contains 2,599 unigram (43.22%), 1,837 bigram (30.50%) and 1,578 trigram (26.24%) insertions. Table 2 shows examples of references and insertions and how they are distributed over different lengths. The numbers indicate that a majority of references are unigrams ($N = 3,854$) and that only a small proportion are trigrams. The table also shows that most references consist of the full insertion (56%), which are 2,599 unigrams, 700 bigrams and 90 trigrams.

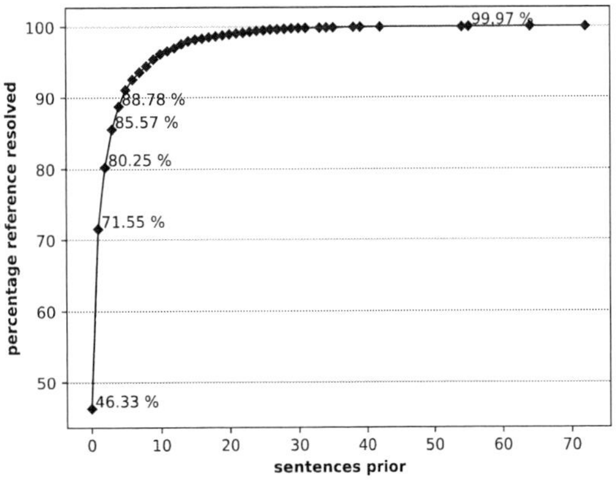


Figure 1: The likelihood that a reference can be found within the previous *x* sentences in the original context.

Figure 1 indicates the positions of the closest antecedent to resolve an implicit reference. The distribution shows that most references refer to an entity in the same sentence (46.33%, $N = 2,786$) or to an entity in the previous sentence (25.21%, $N = 1,517$). The remaining instances can be resolved within 3 up to 75 sentences. Finally, we observe that in the majority of the 6,014 instances, the reference is mentioned only once (43.15%, $N = 2,595$), twice (18.12%, $N = 1,090$) or three times (9.38%, $N = 564$) in the original context.

In the remainder of this paper, we conduct experiments with our collection of 6,014 implicit references, which we split into a train (81.09%, $N = 4,877$), development (9.83%, $N = 591$) and test (9.08%, $N = 546$) set, following the original split by article of wikiHowToImprove.[5]

# 5 Language Model Experiments

In this section, we describe a set of experiments in which we investigate the use of a transformer-based language model for the task of resolving implicit references. In particular, we aim to answer the

[5]https://github.com/irshadbhat/wikiHowToImprove

following research questions: Can we find the manually inserted reference among the top completions predicted by a language model, and is it possible to select a correct prediction based on its fit in the sentence or paragraph context? We describe our experimental set-up in Section 5.1 and our results in Section 5.2. Further analyses are provided in Section 6.

### 5.1 Experimental setting

**Data.** The starting point for our investigation are the 6,014 instances of original–revised sentence pairs described in Section 4. Each revision involves the insertion of a reference into the given sentence. That is, the revised sentence always contains a reference that was not explicitly present in the original sentence. The full insertion may consist of one, two or three tokens, and it may contain function words in addition to the reference itself.

**Method.** Resolving implicit references of varying length requires a generative model. We chose the Generative Pre-trained Transformer model (**GPT**) described by Radford et al. (2018) as a benchmark model because it fulfils this requirement and because it is pre-trained on data that does not overlap with our development and test sets.[6] Since GPT is an auto-regressive language model, which means that predictions are made word-by-word (unidirectional), we apply an additional re-ranking procedure over the top-100 generated sequences and their full (left and right) context. For re-ranking, we use the same GPT model and compute its perplexity score for whole sequences on two levels of context: (a) full sentence (**+S-perplexity**) and (b) sentence plus preceding paragraph context (**+P-perplexity**). Finally, we also fine-tune the GPT model on our training set to improve its fit to how-to guides (**+fine-tuning**).

**Upper bound and baselines.** We approximate an upper bound on our data by assessing the performance of a model that has access to the inserted reference itself, namely the coreference parser used during data creation (see Section 4.1). We further compare GPT to the following baselines: **Most-Frequent** always selects the most frequent referring expression of the most frequent entity in the context, **ClosestRef** selects referring expression(s) from the preceding context by how close they are to the point of the insertion, and **TF-IDF** ranks possible n-grams (where $n$ equals the number of tokens in the manually inserted reference) by their tf-idf score (Jones, 1972), for which we take into account all training and development documents.

**Evaluation.** We evaluate each model by its ability to generate the tokens that are part of the reference inserted in the revised version of a sentence.[7] We count a generated reference as correct if all generated tokens match the tokens in the human-produced reference. To allow for minor variations in spelling, we ignore case when measuring recall (i.e., the relative number of correctly retrieved references) among the top-1 ($R@1$), top-10 ($R@10$) and top-100 ($R@100$) generated sequences.

### 5.2 Results

We first address our initial question: Can we find manually inserted references among the top completions predicted by a language model? The scores listed in Table 3 indicate the proportion of exact matches that are found within the top-1, top-10 and top-100 references generated by the pre-trained GPT model. The numbers show a similar performance of GPT on the development and test set: In about 37% of the cases, the first-best generated reference is identical to the manually inserted reference. In about 83% of the cases, the manually inserted reference can be found within the top-100 generated references. This result is close to our approximated upper bound: in a random sample from the development set, we found a coreference model, which has access to the manually inserted reference itself, to predict the correct co-reference chain in 86 out of 100 cases (for details, see Appendix A in the supplementary material).

**Model comparison.** We next attempt to answer our second question, namely is it possible to select the correct reference based on its fit in the sentence or paragraph context? We evaluate two additional steps for selecting references based on the top sequences generated by GPT: model fine-tuning and re-ranking based on sentence-level or paragraph-level perplexity. Table 4 shows the results of each selection approach, combinations and baselines.

[6] Some models, such as GPT-2, were pre-trained on data that includes wikiHow, which could make it possible for them to make correct predictions in our data based on training memory. However, we also experimented with other models in a preliminary study (e.g., XLNet (Yang et al., 2020), TransformerXL (Dai et al., 2019) and BART (Lewis et al., 2019)) and did not observe any advantages over GPT.

[7] Note that a model only needs to generate the reference part of an insertion. Additional words, as described in Section 4, are provided to all models as part of the context.

| dataset | $R@1$ | $R@10$ | $R@100$ |
|---|---|---|---|
| develop | 37.06% (219 TPs) | 67.85% (401 TPs) | 82.91% (490 TPs) |
| test | 36.36% (198 TPs) | 71.61% (391 TPs) | 83.89% (458 TPs) |

Table 3: Relative and absolute number of exact matches among the top sequences generated by the GPT model and the manually inserted reference found in a revised sentence.

We observe that GPT substantially outperforms all three baselines. Combining GPT with fine-tuning and paragraph-level perplexity re-ranking leads to an accurate top-1 prediction of the inserted reference in 57.4% of the cases on the test set. In 80.8% of the cases, the inserted reference can be found within the top-10 re-ranked sequences. In ablation experiments on the development set, we find that a combination of fine-tuning and perplexity-based re-ranking is necessary to achieve such high results. Fine-tuning and re-ranking based on sentence-level perplexity only improve $R@1$ by 2.5 to 3 percentage points, respectively. Without fine-tuning, re-ranking on the sentence level even reduces the chance of finding the correct reference within the top-10 sequences ($R@10$). Only re-ranking on the paragraph level consistently improves results, up to 8.2 and 16.8 percentage points in $R@10$ and $R@1$, respectively.

**Discussion.** We qualitatively analyzed the top-1 predictions of each method on the development set and observed the following trends: re-ranking on the sentence level generally helps in selecting grammatically suitable candidates when the top generated sequences by the original or fine-tuned model does not fit syntactically, for example, due to number or case disagreements. Fine-tuning GPT seems to adapt the scoring of generated references to better match their occurrences in how-to guides: for example, the pronouns *you* and *them* are more frequent in this genre than *I* and *we*. Finally, we observe that re-ranking on the paragraph level considerably improves the selection of noun phrases that resemble references to entities in the discourse. Whereas the sentence-level method often produces generic references (underlined) that make sense superficially (e.g., *Clean off the surface of the glass*), top candidates in the paragraph-level method plausibly fit also in the specific context (e.g., *Clean off the surface of your typewriter*). We discuss the top predictions of both re-ranking methods in more detail in Section 6.

| method | dataset | $R@1$ | $R@10$ |
|---|---|---|---|
| Upper bound | sample | 86.0% | |
| **MostFrequent** | develop | 28.8% | |
| **ClosestRef** | | 16.9 % | 59.9 % |
| **TF-IDF** | | 11.0 % | 30.8 % |
| **GPT** | | 37.1% | 67.9% |
| +**fine-tuning** (FT) | | 39.6% | 73.4% |
| +**S-perplexity** | | 40.1% | 63.8% |
| +**P-perplexity** | | 52.7% | 76.1% |
| +**FT+S-perp.** | | 46.2% | 67.3% |
| +**FT+P-perp.** | | **56.4%** | **78.0%** |
| **GPT+FT+P-perp.** | test | 57.4% | 80.8% |

Table 4: Results of re-ranking the top-100 generated predictions by the GPT model in terms of recall (relative number of retrieved references); S-perplexity and P-perplexity indicate the application of re-ranking based on GPT's perplexity scores on the full sentence and paragraph, respectively.

## 6 Analysis

In this section, we aim to answer two questions evoked by the results in Section 5. First, we ask how fine-tuning and perplexity-based re-ranking improved the scoring of the top-100 generated sequences and what differences can be seen among the re-ranked top-10 sequences (Section 6.1). Secondly, we investigate the plausibility of the two highest ranked fillers generated by the model (Section 6.2). The latter analysis provides us with insights regarding the existence of a single most plausible filler (or whether none/two fillers can be plausible) given the discourse context. In cases where the human-inserted reference is among the top-2, the analysis also makes it possible for us to find if/when the human-inserted reference is identified as the most plausible.

### 6.1 Sentence vs. Paragraph Perplexity

We compare the generated top-10 sequences of the fine-tuned GPT model and the re-ranked variants on the development set. Predictions for three example sentences are shown in Table 5. The examples indicate that sequences generated by the fine-tuned GPT model often lead to ungrammatical sentences (highlighted in italics). For the re-ranked variants, we observe that such sequences are scored lower and no longer appear among the top ranks.

The examples based on sentence-level re-ranking reveal two unfortunate side-effects: The first is that non-referential candidates may end up in higher positions, simply because they lead to a grammatical sequence. This is particularly visible in Example (2), where the correct sequence was generated by GPT+FT, but ended up outside the top-10 when using GPT+FT+S-perplexity. The second caveat is that sentence-level perplexity increases the rank of entities that are plausible within the sentence but unrelated to the activity described in the article. This is especially visible in Example (3) in Table 5: the phrases *the number*, *the office*, *a friend*, *the person* all seem reasonable candidates in the context of *calling someone*, but none of them directly correspond to *the salon* mentioned in the article. The same applies to Example (1), in which the context mentioned a *container* but contains no references to a *pot*, *bowl*, *cage* or *bag*. It seems that these candidates simply mimic the usage of common knowledge, especially because none of the candidates occur in the preceding context. The aforementioned reasons could explain why sentence-level perplexity without fine-tuning decreased the recall of the manually-inserted reference among the top-10 candidates (see Section 5).

A final interesting observation is that the caveats caused by the sentence-based re-ranking are less present when applying paragraph-level perplexity. After re-ranking on the paragraph level, we find many of the top candidates to be either repetitions of words and phrases from the context or to be closely related to the manually-inserted sequence. This is illustrated by all examples in Table 5. A quantitative analysis further confirmed this insight: based on paragraph-level perplexity, over 20% of the top-10 ranked bigrams and trigrams appear literally in the preceding context, compared to 11% when using sentence-level perplexity.

### 6.2 Plausibility of Generated Fillers

In the first analysis, we discussed the impact of re-ranking the top-100 sequences generated by the fine-tuned model. However, even the best re-ranking procedure is insufficient to avoid errors in our approach when the manually inserted reference from a revised sentence does not appear among the generated sequences. In this section, we address two questions. First, we investigate whether the human-inserted reference is always the one that best fits the sentence given the context. Secondly, we assess the plausibility of the top-2 completions by the model in case both are different from the human-inserted reference. These questions are motivated by the results from an internal analysis, in which we found a few instances where an annotator preferred a model-generated reference over the human-inserted reference or had no preference between the two options (a full report is provided in the supplementary material, Appendix B).

**Set-up.** We take 100 instances from the development set with their top-2 completions provided by the fine-tuned model and ask a student assistant with a background in Computational Linguistics to provide annotations. We randomly select 50 instances where the human-inserted reference is identical with the best generated sequence ("human-insertion among top-2") and 50 where this is not the case ("human-insertion not among top-2"). We show an annotator two versions of the sentence in randomized order: one with the highest ranked sequence and one with the second-highest ranked sequence generated by the model. We show each version together with the preceding sentences from the paragraph and highlight the generated reference. We ask the annotator to indicate the sentence that fits the context better, whether they both fit or whether neither fits. We discuss the main findings of this experiment below, and provide additional examples in the supplementary material (Appendix C). In the examples below, we underline the human-inserted reference.

**Human-insertion among top-2 ($N = 50$).** The annotator indicated a strong preference for the human-inserted reference in most cases ($N = 34$). However, there were also cases in which the annotator indicated no preference ($N = 13$). This is likely the case because many generated sequences involved paraphrases of the human-inserted reference in the given context (e.g., *the button/<u>this button</u>*, *the party/<u>your party</u>*). The same holds for the remaining instances ($N = 3$), in which the annotator preferred the other generated sequence over the human-inserted reference (e.g., *the sequence/<u>the process</u>*). In these cases, it seems like annotations simply reflect personal preferences. Finally, we found no cases in which the annotator indicated that neither insertion was fitting.

| correct sequence | GPT+FT | GPT+FT+S-perplexity | GPT+FT+P-perplexity |
|---|---|---|---|
| (1) Put the grasshoppers in **the container**. | **the container**, *it and*, a container, the bottom, the lid, it. , *it,* , a plastic, a large, the plastic | the water, the pot, the basket, a bowl, the cage, a bag, a pot, the bag, the refrigerator, a jar | **the container**,. 5, the lid, a container, the bag, the bottom, the box, the water, a bag, the hole |
| (2) Rinse **the parts** before assembling. | **the parts**, *out the*, *off the*, them off, and dry, your ke, them thoroughly, *them with*, them in, them out | them out, them thoroughly, it out, them off, it off, the area, and rinse, each piece, and dry, each section | **the parts**, them thoroughly, them off, them out, all parts, each part, the components, the pipes, both parts, and dry |
| (3) Call **the salon** and ask questions | **the salon**, your salon, a salon, a local, the sal, a sal, up the, a hair, the hair, *them and* | the number, the office, a friend, this number, them up, the person, a number, the store, the owner, them in | **the salon**, your salon, a salon, their website, the spa, the stylist, them in, your stylist, each salon, a stylist |

Table 5: The top-10 predictions for the fine-tuned GPT model and the reranked predictions using sentence-level and paragraph-level perplexity. Bold sequences represent the correct sequence, italic sequences are ungrammatical in context, and underlined sequences are references to entities that are not mentioned in the context.

**Human-insertion not among top-2 ($N = 50$).** In a majority of these cases, we found the annotator to select one of the model-generated sequences as best fitting, confirming that completions other than the human-inserted reference can be plausible ($N = 29$). A number of the selected sequences are paraphrases ($N = 11$) of the human-inserted reference, such as: *the form/the application*, *the school/this school* or semantically related sequences ($N = 8$) that differ from the human-inserted reference in terms of specificity (e.g., *let the paint/the nails dry*, *wipe and dry the wood/the floors*, *remove the pan/the vegetables from the heat*, *your laptop/your mac*).

The remaining instances ($N = 10$) involve generated sequences that the annotator indicated as best fitting, although they are incompatible with the human-inserted reference (e.g., *Islam/Christianity*, *the microwave/the freezer*). We take these findings as an indicator that implicit references can be resolved incorrectly and therefore lead to misunderstandings, which could be modelled and anticipated by a language model. Finally, the annotator judged both top-2 sequences to be fitting in 17 cases and none to be fitting in 4 cases. In case of the latter, the completions led to an ungrammatical sentence.

## 7 Conclusions

In this paper, we introduced the task of resolving implicit references in instructional texts, which might be problematic for readers without prior knowledge of the instructed task. We approached the resolution of implicit references as a generation problem for which we leveraged original-revised sentence pairs from wikiHow. The considered pairs contained an explicit reference in the revised sentence which was non-verbalized in the original sentence. Our dataset is one of the largest datasets with implicit references and contains texts from the multiple different domains covered in wikiHow.

We showed that a pre-trained language model is capable of predicting the human-produced insertion in a majority of cases. The best-performing method, which combines a fine-tuned GPT model and perplexity-based re-ranking, achieved results up to 57.4% (top-1) and 80.8% (top-10). Even without fine-tuning and re-ranking, 71.6% of the human-inserted references appeared in the top-10.

We found sentence-level re-ranking useful to eliminate generated sequences that cause ungrammatical sentences and paragraph-level re-ranking to prioritize sequences that also occur in the preceding discourse. Our analysis revealed that the human-inserted reference is commonly found to fit the discourse better than a model-generated alternative. However, we also found cases where other completions were plausible. In the future, we will extend this study and take it as a starting point for examining potential sources of misunderstanding.

## Acknowledgements

The research presented in this paper was funded by the DFG Emmy Noether program (RO 4848/2-1).

## References

Talita Anthonio, Irshad Bhat, and Michael Roth. 2020. wikiHowToImprove: A resource and analyses on edits in instructional texts. In *Proceedings of the 12th Language Resources and Evaluation Conference*, pages 5721–5729, Marseille, France. European Language Resources Association.

Talita Anthonio and Michael Roth. 2020. What can we learn from noun substitutions in revision histories? In *Proceedings of the 28th International Conference on Computational Linguistics*, pages 1359–1370, Barcelona, Spain (Online). International Committee on Computational Linguistics.

Meng Cao and Jackie Chi Kit Cheung. 2019. Referring expression generation using entity profiles. In *Proceedings of the 2019 Conference on Empirical Methods in Natural Language Processing and the 9th International Joint Conference on Natural Language Processing (EMNLP-IJCNLP)*, pages 3163–3172, Hong Kong, China. Association for Computational Linguistics.

Thiago Castro Ferreira, Emiel Krahmer, and Sander Wubben. 2016. Towards more variation in text generation: Developing and evaluating variation models for choice of referential form. In *Proceedings of the 54th Annual Meeting of the Association for Computational Linguistics (Volume 1: Long Papers)*, pages 568–577, Berlin, Germany. Association for Computational Linguistics.

Pengxiang Cheng and Katrin Erk. 2018. Implicit argument prediction with event knowledge. In *Proceedings of the 2018 Conference of the North American Chapter of the Association for Computational Linguistics: Human Language Technologies, Volume 1 (Long Papers)*, pages 831–840, New Orleans, Louisiana. Association for Computational Linguistics.

Pengxiang Cheng and Katrin Erk. 2019. Implicit argument prediction as reading comprehension. *Proceedings of the AAAI Conference on Artificial Intelligence*, 33(01):6284–6291.

Christian Chiarcos and Niko Schenk. 2015. Memory-based acquisition of argument structures and its application to implicit role detection. In *Proceedings of the 16th Annual Meeting of the Special Interest Group on Discourse and Dialogue*, pages 178–187, Prague, Czech Republic. Association for Computational Linguistics.

Zihang Dai, Zhilin Yang, Yiming Yang, Jaime Carbonell, Quoc V. Le, and Ruslan Salakhutdinov. 2019. Transformer-xl: Attentive language models beyond a fixed-length context.

Seth Ebner, Patrick Xia, Ryan Culkin, Kyle Rawlins, and Benjamin Van Durme. 2020. Multi-sentence argument linking. In *Proceedings of the 58th Annual Meeting of the Association for Computational Linguistics*, pages 8057–8077, Online. Association for Computational Linguistics.

Matthew Gerber and J. Y. Chai. 2012. Semantic role labeling of implicit arguments for nominal predicates. *Computational Linguistics*, 38:755–798.

Matthew Gerber and Joyce Chai. 2010. Beyond NomBank: A study of implicit arguments for nominal predicates. In *Proceedings of the 48th Annual Meeting of the Association for Computational Linguistics*, pages 1583–1592, Uppsala, Sweden. Association for Computational Linguistics.

Charles Greenbacker and Kathleen McCoy. 2009. UDel: Generating referring expressions guided by psycholinguistc findings. In *Proceedings of the 2009 Workshop on Language Generation and Summarisation (UCNLG+Sum 2009)*, pages 101–102, Suntec, Singapore. Association for Computational Linguistics.

Kenji Imamura, Kuniko Saito, and Tomoko Izumi. 2009. Discriminative approach to predicate-argument structure analysis with zero-anaphora resolution. In *Proceedings of the ACL-IJCNLP 2009 Conference Short Papers*, pages 85–88, Suntec, Singapore. Association for Computational Linguistics.

Hideki Isozaki and Tsutomu Hirao. 2003. Japanese zero pronoun resolution based on ranking rules and machine learning. In *Proceedings of the 2003 Conference on Empirical Methods in Natural Language Processing*, pages 184–191.

Yiwei Jiang, Klim Zaporojets, Johannes Deleu, Thomas Demeester, and Chris Develder. 2020. Recipe instruction semantics corpus (RISeC): Resolving semantic structure and zero anaphora in recipes. In *Proceedings of the 1st Conference of the Asia-Pacific Chapter of the Association for Computational Linguistics and the 10th International Joint Conference on Natural Language Processing*, pages 821–826, Suzhou, China. Association for Computational Linguistics.

Karen Spärck Jones. 1972. A statistical interpretation of term specificity and its application in retrieval. *Journal of Documentation*, 28:11–21.

Andrej A. Kibrik, Mariya V. Khudyakova, Grigory B. Dobrov, Anastasia Linnik, and Dmitrij A. Zalmanov. 2016. Referential choice: Predictability and its limits. *Frontiers in Psychology*, 7(1429).

Egoitz Laparra and German Rigau. 2013a. ImpAr: A deterministic algorithm for implicit semantic role labelling. In *Proceedings of the 51st Annual Meeting of the Association for Computational Linguistics (Volume 1: Long Papers)*, pages 1180–1189, Sofia, Bulgaria. Association for Computational Linguistics.

Egoitz Laparra and German Rigau. 2013b. Sources of evidence for implicit argument resolution. In *Proceedings of the 10th International Conference on Computational Semantics (IWCS 2013) – Long Papers*, pages 155–166, Potsdam, Germany. Association for Computational Linguistics.

Mike Lewis, Yinhan Liu, Naman Goyal, Marjan Ghazvininejad, Abdelrahman Mohamed, Omer Levy, Ves Stoyanov, and Luke Zettlemoyer. 2019. Bart: Denoising sequence-to-sequence pre-training for natural language generation, translation, and comprehension.

Adam Meyers, Ruth Reeves, Catherine Macleod, Rachel Szekely, Veronika Zielinska, Brian Young, and Ralph Grishman. 2004. The NomBank project: An interim report. In *Proceedings of the Workshop Frontiers in Corpus Annotation at HLT-NAACL 2004*, pages 24–31, Boston, Massachusetts, USA. Association for Computational Linguistics.

Tatjana Moor, Michael Roth, and Anette Frank. 2013. Predicate-specific annotations for implicit role binding: Corpus annotation, data analysis and evaluation experiments. In *Proceedings of the 10th International Conference on Computational Semantics (IWCS 2013) – Short Papers*, pages 369–375, Potsdam, Germany. Association for Computational Linguistics.

Hiromi Nakaiwa. 1997. Automatic extraction of rules for anaphora resolution of japanese zero pronouns from aligned sentence pairs. In *Proceedings of a Workshop on Operational Factors in Practical, Robust Anaphora Resolution for Unrestricted Texts*, ANARESOLUTION '97, page 22–29, USA. Association for Computational Linguistics.

Ani Nenkova and Kathleen McKeown. 2003. References to named entities: a corpus study. In *Companion Volume of the Proceedings of HLT-NAACL 2003 - Short Papers*, pages 70–72.

Alec Radford, Karthik Narasimhan, Tim salimans, and Ilya Sutskever. 2018. Improving language understanding by generative pre-training. OpenAI.

Ehud Reiter and Robert Dale. 2000. *Building Natural Language Generation Systems*. Studies in Natural Language Processing. Cambridge University Press.

Michael Roth and Anette Frank. 2013. Automatically identifying implicit arguments to improve argument linking and coherence modeling. In *Second Joint Conference on Lexical and Computational Semantics (*SEM), Volume 1: Proceedings of the Main Conference and the Shared Task: Semantic Textual Similarity*, pages 306–316, Atlanta, Georgia, USA. Association for Computational Linguistics.

Josef Ruppenhofer, Caroline Sporleder, Roser Morante, Collin Baker, and Martha Palmer. 2009. SemEval-2010 task 10: Linking events and their participants in discourse. In *Proceedings of the Workshop on Semantic Evaluations: Recent Achievements and Future Directions (SEW-2009)*, pages 106–111, Boulder, Colorado. Association for Computational Linguistics.

Fahime Same and Kees van Deemter. 2020. A linguistic perspective on reference: Choosing a feature set for generating referring expressions in context. In *Proceedings of the 28th International Conference on Computational Linguistics*, pages 4575–4586, Barcelona, Spain (Online). International Committee on Computational Linguistics.

Niko Schenk and Christian Chiarcos. 2016. Unsupervised learning of prototypical fillers for implicit semantic role labeling. In *Proceedings of the 2016 Conference of the North American Chapter of the Association for Computational Linguistics: Human Language Technologies*, pages 1473–1479, San Diego, California. Association for Computational Linguistics.

Kazuhiro Seki, Atsushi Fujii, and Tetsuya Ishikawa. 2002. A probabilistic method for analyzing Japanese anaphora integrating zero pronoun detection and resolution. In *COLING 2002: The 19th International Conference on Computational Linguistics*.

Carina Silberer and Anette Frank. 2012. Casting implicit role linking as an anaphora resolution task. In **SEM 2012: The First Joint Conference on Lexical and Computational Semantics – Volume 1: Proceedings of the main conference and the shared task, and Volume 2: Proceedings of the Sixth International Workshop on Semantic Evaluation (SemEval 2012)*, pages 1–10, Montréal, Canada. Association for Computational Linguistics.

Hirotoshi Taira, Sanae Fujita, and Masaaki Nagata. 2008. A Japanese predicate argument structure analysis using decision lists. In *Proceedings of the 2008 Conference on Empirical Methods in Natural Language Processing*, pages 523–532, Honolulu, Hawaii. Association for Computational Linguistics.

Zhilin Yang, Zihang Dai, Yiming Yang, Jaime Carbonell, Ruslan Salakhutdinov, and Quoc V. Le. 2020. Xlnet: Generalized autoregressive pretraining for language understanding.

Ching-Long Yeh and Yi-Chun Chen. 2003. Using zero anaphora resolution to improve text categorization. In *Proceedings of the 17th Pacific Asia Conference on Language, Information and Computation*, pages 423–430, Sentosa, Singapore. COLIPS PUBLICATIONS.

## A Co-reference Quality Analysis

| Human-inserted reference co-refers |
| --- |
| 1. Take your pregnant cat to the vet . As soon as you know , or suspect , that your cat might be pregnant , you should take **her** to the vets to get **<u>her</u>** checked over . |
| 1. On the sheet of **foam**, draw an outline like the one in the image. Make sure it can wrap around your bottle around once, and the strip pointing down can fold under the bottom of the bottle. 2. Cut the foam shape out. 3. Cut a piece of duct tape off the roll, so it will cover part of the bottom of **the foam** and about on each side. Take a new piece and start rolling it around the sides of **<u>the foam</u>** . |

Table 6: Examples where the human-inserted reference co-refers with an entity in the context according to Stanza. The human-inserted reference is highlighted and underlined. The referring expressions within the same co-reference chain are highlighted.

| Human-inserted reference does not co-refer |
| --- |
| 1. Know what kind of games you like (strategy, action, adventure, racing, rpg, simulators, etc. 2. Strategy games are good for you when thinking. They help you reinforce what you learned. **Some strategy games** are : Age Of Empires, The Settlers, City Of Heroes. Action games: **<u>these</u>** are liked by many people. |
| 1. Go get an ' on the floor ' cat scratch pad from anywhere. This one cost $6. My cats wo n't use it flat on the floor, like this. 2. Remove the corrugated cardboard from the box. They usually glue it down, probably because they do n't want you to flip it and re-use the back - side. (You can.) 3. Using the edge of **a counter** or table or other sturdy piece of furniture, break **<u>it</u>** to fit. |

Table 7: Examples where the human-inserted reference did not co-refer with the referring expressions within the same co-reference chain according to Stanza. The human-inserted reference is highlighted and underlined, whereas the referring expressions within the same co-reference chain are highlighted.

In this section, we describe a study that we conducted to investigate the quality of the obtained co-reference chains from Stanza.

**Method.** To investigate the quality of the co-reference chains, we asked an annotator to identify whether the human-inserted reference occurred earlier in the context. We specifically showed the annotator the context and the revised sentence, in which we marked the human-inserted referring expression. We additionally highlighted the referring expressions that co-referred with the human-inserted reference. We asked the annotator to annotate 100 instances, which we randomly extracted from the development set of our data (see Section 4). The annotator was a student in a Computational Linguistics program.

**Results.** The annotator found 86 instances where the human-produced reference co-referred with the referring expressions indicated by the Stanza co-reference parser. We show two examples of these instances in Table 6. In the remaining instances ($N = 14$), the human-inserted referring expression did not co-refer with the referring expressions indicated by Stanza. Nonetheless, it is still possible to find a suitable antecedent in such cases, as shown by the examples in Table 7. We conclude from the obtained results that implicit references in our dataset (described in Section 4) are generally co-referent with an entity mentioned in the context.

## B Error Analysis

In Section 6.1, we discussed the impact of re-ranking the top-100 sequences generated by the fine-tuned GPT model. However, even the best re-ranking procedure is insufficient to avoid errors in our approach when the manually inserted reference from a revised sentence does not appear among the generated sequences. Therefore, we perform an additional study in which we analyze cases of human-produced references that do not show up among the top-100 candidates generated by the fine-tuned GPT model.

**Set-up.** We select all instances for which the fine-tuned GPT model did not generate the human-produced reference among the top-100 ($N = 84$) and ask one annotator to provide judgements. We show the annotator two versions of the revised sentence in randomized order: one containing the human-produced reference and the other containing the top-1 generated completion by GPT. Each version is shown together with the preceding sentences from the paragraph.

In the annotation interface, we highlight the references and ask the annotator to select the version that fits the sentence better, given the context, or whether "both fit". We discuss the three different outcomes below.

**Preference for human insertion** ($N = 57$). In most cases, the annotator labeled the human-produced reference as being a better fit than the generated sequence. In 26 of these cases, the model-generated sequence was not a reference or the reference was accompanied by function words or punctuation. Both types of sequences usually yield an ungrammatical sentence.

The remaining 31 instances can be categorized into three groups: The first are cases where the generated sequence does not make sense in the given sentence position ($N = 12$), such as *Rub the dog's coat with* ***the chamois***. Another subset ($N = 13$) consists of sequences that are referential but the insertion yields an ungrammatical sentence, for example: *It can also be unpleasant to withdraw from* ***your***. The rest ($N = 6$) seem to be sensible references according to our observations, such as:

> (1) Leave your diya uncovered at room temperature, and do your best to keep it away from moisture. The clay should set after 24 hours. If you put your diya on a plate or mat and notice it starts drooping, lightly grease a sheet of aluminum foil with **your spatula**/vegetable oil.

Here, the generated (boldface) sequence *your spatula* seems to fulfil a plausible but different semantic role than the human-produced (underlined) sequence *vegetable oil*. Even though it remains unclear why the annotator preferred the human-produced sequence in these cases, it is interesting to see that the model managed to generate a reference that fills a different semantic role in the given sentence (cf. summary below).

**No preference** ($N = 20$). In 20 out of 84 instances (23.81%), the annotator marked both sequences as being equally fitting in the context. Some of the produced sequences were not references or entities ($N = 3$), but still plausible insertions in the sentence, for example, *Open or create a* ***new*** *word document*. The remaining cases ($N = 17$) contain generated references which are plausible but different from the human-produced reference, such as: *Many of your answers on* ***the subject****/the regents*... (the context here is an article on regents exams). The high relative frequency of such cases suggests that the model-generated sequences might be able to reflect alternate, plausible fillers for an implicit reference.

**Preference for model insertion** ($N = 7$). In 7 cases (8.33%), the annotator marked the generated sequence as fitting better than the human-produced sequence. In 4 cases, the human-produced reference caused fluency or grammatical issues.[8] In two instances, the generated sequence referred to a different entity than the human-produced reference, such as:

> (2) Look closely and carefully at the grain pattern on the handbag. The pattern of the grain on a crocodile leather handbag will have some irregularities. If the grain pattern of **the leather**/the scales is very uniform , it has probably been stamped on .

Given the annotator's preference, these examples support the finding that model-generated sequences may reflect alternate, plausible fillers of an implicit reference. We also noticed one instance where a generated sequence filled the same semantic role as the human-produced reference, but differed in terms of granularity.

> (3) Click the tab at the top left that says "Themes". This will take your sidebar to the theme garden, which looks like this. Make sure to choose from the type of theme you want to look at first from **the sidebar**/wikihow.

In this case, the annotator might have chosen the generated sequence because it was mentioned in the previous sentence.

**Summary.** We showed that most incorrect predictions of the fine-tuned GPT model are indeed errors, as confirmed by the annotator's preference for the human-produced reference over the generated references. We further found the annotator's preference to reflect the effects of re-ranking when the correct reference can be found among the top-100 candidates: The annotator also preferred references that do not disrupt grammaticality and that

[8] It might be that further revision is needed or that they refer to an external link/image.

also occur in the preceding discourse. Finally, there are a fair number of cases in which the annotator had no preference or preferred the model-generated sequence, indicating that there exist plausible, alternate references. In cases like Example (1), such references can be distinguished by the semantic role they fill. However, we also find examples, such as (2) and (3), in which different references can fill the same role at varying levels of granularity. Therefore, it seems unclear whether semantic roles would be helpful in this task and what a suitable role inventory would be.

## C Additional Examples for Section 6.2

In this section, we provide additional examples for the analysis conducted in Section 6.2. In the examples, we highlight the preferred filler by the annotator and underline the human-inserted reference.

### C.1 Human-insertion among top-2

An example where the annotator preferred the human-insertion is:

> (1) 1. Read books or go to the Library. Kids love it when you take them there. 2. Play games with them. Little kids like games like 'Simon says', 'Hide and seek', 'Tag', etc. Older kids might play board games or video games. 3. Make up your own games. Kids have a great time doing this ! Watch a movie with friends/**them**.

In this example, the annotator probably preferred the human-inserted reference because the top-2 completion *friends* does not make sense in the given context. Instead, the referring expression *them* seems more plausible because it can be used to refer to *children*.

In addition, we show an example where the annotator had no preference below:

> (2) Has a friend of yours read something personal or embarrassing that belongs to you? Here 's some tips on how to deal with **that**/**it**.

Example (2) shows a common phenomenon that we noticed for all the instances where the annotator had no preference, namely that the fillers are paraphrases in the given context.

Finally, we show two examples where the annotator preferred the top-2 generated completion by the model, instead of the human-insertion.

> (3) The corks will retain moisture longer than traditional milch and help maintain your plant's health between waterings. 2. Use as a fire starter. When you need to start a fire, remove a cork or two and place them under the wood to be kindled before lighting **the fire**/a fire.

> (4) it's as if you're trying to brush some debris off your pants. Return to the original position. repeat the process with your left knee. 5. Practice the two - step. the two - step is a very basic dance move that can help you get into the rhythm of the music. practicing the two - step can help you form a dance routine. Repeat **the process**/the sequence with your left food.

Both examples are instances for which we concluded that the annotations reflect personal preferences, since the human-insertion and top-2 filler are paraphrases.

### C.2 Human-insertion not among top-2

**Annother has preference.** The two examples below are instances where the annotator preferred either of the top-2 generated sequences.

> (5) Use the pie within several months. While a properly frozen pecan pie will last for a while in a freezer, it won't last forever. Try to use the pie within 2 months, as after that it is at risk of developing freezer burn. * To reheat a frozen pie, let it thaw overnight in the refrigerator. Then warm it in a oven for 15 to 20 minutes. The pie will do better if it is kept at a constant temperature in **the oven**/the microwave.

In example (5), the human-inserted reference was the freezer, which also differs from the top-1 and top-2 completions by the fine-tuned model. This example indicates the possibility of the annotator preferring a different filler than the human-inserted reference and therefore a mismatch between the interpretation of the implicit reference of the writer

and a reader.
The second example shows differences between the top-2 in terms of granularity:

> (6) Wash your face/**your mouth** with warm water in the morning.

In this case, the human-inserted reference was your lips. The annotator therefore preferred the filler that was the closest to the human-inserted reference.

**Annotator has no preference.** Finally, we show an example from the set where the annotator had no preference. This subset consisted of paraphrases, such as:

> (..) It's recommended that you use the manual setting in order to manipulate the flash to produce the highest quality photos. Change the power of **a flash/the flash** depending on the ambient light and the subject you are shooting .

The high occurrence of paraphrases in the generated fillers shows that GPT can generate several plausible fillers for a given implicit reference and is an interesting point for future research.

# A practical perspective on connective generation

**Frances Yung**[1], **Merel C.J. Scholman**[1], and **Vera Demberg**[1,2]
[1]Language Science and Technology, [2]Computer Science, Saarland University
Saarbrücken, Germany
{frances,m.c.j.scholman,vera}@coli.uni-saarland.de

## Abstract

In data-driven natural language generation, we typically know what relation should be expressed and need to select a connective to lexicalize it. In the current contribution, we analyse whether a sophisticated connective generation module is necessary to select a connective, or whether this can be solved with simple methods, such as random choice between connectives that are known to express a given relation, or usage of a generic language model. Comparing these methods to the distributions of connective choices from a human connective insertion task, we find mixed results: for some relations, it is acceptable to lexicalize them using any of the connectives that mark this relation. However, for other relations (temporals, concessives) either a more detailed relation distinction needs to be introduced, or a more sophisticated connective choice module would be necessary.

## 1 Introduction

We assume a natural language generation setting in which we know, based on content planning, what coherence relation we wish to express, and the problem consists of choosing a suitable connective to express this relation. Of course, this problem is not independent of the discourse relation framework that is used – in the current study, we work with the relation distinctions proposed by PDTB-3 (Webber et al., 2019). From a generation perspective, the task would be easiest if, within relation distinctions, the connectives would be substitutable with each other. For instance, consider a framework that distinguishes causal relations from others, but within this class does not distinguish reason relations from result relations. Using such a framework, we would not be able to correctly select between connectives such as "because" and "therefore" as we wouldn't be able to express their difference. In this case, our connective insertion method would have to be able to learn this distinction in order to allow for fitting choices.

In this study, we aim to answer the following questions:

1. Does the discourse relation hierarchy of PDTB-3 make sufficiently fine-grained distinctions, such that choosing any one of the connectives that can express the relation will lead to a coherent text, or are finer-grained distinctions necessary?

2. Is there a practical value in developing sophisticated methods for connective choice, or are comprehenders largely insensitive to the choice among meaning-equivalent connectives?

We conduct two empirical connective insertion studies to test whether humans have a preference for the connective that was originally present in the text when being asked to lexicalize a relation. Several findings seem possible:

a) All connectives that express a specific coherence relation are fully interchangeable – in this case, we expect to see that human participants do not have any specific preference among the connectives that express the relation. We could conclude that the PDTB distinctions are sufficient, and using a simple connective choice method is sufficient.

b) All connectives are correct, but there are other factors, such as information-theoretic aspects, that influence which connective is preferred (e.g., a short vs. a longer / rarer connective). Again, we would conclude that PDTB distinctions are sufficient, but that other factors such as information density need to be taken into account.

c) Some instances of connectives would not be good choices for lexicalizing a specific in-



*Proceedings of the 2nd Workshop on Computational Approaches to Discourse*, pages 72–83
November 10–11, 2021. ©2021 Association for Computational Linguistics

stance of a relation, even though they can express other instances of that relation – in this case, a relevant distinction in relation sense may be missing or additional features may have to be learned in order to choose a fitting connective.

In both cases b) and c), we would expect to find that humans show a peaked distribution, preferring a specific connective or dispreferring a specific connective to express a relation. A more detailed analysis on these cases is conducted in order to check whether the preference is due to a lack of substitutability or rather a softer factor.

Our first study uses as material a naturalistic distribution of relations and finds that random choice among fitting connectives would achieve good accuracy on this problem – however, the coherence relation distribution in this first study is dominated by a small number of frequent relations. The second study therefore uses a more balanced design to better represent less frequent coherence relations. In this study, we find more nuanced results: while there are indeed some relations for which any of the matching connectives can be inserted, and a language model like GPT-2 (Radford et al., 2019) would perform well, there are also some relations for which simple automatic methods would systematically choose unsuitable lexicalizations. We analyse the latter cases in more detail in section 5.2.

## 2 Related work

There has been continuing interest in the task of connective prediction in recent years, but mostly as an auxiliary task to coherence relation classification. Zhou et al. (2010) use a language model for the task of connective prediction and Xu et al. (2012) deploy word pairs as well as a set of linguistically motivated features. More recently, Qin et al. (2017); Shi and Demberg (2019) and Kurfalı and Östling (2021) have used connective prediction for implicit relations as a secondary or adversarial task to improve discourse relation classification. The current study tackles a different task than these studies, where the relation label is assumed not to be available. Instead, we assume that the generation system knows what relation should be conveyed, and the remaining problem is the lexicalization using a connective.

Another related study is Ko and Li (2020), who analyse the discourse abilities of GPT-2 and find that connectives are sometimes incorrect. They propose to use a specific discourse component to address connective generation. Again, however, their setting is different from ours, as we assume that connectives need to be inserted into a text which is generated with a known discourse intention.

An experimental study closely related to the current contribution was conducted by Malmi et al. (2018). Crowd-workers were asked to guess the original connective in a text where the explicit connective had been removed. Our analysis of their results shows that the omission of an explicit connective often leads to a change in interpretation of the relation: for ca. 80% of explicitly marked relations, participants did not recover the original connective. Therefore, our study is designed differently: we ensure that workers express the intended relation by providing them with a choice among connectives that can mark the original relation.

The substitutability of connectives has been studied in previous literature. Most notably, Knott (1996); Knott et al. (2002) explored this topic using a connective substitution task, and created a hierarchy of connectives based on these results. Our study adds quantitative data on connective insertion preferences, as well as a practical perspective by investigating connective choice based on PDTB-3 discourse relation labels (and not just substitutability with respect to other connectives).

## 3 Methodology

We use crowdsourced human experiments to examine whether a specific DC is preferred for a given discourse relation instance. The approach is straight-forward: from discourse-annotated corpora, we sample a set of explicitly marked discourse relations. The original connectives are then removed from the instances and crowdworkers are asked to select the best-suiting connective. Several options of connectives, which are all valid explicit markers of the annotated discourse relation sense, are given to the workers to choose from.

If the choices of connectives made by the crowdworkers reproduce the original connective in the data, it indicates that this particular connective should be preferred over the other alternatives for that specific discourse relation instance. On the other hand, if the choices made by the crowdworkers are evenly distributed per instance, it indicates that the discourse relation instance in question could be interchangeably marked by alternative connectives.

In addition, we test whether a language model (here, GPT-2, Radford et al., 2019) can select the appropriate connective from the same set of options also given to the human participants. The preferred connective is chosen based on the cross entropy loss of the language model. If the connective with the highest probability based on the language model is identical to the preferred choice by humans, this suggests that a language model is sufficient for generating an appropriate connective for a given discourse relation. If, on the other hand, the language model prefers a connective which is not preferred by humans, this indicates that the language model is missing a relevant aspect of the coherence relation.

### 3.1 Data

We used discourse-annotated data where each explicit connective is labelled with a discourse relation type. Two datasets were used: 1) the complete English part of the TED Multilingual Discourse Bank (TED-MDB) (Zeyrek et al., 2019); 2) a balanced sample of the Penn Discourse Treebank 3.0 (PDTB-3; Prasad et al., 2018).

**The English portion of the TED-MDB** consists of the transcription of six English TED talks, which are videos of presentations on various topics. The transcription is annotated with discourse structure following the annotation scheme of PDTB-3 (Webber et al., 2019). Our focus are the explicit connectives and their annotated discourse relation types.

Since our objective is to evaluate the preference for alternative connectives, we exclude cases where the acceptability of the connective is highly restrictive. The majority of such cases is where two verb phrases are linked by a coordinating conjunction. For example, it is not grammatically acceptable to mark the CONJUNCTION relation with other connectives, e.g. *in addition* or *also*, instead of the original *and* in the sentence *"We have a population that is both growing **and** aging"*. Other items that were removed from our experiment include pragmatic markers (e.g. ***but** let's move yet again...*), prepositions (e.g. ***for** committing these so-called crimes*), and annotation errors (e.g. ***so** awesome*).

From the original set of 290 annotated explicit connectives, 210 are included in the experiment after screening. The distribution of the relation and connective types are shown in Table 3 in the appendix. The options of alternative connectives given to the crowdworkers primarily include the connectives used for the same relation type in the same dataset. Additional common connectives are included such that there are three to five options for each question.

The items from TED-MDB were divided into 4 batches, each consisting of 1 to 2 talks and approximately 50 items. They were presented to the crowdworkers paragraph by paragraph in the same order as the original data (see Figure 1).

The distributions of the relations and connective types in the TED-MDB are highly skewed. While this is representative of distributions found in natural language, it also means that we have very few observations for some relation types. We thus ran an additional study using the same setup on a balanced sample, in order to assess the preference of connectives for less frequent relations.

**The balanced sample from PDTB-3** consists of the 12 most frequent explicit relation types in PDTB-3. For each of these, we selected approximately 18 items per relation, resulting in a set of 206 items. We furthermore balanced the number of items marked by different connectives for each relation type. For instance, the ARG2-AS-DENIER relation can be marked using a range of different connectives, including *but*, *however*, *though*, *still* and *yet* as the most frequent ones. We selected the most common connectives with respect to the relation type and included a similar number of instances of relations marked with each of these five connectives in our study. The instances were selected randomly, except for instances with highly restrictive connective usage (as discussed above), instances with multiple labelled relation types and instances where the connective is embedded in the middle of the argument span (because this restricts substitutability). The distribution of the relations and connectives is shown in Table 4 in the appendix.

In the human connective choice experiment, the top 5 most frequent explicit connectives for each relation type are used as connective options. The items from PDTB-3 were presented to workers including one or two sentences of context before and after the discourse relational arguments, depending on sentence length. The items were randomly divided into 8 batches of about 28 items each. Smaller batch sizes were used in this experiment because the workers needed to read more context per item than for the TED-MDB (since the PDTB-3 items do not represent consecutive text).

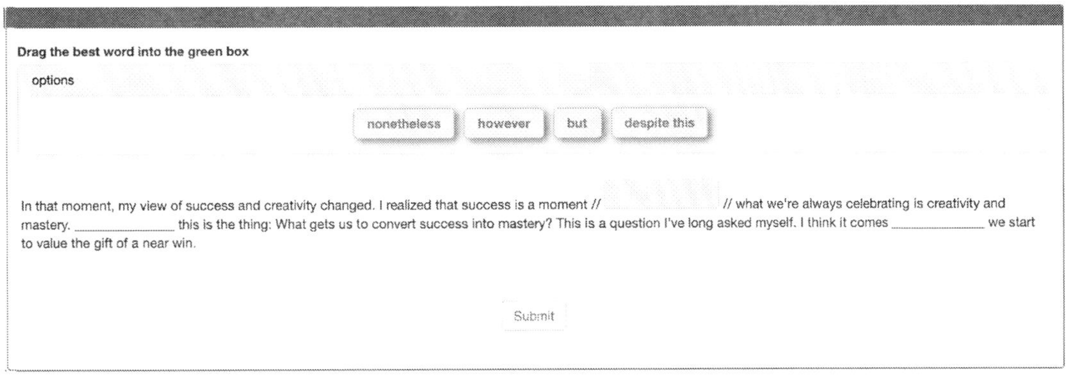


Figure 1: A screenshot of the human evaluation task.

### 3.2 Procedure

The connective selection task was implemented as a drag-and-drop task, as shown in Figure 1, on the LingoTurk platform (Pusse et al., 2016) and hosted on Prolific. The order of the connective options was randomized. We obtained 10 judgments for each item.

A total of 130 crowdworkers (83 females; average age = 31 years) were recruited to take part in either of the studies. All participants were native English speakers residing in English-speaking countries and registered on Prolific as participant. In Study 1 (TED-MDB), the experiment took 15 minutes on average, and participants were remunerated with 1.25 GBP. We anticipated that Study 2 would take longer because it required more reading, we therefore remunerated it with 2.50 GBP, but it turned out to only take 17 minutes on average.

## 4 Language Model

Connectives were compared with respect to the average negative log likelihood of the sentence including the connective, using OpenAI's pretrained Generatively Pre-trained Transformer (GPT-2) language model (Radford et al., 2019) implemented in the Transformers library of huggingface (Wolf et al., 2020). GPT-2 is a unidirectional transformer-based language model trained on a dataset of 40 GB of web crawling data.

The model compared the same set of connective choices as given to the human crowdworkers. The connective choice resulting in the best sequence according to GPT-2 was selected as the predicted connective.

| | Agreement | | |
|---|---|---|---|
| Data | majority | random | most common |
| TED-MDB | .723 | .223 | .852 |
| PDTB-3 | .454 | .242 | .304 |

Table 1: Agreement of the majority, random and most common connective choices with the original connective.

## 5 Results

### 5.1 Agreement between original connective, crowd choices and simple heuristic

Table 1 compares, per corpus, the original connective to three connective choices. The first column presents the agreement between the original connective and the majority choice; that is, the connective most frequently chosen by the workers for each instance. The second column presents the agreement with a randomly chosen connective; this was based on a baseline where a connective was chosen at random from the list of connectives that can express that relation type. Finally, the third column presents the agreement with the most common connective: a simple heuristic was used to select the connective that was most frequently chosen by workers for a discourse relation type, i.e. collapsing across the different instances of a discourse relation type. This last metric measures whether crowd workers use a default connective for every relation sense (e.g., always use *and* to express a conjunction, irrespective of the original connective that may have expressed that relation.)

We see large differences between the studies: In the TED-MDB dataset, which represents the natural distribution of the types of discourse relation, agreement between the majority choice among workers and the original connective is relatively high (72.3%): most workers chose the connective that matches the original connective in the corpus (mostly *and*, *but*, *because*, *so*). The agreement between the original connective and the "most common" baseline is even higher (85.2%), implying that the original connective of an instance is usually the most common connective for the particular relation type. This high agreement is due to the skewed distribution of the relations in TED-MDB: out of the 210 samples, there are 78 instances of *and* for CONJUNCTION and 34 instances of *but* for ARG2-AS-DENIER or CONTRAST (see Table 3), and these connectives are the most common connectives for these relation types. Such a skew towards a small number of highly frequent connectives is particularly strong in spoken language, while a larger variety of connectives is usually observed in written domains (Crible and Cuenca, 2017).

We conclude that for the spoken domain, simply generating the most frequent connective for a given relation sense already yields quite high accuracy. However, from this analysis, we cannot assess what happens in the cases where a less frequent relation needs to be expressed, as the number of these cases in the TED-MDB set is too small for reliable analysis, and we cannot tell whether this result would transfer to the written domain. Therefore, we next conducted an analysis using a balanced dataset based on the PDTB-3.

As Table 1 shows, the agreement is a lot lower for the PDTB-3-based balanced dataset. Here, the majority choice among crowdworkers agreed with the original connective for 45% of the items, while the most frequently selected connective of a relation type is identical with the original connective in only 30% of cases (this makes sense, as it reflects how the dataset was assembled). We will analyse these cases in more detail in the next section.

### 5.2 Analysis per relation type – PDTB-3

Table 2 shows that the accuracy for humans in recovering the original connective differs quite a lot depending on the relation and the original DC (ranging from 15% to 67%). Table 4, in the Appendix, presents more results on the agreement per relation type (collapsing across the original connectives) and statistics to test whether there is a significant difference between the human label distributions among items of different original connectives but the same relation sense.

In the remainder of this section, we present a more fine-grained analysis, for which we classified the results per relation sense and connective into the following broad categories: 1) Freely interchangeable connectives – humans don't show a preference for the original connective, several connectives are equally preferred. 2) Human preference is in line with original. 3) Human preference is for a specific connective which is different from the original.

**Case 1: Freely interchangeable connectives** We observe some relations for which participants chose a wide variety of connectives, and where their choice does not necessarily agree with the original connective. Consider, for example, the relation sense `Arg2-as-denier`: here, the distribution of insertions is nearly identical for all of the original connectives. These cases are unproblematic from a generation perspective, as any choice would be acceptable. Note though that the language model gives higher probability to the more generic connective *but*, while humans have a slight preference for the more specific connective *however*.

We also observe a high rate of interchangeability between *for example* and *for instance*, which mark the relation `Arg2-as-instance`, as well as the connectives for the `Arg2-as-detail` relation. In these cases, the distributions of the human choices are not significantly different from a uniform distribution.

For `Result` relations, the connectives *thus*, *as a result* and *therefore* seem to be freely interchangeable, while *and* and *so* have slightly different distributions. Interestingly, the language model seems to be able to pick up on cues that indicate the connective *so*. We note, though, that it incorrectly assigns the connective *and* to relations which were originally marked by *so* or *thus*, and for which *and* is not a preferred option according to human insertions – the language model here prefers a connective which is too generic.

**Case 2: Crowd-workers agree with the original** An interesting case are instances for which the humans prefer a connective that strongly matches with the original connective, while not selecting alternatives from the set of connectives for the same relation. In these cases, the results suggest that the relation sense is not sufficiently detailed, and there are relevant aspects of meaning of the relation which is not captured by the relational label.

Among these cases, we can then further distin-

| Relations (count) | Original connectives (count) | Distribution of humans' choices | | | | | Most frequent LM choice |
|---|---|---|---|---|---|---|---|
| | | *but* | *however* | *though* | *still* | *yet* | |
| **Arg2-as-denier** | but (4) | 23% | **33%** | 10% | 5% | 30% | but |
| **(20)** | however (4) | 23% | **30%** | 18% | 15% | 15% | but |
| Case 1 | though (4) | 28% | **38%** | 15% | 8% | 13% | but |
| | still (4) | 25% | **35%** | 23% | 5% | 13% | but |
| | yet (4) | 23% | **35%** | 13% | 10% | 20% | but |
| **Arg2-as-inst.** | | *for example* | *for instance* | *in particular* | *in fact* | *as* | |
| **(18)** | for example (9)*** | 30% | **41%** | 18% | 1% | 10% | for example |
| Case 1 | for instance (9) | **29%** | 20% | 18% | 17% | 17% | for example |
| | | *so* | *thus* | *as a result* | *therefore* | *and* | |
| **Result** | so (6)** | **40%** | 13% | 17% | 28% | 2% | so |
| **(18)** | thus (6) | 8% | 23% | **33%** | 25% | 10% | and |
| Case 1 | as a result (6) | 10% | 25% | **32%** | 15% | 18% | and, as a result |
| | | *indeed* | *in fact* | *specifically* | *in particular* | *and* | |
| **Arg2-as-detail** | indeed (4)* | 13% | **53%** | 5% | 13% | 18% | and, in fact |
| **(16)** | in fact (4) | 5% | 25% | 25% | 15% | **30%** | and |
| Case 1/3 | specifically (4) | 13% | 23% | **25%** | 18% | 23% | and |
| | in particular (4) | 8% | 13% | 20% | 25% | **35%** | and |
| | | *although* | *though* | *even if* | *even though* | *while* | |
| **Arg1-as-denier** | although (4)** | 23% | 8% | 3% | **60%** | 8% | even though |
| **(16)** | though (4)* | 35% | 8% | 8% | **43%** | 8% | even though |
| Case 2A | even if (3) | 10% | 10% | **50%** | 23% | 7% | even if |
| | even though (5)*** | 10% | 0% | 18% | **66%** | 6% | even though |
| | | *then* | *before* | *until* | *later* | *ultimately* | |
| **Precedence** | then (5) | 28% | 8% | 26% | 8% | **30%** | then |
| **(14)** | before (5)*** | 0% | **84%** | 14% | 2% | 0% | before |
| Case 2A | until (4)*** | 3% | 8% | **90%** | 0% | 0% | until |
| | | *because* | *as* | *since* | *for* | *when* | |
| **Reason** | because (6)*** | **38%** | 35% | 25% | 0% | 2% | because |
| **(18)** | as (6)* | 25% | **32%** | 17% | 2% | 25% | as |
| Case 2A | since (6)*** | 22% | 32% | **38%** | 0% | 8% | as |
| | | *and* | *also* | *in addition* | *moreover* | *or* | |
| **Conjunction** | and (6)*** | **57%** | 3% | 20% | 17% | 3% | and |
| **(19)** | also (6)*** | **53%** | 10% | 18% | 17% | 2% | and |
| Case 2A/B | in addition (7)*** | **41%** | 3% | 27% | 29% | 0% | and |
| | | *after* | *when* | *since* | *once* | *previously* | |
| **Succession** | after (4)** | **48%** | 15% | 5% | 33% | 0% | after, when |
| **(17)** | when (4)** | 13% | **48%** | 5% | 35% | 0% | once |
| Case 2B | since (3)*** | 7% | 7% | **83%** | 3% | 0% | since |
| | once (3)*** | 10% | 33% | 0% | **57%** | 0% | once |
| | previously (3) | **40%** | 3% | 17% | 10% | 30% | when |
| | | *but* | *while* | *however* | *still* | *on the other hand* | |
| **Contrast** | but (4)** | **40%** | 8% | 40% | 5% | 8% | but |
| **(15)** | while (4)** | 10% | **60%** | 18% | 3% | 10% | but, while |
| Case 2B | however (3)* | 13% | 20% | **57%** | 7% | 3% | but |
| | still (4) | **38%** | 10% | 25% | 3% | 25% | but |
| **Arg2-as-cond.** | | *if* | *when* | *until* | *as long as* | *in case* | |
| **(18)** | if (9)*** | 30% | 16% | 2% | **43%** | 9% | as long as |
| Case 2B | when (9)*** | 16% | **49%** | 9% | 19% | 8% | when |
| | | *when* | *as* | *while* | *meanwhile* | *at the same time* | |
| **Synchronous** | when (4)* | **45%** | 20% | 23% | 3% | 10% | when |
| **(18)** | as (4)*** | 15% | **55%** | 25% | 0% | 5% | as |
| Case 2B | while (3)*** | 13% | 8% | **80%** | 0% | 0% | at the same time |
| | meanwhile (3) | 3% | 13% | 30% | **43%** | 10% | at the same time |
| | at the same time (3) | 7% | 27% | **30%** | 20% | 17% | at the same time |

Table 2: Distribution of connectives per relation sense chosen by crowd workers in the PDTB data. The relation senses are ordered according to their case classification in section 5.2. Under the column "Distribution of humans' choices", the majority choice per original connective type is in marked in bold, and the choice matching with the original connective is underlined. $\chi^2$ **tests** are performed to test whether the distributions are significantly different from a uniform distribution ($^{*}$:$p < 0.05$;$^{**}$:$p < 0.01$;$^{***}$:$p < 0.001$).The final column presents the language model's (GPT2) prediction.

guish between cases where a language model successfully picks up on the distinction (Case 2A) vs. cases where the language model assigns a dispreferred connective (Case 2B).

**Examples of cases of type 2A** include the relation `Arg1-as-denier`: here, the crowd workers had a strong preference for the connective *even though*, which they inserted for sentences originally marked with *although*, *though* and *even though*. These connectives seem to be fully interchangeable, and could even be classified as Case 1, if it wasn't for the connective *even if*, which shows a different distribution. Interestingly, the language model agrees with human preferences for these cases – it generally assigns highest likelihood to the connective *even though*, but also correctly marks the original cases that were marked with *even if*.

A similar case is `Precedence`: the connectives *then*, *before* and *until* can be successfully recovered based on the language model.

Next, we take a look at the `Reason` relation. Here, participants largely recover the original connective, indicating that these connectives are not fully interchangeable. In particular, the connective *because* places more emphasis on the reason, and so it should be used in cases where the information given as the reason is new. *As* and *since* place emphasis on the result and are more commonly used when the speaker believes that the content of the reason is something that the addressee already knows. Interestingly, the language model successfully recovers the difference between connectives *because* and *as*, but prefers *as* also for cases where the original connective is *since*. This confusion might be related to both connectives being able to express a purely temporal relation as well. We can also see that only those `Reason` relations originally marked by *as* can be marked using *when*, which indicates that relations marked with *as* have a stronger temporal aspect than ones marked with *because*. A model that captures this aspect would have to learn when a reason is not temporal.

Finally, for `Conjunction` relations, we observe that both humans and the language model prefer to simply use the connective *and*. A small difference in human insertions is present between the instances containing the connective *in addition* originally vs. *and* or *also*: the heavier connective *in addition* can be more easily replaced by *moreover* compared to lighter connectives. A model using these connectives correctly would hence have to learn to pick up on heaviness effects relating to the prominence and length of relational arguments.

**Examples of Case 2B** are found in `Succession` relations. Here, the connectives *after*, *since* and *once* are successfully recovered by the workers as well as the language model, but for instances originally expressed by the connective *when*, the language model prefers *once*. A closer look at the data for the connective *when* reveals that in two cases, *once* is also the preferred connective for humans. For the other two items, *once* is not used at all. We find that this difference is related to tense/time frame: *Once* is interchangeable with *when* when the items speaks of future possibilities, not about the past. To illustrate, compare (1), which can be expressed with both *once* and *when*, with (2), can only be expressed with *when*.

(1) (...) [the plant can be reactivated quickly] ___ [the market improves.]

(2) [The controls on cooperatives appeared relatively liberal] ___ [first introduced.]

For `Succession` instances originally marked with *previously*, the language model assigns the connective *when*. However, humans only inserted *when* in 3% of cases. Manual analysis shows that this is because *previously* is used for a change in state/event, as in (3). The connective *when* is dispreferred in such cases, because it implies a shorter time frame.

(3) [Equus Capital Corp. would pay $12 cash for each of Tony Lama's 2.1 million shares outstanding] ___ [it offered $13.65 a share in cash, or $29 million.]

In `Contrast` relations, the human participants mostly recovered the original connective, indicating that they are not freely interchangeable. However, the language model uniformly selects *but* as the connective with highest likelihood. This seems to be particularly problematic for the instances originally marked with *while* and *however*, as they exhibit a low rate of *but*-choices among the humans. An example item for a case originally marked with *while* is shown in (4). An important factor here seems to be related to the simultaneous nature of the two facts that are contrasted.

(4) [Among liberals, 60% have positive views of her] ___ [50% approve of the president's job performance.]

For items originally marked with *however*, *but* also seems acceptable , but *however* gives a slightly stronger marking and breaks up the two arguments into two separate sentences. Information-theoretic aspects might be at play here. To illustrate this, consider the following example:

(5) One of the fastest growing segments of the wine market is the category of super-premiums (...). [For years, this group included a stable of classics – Bordeaux first growths (Lafite-Rothschild, Latour, Haut-Brion, Petrus), Grand Cru Burgundies (Romanee-Conti and La Tache) deluxe Champagnes (Dom Perignon or Roederer Cristal), rarefied sweet wines (Chateau Yquem or Trockenbeerenauslesen Rieslings from Germany, and Biondi-Santi Brunello Riserva from Tuscany)] ___ [in the last year or so, this exclusive club has taken in a host of flashy new members.]

*But* would be felicitous in this example, yet only one participant selected *but*, and eight selected *however*. Note that the first argument of this relation is rather long, and so participants might prefer however because it provides a clearer break between the arguments: in natural language, *however* is more frequently used to start a new sentence than *but*, which is more frequently used sentence-medially.

In `Arg2-as-condition` relations, we observe a low prediction accuracy because workers avoid the strong connective *if* – they might have interpreted multiple relations (and thus prefer multi-sense DCs over single-sense DCs). Instead of *if*, most participants and the language model chose *when* or *as long as*. These are however not suitable for all usages of *if*, as there may be differences in whether an event will actually happen, or whether there is uncertainty about it happening at all. Consider (6) and (7). Both were originally marked with *if*, but *as long as* was the preferred choice for (6). For (7), however, *as long as* would be infelicitous, and *if* was indeed the preferred crowd-choice.

(6) [The IRS says people in the disaster areas won't be penalized for late filing] ___ [their returns are marked "Hugo" and postmarked by Jan. 16.]

(7) [What will Mr. Sagan do with his new theater building] ___ [the allure of Hollywood and Broadway proves too much for such Steppenwolf stalwarts as John Malkovich (...).]

Finally, for the temporal `Synchronous` relations, the language model prefers the connective *at the same time* for relations marked originally by *at the same time*, *while* or *meanwhile*. By contrast, the workers agreed with the original connectives for both *while* and *meanwhile* items. For *at the same time* items, the workers also preferred *while*. A closer look at the instances reveals that *while* works particularly well when there is also a possible contrastive aspect in the item, as in (8).

(8) [Personal spending grew 0.2% in September to a $3.526 trillion annual rate] ___ [personal income was held down by the effects of Hurricane Hugo.]

**Case 3: Humans disagree with original** We found disagreements between humans and original connectives mostly in cases where the original connective was relatively unusual in sentence-initial position, such as *yet*, *also*, *still* or *indeed*. It is possible that this results from our experimental design, as the connective options were presented without a comma, which would be needed for many of these cases if used in sentence-initial position.

## 6 Discussion

We set out to investigate the extent to which the choice of connective to realize a particular relation is constrained. Specifically, we saw three possible outcomes: connectives that express a relation are fully interchangeable for the PDTB-3 relations that we work with here, other factors (e.g., information-theoretic ones) lead to preferences even though interchangeability is given, or the relation sense distinctions are not sufficiently fine-grained, so that an inappropriate connective might be chosen.

The main result is that connective choice varies depending on the dataset: in TED-MDB, high accuracy is achieved by choosing the most probable realization according to GPT-2 or choosing the most common connective per relation type. In PDTB, accuracy of the connective choice model is a lot lower.

We identified a set of different cases: a very simple connective selection strategy of randomly choosing among fitting connectives, might be good enough for some relations (Case 1). For other relations (identified as Case 2A above), a language-model-based strategy seems to perform well.

However, we also identified some more problematic cases (classified as 2B above): for these cases, we would either need to extend the relation inventory in order to capture the more fine-grained distinctions, such as temporal aspects (in `Succession` relations), factuality of events (in `Arg2-as-condition`) or whether there is a shared common ground (`Reason` relations). Alternatively, a more sophisticated language model would have to be developed, which can learn to use the correct connective in these cases. In future work, we aim to evaluate to what extent this could be learned by a transformer model which has been fine-tuned on a connective insertion task where the arguments and the target relation is given, and the correct connective needs to be selected.

We also found some limited evidence for other factors influencing connective choice – for the selection of a rather common and light connective like *and* or *but* vs. a more heavy and longer connective like *in addition* or *on the other hand*, it seems that while substitutability is given, preferences in terms of focus on the relation and heaviness and distance of the relational arguments may play an important role in connective choice. Again, it would be interesting to see whether a more sophisticated language model could pick up on these aspects.

The analyses performed here are clearly empirical. We do not claim that our method has allowed us to detect all possible cases where substitutability of connectives might not be given. Instead, our analyses provide a practical perspective indicating how a simple generation system for connectives would fare for frequent relations and connectives.

In relation to this, the difference in performance of the generation system on TED-MDB and PDTB provides interesting insights. These datasets represent different domains: the TED-MDB dataset consists of spoken data, whereas the PDTB dataset consists of written data. Spoken data tends to be characterized by a smaller range of connective types, as was the case in our data. The model's performance on this dataset seems promising, as it generally selects the same connective as the original one. As our subsequent analysis shows, this is mostly because these relations are "easy" – the original connective in TED-MDB is often the most common connective for a given relation type (e.g., *and*, *but*).

In the PDTB dataset, we manipulated the range and distribution of connectives by specifically choosing instances of a larger number of connectives, to give a more representative picture of the limitations of the simple GPT-2 based model. Some of the connectives in this set are infrequent in natural language. We find that the GPT-2 tends to default to frequently occurring connectives within relation senses (e.g., *but*, *and*, *even though*), irrespective of the original connective.

Finally, we note that the results of our analysis of course also depend on our choice of using PDTB as a framework here – other frameworks can differ in what coherence relations they distinguish, and accordingly, the results regarding which relations need to be distinguished at a more fine-grained level might vary. The methodology used here can also be applied to data from other frameworks to evaluate whether those distinctions are sufficient for computational purposes such as connective generation.

## 7 Conclusion

The current study showed that, in spoken data, a language generation system can predict the connective that should be used to express a discourse relation with high accuracy. This is partially because the relations tend to be quite simple and be marked by high-frequency connectives: even simply choosing the most prototypical connective for a given relation sense shows high accuracy on this data set.

On the other hand, our subsequent analysis of written data, using a more balanced set of relations and connectives, highlighted that there is a clear need for a more sophisticated method for connective choice. The results from human annotators indicated that connectives for many relational classes are not fully interchangeable. In some cases (`Succession`, `Condition`, and `Reason` relations), additional finer-grained relation types are needed to capture more information. In other cases (relating to specific connectives, such as *in addition* and *however*), information-theoretic constraints appear to influence connective choice. These insights can be useful for natural language generation researchers as well as research on automatic discourse parsing.

## Acknowledgements

This research was funded by the German Research Foundation (DFG) as part of SFB 1102 "Information Density and Linguistic Encoding".

## References

Ludivine Crible and Maria-Josep Cuenca. 2017. Discourse markers in speech: characteristics and challenges for corpus annotation. *Dialogue and Discourse*, 8(2):149–166.

Alistair Knott. 1996. *A data-driven methodology for motivating a set of coherence relations*. Ph.D. thesis, The University of Edinburgh: College of Science and Engineering: School of Informatics.

Alistair Knott, Ted Sanders, and Jon Oberlander. 2002. Levels of representation in discourse relations.

Wei-Jen Ko and Junyi Jessy Li. 2020. Assessing discourse relations in language generation from gpt-2. In *Proceedings of the 13th International Conference on Natural Language Generation*, pages 52–59.

Murathan Kurfalı and Robert Östling. 2021. Let's be explicit about that: Distant supervision for implicit discourse relation classification via connective prediction. *arXiv preprint arXiv:2106.03192*.

Eric Malmi, Daniele Pighin, Sebastian Krause, and Mikhail Kozhevnikov. 2018. Automatic prediction of discourse connectives. In *Proceedings of the Eleventh International Conference on Language Resources and Evaluation (LREC 2018)*.

Rashmi Prasad, Bonnie Webber, and Alan Lee. 2018. Discourse annotation in the PDTB: The next generation. In *Proceedings 14th Joint ACL-ISO Workshop on Interoperable Semantic Annotation*, pages 87–97.

Florian Pusse, Asad Sayeed, and Vera Demberg. 2016. Lingoturk: managing crowdsourced tasks for psycholinguistics. In *Proceedings of the 2016 Conference of the North American Chapter of the Association for Computational Linguistics: Demonstrations*, pages 57–61.

Lianhui Qin, Zhisong Zhang, Hai Zhao, Zhiting Hu, and Eric P Xing. 2017. Adversarial connective-exploiting networks for implicit discourse relation classification. *arXiv preprint arXiv:1704.00217*.

Alec Radford, Jeff Wu, Rewon Child, David Luan, Dario Amodei, and Ilya Sutskever. 2019. Language models are unsupervised multitask learners.

Wei Shi and Vera Demberg. 2019. Learning to explicitate connectives with Seq2Seq network for implicit discourse relation classification. In *Proceedings of the 13th International Conference on Computational Semantics - Long Papers*, pages 188–199, Gothenburg, Sweden. Association for Computational Linguistics.

Bonnie Webber, Rashmi Prasad, Alan Lee, and Aravind Joshi. 2019. The Penn Discourse Treebank 3.0 annotation manual. *Philadelphia, University of Pennsylvania*.

Thomas Wolf, Lysandre Debut, Victor Sanh, Julien Chaumond, Clement Delangue, Anthony Moi, Pierric Cistac, Tim Rault, Remi Louf, Morgan Funtowicz, Joe Davison, Sam Shleifer, Patrick von Platen, Clara Ma, Yacine Jernite, Julien Plu, Canwen Xu, Teven Le Scao, Sylvain Gugger, Mariama Drame, Quentin Lhoest, and Alexander Rush. 2020. Transformers: State-of-the-art natural language processing. In *Proceedings of the 2020 Conference on Empirical Methods in Natural Language Processing: System Demonstrations*, pages 38–45, Online. Association for Computational Linguistics.

Yu Xu, Man Lan, Yue Lu, Zheng Yu Niu, and Chew Lim Tan. 2012. Connective prediction using machine learning for implicit discourse relation classification. In *The 2012 International Joint Conference on Neural Networks (IJCNN)*, pages 1–8. IEEE.

Deniz Zeyrek, Amália Mendes, Yulia Grishina, Murathan Kurfalı, Samuel Gibbon, and Maciej Ogrodniczuk. 2019. Ted multilingual discourse bank (ted-mdb): A parallel corpus annotated in the pdtb style. *Language Resources and Evaluation*, pages 1–27.

Zhi Min Zhou, Yu Xu, Zheng-Yu Niu, Man Lan, Jian Su, and Chew Lim Tan. 2010. Predicting discourse connectives for implicit discourse relation recognition. In *Coling 2010: Posters*, pages 1507–1514.

## A Appendix

| **Relations (count)** | **Original connectives (count)** | **Options of alternative connectives** |
|---|---|---|
| **Conjunction (80)** | and (78), also (2) | and, also, in addition, furthermore, (nothing) |
| **Disjunction (3)** | or (3) | or, alternatively, otherwise |
| **Arg1-as-detail (1)** | in short (1) | in short, in summary, to sum up, in general, to conclude |
| **Arg2-as-detail (4)** | in fact (2), clearly (1), especially (1) | in fact, clearly, especially, in more detail, in particular |
| **Arg2-as-manner (6)** | by (4), through (2) | by, through, by means of, by way of |
| **Reason (17)** | because (16), since (1) | because, since, as |
| **Result (17)** | so (15), because of that (1), that's why (1) | so, because of that, that's why, therefore, as a result |
| **Arg2-as-condition (20)** | if (17), when (3) | if, when, provided that, given that, in case |
| **Contrast (15)** | but (10), and (2), when (1), where (1), where, on the one hand (1) | and, but, when, on the contrary, on the one/other hand |
| **Arg2-as-denier (26)** | but (24), however (1), though (1) | but, however, though, nonetheless, despite this |
| **Similarity (1)** | also (1) | also, similarily, in the same vein |
| **Precedence (5)** | and then (4), then (1) | and then, then, and next, and afterwards |
| **Synchronous (15)** | as (7), when (6), while (1), at the same time (1) | as, when, at the same time, while, meanwhile |

Table 3: Distribution of discourse relation and connective types of the items from TED-MDB and the choices of alternative connectives given to the human crowdworkers

| Relation types (item count) | Original connectives (item count) / connective options | Agree with org. Maj. | LM | $\chi^2$ test $\chi^2$ | *df* | |
|---|---|---|---|---|---|---|
| **Conjunction (19)** | and (6), also (6), in addition (7), *moreover, or* | .316 | .632 | 12.01 | 8 | |
| **Arg2-as-detail (16)** | indeed (4), in fact (4), specifically (4) in particular (4), *and* | .200 | .067 | 24.81 | 12 | * |
| **Arg2-as-instance (18)** | for example (9), for instance (9), *in particular, in fact, as* | .278 | .389 | 20.33 | 4 | *** |
| **Reason (18)** | because (6), as (6), since (6), *for, when* | .444 | .555 | 20.78 | 8 | ** |
| **Result (18)** | so (6), thus (6), as a result (6), *therefore, and* | .444 | .500 | 36.51 | 8 | *** |
| **Arg2-as-condition (18)** | if (9), when (9), *until, as long as, in case* | .444 | .278 | 31.95 | 4 | *** |
| **Arg1-as-denier (16)** | although (4), though (4), even if (3), even though (5), *while* | .500 | .500 | 46.82 | 12 | *** |
| **Arg2-as-denier (20)** | but (4), however (4), though (4), still (4), yet (4) | .150 | .250 | 11.23 | 16 | |
| **Contrast (15)** | but (4), while (4), however (3), still (4), *on the other hand* | .530 | .400 | 58.30 | 12 | *** |
| **Precedence (14)** | then (5), before (5), until (4), *later, ultimately* | .786 | .929 | 142.60 | 8 | *** |
| **Succession (17)** | after (4), when (4), since (3), once (3), *previously* | .611 | .500 | 179.72 | 16 | *** |
| **Synchronous (18)** | when (4), as (4), while (3), meanwhile (3), at the same time (3) | .611 | .389 | 116.84 | 16 | *** |
| **Overall (215)** | | .423 | .433 | | | |

Table 4: Distribution of discourse relation and connective types of the experimental items from PDTB-3. The **connective options** given to the human crowdworkers primarily include the original connectives of the same relation in the sample set. Further options (in *italics* and without item counts) are added such that there are five choices per question. **Agree with org.** is the percentage of items per relation where the majority choice by the crowdworkers (**Maj.**) or the choice with the lowest perplexity based on GPT-2 (**LM**) matches the original connective. Here, the $\chi^2$ **test** is performed to test if there is significant difference between the human label distributions among items of different original connectives but the same relation (*:$p < 0.05$;**:$p < 0.01$;***:$p < 0.001$).

# Semi-automatic discourse annotation in a low-resource language: Developing a connective lexicon for Nigerian Pidgin

**Marian Marchal**[1], **Merel Scholman**[1], and **Vera Demberg**[1,2]
[1]Language Science and Technology, [2]Computer Science, Saarland University
Saarbrücken, Germany
{marchal,m.c.j.scholman,vera}@coli.uni-saarland.de

## Abstract

Cross-linguistic research on discourse structure and coherence marking requires discourse-annotated corpora and connective lexicons in a large number of languages. However, the availability of such resources is limited, especially for languages for which linguistic resources are scarce in general, such as Nigerian Pidgin. In this study, we demonstrate how a semi-automatic approach can be used to source connectives and their relation senses and develop a discourse-annotated corpus in a low-resource language. Connectives and their relation senses were extracted from a parallel corpus combining automatic (PDTB end-to-end parser) and manual annotations. This resulted in Naija-Lex, a lexicon of discourse connectives in Nigerian Pidgin with English translations. The lexicon shows that the majority of Nigerian Pidgin connectives are borrowed from its English lexifier, but that there are also some connectives that are unique to Nigerian Pidgin.

## 1 Introduction

Resources such as discourse-annotated corpora (e.g. PDTB, Prasad et al., 2008) and connective lexicons (e.g. DimLEX, Stede and Umbach, 1998) have proven highly valuable in investigating discourse structure and coherence marking, but they are only available for a limited number of languages. One promising way to expand these resources is to project annotations from languages for which such resources are available to under-resourced languages. The current paper sets out to investigate how automatic discourse parsing can be combined with manual annotation to construct a connective lexicon in a low-resource language. We apply this method to create Naija-Lex, a lexicon of Nigerian Pidgin, but the method can also be adapted to apply to other low-resource languages.

Pidgin and creole languages, such as Nigerian Pidgin (commonly referred to as 'Pidgin' or 'Naija'), tend to be less complex on a syntactic and morphological level than their lexifiers (Szmrecsanyi et al., 2009). This raises interesting questions with respect to their discourse complexity, such as: how is discourse structure realized in contact languages? And how does this affect discourse marking? In addition, because pidgins are still in an evolutionary stage, they are a testing ground for examining how connectives emerge. However, the scarcity of linguistic resources, such as discourse-annotated corpora, for these languages makes it difficult to answer these questions. Another contribution of this paper is the creation of a discourse-annotated layer for a parallel corpus of Nigerian Pidgin, which can be used to study these questions.

We adopt a semi-automatic approach using automatic connective identification and annotation projection, combined with manual annotation, to initialize a list of discourse connective candidates in Nigerian Pidgin. This allows us to evaluate how existing tools can be adopted to investigate low-resource languages. More specifically, we assess the usefulness of the PDTB end-to-end parser (Lin et al., 2014) in identifying connectives in informal spoken English translated text, to source connectives in the target language.

The main contributions of the present research are the following:

- We identify challenges in constructing a lexicon in an under-resourced language and present a methodology for sourcing discourse connectives and their associated relation senses in such a language.
- We create a lexicon of discourse connectives in Nigerian Pidgin with English translations (Naija-Lex), which enables further research on discourse structure and coherence marking in Pidgin.
- We add a discourse-annotated layer to an existing Nigerian Pidgin-English parallel corpus



*Proceedings of the 2nd Workshop on Computational Approaches to Discourse*, pages 84–94
November 10–11, 2021. 

containing explicit connectives and their relation senses.

Section 2 discusses earlier work on automatic discourse annotation and lexicon construction, after which Nigerian Pidgin is introduced in Section 3. Section 4 describes the method used to identify the connectives in Pidgin. We elaborate on the Naija-Lex lexicon that we created using this method in Section 5 and evaluate our method in Section 6.

## 2 Related work

### 2.1 Lexicon creation

Connective inventories have been developed for various languages, including German (Stede and Umbach, 1998), French (Roze et al., 2012), Chinese (Zhou and Xue, 2015) and English (Das et al., 2018), among others (see also Stede et al., 2018). Recently, these efforts have been extended with several multi-lingual connective databases (Bourgonje et al., 2017; Kurfalı et al., 2020).

One challenging aspect about constructing a connective lexicon for a new language is defining the category of connectives. Traditionally, the PDTB (Prasad et al., 2008) has placed strong syntactic restrictions on which lexical items can function as connectives, considering only subordinating and coordinating conjunctions and adverbials. Stede et al. (2018) point out that for multilingual lexicons, such a strict definition is not feasible, as languages differ highly in the way coherence relations are expressed. Still, Stede et al. (2018) restrict the class of connectives syntactically, by posing that a connective cannot be inflected or modified, and that verbs should be excluded for this reason.

Similar to certain other lexicons (e.g. LDM-PT, Mendes and Lejeune, 2016), the lexicon we present here will maintain less strict requirements on the syntactic category and modifiability of the lexical item. In this way, we can allow for more variation that might be present in a relatively young language and obtain a more complete overview of discourse marking in Nigerian Pidgin.

### 2.2 Connective identification

In the last decade, shallow discourse parsing of explicit connectives has received considerable attention in the computational discourse community (e.g. Lin et al., 2014; Pitler and Nenkova, 2009; Wang and Lan, 2015; Zeldes et al., 2019). One challenge for such automatic parsers is that a discourse connective often also has a non-connective function, which is difficult to distinguish. Still, automatic discourse parsers for English achieve an F1 of almost 95% in identifying explicit connectives (Lin et al., 2014; Wang and Lan, 2015).

Discourse parsers are still very much restricted in terms of language and domain, because of a strong focus on the use of the PDTB for training. Parsers on languages other than English often reach much lower performance (e.g. Xue et al., 2016), although the recent DisRPT connective detection task (Zeldes et al., 2019) has yielded some high performing systems in other languages as well (Muller et al., 2019; Yu et al., 2019). However, these parsers still require training data, which is not available for low-resource languages.

Using parallel corpora might therefore be a promising method to identify connectives and then project their annotations to a low-resource language. One possible difficulty is that these corpora might be from different domains than what the parsers have been trained on, which leads to lower performance (Ramesh and Yu, 2010; Knaebel and Stede, 2020; Scholman et al., 2021).

We will use the PDTB end-to-end parser (Lin et al., 2014), as it has been shown to perform better on spontaneous spoken data than other parsers (Scholman et al., 2021). However, performance of the parser drops considerably when comparing spoken language with the newspaper text data it was trained on. We will therefore also assess its reliability on an out-of-domain translated text.

### 2.3 Connective projection

Several previous studies have used research available on connectives in one language (mostly English) to identify connectives in another language. Zhou and Xue (2012) and Das et al. (2020) have used bilingual dictionaries to translate English connectives to Chinese and Bangla respectively as part of identifying connectives in these target languages to construct a lexicon. However, no dictionaries are available for Nigerian Pidgin.

Another line of research in using cross-lingual information to source connectives is to use parallel corpora. Versley (2010) projected discourse connectives across an English-German parallel corpus, but found that simple word alignment is not enough to reliably identify connectives in text and that performance increased when bootstrapping using an established connective list. Bourgonje et al. (2018) combined a German connective lexicon with parallel text corpora to find Dutch connectives and subsequently manually checked and annotated them for relation sense. However, this approach does not automatically distinguish between connective and non-connective usages of connectives in the source languages, which always needs to be resolved manually. The current research attempts to resolve this by using a shallow discourse parser to identify connectives in the translation text automatically.

A more similar approach to that adopted in the current study is that of Laali and Kosseim (2014). They used the PDTB end-to-end parser to identify English discourse connectives in the Europarl corpus source text, after which they used word alignment to identify connectives in the parallel French texts. This mapping was further improved with additional filtering based on frequency and syntactic information. However, performance is highly dependent on the length and syntactic categories of discourse connectives, which vary between languages. In addition, automatic word alignment can only be applied successfully if enough parallel data is available, while resources for the language under consideration here are limited.

One possible drawback of using translation text to source connectives is that it draws on the assumption that coherence relations in the source text and the translated text remain the same. However, this is not necessarily the case. Discourse relations often allow multiple interpretations, but a translated text might only contain the interpretation of the translator (i.e. in cases where the original connective is disambiguated). Secondly, there are several factors guiding when discourse relations are implicitated or explicitated in translation text, such as specific features of the target language and the relation sense (Becher, 2011; Zufferey and Cartoni, 2014). The distribution of explicit relations in the translation text thus does not necessarily reflect the distribution of explicit relations in the source text. This would influence the likelihood of connectives found in the source language by only taking into account the connectives in the translation text. We will therefore also assess how well the explicit connectives in the translated text reflect the discourse relations in the source text.

Finally, connective lexicons contain information about the relation senses that can be signalled by a certain connective. The PDTB end-to-end parser provides relation sense labels for the connectives it identifies, which could be projected to the connectives in the parallel text. This was, however, not taken into account by Laali and Kosseim (2014). The present research therefore evaluates and extends their methodology for lexicon creation with a parallel corpus.

## 3 Nigerian Pidgin

Nigerian Pidgin is a contact language spoken all over Nigeria. Although officially a pidgin, it is also often considered a creole (e.g., Courtin et al., 2018), as it is a relatively stable language with a fully-developed vocabulary and grammar. In addition to approximately 5 million native speakers, there are estimated to be almost 100 million speakers of Nigerian Pidgin as a second language. It is often also referred to simply as 'Pidgin' by Nigerian Pidgin speakers themselves.

English is one of the main lexifiers of Nigerian Pidgin, with many words having a similar form and meaning as the English origin, as can be seen in Example (1).

(1) I say 'toh, me I sabi operate computer small small'.
*I said 'well, I know a bit about computers'.*

Nigerian Pidgin is also influenced by other European languages (e.g. Portuguese, illustrated by *sabi* in the example above) as well as various indigenous languages it has been in contact with, such as Hausa, Igbo and Yoruba. Nigerian Pidgin is characterized by focus constructions (see e.g. *me* in (1)), which are often indicated with the focus particle *na* (Caron et al., 2019). In addition, serial verb constructions are typical for Nigerian Pidgin. As a result, coordinating conjunctions are less frequent in Nigerian Pidgin than in English (Courtin et al., 2018). An example of such a serial verb construction is provided in Example (2), which has been translated in English with the coordinating conjunction *and*. This suggests that discourse relations might be expressed differently in Nigerian Pidgin.

(2) Con dey hustle, con hustle money go give am.
*Then we hustled, got money <u>and</u> went to give it to her.*

Linguistic research and resources on Nigerian Pidgin are limited, although this has shifted in recent years. As part of a larger project studying the syntactic and prosodic structure of Nigerian

Pidgin, Caron et al. (2019) are in the process of creating a 500,000 word corpus of spoken data, part of which is already available and will be used in the current study. We also note related work from the NLP community in studying Pidgin to explore new approaches for low-resource natural language generation (Chang et al., 2020) and translation (Ogueji and Ahia, 2019). However, no previous research has examined the discourse structure of Nigerian Pidgin.

## 4 Methodology

### 4.1 Data

The data we use in our analysis comes from the gold section of the Naija Treebank (UD NSC Corpus),[1] a parallel corpus of Nigerian Pidgin utterances with English translations. This dataset consists of 140,859 words collected in various locations, and represents 87 speakers. The sampling of speakers aimed at balancing age, sex, education, linguistic and geographic background. The genres recorded cover life stories, speeches, radio programs, free conversations, cooking recipes, comments on current state of affairs, etc. The translation of the Nigerian Pidgin sentences into English was done by a team of native speakers of Nigerian Pidgin, and aimed at remaining as faithful as possible to the structure and style of the original utterances (Caron et al., 2019).

We extracted the original Nigerian Pidgin utterances (referred to as Source Text – ST), together with their English translations (referred to as Translated Text – TT) and the Nigerian Pidgin POS tags from the NSC corpus. In total, the dataset used in this study contains 9,242 Nigerian Pidgin utterances, divided into three subsets: dev (n=991), train (n=7,279), and test (n=972).

### 4.2 Construction of the lexicon

Figure 1 displays the workflow used in this study. As Step 1, we ran an automatic end-to-end PDTB classifier on the English text to extract the TT connectives, by disambiguating between connective and non-connective usages of connective tokens. This resulted in the extraction of 4,592 TT connective tokens (dev: n=454, train: n=3,691, test: n=446), consisting of 41 different TT connective types, in 3,389 utterances. In addition, the parser provides the relation sense (PDTB 2.0) of each English connective.

As a next step, the first two authors both manually annotated the Nigerian Pidgin counterpart of all English connectives in the dev set in order to obtain an initial dictionary of English-Nigerian Pidgin connective mappings. Following the criteria from the PDTB (Prasad et al., 2008), only Nigerian Pidgin words from the following syntactic categories were initially considered as connective candidates: coordinating conjunctions, subordinating conjunctions, adverbs, and adpositions. Of 446 TT connectives, 336 were mapped onto an equivalent in the ST. This mapping functioned as input for an initial (seed) connective dictionary, which contained 30 Pidgin connective candidates and 52 unique co-occurrence types (excluding TT connective$\sim$implicit ST pairing).

This initial dictionary was then used to predict the Nigerian Pidgin equivalent of the extracted English connectives in the train set in Step 3. For each utterance containing an English connective in the TT, the POS-tagged ST was searched for one of the Nigerian Pidgin equivalents that had been mapped onto this connective in the dev set. In order to predict a mapping for cases where a single Pidgin connective was mapped to multiple English connectives or vice versa we calculated normalized pointwise mutual information (NPMI) of co-occurrences in our dictionary. The connective match with the highest NPMI was selected as the target connective. For example, English *until* could be a translation of Nigerian Pigin *till* or *sotay*. If the ST of a TT containing *until* would contain both *till* and *sotay*, *sotay* would be selected as its association with *until* is stronger than that of *till*.

In cases where the NPMI did not resolve to a one-to-one mapping (e.g. the TT text contained two instances of *until*, with only one equivalent in the ST), the Nigerian Pidgin connective with the closest relative position in the sentence was selected. When no Pidgin translation equivalent was found, the four words closest to the relative position in the TT were searched for another Pidgin connective that had not been mapped to this English connective yet to extend the initial dictionary with new candidate mappings.

To examine whether the data set contained other Nigerian Pidgin connectives that did not occur in the dev subset, we manually annotated selected instances from the train set where (a) an English

[1] `https://universaldependencies.org/treebanks/pcm_nsc/index.html`

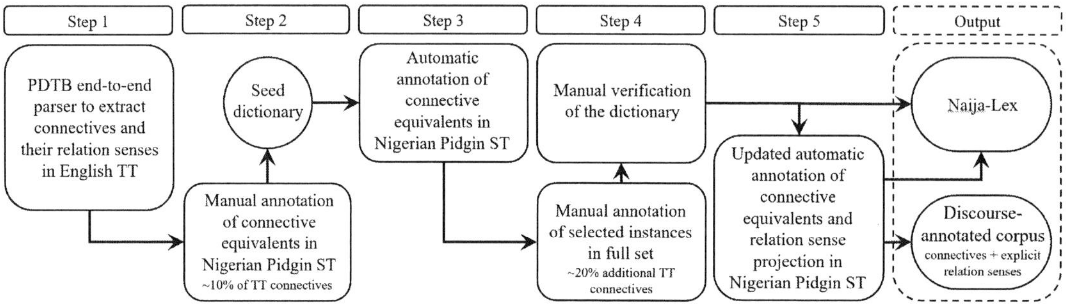


Figure 1: Schematic overview of the workflow for the construction of the connective lexicon (and discourse-annotated corpus) for Nigerian Pidgin.

connective had been identified in the TT that did not appear in the dev set and (b) where no Nigerian Pidgin translation equivalent was found (Step 4). We also manually examined all instances where the Pidgin connective candidates 'wey' or 'sey' were extracted from the ST, since these are frequently used as complementizers rather than connectives. In this annotation round we expanded the connective dictionary by relaxing restrictions on the syntactic category, due to high co-occurrence of English connectives with certain auxiliary verbs and lexical phrases in Pidgin. We then further verified the dictionary by checking the new English-Nigerian Pidgin connective mappings that did not occur in the seed dictionary and consulted a native Pidgin-speaking linguist to verify (a) whether connectives that did not have an English origin were indeed a connective in Pidgin and (b) whether the English translations were valid.

The updated dictionary was used to improve the automatically identified Nigerian Pidgin connectives in the train set (Step 5) and to construct the connective lexicon. The lexicon was complemented with automatic relation sense labels and the frequency data from the corpus.

## 5 Naija-Lex: A lexicon of Nigerian Pidgin connectives

In total, 4,186 Nigerian Pidgin connective tokens were identified. They were retrieved based on 40 English connective types in the translation text. The Nigerian Pidgin connective tokens consisted of 77 types, which were categorized in 57 entries in the lexicon. Naija-Lex is made available online.[2] For each connective entry, the lexicon contains information on its frequency, alternative forms, syntactic category(/ies), English translation equivalents and non-connective usage. In addition, the various relation senses that the connective can signal are included, together with an example of the Nigerian Pidgin connective in every sense and the relation sense distribution.

### 5.1 Connective origin and syntactic category

The majority of the connective entries (n=39) are derived from connectives in the English lexifier. Their phonology has often been adapted slightly to that of Nigerian Pidgin, leading to multiple variants of the same connective. For example, *because* occurs in Nigerian Pidgin as *because*, but also as *cause* and *cos*, and *dough* has been adapted from English *though*. Only 18 connective types in the lexicon did not originate from English connectives. Examples of these are *abi* (English: *or*), *wey be sey* (English: *when*) and *sotay* (English: *until*).

Some of these Pidgin connectives have evolved from English non-connective words. Consider *con* (originating from English 'come') and *make*. Both have evolved from an English verb and can now be used as a main verb in Pidgin, in which case they do not function as connectives, as well as an auxiliary, in which case they are frequently translated as connectives expressing causal and temporal connectives in English (see Examples (3) and (4)).

(3) I **con** realise sey omo na dis Pidgin na im make us connect like dat.
*Then I realized that, wow, this Pidgin brought us together.*

(4) De want hold am **make** e no fall.
*They want to hold them* ***so*** *they won't fall off.*

*Con* is used frequently in narration, connecting the events in one utterance with the following events in the next utterance. Like many other

[2] https://osf.io/xns9z/?view_only=710a1eca318f46b9b10584c3b980beec

Nigerian Pidgin auxiliary verbs, *con* is positioned between the subject and the main verb of the clause. By contrast, *make* is only found in clause-initial position. In a non-connective usage, it often functions as a directive, its meaning equivalent to 'should' in English. This causal function has likely extended to its usage as a causal discourse connective. Note that *make* does not satisfy the criterion of not being modifiable (cf. Stede et al., 2018): depending on the pronoun, it is inflected to *meh* or *mey*. We still consider it a connective, because it can also be used to signal a causal relation between two abstract, clausal arguments (similar to causal discourse verbs, see e.g. Danlos, 2006).

Other unique Pidgin connectives have evolved from Pidgin words that originally did not express a discourse function. The connective *naim* is a contraction of the auxiliary verb *na*, which is often used as a focus particle, and the 3SG pronoun *im* and has been lexicalized to a causal/temporal connective, equivalent to *then* or *so*. An example of its connective and non-connective use can be found in (5) and (6) respectively:

(5) E get one lady, hm she just enter inside shop o. **Naim** she say she wan do facials.
*There was one lady, she just went into the shop. **Then** she said she wanted to do facials.*

(6) And **na im** dey give am.
*And **he's the one** giving it to her.*

The most frequent syntactic category of the connective variants was subordinating conjunctions (n=16), followed by adverbs (n=15) and adpositions (n=11). The lexicon also contains one particle as Pidgin connective (*shey*, English *so*), which is another syntactic class traditionally not considered to contain connectives in English.

### 5.2 Connective and relation sense distribution

In terms of frequency of connectives in the Nigerian Pidgin data, the data shows that *if* was the most frequent (n=643), followed by *so* (n=606) and *and* (n=511). The most frequent connectives that are not English cognates are *con* and *naim*, with 394 and 77 occurrences respectively.

Table 1 provides information regarding the relation sense distribution found in the corpus, based on projected labels originally assigned to the English connectives. Connectives in Nigerian Pidgin were used to express a total of eight different relation classes (based on PDTB2 level 2 relation labels). Temporal and Cause were the most frequent explicit relations in the corpus. Table 1 also shows that Conjunction relations were frequently implicit in the ST and had been explicitated in the TT. Importantly, the distribution is similar in the manually annotated dev set, indicating that this distribution is not an artefact of the automatic annotation.

| Relation sense | Explicit | Implicit |
|---|---|---|
| Temporal | 30.4 | 17.8 |
| Cause | 25.8 | 10.3 |
| Conjunction | 14.1 | 52.8 |
| Contrast | 11.1 | 6.4 |
| Condition | 15.4 | 10.6 |
| Alternative | 1.4 | 0.8 |
| Restatement | 1.5 | 1.0 |
| Instantiation | 0.3 | 0.3 |

Table 1: Relation sense distribution in percentages for connectives that were explicit (n=4049) and implicit (n=388) in Nigerian Pidgin (but explicit in English).

When considering the relational distribution of each connective, we find that most connectives have one clear dominant meaning. This is illustrated in Figure 2. For example, Nigerian Pidgin *den* is almost exclusively used in temporal relations. The connective *as* is predominantly used as a temporal connective, but similar to English, has also maintained its causal meaning. The non-cognate connectives *con* and *naim*, however, are used in various relations, mostly Temporal and Cause. Although it might seem surprising that additional connectives have developed for relations that can also be signalled by English cognate connectives (e.g. *den* for Temporal and *so* for Cause), we note that these relations are also the most frequent, which might explain why speakers are more likely to find new ways to express them. Alternatively, these new connectives might have evolved precisely because of the polyfunctional usage. The connectives borrowed from English clearly signal one dominant relation, whereas *con* and *naim* can be used to underspecify these discourse relations.

## 6 Evaluation of the method

### 6.1 Automatic connective identification in TT

To evaluate accuracy of the first step in our pipeline we manually annotated the TT in the development set for presence of connectives, according to the criteria set by Stede et al. (2018).

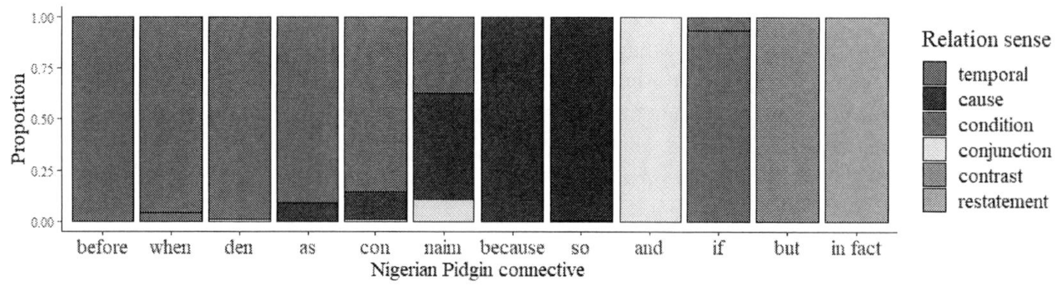


Figure 2: Relation sense distribution of the twelve most frequent Nigerian Pidgin connectives.

Connectives were identified in the English TT by the PDTB end-to-end parser with relatively high reliability (precision = 85.2%, recall = 85.6%, F1 = 85.4%). This is lower than the parser's performance on the test set of the PDTB (i.e. 95.76%), but that was expected, because the parser was trained on text from the written newspaper domain.

A closer examination of the performance per connective shows that precision is especially low on *so, so that, also* and *later* (<= 50%). In spoken language, *so* is often used as a discourse marker rather than a connective.[3] For *so that*, the majority of mistakes were caused by the parser identifying *so* with a demonstrative *that* as a connective. Low recall was reached for *afterwards* and *yet*, which occurred infrequently and were not detected by the parser. The inaccuracy of automatic connective identification is thus mainly due to a small number of connectives. Manual examination of these instances can improve the accuracy significantly.

### 6.2 Relation sense identification in TT

The PDTB end-to-end parser was also used to extract relation senses for the connectives in the TT. In order to evaluate the parser's reliability, the second author and an independent coder annotated the English connectives in the dev set using PDTB2 labels. Agreement was high (Cohen's $\kappa$: 0.88, CI [0.85, 0.92]; $AC_1$ = 0.89, CI [0.86, 0.92], level 2 labels) (see Spooren and Degand, 2010, for IAA standards in discourse relation annotation). Disagreements were resolved by the first author.

For the connectives that the parser had identified correctly, the label provided by the parser was identical to the gold label in 78.8% of cases (Cohen's $\kappa$: 0.74, CI [0.70, 0.79]; $AC_1$ = 0.77, CI [0.72, 0.81]). Again, reliability was characterized by low performance on a small number of relation senses. More specifically, there was extremely low precision on Concession relations (0.04), as well as low recall on Contrast relations (0.23), because many Concession relations were identified as Contrast relations by the parser. Since the parser cannot distinguish between these relations reliably, these senses were merged in further analyses. Note that these distinctions are notoriously difficult to annotate, even by experts (Robaldo and Miltsakaki, 2014; Zufferey et al., 2012). Similarly, recall was low on Synchrony relations (0.30), since many of them were considered Asynchronous in manual annotation. These senses were therefore also collapsed. Adopting this 8-way classification resulted in very high reliability: (Cohen's $\kappa$: 0.90, CI [0.86, 0.94]; $AC_1$ = 0.91, CI [0.88, 0.95]).

The connective *in fact* was classified by the parser as signalling a Conjunction relation instead of Restatement, leading to a low precision (0.20) on this relation sense as well. The parser classified the two instances of *as if* in the development set as Concession, whereas the manual annotation was Expansion. Note that the PDTB 2.0 manual also indicates that both of these interpretations are possible for these connectives.

### 6.3 Connective mapping from TT to ST

To evaluate how reliable the automatic connective mapping was with the updated dictionary (i.e. Step 5 in Figure 1) and how the lexicon extends to new data, the accuracy of the final dictionary was determined based on its performance on the test set. 87.9% of the English connectives in the test set were correctly matched with their Pidgin connective. Sixteen connectives in the test set (3.6% of the total TT connectives) were incorrectly identified as implicit in ST, because their Pidgin translation had not co-occurred with this TT connective in the

[3]Note that the difference between discourse marker and connective *so* was reflected in the Pidgin POS-tags. Discourse marker uses of *so* were mostly annotated as adverbs, whereas connective uses of *so* were mostly subordinating conjunctions.

initial set. When allowing for the automatic mapping to identify new TT-ST pairings, the overall accuracy of the mapping in the test set increased to 90.9% (precision: 92.0, recall: 97.9, F1: 94.9).

The remainder of the incorrect mappings were mostly due to the English connective being incorrectly identified by the parser as a connective (n=12) or to one or multiple possible Nigerian Pidgin translations of the English connective occurring in the utterance, while they were not a translation of the English connective. Again, performance on individual connectives was high, except for a few Nigerian Pidgin connectives: *sey, wey, for, na* and *like* all reached F1 scores lower than 70%. This is likely because they also frequently occur with a non-connective meaning.

Finally, we evaluate how many Nigerian Pidgin connectives are missed when annotating only a subset of the corpus manually. In the Pidgin test set, we identified six Pidgin connectives that did not occur in the lexicon so far. Two of them were corpus annotation variants (i.e. different spelling/POS-tag) of connectives that had already been extracted from the initial set. The remainder of the new Pidgin connectives were separate entries and their English TT equivalent had either been mapped onto a new mapping or had incorrectly been identified as implicit in the ST. Extending the lexicon using additional datasets can therefore be reliably done using manual annotation of only those English TT connectives that either have not occurred previously or that are mapped onto a ST connectives that so far has not co-occurred with the English connective.[4]

### 6.4 Relation sense projection from ST to TT

A final premise of this method is that the relation marked in the TT reflects the relation expressed by the connective in the ST (cf. Laali and Kosseim, 2014). To evaluate this assumption, we manually annotated the relation sense of the Nigerian Pidgin connectives that had been identified in the dev set. Inter-annotator agreement on a subset of the data was sufficient (Cohen's $\kappa$: 0.77, CI [0.59, 0.94]; $AC_1$ = 0.82, CI [0.68, 0.96]). These manual annotations of the ST were then compared with the projected automatic annotations of the PDTB parser. Since the analysis above shows that distinctions within the class of Temporal relations and Comparison are not reliably annotated, these classes were combined. Agreement between the parser's label and the manual annotation on this 8-way classification was high (Cohen's $\kappa$: 0.90, CI [0.86, 0.94]; $AC_1$ = 0.91, CI [0.88, 0.94]) and only slightly lower than the reliability of the parser on the translation text. Using automatic annotation of a translation text to extract the relation sense of connectives in a source text is therefore well feasible.[5]

## 7 Discussion

The present research shows how extending discourse research to contact languages provides more insight in how discourse structure is realized cross-linguistically. We find a similar relational distribution between English and Pidgin. Moreover, we identified a relatively large variety of discourse markers in Nigerian Pidgin. Taken together, this indicates that the discourse structure of Pidgin is not necessarily less complex than in English, even though pidgins are generally considered to be less syntactically complex.

Furthermore, the analysis reveals that most of the discourse connectives in Nigerian Pidgin are derived from English discourse markers. However, discourse relations in Pidgin are not always marked by lexical items from a limited set of syntactic categories (cf. Stede et al., 2018): Auxiliary verbs can also signal coherence relations in Nigerian Pidgin. We therefore recommend researchers working on identifying connectives in different languages to be flexible in what items might signal coherence relations. Cross-linguistic variation should be taken into account when defining restrictions on what can constitute a discourse connective. In order to do so, more research on coherence marking in different languages (especially non-Indo-European languages) is needed.

Nigerian Pidgin is mainly a spoken language. This affects our analysis in several ways. Firstly, the nature of spoken language influences the distribution of connectives and the relation senses they mark. A smaller number of connective types are used in spoken compared to written text (Crible and Cuenca, 2017). At the same time, connectives in spoken language are used in a wider variety of functions. This should therefore be taken into account when considering the frequency of connectives and their relation sense distribution in the lexicon.

Secondly, the performance of the parser is in-

[4]This amounts to less than 5% of the data for our corpus.

[5]To reduce noise in the corpus and the lexicon, we manually checked the relation senses that accounted for less than 5% of the cases for a given Pidgin connective.

fluenced by the change in domain. A comparison with the parser's performance on a different English discourse-annotated spoken corpus (DiscoSPICE, Rehbein et al., 2016) revealed that the parser makes comparable mistakes in identifying connectives in dialogues by native speakers of English (see also Scholman et al., 2021). Inaccuracies of the parser in the current study are thus for the most part due to the fact that our data is spoken.

Despite the fact that the process described in this paper contains a number of manual steps, we believe that this method can easily be extended to other low-resource languages. The annotations were for the most part done by the second author, who is semi-proficient in Pidgin. In addition, comparing instances of connective candidates that were automatically identified in the corpus allowed a non-native speaker with little knowledge of the language (the first author) to manually verify the data. Although the native speaker we consulted was a trained linguist, the additional required judgments can be also be obtained in such a way that no linguistic knowledge is required from the native speaker. Furthermore, the required amount of manual annotations does not increase considerably with larger datasets. Firstly, by annotating the dev set alone, only a few infrequent connectives had been missed (6 out of 77 connective variants) and annotating a small subset of the data helps to identify these cases. Secondly, larger resources lead to a stronger reliability of statistical approaches. A combination of manual and automatic approaches therefore seems a fruitful way to construct resources for other under-researched languages as well.

Another challenge in identifying connectives in contact languages specifically, is the large amount of variation and the frequent use of code-switching. Especially for an English-lexified language like Nigerian Pidgin, it can be difficult to distinguish between cases in which the utterance is English or Nigerian Pidgin. In fact, some of the connectives that we initially identified as ST connectives were in fact English connectives that had been used during code-switching. Frequency filters, which have also been adopted in fully-automatic approaches to cross-lingual connective identification (Laali and Kosseim, 2014), are therefore crucial. Lexical items that only occur a few times or are only used by a small number of speakers should be checked manually. To distinguish between code-switched and infrequent connective uses, the context should be taken into account. If the connective is embedded in an English-only sentence, it is likely not a connective in the target language.

The similarities between Nigerian Pidgin and English could also have been employed as an advantage. For example, as one reviewer suggests, Levenshtein's distance can be used to find Nigerian Pidgin connective candidates that are similar to the English connective. However, there are a few drawbacks to such an approach. The Nigerian Pidgin version of an English connective sometimes diverged strongly from its English cognate (e.g. *because - cos)* and some of the Nigerian Pidgin connectives with an English origin were not cognates of the English connective, but of a synonym (e.g. the Pidgin meaning-equivalent of *instead* is *rader*). Levenshtein's distance might therefore not always be a reliable measure. More importantly, our goal was to establish the usefulness of existing resources to research discourse structure in low-resource languages in general, not English-lexified contact languages only. In addition, in searching for Nigerian Pidgin connectives, we did not want to create a bias towards English connective cognates, as one of our research goals was to examine how discourse connectives emerge and to establish which connectives would not originate from English.

## 8 Conclusion

This study presents Naija-Lex, a lexicon of connectives in Nigerian Pidgin, which was constructed by combining automatic discourse parsing with manual annotation. In doing so, we showed that automatic discourse parsing is a valuable resource in constructing a discourse-annotated database to extract connectives. However, construction of a seed set based on a subset of the data and manual annotation of selected connectives and relation senses is necessary to obtain a reliable database. In addition, we made a first step to building a Nigerian-Pidgin discourse-annotated corpus by annotating ST connectives that were explicit in the TT. We will extend this corpus with implicit relations in further work.

## Acknowledgements

We are highly grateful to Emeka Felix Onwuegbuzia for his valuable insights on Nigerian Pidgin and evaluating a subset of the connectives. This research was funded by the German Research Foundation (DFG) as part of SFB 1102 "Information Density and Linguistic Encoding".

## References


Viktor Becher. 2011. When and why do translators add connectives?: A corpus-based study. *Target. International Journal of Translation Studies*, 23(1):26–47.

Peter Bourgonje, Yulia Grishina, and Manfred Stede. 2017. Toward a bilingual lexical database on connectives: Exploiting a German/Italian parallel corpus. In *Proceedings of the Fourth Italian Conference on Computational Linguistics (CLiC-it)*, pages 1–6, Rome, Italy.

Peter Bourgonje, Jet Hoek, Jacqueline Evers-Vermeul, Gisela Redeker, Ted Sanders, and Manfred Stede. 2018. Constructing a lexicon of Dutch discourse connectives. *Computational Linguistics in the Netherlands Journal*, 8:163–175.

Bernard Caron, Marine Courtin, Kim Gerdes, and Sylvain Kahane. 2019. A surface-syntactic UD treebank for Naija. In *TLT 2019, Treebanks and Linguistic Theories, Syntaxfest*.

Ernie Chang, David Ifeoluwa Adelani, Xiaoyu Shen, and Vera Demberg. 2020. Unsupervised Pidgin text generation by pivoting English data and self-training. In *International Conference on Learning Representations (ICLR)*.

Marine Courtin, Bernard Caron, Kim Gerdes, and Sylvain Kahane. 2018. Establishing a language by annotating a corpus. In *annDH 2018 Annotation in Digital Humanities*, volume 2155, pages 7–11. CEUR.

Ludivine Crible and Maria-Josep Cuenca. 2017. Discourse markers in speech: Characteristics and challenges for corpus annotation. *Dialogue and Discourse*, 8(2):149–166.

Laurence Danlos. 2006. "discourse verbs" and discourse periphrastic links. In *Proceedings of KONVENS 2006 (Konferenz zur Verarbeitung natürlicher Sprache) Universität Konstanz*, page 160.

Debopam Das, Tatjana Scheffler, Peter Bourgonje, and Manfred Stede. 2018. Constructing a lexicon of English discourse connectives. In *Proceedings of the 19th Annual SIGdial Meeting on Discourse and Dialogue*, pages 360–365.

Debopam Das, Manfred Stede, Soumya Sankar Ghosh, and Lahari Chatterjee. 2020. DiMLex-Bangla: A lexicon of Bangla discourse connectives. In *Proceedings of the 12th Language Resources and Evaluation Conference*, pages 1097–1102.

René Knaebel and Manfred Stede. 2020. Contextualized embeddings for connective disambiguation in shallow discourse parsing. In *Proceedings of the First Workshop on Computational Approaches to Discourse (CoDi 2020)*, pages 65–75, Online. Association for Computational Linguistics.

Murathan Kurfalı, Sibel Ozer, Deniz Zeyrek, and Amália Mendes. 2020. Ted-MDB Lexicons: TrEnConnLex, PtEnConnLex. In *Proceedings of the First Workshop on Computational Approaches to Discourse*, pages 148–153.

Majid Laali and Leila Kosseim. 2014. Inducing discourse connectives from parallel texts. In *Proceedings of COLING 2014, the 25th International Conference on Computational Linguistics: Technical Papers*, pages 610–619.

Ziheng Lin, Hwee Tou Ng, and Min-Yen Kan. 2014. A PDTB-styled end-to-end discourse parser. *Natural Language Engineering*, 20(2):151–184.

Amália Mendes and Pierre Lejeune. 2016. LDM-PT: A Portuguese lexicon of discourse markers. In *Conference Handbook of TextLink–Structuring Discourse in Multilingual Europe Second Action Conference*, pages 89–92. Debrecen University Press.

Philippe Muller, Chloé Braud, and Mathieu Morey. 2019. Tony: Contextual embeddings for accurate multilingual discourse segmentation of full documents. In *Proceedings of the Workshop on Discourse Relation Parsing and Treebanking 2019*, pages 115–124. Association for Computational Linguistics.

Kelechi Ogueji and Orevaoghene Ahia. 2019. PidginUNMT: Unsupervised neural machine translation from West African Pidgin to English. In *NeurIPS 2019 Workshop on Machine Learning for the Developing World (ML4D)*.

Emily Pitler and Ani Nenkova. 2009. Using syntax to disambiguate explicit discourse connectives in text. In *Proceedings of the ACL-IJCNLP 2009 Conference Short Papers*, pages 13–16, Suntec, Singapore. Association for Computational Linguistics.

Rashmi Prasad, Nikhil Dinesh, Alan Lee, Eleni Miltsakaki, Livio Robaldo, Aravind Joshi, and Bonnie Webber. 2008. The Penn Discourse TreeBank 2.0. In *Proceedings of the Sixth International Conference on Language Resources and Evaluation (LREC'08)*, Marrakech, Morocco. European Language Resources Association (ELRA).

Balaji Polepalli Ramesh and Hong Yu. 2010. Identifying discourse connectives in biomedical text. In *AMIA Annual Symposium Proceedings*, volume 2010, page 657. American Medical Informatics Association.

Ines Rehbein, Merel Scholman, and Vera Demberg. 2016. Annotating discourse relations in spoken language: A comparison of the PDTB and CCR frameworks. In *Proceedings of the Tenth International Conference on Language Resources and Evaluation (LREC'16)*, pages 1039–1046, Portorož, Slovenia. European Language Resources Association (ELRA).

Livio Robaldo and Eleni Miltsakaki. 2014. Corpus-driven semantics of concession: Where do expectations come from? *Dialogue & Discourse*, 5(1):1–36.

Charlotte Roze, Laurence Danlos, and Philippe Muller. 2012. Lexconn: a french lexicon of discourse connectives. *Discours. Revue de linguistique, psycholinguistique et informatique. A journal of linguistics, psycholinguistics and computational linguistics*, (10).

Merel C.J. Scholman, Tianai Dong, Frances Yung, and Vera Demberg. 2021. Comparison of methods for explicit discourse connective identification across various domains. In *Proceedings of the First Workshop on Computational Approaches to Discourse (CoDi 2020)*.

Wilbert P. M. S. Spooren and Liesbeth Degand. 2010. Coding coherence relations: Reliability and validity. *Corpus Linguistics and Linguistic Theory*, 6(2):241–266.

Manfred Stede, Tatjana Scheffler, and Amália Mendes. 2018. Connective-Lex: A web-based multilingual lexical resource for connectives. *Discours. Revue de linguistique, psycholinguistique et informatique. A journal of linguistics, psycholinguistics and computational linguistics*, (24).

Manfred Stede and Carla Umbach. 1998. DiMLex: A lexicon of discourse markers for text generation and understanding. In *36th Annual Meeting of the Association for Computational Linguistics and 17th International Conference on Computational Linguistics, Volume 2*, pages 1238–1242.

Benedikt Szmrecsanyi, Bernd Kortmann, Geoffrey Sampson, David Gil, and Peter Trudgill. 2009. Between simplification and complexification: Non-standard varieties of English around the world. In *Language complexity as an evolving variable*, pages 64–79. Oxford University Press.

Yannick Versley. 2010. Discovery of ambiguous and unambiguous discourse connectives via annotation projection. In *Proceedings of Workshop on Annotation and Exploitation of Parallel Corpora (AEPC)*, pages 83–82.

Jianxiang Wang and Man Lan. 2015. A refined end-to-end discourse parser. In *Proceedings of the Nineteenth Conference on Computational Natural Language Learning - Shared Task*, pages 17–24, Beijing, China. Association for Computational Linguistics.

Nianwen Xue, Hwee Tou Ng, Sameer Pradhan, Attapol Rutherford, Bonnie Webber, Chuan Wang, and Hongmin Wang. 2016. CoNLL 2016 shared task on multilingual shallow discourse parsing. *Proceedings of the CoNLL-16 shared task*, pages 1–19.

Yue Yu, Yilun Zhu, Yang Liu, Yan Liu, Siyao Peng, Mackenzie Gong, and Amir Zeldes. 2019. Gum-Drop at the DISRPT2019 shared task: A model stacking approach to discourse unit segmentation and connective detection. In *Proceedings of Discourse Relation Parsing and Treebanking (DISRPT2019)*, pages 133–143.

Amir Zeldes, Debopam Das, Erick Galani Maziero, Juliano Antonio, and Mikel Iruskieta. 2019. The DISRPT 2019 shared task on elementary discourse unit segmentation and connective detection. In *Proceedings of the Workshop on Discourse Relation Parsing and Treebanking 2019*, pages 97–104.

Yuping Zhou and Nianwen Xue. 2012. PDTB-style discourse annotation of Chinese text. In *Proceedings of the 50th Annual Meeting of the Association for Computational Linguistics (Volume 1: Long Papers)*, pages 69–77.

Yuping Zhou and Nianwen Xue. 2015. The Chinese Discourse TreeBank: A Chinese corpus annotated with discourse relations. *Language Resources and Evaluation*, 49(2):397–431.

Sandrine Zufferey and Bruno Cartoni. 2014. A multifactorial analysis of explicitation in translation. *Target. International Journal of Translation Studies*, 26(3):361–384.

Sandrine Zufferey, Liesbeth Degand, Andrei Popescu-Belis, and Ted J. M. Sanders. 2012. Empirical validations of multilingual annotation schemes for discourse relations. In *Proceedings of the 8th Joint ISO-ACL/SIGSEM Workshop on Interoperable Semantic Annotation (ISA-8)*, pages 77–84, Jeju Island, Korea.

# Comparison of methods for explicit discourse connective identification across various domains

**Merel C.J. Scholman**[1], **Tianai Dong**[1], **Frances Yung**[1] and **Vera Demberg**[1,2]
[1]Language Science and Technology, [2]Computer Science, Saarland University
Saarbrücken, Germany
{m.c.j.scholman,tdong,frances,vera}@coli.uni-saarland.de

## Abstract

Existing parse methods use varying approaches to identify explicit discourse connectives, but their performance has not been consistently evaluated in comparison to each other, nor have they been evaluated consistently on text other than newspaper articles. We here assess the performance on explicit connective identification of four parse methods (PDTB e2e, Lin et al., 2014; the winner of CONLL2015, Wang and Lan, 2015; DisSent, Nie et al., 2019; and Discopy, Knaebel and Stede, 2020), along with a simple heuristic. We also examine how well these systems generalize to different datasets, namely newspaper text (PDTB), scientific text (BioDRB), prepared spoken text (TED-MDB) and spontaneous spoken text (Disco-SPICE). The results show that Discopy outperforms the other parse methods in all datasets, with the exception of DiscoSPICE. Moreover, performance drops significantly from the PDTB to all other datasets. We provide a more fine-grained analysis of domain differences and connectives that prove difficult to parse, in order to highlight the areas where gains can be made.

## 1 Introduction

Understanding the discourse relations that hold between segments in natural language text is crucial to many NLP applications, such as text generation, dialogue understanding, and question-answering systems. Shallow discourse parsers are used to uncover such relations by identifying connectives, extracting their arguments, and predicting the sense of the discourse relation. The current contribution focuses on the first step in the pipeline: finding explicit connectives in natural language. This step is not only interesting from the perspective of discourse relation classification, it can also be valuable for downstream applications, as accurate connective identification is crucial to mitigate the effect of cascaded errors downstream (Lin et al., 2014).

Connective identification is not a trivial task, as some connectives are ambiguous and may not consistently function as discourse connectives. A simple dictionary lookup would therefore not be able to distinguish between the discourse connective-usage of *yet* in Example (1), compared to the non-connective usage in (2) and (3).

(1) Julie wants to buy a house. Yet she has not found the right one.

(2) Julie wants to buy a house. She has yet to find the right one.

(3) Julie wants to buy a luxurious, yet affordable house.

In (1), *yet* expresses an adversative relation (equivalent to *nevertheless*). In (2), it functions as an adverb expressing a temporal meaning (i.e. *up until this time*). Finally, in (3), *yet* does not function in a relation with two complete discourse arguments, and would therefore not be annotated as a connective. An accurate parser would need to be able to distinguish between these fine-grained differences in the usage of connective candidates.

Further, connective usage diverges between domains. For example, *but* and *so* are often used as discourse structuring markers in spoken language, rather than discourse connectives. Existing parsers, however, have mainly been evaluated on newspaper text, since the largest discourse-annotated corpus available comes from this domain (PDTB, Prasad et al., 2008). Performance of existing discourse connective identification parsers on domains other than the written one is currently not well known.

Finally, we note that there is a lack of information on which connectives remain difficult to identify, even in state-of-the-art parsers. This is due to the tendency of studies reporting only the general accuracy, without providing detail on the accuracy on specific connectives. However, such information can provide the field with more information on what to focus on.



*Proceedings of the 2nd Workshop on Computational Approaches to Discourse*, pages 95–106
November 10–11, 2021. 

In sum, performance of different parsing methods have not been consistently evaluated in comparison to each other, nor have they been evaluated consistently on text other than newspaper articles. In addition, previous work tends to report only overall accuracy, whereas a more fine-grained analysis of connectives might prove to be valuable for future efforts. The current contribution fills these gaps in the literature.

Specifically, we evaluate the performance on explicit connective identification of four parse methods (PDTB e2e, Lin et al., 2014; the winner of CONLL2015, Wang and Lan, 2015; DisSent, Nie et al., 2019; and Discopy, Knaebel and Stede, 2020), along with a simple heuristic as a baseline. The heuristic will identify all connectives in the data, without being able to distinguish discourse versus non-discourse usages of connectives. We include this "parse method" to provide insight into how discourse usage of connectives affects the performance of such a heuristic.

We also evaluate how well these systems generalize to different datasets from new domains, namely scientific text (BioDRB, Prasad et al., 2011), prepared spoken text (TED-MDB, Zeyrek et al., 2019) and spontaneous spoken text (DiscoSPICE, Rehbein et al., 2016).

## 2 Related work

**Connective identification** In recent years, shallow discourse parsing has received notable attention in the field. Much of this work has focused on the automatic labeling of implicit connectives, as performance there is significantly lacking (the current state-of-the-art achieves an F1 around 64% on a four-way classification, e.g. Ji et al., 2016; Lan et al., 2017; Shi and Demberg, 2019). Explicit relation identification has received less attention since prior work has reported high accuracy on explicit connectives in news articles. An open question is how these parsers perform on out-of-domain data.

Pitler and Nenkova (2009)'s work on explicit connective identification formed the basis for much subsequent research efforts in this direction. They show that syntactic features provide highly useful information for predicting whether a connective candidate functions as a discourse connective (an accuracy of 94.2% F1 on PDTB2 with a 10-fold cross validation on Sec. 02–22). Lin et al. (2014) built on this work to develop the PDTB end-to-end (PDTB e2e) discourse parser. Their parser performs at 95.4% F1 on the PDTB with a 10-fold cross validation on Sec. 02–22. In the context of the CONLL2015 shared task, Wang and Lan (2015) built on both of these approaches and presented the top-ranked system, which achieved an F1 score of 94.2% on connective identification in the PDTB2 section 23 test set and 91.9% in the CONLL 2015 blind test set. All three models rely heavily on various combinations of syntactic and lexical features extracted from texts.

More recent models have taken different approaches. DisSent uses dependency parsing and sentence embeddings to annotate discourse relations (Nie et al., 2019). They report an accuracy of 87.9% F1 on PDTB relations in determining whether a connective is present. Notably, they used sentences extracted from books as training data, rather than PDTB. This might make their approach more stable across domains. Finally, Knaebel and Stede (2020) use a neural approach that integrates contextualized word embeddings and predicts whether a connective candidate is part of a discourse relation or not. They achieve an F1 score of 97% on the PDTB2 section 23 test set.

### 2.1 Domain differences

In the current paper we focus on comparing the parsers' performance on two written corpora with the performance on two spoken corpora. Spoken data differs from written in a number of ways, including shorter sentence length on average and a higher rate of elliptical structures and omissions. Moreover, discourse connectives are used differently across domains. For example, compared to written data, spoken data tends to have a higher rate of explicit connectives, fewer connective types, and more non-discourse connective usage of connectives (see, e.g. Crible and Cuenca, 2017; Rehbein et al., 2016). It is also not uncommon for relations in spoken data to have an incomplete or even implicit sentence argument, as in Example (4), or to have connectives function as a discourse marker rather than connective, as in Example (5) (examples taken from DiscoSPICE):

(4) **And** uhm, bring cos uh unfortunately just she's been up in Belfast this week.

(5) And his face got really red. So I thought oh God. **So** yesterday when he he came back he said what were you saying to me about John.

In Example (4), the second argument (Arg2) for the connective *and* is not fully uttered; instead, the speaker cut off her utterance after the verb *bring* and switched to a different discourse relation. In Example (5), the speaker uses *so* in a non-discourse connective usage (the utterance cannot be paraphrased as "I thought oh God and as a result he asked me..."). It is unclear how parsers developed for the written domain would handle such cases that are more typical of the spoken domain.

Even within the written domain, differences in connective usage can occur between various types of written text. For example, Roman et al. (2016) found a higher rate of discourse connectives used in science textbooks compared to social studies textbooks. Moreover, specific connectives can occur more in one domain than another; for example, *in summary* occurs more commonly in biomedical abstracts than in the general written domain (Gopalan and Devi, 2016).

## 3 Method

### 3.1 Parse methods

**Heuristic** The heuristic is based on the list of 100 connectives from the PDTB2. This method simply extracts all connective candidates from the PDTB connective list, without distinguishing between usages. The heuristic will function as the baseline model.

**PDTB end-to-end** The PDTB end-to-end model is trained using the PDTB dataset sections 02-21, evaluated using sec 22, and tested on sec 23. To distinguish a discourse connective from its non-connective usage, Lin et al. (2014) extract a set of lexical and syntactic features for a connective and its preceding and following word. They also utilize the syntactic parse path from the connective to the root of the tree model, as well as the compressed path where adjacent identical tags are combined.

Note that a version of this parser specifically aimed at parsing BioDRB has been made available. Here, we use the general version of the parser to be able to consistently evaluate its performance on out-of-domain text across datasets.

**CONLL2015** Similar to the PDTB e2e parser, the CONLL2015 winning parser is trained on PDTB sec 02-21, evaluated using sec 22, and tested on sec 23. Wang and Lan (2015) reimplemented well-established techniques from Pitler and Nenkova (2009) and Lin et al. (2014), and added the POS tags of nodes from the connective's parent to capture more syntactic context information from the connective.

As part of the CONLL2015 shared task, competitors had access to the dependency tree, which we do not have access to. Instead, we generated parse trees using Stanford's CoreNLP Natural Language Processing Toolkit (the same parser that was used by the e2e parser). We note that the parse tree result after running Stanford CoreNLP might be different from the one that is given by CONLL2015, which in turn might affect performance of this model.

**DisSent** In this model, connectives are used in the downstream task for learning sentence representation from explicit discourse relations. Nie et al. (2019) used texts from a BookCorpus (Zhu et al., 2015) to train and test their models. They identified common connectives in these texts, choosing those with a frequency greater than 1% in PDTB. As a result, the list of connectives that their parser can identify is much smaller than that used by other parsers (18 connectives compared to approximately 100 used by other parsers). Moreover, the possible dependency patters that are defined for each of these connective types is also restricted, and so this parser runs the risk of missing instances of the 18 connective types that it does aim to identify. We prepared the input for this parser using Stanford's CoreNLP dependency parser.

**Discopy** The final model included is a recent neural model proposed by Knaebel and Stede (2020), which achieves state-of-the-art results in connective identification. Instead of using various combinations of syntactic or lexical features, the method implements a neural model which relies on pre-trained word embeddings. The model concatenates contextualized embeddings of connectives with the embeddings of their contexts. For multi-word connectives, the contextualized embeddings of the single words are averaged. The model is then trained in a multi-task setting, to predict the connective or predict the coherence relation. They used PDTB sec 02–22 for training and sec 23-24 for testing. Here, we assess their best performing bert-based model on connective identification task, with context size of 1.

### 3.2 Data

Parser performance was measured on four different datasets in order to determine how well the parsers can identify connectives in various domains.

All datasets have already been annotated with discourse relations, and therefore we can use the gold connectives from these annotations.

**PDTB2 sec 23** We evaluated all parsers on the Penn Discourse Treebank 2.0 (PDTB2, Prasad et al., 2008). The PDTB consists of discourse annotations on the Wall Street Journal texts. We here evaluate performance on section 23, which is commonly used as test dataset. According to the gold label annotations, the dataset contains 923 explicit connective tokens, with 62 unique types.

**BioDRB** We included text from the Biomedical Discourse Relation Bank (BioDRB; Prasad et al., 2011). This corpus consists of discourse annotations of 24 biomedical research articles from the GENIA corpus, using an adapted version of the PDTB2 annotation framework. These texts represent the biomedical, scientific text genre.

The BioDRB has 2636 gold explicit connective tokens with 180 unique connective types. The higher number of connective types in BioDRB compared to PDTB is mainly due to BioDRB having annotated modified connectives as unique types (e.g. *180 seconds after*, *due mainly to*), and to BioDRB annotating post-modified connectives (because of), which PDTB2 does not annotate. To make the comparison consistent across datasets, we mapped the gold connectives in BioDRB to the corresponding connective heads annotated in PDTB. We removed connectives considered to be alternative lexicalizations in PDTB. The final dataset contains 2574 connective tokens with 134 unique connective types.

**TED-MDB** TED-MDB (Zeyrek et al., 2019) is a resource of TED talk transcripts manually annotated for discourse relations. TED talks are highly structured speeches that are often minutely prepared and are meant to provide targeted information on various topics or ideas. The resource is multilingual, but we focus only on English in the current contribution.

TED-MDB currently consists of 6 TED talk transcripts annotated in PDTB3-style, with a total of 304 explicit connective tokens and 35 unique connective types. The reduced number of connective types compared to the PDTB can be attributed to the smaller size of this dataset as well as the genre. However, TED-MDB also includes connective types that are not included in PDTB2's connective list (some of which are part of PDTB3's connective list), such as *at, by, in* and *through.*

**Disco-SPICE** Disco-SPICE (Rehbein et al., 2016) is a corpus of transcribed broadcast interviews and telephone conversations from the SPICE-Ireland corpus (Kallen and Kirk, 2008), annotated in PDTB3-style. These texts represent a more informal, spontaneous spoken genre than the TED talks. This dataset contains 1163 explicit connective tokens with 50 unique connective types. Again, the reduced number of connective types can be attributed to the domain.

## 4 Results

### 4.1 Overall accuracy

Table 1 presents the accuracy of each parser. The results show that Discopy is most accurate in identifying connectives in the PDTB, BioDRB and TED-MDB, but the e2e parser displays a higher F1 score in DiscoSPICE. Moreover, we find that, across the board, performance significantly drops for datasets other than the PDTB. This emphasizes the need for out-of-domain evaluation and development. Chi-squared tests confirm that the difference in performance between the parsers and between the datasets are significant, see Appendix A.

**Heuristic** The heuristic uses PDTB's connective list as input to identify connectives, resulting in the highest recall on all datasets.[1] The heuristic's recall on BioDRB is lower than on other datasets because a portion of the connectives annotated in BioDRB are not included in PDTB's connective lexicon.

Its F1 score on spoken data is relatively high compared to other parsers, particularly for DiscoSPICE. This can be attributed to its insensitivity to syntactic requirements for Arg2 that are based on the written domain but are often impractical for the spoken domain. Hence, when syntactic features are too complex/inaccurate for spoken texts, connectives themselves can be used as reliable features.

Nevertheless, of all parse methods included, the heuristic's precision is lowest on all datasets. This reflects its high false positive rate, which is due to the heuristic not being able to distinguish between discourse versus non-discourse usage of connectives. Simply extracting all connectives using a heuristic might therefore be helpful for identifying

[1]Recall on PDTB is not 1 because there was one instance of *if...if...then*, where the gold standard attributed a single instance of *then* to both *if*'s.

| | Heuristic | | | PDTB e2e | | | CONLL2015 | | | DisSent | | | Discopy | | |
|---|---|---|---|---|---|---|---|---|---|---|---|---|---|---|---|
| | P | R | F1 | P | R | F1 | P | R | F1 | P | R | F1 | P | R | F1 |
| PDTB | .29 | .99 | .46 | .92 | .91 | .91 | .92 | .82 | .87 | .75 | .32 | .45 | .97 | .92 | **.95** |
| BioDRB | .21 | .67 | .32 | .80 | .53 | .63 | .86 | .31 | .46 | .48 | .24 | .32 | .86 | .56 | **.68** |
| TED-MDB | .49 | .92 | .64 | .81 | .69 | .74 | .84 | .66 | .74 | .64 | .22 | .33 | .85 | .71 | **.77** |
| DiscoSPICE | .32 | .88 | .46 | .41 | .54 | **.47** | .35 | .37 | .36 | .54 | .20 | .29 | .40 | .48 | .43 |

Table 1: Precision, Recall and F1 per corpus and parse method.

connectives, but human input or additional computational input would still be necessary to then decide on whether the candidate connective functions as a discourse connective.

**PDTB e2e** Performance of the PDTB e2e parser on the PDTB corpus is lower than reported in Lin et al. (2014) (91% versus 95% F1, respectively). This drop in the F1 score may be due to minor differences between our experimental set-up and theirs: we evaluated connective identification from final outputs of the end-to-end parser, while the original paper performed a separate training and testing on connective classifiers.

Applying the parser to datasets other than PDTB leads to a drop in performance. On BioDRB and TED-MDB, the e2e parser shows a high precision score but low recall score, which can be explained in part by the corpora having annotated a larger number of connective types than the PDTB2. Finally, we note low precision and recall scores on DiscoSPICE, with F1 scores on this spoken genre considerably lower than on the PDTB texts.

**CONLL2015** Performance of the CONLL2015 winning parser on PDTB is lower than reported in the original paper (87% versus 94% F1, respectively, Wang and Lan, 2015). This drop in performance is likely caused by the difference in dependency tree parser used to prepare the data.

Further, this parser shows a low recall score on BioDRB, which can again be explained by the difference in connective lists. The performance on TED-MDB is in line with PDTB e2e, but performance on DiscoSPICE is relatively low. This might be attributed to the syntactic structure of the texts: Wang and Lan (2015)'s new features can capture more syntactic features from texts, but this might result in lower accuracy when the parsed structure diverges from that of the trained texts. This indicates that complex lexical and syntactic features are too restrictive and therefore not appropriate for spontaneous spoken texts like those in DiscoSPICE.

**DisSent** As mentioned in Section 3, DisSent targets only the 18 most frequently occurring connective types. Considering DisSent only takes a small portion of PDTB's connective types into account, it has the potential to uncover a relatively high number of connective tokens: a maximum of 86% of all gold connectives in PDTB, 43% in the BioDRB, 87% in TED-MDB, and 89% in DiscoSPICE. However, the results show that it missed a significant portion of these connectives: it identified 26% of all gold connectives in PDTB, 11% in the BioDRB, 19% in TED-MDB, and 18% in DiscoSPICE. Consequently, DisSent shows low recall scores in every corpus. In addition, it shows poor precision in BioDRB and TED-MDB specifically (but relatively high precision in DiscoSPICE compared to other parsers, which might be due to less diverse dependency patterns in DiscoSPICE). We conclude that DisSent can only be competitive if it is extended to include more connective types and syntactic patterns.

**Discopy** Discopy outperforms the other parsers on the PDTB, BioDRB, and TED-MDB. This indicates that word embeddings are more flexible than hand-engineered features, and can perform well without domain knowledge. The outlier for this parser is DiscoSPICE: e2e outperforms Discopy on this dataset (47% versus 43% F1). It seems that none of the parsers can parse connectives in this dataset with high accuracy, which could be explained by the features of transcribed spontaneous spoken language that are very different from written language (such as fragments, disfluencies and interjections).

The performance of the parser on PDTB is slightly lower than reported in the original paper, which could be a result of the implementation of the models.

### 4.2 Analyses of specific connectives

Detailed results on accuracy per connective for every dataset and parser are provided as an online appendix.[2] We here highlight some observations based on this data. We focus on results from the PDTB e2e, CONLL2015, and Discopy, since these provide the most coverage and behave similarly.

Certain connectives were identified accurately in all corpora by the parsers. These include *additionally, although, however, while, instead, meanwhile, nevertheless, therefore, unless,* and *whereas*. Many of these tend to function consistently as discourse connectives (i.e. they do not occur frequently in a non-connective usage), which might explain why they are easier to identify.

The remainder of this section presents a qualitative analysis, in which we consider in particular connectives that were included in the PDTB connective list, but were not identified correctly. We take the PDTB dataset as our reference model, and compare the other datasets to performance in this dataset. Most findings can be classified as an issue relating to the gold label, an issue relating to the parser, or an issue relating to token frequency. We end with general observations regarding DisSent. Table 4 in Appendix B presents a summary of the findings.

**Performance on the PDTB dataset** All three parsers show relatively poor accuracy on *or, nor, once* and *previously*. Moreover, all parsers miss some connective types altogether, such as *finally, specifically, rather, hence* (all parsers), *earlier* (e2e and CONLL), and *consequently* (CONLL and Discopy). Both of these issues are likely related to token frequency: these connectives all occur very infrequently in the test set and relatively infrequently in the training data. The poor performance might therefore be a reflection of the lack of training data; it remains a question whether the performance on these connectives will generalize if the test set would include more instances of them.

Both PDTB e2e and CONLL2015 (but not Discopy) also show poor performance on *as*, which occurs more frequently in the PDTB test set (n=40). The e2e parser shows higher precision than recall, whereas the CONLL2015 parser shows lower precision than recall. Manual inspection of the instances of *as* that were not identified did not reveal any pattern indicating why they might have been missed. As we will see in the next paragraphs, *as* proved to be difficult to identify in the other datasets as well. The divergence between the parsers on this connective is particularly interesting.

**Genre-specific findings: BioDRB versus PDTB** Performance on the following connectives in BioDRB was relatively poor in all parsers: *as, once, still, except,* and *after*. Note that performance for *as, once,* and *after* was also comparatively lower in PDTB (albeit higher than in BioDRB). Difficulty with these connective types is likely due to their frequent usage as non-discourse connectives. Regarding *still*, the e2e parser seems to have a specific issue: it only identified those instances of *still* in BioDRB that occurred argument-initially.

Second, we find an issue with the BioDRB gold label for *until*: the gold BioDRB dataset contains 11 instances of *until*, but all three parsers only identified one instance. For the "false negatives", the Arg2 only contains a verb or noun phrase, as in (7). Such fragments are generally not considered to be full relational arguments and the connectives are therefore usually not annotated. It appears that BioDRB has more relaxed restrictions on what can constitute a relational argument. This can possibly explain the general trend of the parsers displaying relatively low recall compared to precision scores for BioDRB.

(7) E14.5 fetal thymic lobes were collected and stored in the TRIzol (GIBCO BRL) at -70C **until** RNA isolation.

We also find an issue with the gold label for instances of *also* in BioDRB: all parsers perform well on this connective in the PDTB but in the BioDRB, they show low precision. The gold BioDRB lists 92 instances of *also*, PDTB e2e identified 183 instances, CONLL 126 instances and Discopy 156 instances. Consider Example (8), a true positive identified by all parsers, and Example (9), a "false positive" identified by e2e and Discopy. Both relations are very similar, and so it is unclear why one instance of *also* was part of the gold dataset and the other was not.

(8) A much lower, but still significant increase was seen in fetal TN2 cells (25% increase, $p < 0.01$). Proliferation was **also** significantly higher at the fetal TN3 stage compared to adult (50% increase, $p < 0.01$).

(9) In the peripheral blood of OX35-treated rats, the percentage of CD3+ cells was significantly lower than in PBS-treated animals. The percentage of CD4+ cells in the OX35-treated

[2] https://osf.io/xzsa7/?view_only=0cc5d937fa264fb59b5fe5e035c1ac75

group was **also** significantly lower than that of the PBS control.

Similar to performance in the PDTB, the parsers show low performance on *previously* in BioDRB, which appears to be a difficult connective to identify accurately. In BioDRB, the errors can be attributed to both an issue with the gold label as well as an issue with the parsers. The gold contained no instances of *previously*, but the parsers all identified a different number of occurrences (3 to 8 instances). Some of these cases, such as Example (10), appear to be valid.

(10) In agreement with this, western blot analysis demonstrated an upregulation of Id1 protein, while the amount of Id2 and Id3 protein levels remained unchanged. **Previously**, Id1 has been considered not to be expressed in later developmental stages than pro-B cells (...).

**Genre-specific findings: spoken versus written** Spoken data is characterised by certain frequent connectives displaying a higher rate of non-connective usage compared to written data (e.g., *but, so, and*). As expected, these connectives show poorer performance in the spoken domain compared to the written domain.

We also find lower performance on *as, when* and *then* in the spoken domain. Regarding *as*, we can see this is a consistently difficult connective candidate to identify across all datasets. The poor performance of the parsers on *when* in TED-MDB can be attributed to an issue with the gold labels. Certain instances of *when* were not included in the gold TED-MDB, but the parsers were accurate in identifying these "false positives". Example (11) presents an instance of *when* that was not part of the gold dataset but was identified accurately by the parsers.

(11) We thrive **when** we stay at our own leading edge.

Poor performance on *then* in DiscoSPICE can be attributed in part to missed instances in the gold dataset, but also to the common usage of *then* as a non-discourse connective in DiscoSPICE, as in Example (12). Such instances, where no clear arguments or relation sense can be identified for the connective, were not annotated in DiscoSPICE but the parsers did identify them.

(12) Yeah so, so hopefully just the three people are alright and they're not. Cos **then** like with eleven people you'd be assured to have a few good people there but three people you're just.

We also note a peculiarity for *if* in TED-MDB. The parsers identified false positives for *if* in TED-MDB, an issue which can be attributed to annotation standards. The instances were in fact rhetorical "what if" relations (see Example 13), whereby the first argument could be taken to be *what* (or rather, *what* substitutes Arg1). Annotation frameworks would likely not consider such instances as true connectives, since the *what* cannot constitute a full relational argument according to most segmentation conventions.

(13) What **if** they used that firepower to allocate more of their capital to companies working the hardest at solving these challenges or at least not exacerbating them?

Finally, we note two issues specific to transcribed spoken data. First, some connectives are sometimes spelled differently in transcribed text than in normal written text, such as *because* being transcribed as *cos*. Such phonetic spelling variants lead to a higher rate of false negatives. Second, some false negatives in DiscoSPICE can be attributed to disfluencies, interjections or fillers such as *uh* and *ehm*. For example, both PDTB e2e and CONLL (but not Discopy) missed an instance of the connective *after* in DiscoSPICE (Example 14) because the connective is immediately followed by a filler, which affected the syntactic parse of the argument. Both of these issues might be solved by additional preprocessing of the spoken text (correcting spelling variants and removing disfluencies), but a better solution would be to develop a parser for spoken data that can handle such characteristics.

(14) Fintan rang me actually right **after** *uhm* I put down the phone to you.

**Connective-specific findings for DisSent** Of the 18 connectives that DisSent aims to identify, it shows poor performance in most datasets on four connectives in particular: *and, so, as,* and *though*. Furthermore, DisSent fails to identify any instances of *but* in both the PDTB and BioDRB. These results can be explained by DisSent's method:it does not identify connectives based on a heuristic search, but rather based on the syntactic pattern that the connective occurs in. The possible patterns that are provided for every connective are, in some cases, too restricted or coarse-grained, which is why the parser misses many instances of *and*, and all instances of *but*. This parser is hence extremely sensitive to the dependency parse of the dataset.

## 5 Discussion

Explicit connective identification can be done relatively reliably by existing parsers, but gains can still be made in this area. We therefore aimed to evaluate existing parsers and uncover more fine-grained errors. The results showed that Discopy (Knaebel and Stede, 2020) outperformed the other parsers in three out of four datasets: PDTB, BioDRB, and TED-MDB. This indicates that the contextualized embeddings used by Discopy are more flexible predictors of discourse connective usage than the syntactic and lexical features used by other parsers, even on out-of-domain data.

The exception to this is DiscoSPICE, for which the PDTB e2e parser performed best. However, even e2e's performance on this dataset was not sufficient. DiscoSPICE contains features and syntactic patterns that are specific to spoken data, such as disfluencies, incomplete sentence structures, and increased ambiguity of connectives (e.g., whether *so* is used as a connective or marker). These features can explain the low performance of all parsers on this dataset. There is still room for improvement in this area.

The performance of all parsers was lower on out-of-domain text compared to PDTB. This reaffirms earlier findings, which showed that a connective identification classifier trained on PDTB does not perform well on BioDRB even with domain adaptation techniques, compared to a classifier trained on the BioDRB alone (Ramesh and Yu, 2010; Prasad et al., 2011). Of course, these results cannot be considered surprising, given that prior work on discourse parsing has heavily focused on the written domain, with a strong bias towards newspaper text. Similar evaluations have not been done on other domains, nor have the parsers been applied frequently to other domains (but see Laali and Kosseim, 2014; Marchal et al., 2021, for an application of the e2e parser to spoken translated data). This underlines the importance of evaluation of existing parsers on other domains and the need for domain adaption of connective identification models and classifiers.

The results further indicated that performance is affected by the connectives' usage as non-discourse connectives and the connectives' frequency. One solution, as suggested by Lin et al. (2014), is to separately train a model for each highly ambiguous connective and another generic model to identify the remaining connectives. Another solution could be to provide parsers with more training data for infrequent connectives, which can be obtained via connective generation; this approach has recently been applied to address the lack of training data for implicit relations (Shi and Demberg, 2019; Kurfalı and Östling, 2021).

When analyzing connective-specific results, we found that poor performance could often be attributed to issues with the gold label. Some of the false positives seemed to be valid connectives, and might therefore actually be missed instances in the gold dataset. This highlights that in manual annotation, errors are still prevalent and maybe inevitable to some extent, which can affect performance of parsers. One way to remedy this is to support manual annotation with the output of SOTA parsers or even a simple heuristic, so that inconsistencies or false negatives would be less likely to occur.

We also found divergences between what frameworks and parsers consider relational arguments: BioDRB identified instances of *until* with only a noun phrase as the second argument, which the parsers consistently did not consider a relational connective. Conversely, Discopy consistently identified instances of *what if*-relations, which the gold standard did not consider to be relations. Discourse segmentation therefore has an impact on connective identification as well. Unfortunately, the issue of segmentation is still not entirely resolved in the field of discourse relation annotation (see, e.g., Hoek et al., 2018).

Many connectives annotated in the gold datasets could not be identified at all by the parsers because they rely on PDTB2's connective list. This list is not exhaustive and would need to be expanded for the parsers to provide more coverage. One place to start would be PDTB 3.0's connective list (Webber et al., 2019). However, even this list will not cover all connective types that might also occur in other genres (e.g. *hereafter* occurs in BioDRB but not PDTB). Extending connective lists with a general lexicon of English connectives (Das et al., 2018) can provide new connective candidates as well.

With regards to running the models, we observed a trade-off between accuracy and computational cost: the training and testing of Discopy (a bert-based model) required much more computational energy than any traditional parser (Bender et al., 2021). When comparing the success of neural methods and the other three parsers, it is important to be clear about the context in which they are used (Bender and Koller, 2020).

Finally, we note that our results did not perfectly replicate those of the original authors. This is likely due to a difference in the experimental set-up used (e.g., the dependency parse method used by Wang and Lan (2015) was not publicly available) and a difference in evaluation methods. To ensure that the lack of replicability was not due to incorrect implementation, the second author and another, unrelated researcher independently implemented all parse methods, and neither were able to perfectly replicate the results. Note that Han et al. (2020) also obtained different results than the original when replicating the e2e parser (although they observed improved scores), and attributed these divergences to minor variations between experimental set-ups in terms of implementations, hyperparameter settings and/or choice of the type of F1 score reported on. These results emphasize the general need in the field for more transparent reporting and a more consistent approach to evaluation (see also Kim et al., 2020, for implicit relation classification).

## 6 Conclusion

A comparison of different parse methods revealed that Discopy, a neural parser using sentence embeddings, generally outperforms parsers using syntactic and lexical features. The results also showed a severe performance drop when applying the parsers to other domains, especially spontaneous spoken discourse. This can be attributed to genre-specific syntactic structures, issues with the gold standards, and differences between connective lexicons. These results emphasise the need for out-of-domain training and evaluation, and provide insight as to where gains can be made.

## Acknowledgements

This research was funded by the German Research Foundation (DFG) as part of SFB 1102 "Information Density and Linguistic Encoding". We are grateful to Ida Novindasari and Anam Sadiq for their contributions to the implementations of the parsers.

## References

Emily M. Bender, Timnit Gebru, Angelina McMillan-Major, and Shmargaret Shmitchell. 2021. On the dangers of stochastic parrots: Can language models be too big? . *Proceedings of the 2021 ACM Conference on Fairness, Accountability, and Transparency.*

Emily M. Bender and Alexander Koller. 2020. Climbing towards NLU: On meaning, form, and understanding in the age of data. In *Proceedings of the 58th Annual Meeting of the Association for Computational Linguistics*, pages 5185–5198, Online. Association for Computational Linguistics.

Ludivine Crible and Maria-Josep Cuenca. 2017. Discourse markers in speech: characteristics and challenges for corpus annotation. *Dialogue and Discourse*, 8(2):149–166.

Debopam Das, Tatjana Scheffler, Peter Bourgonje, and Manfred Stede. 2018. Constructing a lexicon of English discourse connectives. In *Proceedings of the 19th Annual SIGdial Meeting on Discourse and Dialogue*, pages 360–365.

Sindhuja Gopalan and Sobha Lalitha Devi. 2016. BioDCA Identifier: A System for Automatic Identification of Discourse Connective and Arguments from Biomedical Text. In *Proceedings of the Fifth Workshop on Building and Evaluating Resources for Biomedical Text Mining (BioTxtM2016)*, pages 89–98.

Kelvin Han, Phyllicia Leavitt, and Srilakshmi Balard. 2020. Comparing PTB and UD information for PDTB discourseconnective identification. In *Actes de la 6e conférence conjointe Journées d'Études sur la Parole (JEP, 33e édition), Traitement Automatique des Langues Naturelles (TALN, 27e édition), Rencontre des Étudiants Chercheurs en Informatique pour le Traitement Automatique des Langues (RÉCITAL, 22e édition). Volume 3: Rencontre des Étudiants Chercheurs en Informatique pour le TAL*, pages 123–136.

Jet Hoek, Jacqueline Evers-Vermeul, and Ted JM Sanders. 2018. Segmenting discourse: Incorporating interpretation into segmentation? *Corpus Linguistics and Linguistic Theory*, 14(2):357–386.

Yangfeng Ji, Gholamreza Haffari, and Jacob Eisenstein. 2016. A latent variable recurrent neural network for discourse-driven language models. In *Proceedings of the 2016 Conference of the North American Chapter of the Association for Computational Linguistics: Human Language Technologies*, pages 332–342, San Diego, California. Association for Computational Linguistics.

Jeffrey L Kallen and John Monfries Kirk. 2008. *ICE-Ireland: A User's Guide: Documentation to Accompany the Ireland Component of the International Corpus of English (ICE-Ireland).* Cló Ollscoil na Banríona.

Najoung Kim, Song Feng, Chulaka Gunasekara, and Luis Lastras. 2020. Implicit discourse relation classification: We need to talk about evaluation. In *Proceedings of the 58th Annual Meeting of the Association for Computational Linguistics*, pages 5404–5414. Association for Computational Linguistics.

René Knaebel and Manfred Stede. 2020. Contextualized embeddings for connective disambiguation in shallow discourse parsing. In *Proceedings of the First Workshop on Computational Approaches to Discourse*, pages 65–75, Online. Association for Computational Linguistics.

Murathan Kurfalı and Robert Östling. 2021. Let's be explicit about that: Distant supervision for implicit discourse relation classification via connective prediction. *arXiv preprint arXiv:2106.03192*.

Majid Laali and Leila Kosseim. 2014. Inducing discourse connectives from parallel texts. In *Proceedings of COLING 2014, the 25th International Conference on Computational Linguistics: Technical Papers*, pages 610–619.

Man Lan, Jianxiang Wang, Yuanbin Wu, Zheng-Yu Niu, and Haifeng Wang. 2017. Multi-task attention-based neural networks for implicit discourse relationship representation and identification. In *Proceedings of the 2017 Conference on Empirical Methods in Natural Language Processing*, pages 1299–1308, Copenhagen, Denmark. Association for Computational Linguistics.

Ziheng Lin, Hwee Tou Ng, and Min-Yen Kan. 2014. A PDTB-styled end-to-end discourse parser. *Natural Language Engineering*, 20(2):151–184.

Marian Marchal, Merel CJ Scholman, and Vera Demberg. 2021. Semi-automatic discourse annotation in a low-resource language: Developing a connective lexicon for Nigerian Pidgin. In *Proceedings of the Second Workshop on Computational Approaches to Discourse*.

Allen Nie, Erin Bennett, and Noah Goodman. 2019. DisSent: Learning sentence representations from explicit discourse relations. In *Proceedings of the 57th Annual Meeting of the Association for Computational Linguistics*, pages 4497–4510, Florence, Italy. Association for Computational Linguistics.

Emily Pitler and Ani Nenkova. 2009. Using syntax to disambiguate explicit discourse connectives in text. In *Proceedings of the ACL-IJCNLP 2009 Conference Short Papers*, pages 13–16, Suntec, Singapore. Association for Computational Linguistics.

Rashmi Prasad, Nikhil Dinesh, Alan Lee, Eleni Miltsakaki, Livio Robaldo, Aravind Joshi, and Bonnie Webber. 2008. The Penn Discourse TreeBank 2.0. In *Proceedings of the Sixth International Conference on Language Resources and Evaluation (LREC'08)*, Marrakech, Morocco. European Language Resources Association (ELRA).

Rashmi Prasad, Susan McRoy, Nadya Frid, Aravind Joshi, and Hong Yu. 2011. The biomedical discourse relation bank. *BMC bioinformatics*, 12(1):1–18.

Balaji Polepalli Ramesh and Hong Yu. 2010. Identifying discourse connectives in biomedical text. In *AMIA Annual Symposium Proceedings*, volume 2010, page 657. American Medical Informatics Association.

Ines Rehbein, Merel Scholman, and Vera Demberg. 2016. Annotating discourse relations in spoken language: A comparison of the PDTB and CCR frameworks. In *Proceedings of the Tenth International Conference on Language Resources and Evaluation (LREC'16)*, pages 1039–1046, Portorož, Slovenia. European Language Resources Association (ELRA).

Diego Xavier Roman, Allison Briceño, Hannah Rohde, and Stephanie Hironaka. 2016. Linguistic cohesion in middle-school texts: A comparison of logical connectives usage in science and social studies textbooks. *The Electronic Journal for Research in Science & Mathematics Education*, 20(6).

Wei Shi and Vera Demberg. 2019. Learning to explicitate connectives with Seq2Seq network for implicit discourse relation classification. In *Proceedings of the 13th International Conference on Computational Semantics - Long Papers*, pages 188–199, Gothenburg, Sweden. Association for Computational Linguistics.

Jianxiang Wang and Man Lan. 2015. A refined end-to-end discourse parser. In *Proceedings of the Nineteenth Conference on Computational Natural Language Learning - Shared Task*, pages 17–24, Beijing, China. Association for Computational Linguistics.

Bonnie Webber, Rashmi Prasad, Alan Lee, and Aravind Joshi. 2019. The Penn Discourse Treebank 3.0 annotation manual. *Philadelphia, University of Pennsylvania*.

Deniz Zeyrek, Amália Mendes, Yulia Grishina, Murathan Kurfalı, Samuel Gibbon, and Maciej Ogrodniczuk. 2019. Ted multilingual discourse bank (ted-mdb): a parallel corpus annotated in the pdtb style. *Language Resources and Evaluation*, pages 1–27.

Yukun Zhu, Ryan Kiros, Rich Zemel, Ruslan Salakhutdinov, Raquel Urtasun, Antonio Torralba, and Sanja Fidler. 2015. Aligning books and movies: Towards story-like visual explanations by watching movies and reading books. In *Proceedings of the IEEE international conference on computer vision*, pages 19–27.

## A Model comparisons

$Chi^2$ tests confirm that the difference in performance (TP and FN distribution) between the top three parsers is significant in each dataset, with the exception of TED-MDB, as displayed in Table 2. The top three parsers considered here because these were most competitive. $Chi^2$ tests confirm that the difference in performance (TP and FP distribution) between the datasets is significant in each parser, as shown in Table 3.

| Dataset | $\chi^2$ | *df* | |
|---|---|---|---|
| PDTB | 52.45 | 2 | *** |
| BioDRB | 369.88 | 2 | *** |
| TED-MDB | 1.74 | 2 | |
| DiscoSPICE | 69.25 | 2 | *** |

Table 2: $Chi^2$ statistics to test whether there is a significant difference between the parsers per dataset.

| Parser | $\chi^2$ | *df* | |
|---|---|---|---|
| e2e | 879.32 | 3 | *** |
| CONLL | 1005 | 3 | *** |
| Discopy | 1204.8 | 3 | *** |

Table 3: $Chi^2$ statistics to test whether there is a significant difference between the datasets per parser.

## B Summary of connective-specific results

Table 4 presents the highlights of the connective-specific results per dataset.

|  | Poor performance | Unidentified connectives | Issues with gold label | Other observations |
|---|---|---|---|---|
| PDTB2 | *as, or, nor, once, previously* | *finally, specifically, rather, hence* | - | PDTB e2e and CONLL2015 show low performance on *as*, but Discopy performs better. |
| BioDRB | *after, as, except, once, still* | *besides* | *until, also, previously* | BioDRB maintains different segmentation rules; New connective types not on PDTB2's list; PDTB e2e parser only identifies argument-initial instances of *still*. |
| TED-MDB | *and, as, so, then, when* | *for, on the one hand, rather* | *when* | Rhetorical "what if" relations present false positives; New connective types not on PDTB2's list. |
| Disco-SPICE | *and, as, but, so, then* | *after, also, finally, for, later, otherwise, still* | *then* | Phonetic spelling of connectives cannot be identified; Syntactic structures affect performance; PDTB e2e and CONLL are affected by interjections. |

Table 4: Summary of connective-specific analysis per dataset.

# Revisiting Shallow Discourse Parsing in the PDTB-3: Handling Intra-sentential Implicits

**Zheng Zhao** and **Bonnie Webber**
Institute for Language, Cognition and Computation
School of Informatics, University of Edinburgh
10 Crichton Street, Edinburgh, EH8 9AB
{zheng.zhao,bonnie.webber}@ed.ac.uk

## Abstract

In the PDTB-3, several thousand implicit discourse relations were newly annotated *within* individual sentences, adding to the over 15,000 implicit relations annotated *across* adjacent sentences in the PDTB-2. Given that the position of the arguments to these *intra-sentential implicits* is no longer as well-defined as with *inter-sentential implicits*, a discourse parser must identify both their location and their sense. That is the focus of the current work. The paper provides a comprehensive analysis of our results, showcasing model performance under different scenarios, pointing out limitations and noting future directions.

## 1 Introduction

Discourse parsing is the task of identifying and categorizing discourse relations between discourse segments in a given text. The task is considered to be important for downstream tasks such as question answering (Jansen et al., 2014), machine translation (Li et al., 2014), and text summarization (Cohan et al., 2018). There are various approaches to discourse parsing, corresponding to different views of (1) what constitutes the segments of discourse, (2) what structures can be built from such segments, and (3) what semantic and/or rhetorical relations can hold between such segments (Xue et al., 2015; Zeldes et al., 2019).

Approaches to discourse structure generally allow discourse relations to hold between segments within a sentence (i.e., *intra-sentential discourse relations*) or across sentences (i.e. *inter-sentential discourse relations*) (Joty et al., 2012; Muller et al., 2012; Stede, 2011; Stede et al., 2016).

In the Penn Discourse Treebank (PDTB; Prasad et al., 2008), all discourse relations have two arguments, called *Arg1* and **Arg2**. Discourse relations are termed *explicit*, if the evidence for the relation is an explicit discourse connective (word or phrase). For *implicit discourse relations*, evidence is in the form of argument adjacency (with or without intervening punctuation), though annotators were asked to record one or more discourse connectives that, if present, would explicitly signal the sense(s) they inferred to hold between the arguments. Where annotators felt that the relation was already signalled by an alternative (non-connective) expression, the expression was annotated as evidence for what was called an *AltLex relation* (Prasad et al., 2010).

The first major release of the PDTB was the PDTB-2 (Prasad et al., 2008) whose guidelines limited annotation to (a) Explicit relations lexicalized by discourse connectives, and (b) Implicit and AltLex relations between paragraph-internal adjacent sentences and between complete clauses within sentences separated by colons or semi-colons. Since there were only ~530 intra-sentential implicit relations among the ~15,500 implicit relations annotated in the PDTB-2, they were ignored in work on discourse parsing (Lin et al., 2014; Wang and Lan, 2015; Xue et al., 2015, 2016), which took implicit relations to hold only between adjacent sentences.

The situation changed with the release of the PDTB-3 (Webber et al., 2019). Among the ~5.6K sentence-internal implicit relations annotated in the PDTB-3 are relations between VPs or clauses conjoined implicitly by punctuation (Ex. 1), between a free adjunct or free to-infinitive and its matrix clause (Ex. 2), and between a marked syntactic construction and its matrix clause. There are also implicit relations co-occurring with explicit relations (Webber et al., 2019), as noted in Section 3.1.

(1) Father McKenna moves through the house *praying in Latin*, (Implicit=and) **urging the demon to split**. [wsj_0413]

(2) *Father McKenna moves through the house* (Implicit=while) **praying in Latin**, **urging the demon to split**. [wsj_0413]

Why are implicit *intra-sentential* relations a problem for shallow discourse parsing? First, as already noted, unlike *inter-sentential* implicits, they do not occur at sentence boundaries, with material



*Proceedings of the 2nd Workshop on Computational Approaches to Discourse*, pages 107–121
November 10–11, 2021. ©2021 Association for Computational Linguistics

to the left of the boundary as *Arg1* and material to the right as **Arg2**. Secondly, *Arg1* and **Arg2** can appear in either order: *Arg1* before **Arg2**, as in Ex 1–2, or **Arg2** before *Arg1*, as in Ex. 3. Parsing implicit intra-sentential relations therefore requires both locating and labelling their arguments, as well as identifying the sense(s) in which they are related.[1]

(3) (Implicit=if it is) **To slow the rise in total spending**, *it will be necessary to reduce per-capita use of services.* [wsj_0314]

This work takes up some of the challenges of parsing implicit intra-sentential discourse relations. Overall, it contributes: (1) a set of BERT-based models used as a pipeline for recognizing intra-sentential implicit discourse relations as well as classifying their senses; (2) experimental evidence that these BERT-based models perform better than comparable LSTM-based models on the relation recognition task; (3) evidence that the use of parse tree features can improve model performance, as was earlier found useful in simply recognizing when a sentence contained at least one implicit intra-sentential relation (Liang et al., 2020).

## 2 Related Work

The focus of the current work is parsing implicit intra-sentential discourse relations in the framework of the PDTB-3. As most of the implicit relations in the PDTB-2 were inter-sentential (i.e., ~95% of its 15.5K implicit relations), its intra-sentential implicits were ignored in parser development. Nearly all recent work on recognizing inter-sentential implicits in the PDTB-2 used neural architectures. This included multi-level attention in work by Liu and Li (2016), multiple text representations in work by Bai and Zhao (2018), including character, subword, word, sentence, and sentence pair levels, to more fully capture the text. Dai and Huang (2018) introduced a paragraph-level neural architecture with a conditional random field (CRF, Lafferty et al., 2001) layer which models inter-dependencies of discourse units and predicts a sequence of discourse relations in a paragraph. Varia et al. (2019) introduced an approach to distill knowledge from word pairs for discourse relation with CNN by joint learning of implicit and explicit relations. Shi and Demberg (2019) discovered that BERT-based models, which were trained on the next sentence prediction task, benefited implicit inter-sentential discourse relation classification. Here we assess whether they also benefit classifying intra-sentential implicit relations.

Looking at implicit relations in the PDTB-3, Prasad et al. (2017) consider the difficulty in extending implicit relations to relations that cross paragraph boundaries. Kurfalı and Östling (2019) examine whether implicit relation annotation in the PDTB-3 can be used as a basis for learning to classify implicit relations in languages that lack discourse annotation. Kim et al. (2020) explored whether the PDTB-3 could be used to learn fine-grained (Level-2) sense classification in general, while Liang et al. (2020) looked at whether separating inter-sentential implicits from intra-sentential implicits could improve their sense classification. They also took a first step towards recognizing what sentences contained intra-sentential implicit relations, finding this benefitted from the use of linearized parse tree features.

Outside the PDTB-3 framework, intra-sentential discourse relations are handled by (1) identifying discourse units (DUs), (2) attaching them to one another, and (3) associating the attachment with a coherence relation (Muller et al., 2012). One can therefore ask why we did not simply adopt this framework in the PDTB-3 and exploit the relatively good performance by systems in the DISRPT shared task on sentence-level discourse unit segmentation (Zeldes et al., 2019). There are two main reasons: First, DISRPT (and the approaches to discourse structure it covers) assumes that discourse segments cover a sentence with a non-overlapping partition. This is not the case with the PDTB, where the presence of overlapping segments (both within and across sentences) has been well documented (Lee et al., 2006). Second, discourse segments in these approaches are taken to correspond to syntactic units, which leads to both over-segmentation and under-segmentation in the PDTB-3. Of course, there are "work-arounds" for over-segmentation, such as RST's use of a SAME-SEGMENT relation (Mann and Thompson, 1988), and under-segmentation can be addressed through additional segmentation. However, we decided that starting from scratch would allow us to clearly identify the problems of parsing intra-sentential implicits, at which point, we could consider what we

[1] While the arguments to some explicit discourse relations can also appear in either order, **Arg2** is still bound to the explicit conjunction, so its relative position can be easily identified.

could adopt from work done on the DISRPT shared task on sentence-level discourse unit segmentation (Zeldes et al., 2019).

## 3 Methodology

Given an input sentence $S$ represented as a sequence of tokens $s_1 \cdots s_n$, our aim is to identify the span of *Arg1* and **Arg2** if there exist an implicit discourse relation in that sentence and then to predict its corresponding sense relation. We treat the identification of argument spans as a sequence tagging problem, and the prediction of senses as a classification task. Thus, given $S$, our aim is to output both a tag sequence $Y$ of length $n$ and a sense label $c$ for the identified relation. The generated tag sequence $y_1 \cdots y_n$ contains token-level labels where $y_j \in \{\texttt{B-Arg1}, \texttt{B-Arg2}, \texttt{I-Arg1}, \texttt{I-Arg2}, \texttt{O}\}$ indicating whether the token belongs to *Arg1*, **Arg2**, or Other. We adopt the BIO format (Ramshaw and Marcus, 1999) since arguments (1) can span multiple tokens, (2) can occur in either order, (3) need not be adjacent, and (4) do not overlap. (Future work will address two additional properties of intra-sentential implicits: (1) as shown in Sec 3.1, a sentence can contain more than one such relation and (2) even though most arguments are continuous spans, 264 intra-sentential implicit relations (4.2%) have discontinuous spans.)

This section describes the two parts of our approach. Section 3.1 describes the creation of two datasets based on the PDTB-3: $\mathcal{D}_1 = \{(S^{(i)}, P^{(i)}, Y^{(i)}) \mid i \in \{1 \ldots N\}\}$, $\mathcal{D}_2 = \{(A_1^{(i)}, A_2^{(i)}, P^{(i)}, c^{(i)}) \mid i \in \{1 \ldots M\}\}$ consisting of $N$ and $M$ input-output pairs, where $S$ is the input sentence, $P$ is its parse tree, $A_1$ and $A_2$ are *Arg1* and **Arg2** of the intra-sentential relation, $Y$ is the output sentence label, and $c$ is the sense label. Sections 3.2–3.3 describe models to recognize the argument spans and classify the relations. We provide detailed descriptions for these two steps in the rest of this section.

### 3.1 Dataset Generation

As we have two tasks, we built two datasets. Dataset $\mathcal{D}_1$ is used to train our argument identification models. It simply comprises individual sentences from the PDTB-3 and a sequence of labels of these sentences. Some models also contain parse tree features (Marcus et al., 1993). To generate the sequence of labels $Y$, we take annotations of intra-sentential implicit relations from the PDTB-3. *Arg1* tokens in the sentence are labelled `Arg1`, and **Arg2** tokens are labelled `Arg2`. Tokens with `O` labels means they belong to neither *Arg1* nor **Arg2**. If a sentence does not have any intra-sentential implicit relation, then all of its tokens will be labelled `O`. In BIO format, these labels then become `B-Arg1`, `B-Arg2`, `I-Arg1`, `I-Arg2`, and `O`.

| Number of relations | Count | % |
|---|---|---|
| 0 | 41,734 | 89.89% |
| 1 | 4,314 | 9.29% |
| 2 | 321 | 0.69% |
| 3 | 42 | 0.09% |
| 4 | 15 | 0.03% |
| 5 | 4 | 0.01% |
| total | 46,430 | 100% |

Table 1: The distribution of intra-sentential implicit relations per sentence for our dataset.

The dataset comprises the 46,430 sentences in the PDTB-3, with 24,369 intra-sentential relations, of which 6,234 are implicit. Table 1 shows that a single sentence can have zero, one or more intra-sentential implicit relations, with over 99% of the sentences having no more than one. So as not to lose any training data, the 321 sentences with two relations are duplicated, with each duplicate containing one of the relations. So while we do not currently try to learn multiple implicit relations within a sentence, this approach means we don't prejudice which relation is learned.

Another way of not losing data is to treat intra-sentential AltLex relations as intra-sentential implicits because they only differ from the latter in signalling its sense in its lexicalization (Liang et al., 2020). For instance, free-adjuncts are generally **Arg2** of an intra-sentential implicit. However, those free adjuncts headed by "avoiding", "contributing to", "resulting in", etc. are labelled AltLex relations because the head uniquely signals a RESULT sense. Structurally, however, it is still an intra-sentential implicit.

Finally, the dataset does not include implicit relations that are linked to an explicit relation. Such linking is used to convey that the arguments are semantically related in a way that cannot be attributed to the explicit discourse connective alone (Webber et al., 2019). A dedicated model to recognize implicits "linked" to explicit relations is included in work by Liang et al. (2020).

Dataset $\mathcal{D}_2$ is used to train the sense classi-

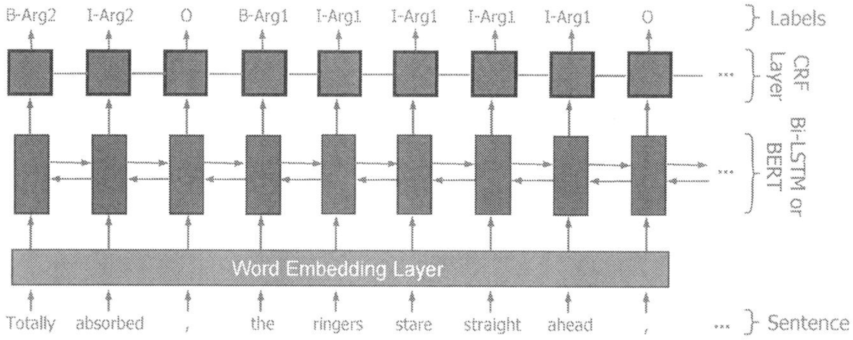


Figure 1: Architecture of our proposed argument identification model.

fier. It only contains data on sentences with intra-sentential implicits, and is thus smaller than $\mathcal{D}_1$. Each entry in $\mathcal{D}_2$ includes *Arg1*, **Arg2**, the parse tree for the sentence in which they lie, and a sense label for the *Arg1*–**Arg2** pair. Similar to $\mathcal{D}_1$, we also include AltLex relations. The current effort uses Level-2 sense labels to avoid data sparsity, while still providing a more meaningful sense than the 4 coarse labels in Level-1. The distribution of Level-2 sense labels is shown in Table 7 in Appendix A.1.

### 3.2 Argument Identification

The architecture for our argument identification model is shown in Figure 1. The input sentence first goes through the word embedding layer and then passes through either a BiLSTM (Hochreiter and Schmidhuber, 1997) or BERT module. Then the learned representation over the input sentence is fed into a CRF layer to generate a sequence of labels $Y$.

**Baseline model** The baseline model uses pre-trained GloVe (Pennington et al., 2014) vectors with BiLSTM and no additional parse tree features. For input sentence $S$ where $S = \{s_1, \ldots, s_n\}$ and $s_i$ denotes the $i$th token in $S$, the word vector $e_i$ is obtained from the word embedding module. Then a contextualized token-level encoding $h_i$ is obtained via a BiLSTM module:

$$\overrightarrow{h}_i = \mathbf{LSTM}_f(e_i, \overrightarrow{h}_{i-1}),$$

$$\overleftarrow{h}_i = \mathbf{LSTM}_b(e_i, \overleftarrow{h}_{i+1}),$$

$$h_i = [\overrightarrow{h}_i; \overleftarrow{h}_i],$$

where $\overrightarrow{h}_i$ and $\overleftarrow{h}_i$ are hidden states of forward and backward LSTMs at time step $i$, and ; denotes concatenation.

The resulting contextual word representations are then fed to the CRF layer to predict the $Y$ label.

**BERT-based models** Shi and Demberg (2019) observed that BERT-based models can benefit the task of classifying implicit *inter-sentential* discourse relations. Here we ask whether they can help in the task of argument recognition for *intra-sentential* implicit relations by creating variants of the baseline model where some parts of the model are replaced by BERT-based models.

The first variant of the model we implemented replaces the pre-trained GloVe word vectors with a pre-trained BERT model for word embedding initialization. We then construct a second variant on top of this, which also contains parse tree features. (These come from Penn TreeBank parse trees (Marcus et al., 1993), since we already know from Liang et al. (2020) that performance will drop when automated parse tree features are used.) The parse trees are first linearized and then fed to a separate BiLSTM module. The learned parse tree representations are concatenated with learned representations of the input sentence to a single vector. This vector, containing both lexical and syntactic information of the input, is then fed to the CRF layer for output prediction.

These model variants use a pre-trained BERT model. We also implemented models that fine-tune BERT on our task. One variant uses the vanilla BERT model, replacing the BiLSTM module, and another variant has the same architecture but also uses parse tree features of the input sentences.

### 3.3 Sense Classification

The sense classifier uses a BERT model whose input is the pair of arguments, *Arg1* and **Arg2**, and whose output is a Level-2 discourse relation sense.

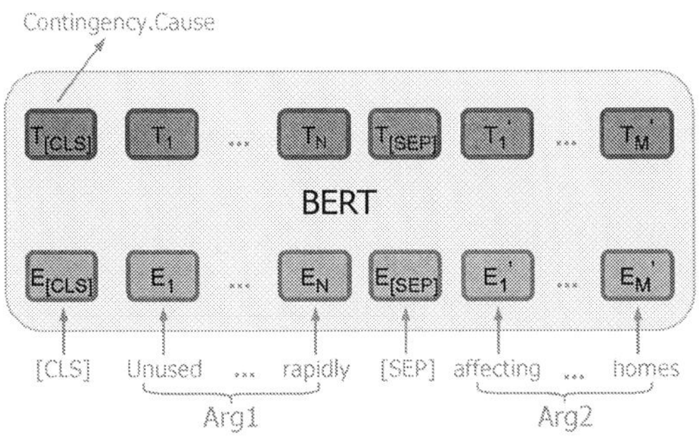


Figure 2: Architecture of our sense classifier.

The model architecture is illustrated in Figure 2. Following Shi and Demberg (2019), we concatenate *Arg1* and **Arg2** into a sequence separated with the special token [SEP]. We also insert the special token [CLS] at the beginning of the sequence. We use the output of BERT on the [CLS] token for sense classification. In addition, we also use parse trees as additional features to BERT. Similar to the method for argument identification, the learned parse tree features are concatenated with the representations of the [CLS] token to a single vector. This vector is then used for predicting the sense label.

### 3.4 Training and Inference

Given the training set for argument identification with labelled sequence $\{S^{(i)}, P^{(i)}, Y^{(i)} \mid i \in \{1 \dots N\}\}$, we maximize the conditional log likelihood for the sequence tagging objective:

$$\bar{w} = \underset{w}{\operatorname{argmax}} \sum_{i=1}^{N} \log p(Y^{(i)} \mid S^{(i)}, P^{(i)}, w),$$

where $w$ denotes the model's parameters including the weights of the LSTM/BERT module and the transition weights of the CRF layer. The loss function for $Y$ labels is the negative log-likelihood based on $Y^{(i)} = \{y_1, \dots, y_n\}$:

$$\mathcal{L}_Y = -\sum_{i=1}^{N}\sum_{j=1}^{n} \log p(y_j),$$

where $y_j \in Y^{(i)}$.

For sense classification which is predicting $c$ label, the loss function is cross entropy:

$$\mathcal{L}_c = -\sum_{i=1}^{M}\sum_{j=1}^{C} c_j^{(i)} \log p(c_j^{(i)}),$$

where $C$ denotes the number of classes.

At test time, inference for labels of a sentence $S$ involves applying the Viterbi algorithm to the CRF module to find the sequence with maximum likelihood $\hat{Y}$:

$$\hat{Y} = \underset{Y}{\operatorname{argmax}} P(Y \mid S, P, \bar{w}).$$

## 4 Experiments

For our experiments with LSTM-based models, we set the hidden dimensions to 256, the word embeddings to 100, and the vocabulary size to 50K. The word embeddings are initialized either using pre-trained Glove vectors (6B tokens, *uncased*) or a pre-trained *base-uncased* BERT. For experiments with BERT-based models, we use the same configuration with *base-uncased* BERT from Devlin et al. (2019). All of our training used the Adam optimizer (Kingma and Ba, 2015). LSTM-based models used a learning rate of 1e-3 and BERT-based models used a learning rate of 5e-5. We also use gradient clipping with a maximum gradient norm of 1 and we do not use any form of regularization. For sense classification, the gradient clipping is set with a maximum gradient norm of 0.5. We carry out assessment on the datasets mentioned in Section 3.1 in two different ways: (1) using a random split of each dataset into training (60%), development (20%) and test (20%) subsets, and (2) accepting the argument in Shi and Demberg (2017) that there is too much variation across the corpus for a single random split to produce representative results and that N-fold cross-validation will deliver more reliable and predictive results. In this work, we perform 10-fold cross-validation. We use loss on the development set to perform early stopping. All of our models were trained on a single Tesla P100 GPU with a batch size of 32. Our model implementation uses PyTorch (Paszke et al., 2019). We used the BERT implementation from the Transformers library (Wolf et al., 2020), and the CRF implementation from AllenNLP library (Gardner et al., 2018) for constrained decoding for the BIO scheme.

## 5 Results

**Argument Identification** The best results here on the sequence labelling objective for all model variants come from the fine-tuned BERT-based model with additional parse tree features. In general, BERT-based models outperform LSTM-based models, and models that use parse tree features

| model | *Arg1* | | | **Arg2** | | |
|---|---|---|---|---|---|---|
| | Precision | Recall | $F_1$ | Precision | Recall | $F_1$ |
| LSTM + GloVe (baseline) | 35.50 | 30.73 | 32.79 | 43.14 | 41.57 | 42.06 |
| LSTM + BERT$^\dagger$ | 39.83 | 49.01 | 43.44 | **56.93** | 59.88 | **58.22** |
| LSTM + BERT$^\dagger$ + parse tree | 43.55 | 50.56 | 46.66 | 53.45 | **61.53** | 57.19 |
| BERT fine-tuned | 45.80 | 50.63 | 48.06 | 54.56 | 59.04 | 56.64 |
| BERT fine-tuned + parse tree | **49.62**$*$ | **51.39** | **50.43**$*$ | 56.47 | 58.31 | 57.28 |

Table 2: Results of exact match for *Arg1* and **Arg2**. † denotes that a pre-trained BERT is used for word embedding, and $*$ denotes significant improvement over BERT fine-tuned with $p < 0.05$. Significance test was performed by estimating variance of the model from 5 random initialization.

| model | *Arg1* | | | **Arg2** | | |
|---|---|---|---|---|---|---|
| | Precision | Recall | $F_1$ | Precision | Recall | $F_1$ |
| LSTM + BERT$^\dagger$ | 44.51±6.14 | 51.23±5.48 | 47.59±4.76 | 58.59±2.82 | 62.70±2.21 | 60.51±1.70 |
| LSTM + BERT$^\dagger$ + parse tree | 44.82±5.88 | 53.58±2.79 | 48.54±3.56 | **60.48±2.30** | **61.64±2.68** | **61.00±1.70** |
| BERT fine-tuned | 48.22±5.55 | 53.26±2.94 | 50.42±3.58 | 58.59±3.29 | 58.64±2.24 | 58.64±1.86 |
| BERT fine-tuned + parse tree | **49.74±3.41** | **53.94±2.93** | **51.62±1.85** | 60.17±2.49 | 60.37±2.52 | 60.22±1.78 |

Table 3: Cross-validation results of exact match for *Arg1* and **Arg2**. † denotes that a pre-trained BERT is used for word embedding.

outperform those that don't. (All results appear in Appendix A.2. The overall higher results for O (i.e., neither *Arg1* nor **Arg2**) come simply from label imbalance.)

The standard automatic evaluation metrics for discourse argument recognition are Precision, Recall and $F_1$, computed on predicted arguments for relations that match the gold annotations. We follow Xue et al. (2015) in counting an argument as correctly recognized if and only if its span exactly matches the gold argument. No reward is given for partial match. Results on the test set from the 60/20/20 random split are shown for all models in Table 2. Cross-validation results are shown in Table 3 for BERT-based models. The best overall performance comes from the fine-tuned BERT model with parse tree features. The cross-validation results also show that the use of parse tree features improves Precision, if not Recall in all cases. This makes sense as the parse tree features can be used to reject what would otherwise be False Positives. In addition, we can see that for **Arg2**, the LSTM models with pre-trained BERT perform better than fine-tuned BERT. We haven't yet figured out any reason for this. Finally, we can see that models perform better on **Arg2** (both Recall and Precision) than on *Arg1*. We attribute this to the fact that, even though **Arg2** is not marked with an explicit connective (i.e., these are all implicit relations), there may still be positional and/or syntactic cues to its identity.

Supporting these observations are statistics from the test set. First, of its 987 sentences with intra-sentential implicit relations, the leftmost argument aligns with the beginning of the sentence 495 times (50.2%). Of these, *Arg1* is the leftmost argument 430 times (86.9%). At the other end of the sentence, 685 (69.4%) relations have their rightmost argument ending at the end of the sentence, almost 200 more than those with an argument at the beginning. Of these 685 relations, 614 (89.6%) have **Arg2** at their rightmost boundary. Note that whenever an argument starts or ends at a sentence boundary, the model just needs to predict the other end of the span, which is easier than predicting both ends. With **Arg2** appearing more often at a sentence boundary than *Arg1*, this is consistent with our observation of model performance.

Even though the training data for the argument identification model contains at most one relation per sentence and the model only predicts continuous argument spans, we purposely relax the constraint for the model to predict at most one relation per sentence. We find that for all test set predictions, our best model predicts 77 sentences with more than one *Arg1* (7.53% of all sentences predicted to have a relation). It also predicts 44 sentences with more than one **Arg2** (4.31% of all sentences predicted to have a relation). This probably arises from duplicating those training instances with more than one relation (cf. Section 3.1). Later in this section, we show how the sense classifier can be used

| model | *Arg1*-**Arg2** | | | **Arg2**-*Arg1* | | |
|---|---|---|---|---|---|---|
| | Precision | Recall | $F_1$ | Precision | Recall | $F_1$ |
| LSTM + GloVe (baseline) | 70.50 | 42.94 | 53.37 | 45.16 | 18.92 | 26.67 |
| LSTM + BERT† | 70.03 | 75.03 | 74.01 | 51.85 | 56.76 | 54.19 |
| LSTM + BERT† + parse tree | 70.82 | 70.97 | 70.90 | 39.22 | 27.03 | 32.00 |
| BERT fine-tuned | **83.77** | 73.49 | **78.30** | 59.09 | 70.27 | 64.20 |
| BERT fine-tuned + parse tree | 78.35 | **76.12** | 77.22 | **62.22** | **75.68** | **68.29** |

Table 4: Results of argument order prediction with either *Arg1*-**Arg2** (914 instances from the test set) and **Arg2**-*Arg1* (73 instances from the test set). † denotes a pre-trained BERT is used for word embedding.

to choose among multiple predicted arguments.

As noted earlier, the order of arguments in an intra-sentential implicit relation is not fixed. So we have also correlated model performance with argument order. Of the 5,157 sentences overall with intra-sentential implicit relations, 4,665 (90.5%) have arguments in *Arg1*-**Arg2** order. In the 60/20/20 split test set, this imbalance is higher across the 987 intra-sentential implicit relations, with 914 (92.6%) showing the more common *Arg1*-**Arg2** order. Performance of the model in predicting argument order is shown in Table 4. Note that a match of argument order here does not imply exact match of arguments in the previous evaluation. However, all models are more accurate in predicting the more frequent *Arg1*-**Arg2** order than **Arg2**-*Arg1* order, although the performance difference is less with BERT-based models than with LSTM-based models, suggesting BERT can deal with under-represented data better.

For completeness, we also analyze the best model's argument identification performance under different conditions. First, we consider that part of the 60/20/20 split test set whose sentences contain more than one intra-sentential implicit relations. For a fair comparison, we ensure that all single-relation tokens derived from the same sentence are in the test set (36 tokens). We further divide these tokens into ones whose relation is further left in the sentence and ones whose relation is further right. The top part of Table 5 shows the performance of the fine-tuned BERT model with parse tree features on these sets. Compared with the original test set, the overall performance on relations derived from sentences with multiple relations is much worse. This is expected as the training set for argument identification assumed that a sentence can only have at most one intra-sentential implicit relation.

We next examine performance for different sense labels, based on the four most frequent senses in the test set – those that appear more than 100 times. The bottom part of Table 5 shows that our model performed best on CONTINGENCY.CAUSE. Inspection of the True Positives shows this to result from **Arg2** of these relations often being headed by a AltLex token with Part-of-speech tag VBG, which uniquely conveys the sense CONTINGENCY.CAUSE.RESULT. The model can thus easily learn to recognize these arguments using the parse tree features.

**Sense Classification** Cross-validation results for Precision, Recall, and $F_1$ for the top four senses recognized by our sense classifier are shown in Table 6. The complete performance breakdown is given in Table 14 in Appendix A.3, along with a confusion matrix (Figure 3) and results on the test set in the 60/20/20 random split (Table 13). As the distribution of senses is imbalanced, we calculate overall performance by averaging performance for each sense, weighted by its frequency in the test set. Note that the overall $F_1$ for intra-sentential implicits is much higher than 50.41 reported in Liang et al. (2020) where a LSTM-based model is used. The overall accuracy of our sense classifier on cross-validation is 69.54%, and that on the test set in the 60/20/20 random split is 75.19%. From the results, we can see that the performance for CONTINGENCY.PURPOSE is very high, with $F_1$ exceeding the weighted average by almost 20 points. We speculate that this is due to the fact that over 90% of CONTINGENCY.PURPOSE labels are on relations where **Arg2** begins with a free "to clause" and there are few other intra-sentential implicits labelled CONTINGENCY.PURPOSE.

Our sense classifier is trained using gold argument spans taken from the PDTB-3. In reality, such gold annotations will rarely be available. Thus, we also use predicted arguments from our argument identification model as inputs to test the ability of

| condition | *Arg1* | | | **Arg2** | | | # of rels |
|---|---|---|---|---|---|---|---|
| | Precision | Recall | $F_1$ | Precision | Recall | $F_1$ | |
| multiple relations | 31.25 | 28.57 | 29.85 | 21.95 | 25.71 | 23.68 | 36 |
| multiple relation + left | 25.00 | 23.53 | 24.24 | 10.00 | 11.76 | 10.81 | 18 |
| multiple relation + right | 37.50 | 33.33 | 35.29 | 33.33 | 38.89 | 35.90 | 18 |
| Contingency.Cause | **68.12** | **62.65** | **65.27** | 75.44 | **69.08** | **72.12** | 249 |
| Contingency.Purpose | 63.98 | 47.22 | 54.34 | **78.80** | 57.54 | 66.51 | 252 |
| Expansion.Conjunction | 48.08 | 39.06 | 43.10 | 42.86 | 39.84 | 41.30 | 128 |
| Expansion.Level-of-detail | 59.05 | 56.88 | 57.94 | 60.38 | 58.72 | 59.53 | 109 |
| Original test set | 49.62 | 51.39 | 50.43 | 56.47 | 58.31 | 57.28 | 987 |

Table 5: Results of argument identification for *Arg1* and **Arg2** for our best model under different conditions.

| Sense | BERT + Parse Tree | | |
|---|---|---|---|
| | Precision | Recall | $F_1$ |
| Contingency.Cause | $76.50 \pm 4.22$ | $74.60 \pm 4.89$ | $75.31 \pm 2.14$ |
| Contingency.Purpose | $86.78 \pm 2.05$ | $90.49 \pm 2.66$ | $88.56 \pm 1.57$ |
| Expansion.Conjunction | $73.99 \pm 8.05$ | $70.33 \pm 5.55$ | $71.82 \pm 5.03$ |
| Expansion.Level-of-detail | $57.79 \pm 4.70$ | $48.23 \pm 3.12$ | $52.37 \pm 2.06$ |
| Overall | $70.86 \pm 1.45$ | $69.54 \pm 1.30$ | $69.65 \pm 1.36$ |

Table 6: Cross-validation results for sense classification.

our sense classifier. Specifically, we first obtain test set sentences with intra-sentential implicit relations and their parse trees. Then we feed those to our argument identification model to get predicted arguments. These predicted arguments are then fed in to our sense classifier together with the parse tree features. If the argument identification model fails to predict any arguments for any sentences, we ignore them in our evaluation. Table 15 in Appendix A.3 shows the sense classification results using predicted arguments and, for comparison, the results using the gold arguments. Note that as we dropped some sentences, the results with gold arguments are slightly different from those of the original test set. Because the performance drop is small going from gold arguments to predicted arguments, we can argue that our models can be used as a pipeline for handling intra-sentential implicit relations in shallow discourse parsing with the input simply being a sentence.

We noted in Section 3.1 that our argument identification model might predict multiple *Arg1*s and/or **Arg2**s for a given sentence. We therefore assessed whether the sense classifier could be used to decide which of the predicted arguments to use. Specifically, we identify cases where one argument has a single prediction but there are multiple predictions for the other argument. For each *Arg1*-**Arg2** pair, we use the sense classifier to predict the sense label and its likelihood. Comparing these likelihoods, we select the pair with the highest certainty, ignoring cases where the predicted senses are the same for all pairs. We also implement a baseline of always choosing the pair with the most frequent sense, which is CONTINGENCY.CAUSE. The 60/20/20 split test set shows 34 cases in which there are multiple predictions of *Arg1* for a single **Arg2**. In 23 out of these 34 instances, the correct *Arg1* is associated with the pair with the highest likelihood. The baseline only gets 13 cases correct. Similarly, the test set shows 23 cases in which there are multiple predictions of **Arg2** for a single *Arg1*. In 13 of these 23 instances, the pair for which the sense classifier assigns the highest priority correctly identifies which **Arg2** to use. The baseline only gets 9 cases correct. While further analysis is needed, this does show that the sense classifier can contribute to selecting the right argument from the set of predicted argument candidates.

## 6 Conclusions and Future Work

To the best of our knowledge, this is the first work to attempt to identify the arguments of intra-sentential implicit discourse relations in the framework of the PDTB-3, as well as their order and at least one of their sense relations. We used a model architecture similar to models of a sequence tagging task, and concluded that BERT-based models have better performance than LSTM-based models in both exactly matching gold annotations of arguments and correctly predicting the order of *Arg1* and **Arg2**. We confirmed that using parse trees features as input to the model assists with these tasks. We also provide evidence that our sense classifier, together with the argument recognizer, can be used as a pipeline for handling intra-sentential implicit relations. We also find that the sense classifier can be used to aid the selection of the right argument from the set of predicted argument candidates.

Our methods have several limitations. First, we assumed every sentence can have at most one intra-sentential implicit relation, whereas in reality, multiple such relations are possible (cf. Table 1). Secondly, our approach does not support the case of discontinuous argument spans. Thirdly, we have ignored implicit relations "linked" to explicit relations (either intra-sentential or inter-sentential). Finally, although we have followed the lead of Shi and Demberg (2017) in assessing performance using cross-validation because it is more reliable than choosing a specific test set, we did not cast all our results in those terms. In the future, we plan to address these problems and develop methods that can identify all existing relations within the sentence.

## Acknowledgments

This work was supported in part by the UKRI Centre for Doctoral Training in Natural Language Processing (UKRI grant EP/S022481/1), the University of Edinburgh, and Huawei. We would like to thank Hannah Rohde and anonymous CODI reviewers for their helpful feedback.

## References

Hongxiao Bai and Hai Zhao. 2018. Deep enhanced representation for implicit discourse relation recognition. In *Proceedings of the 27th International Conference on Computational Linguistics*, pages 571–583, Santa Fe, New Mexico, USA. Association for Computational Linguistics.

Arman Cohan, Franck Dernoncourt, Doo Soon Kim, Trung Bui, Seokhwan Kim, Walter Chang, and Nazli Goharian. 2018. A discourse-aware attention model for abstractive summarization of long documents. In *Proceedings of the 2018 Conference of the North American Chapter of the Association for Computational Linguistics: Human Language Technologies, Volume 2 (Short Papers)*, pages 615–621, New Orleans, Louisiana. Association for Computational Linguistics.

Zeyu Dai and Ruihong Huang. 2018. Improving implicit discourse relation classification by modeling inter-dependencies of discourse units in a paragraph. In *Proceedings of the 2018 Conference of the North American Chapter of the Association for Computational Linguistics: Human Language Technologies, Volume 1 (Long Papers)*, pages 141–151, New Orleans, Louisiana. Association for Computational Linguistics.

Jacob Devlin, Ming-Wei Chang, Kenton Lee, and Kristina Toutanova. 2019. BERT: Pre-training of deep bidirectional transformers for language understanding. In *Proceedings of the 2019 Conference of the North American Chapter of the Association for Computational Linguistics: Human Language Technologies, Volume 1 (Long and Short Papers)*, pages 4171–4186, Minneapolis, Minnesota. Association for Computational Linguistics.

Matt Gardner, Joel Grus, Mark Neumann, Oyvind Tafjord, Pradeep Dasigi, Nelson F. Liu, Matthew E. Peters, Michael Schmitz, and Luke Zettlemoyer. 2018. Allennlp: A deep semantic natural language processing platform. *CoRR*, abs/1803.07640.

Sepp Hochreiter and Jürgen Schmidhuber. 1997. Long short-term memory. *Neural Comput.*, 9(8):1735–1780.

Peter Jansen, Mihai Surdeanu, and Peter Clark. 2014. Discourse complements lexical semantics for non-factoid answer reranking. In *Proceedings of the 52nd Annual Meeting of the Association for Computational Linguistics (Volume 1: Long Papers)*, pages 977–986, Baltimore, Maryland. Association for Computational Linguistics.

Shafiq Joty, Giuseppe Carenini, and Raymond Ng. 2012. A novel discriminative framework for sentence-level discourse analysis. In *Proceedings of the 2012 Joint Conference on Empirical Methods in Natural Language Processing and Computational Natural Language Learning*, pages 904–915, Jeju Island, Korea. Association for Computational Linguistics.

Najoung Kim, Song Feng, Chulaka Gunasekara, and Luis Lastras. 2020. Implicit discourse relation classification: We need to talk about evaluation. In *Proceedings of the 58th Annual Meeting of the Association for Computational Linguistics*, pages 5404–5414, Online. Association for Computational Linguistics.

Diederik P. Kingma and Jimmy Ba. 2015. Adam: A method for stochastic optimization. In *3rd International Conference on Learning Representations, ICLR 2015, San Diego, CA, USA, May 7-9, 2015, Conference Track Proceedings*.

Murathan Kurfalı and Robert Östling. 2019. Zero-shot transfer for implicit discourse relation classification. In *Proceedings of the 20th Annual SIGdial Meeting on Discourse and Dialogue*, pages 226–231, Stockholm, Sweden. Association for Computational Linguistics.

John D. Lafferty, Andrew McCallum, and Fernando C. N. Pereira. 2001. Conditional random fields: Probabilistic models for segmenting and labeling sequence data. In *Proceedings of the Eighteenth International Conference on Machine Learning (ICML 2001), Williams College, Williamstown, MA, USA, June 28 - July 1, 2001*, pages 282–289. Morgan Kaufmann.

Alan Lee, Rashmi Prasad, Aravind Joshi, Nikhil Dinesh, and Bonnie Webber. 2006. Complexity of dependencies in discourse: Are dependencies in discourse more complex than in syntax. In *Proceedings of the 5th International Workshop on Treebanks and Linguistic Theories*, pages 12–23.

Junyi Jessy Li, Marine Carpuat, and Ani Nenkova. 2014. Assessing the discourse factors that influence the quality of machine translation. In *Proceedings of the 52nd Annual Meeting of the Association for Computational Linguistics (Volume 2: Short Papers)*, pages 283–288, Baltimore, Maryland. Association for Computational Linguistics.

Li Liang, Zheng Zhao, and Bonnie Webber. 2020. Extending implicit discourse relation recognition to the PDTB-3. In *Proceedings of the First Workshop on Computational Approaches to Discourse*, pages 135–147, Online. Association for Computational Linguistics.

Ziheng Lin, Hwee Tou Ng, and Min-Yen Kan. 2014. A pdtb-styled end-to-end discourse parser. *Natural Language Engineering*, 20(2):151–184.

Yang Liu and Sujian Li. 2016. Recognizing implicit discourse relations via repeated reading: Neural networks with multi-level attention. In *Proceedings of the 2016 Conference on Empirical Methods in Natural Language Processing*, pages 1224–1233, Austin, Texas. Association for Computational Linguistics.

William C Mann and Sandra A Thompson. 1988. Rhetorical structure theory: Toward a functional theory of text organization. *Text*, 8(3):243–281.

Mitchell P. Marcus, Beatrice Santorini, and Mary Ann Marcinkiewicz. 1993. Building a large annotated corpus of English: The Penn Treebank. *Computational Linguistics*, 19(2):313–330.

Philippe Muller, Stergos Afantenos, Pascal Denis, and Nicholas Asher. 2012. Constrained decoding for text-level discourse parsing. In *Proceedings of COLING 2012*, pages 1883–1900, Mumbai, India. The COLING 2012 Organizing Committee.

Adam Paszke, Sam Gross, Francisco Massa, Adam Lerer, James Bradbury, Gregory Chanan, Trevor Killeen, Zeming Lin, Natalia Gimelshein, Luca Antiga, Alban Desmaison, Andreas Kopf, Edward Yang, Zachary DeVito, Martin Raison, Alykhan Tejani, Sasank Chilamkurthy, Benoit Steiner, Lu Fang, Junjie Bai, and Soumith Chintala. 2019. Pytorch: An imperative style, high-performance deep learning library. In H. Wallach, H. Larochelle, A. Beygelzimer, F. d Alché-Buc, E. Fox, and R. Garnett, editors, *Advances in Neural Information Processing Systems 32*, pages 8024–8035. Curran Associates, Inc.

Jeffrey Pennington, Richard Socher, and Christopher D. Manning. 2014. Glove: Global vectors for word representation. In *Empirical Methods in Natural Language Processing (EMNLP)*, pages 1532–1543.

Rashmi Prasad, Nikhil Dinesh, Alan Lee, Eleni Miltsakaki, Livio Robaldo, Aravind Joshi, and Bonnie Webber. 2008. The Penn Discourse TreeBank 2.0. In *Proceedings of the Sixth International Conference on Language Resources and Evaluation (LREC'08)*, Marrakech, Morocco. European Language Resources Association (ELRA).

Rashmi Prasad, Katherine Forbes Riley, and Alan Lee. 2017. Towards full text shallow discourse relation annotation: Experiments with cross-paragraph implicit relations in the PDTB. In *Proceedings of the 18th Annual SIGdial Meeting on Discourse and Dialogue*, pages 7–16, Saarbrücken, Germany. Association for Computational Linguistics.

Rashmi Prasad, Aravind Joshi, and Bonnie Webber. 2010. Realization of discourse relations by other means: Alternative lexicalizations. In *Coling 2010: Posters*, pages 1023–1031, Beijing, China. Coling 2010 Organizing Committee.

Lance A Ramshaw and Mitchell P Marcus. 1999. Text chunking using transformation-based learning. In *Natural language processing using very large corpora*, pages 157–176. Springer.

Wei Shi and Vera Demberg. 2017. On the need of cross validation for discourse relation classification. In *Proceedings of the 15th Conference of the European Chapter of the Association for Computational Linguistics: Volume 2, Short Papers*, pages 150–156, Valencia, Spain. Association for Computational Linguistics.

Wei Shi and Vera Demberg. 2019. Next sentence prediction helps implicit discourse relation classification within and across domains. In *Proceedings of the 2019 Conference on Empirical Methods in Natural Language Processing and the 9th International Joint Conference on Natural Language Processing (EMNLP-IJCNLP)*, pages 5790–5796, Hong Kong, China. Association for Computational Linguistics.

Manfred Stede. 2011. Discourse processing. *Synthesis Lectures on Human Language Technologies*, 4(3):1–165.

Manfred Stede, Stergos Afantenos, Andreas Peldszus, Nicholas Asher, and Jérémy Perret. 2016. Parallel discourse annotations on a corpus of short texts. In *Proceedings of the Tenth International Conference on Language Resources and Evaluation (LREC'16)*, pages 1051–1058, Portorož, Slovenia. European Language Resources Association (ELRA).

Siddharth Varia, Christopher Hidey, and Tuhin Chakrabarty. 2019. Discourse relation prediction: Revisiting word pairs with convolutional networks. In *Proceedings of the 20th Annual SIGdial Meeting on Discourse and Dialogue*, pages 442–452, Stockholm, Sweden. Association for Computational Linguistics.

Jianxiang Wang and Man Lan. 2015. A refined end-to-end discourse parser. In *Proceedings of the Nineteenth Conference on Computational Natural Language Learning - Shared Task*, pages 17–24, Beijing, China. Association for Computational Linguistics.

Bonnie Webber, Rashmi Prasad, Alan Lee, and Aravind Joshi. 2019. The penn discourse treebank 3.0 annotation manual. `https://catalog.ldc.upenn.edu/docs/LDC2019T05/PDTB3-Annotation-Manual.pdf`.

Thomas Wolf, Lysandre Debut, Victor Sanh, Julien Chaumond, Clement Delangue, Anthony Moi, Pierric Cistac, Tim Rault, Remi Louf, Morgan Funtowicz, Joe Davison, Sam Shleifer, Patrick von Platen, Clara Ma, Yacine Jernite, Julien Plu, Canwen Xu, Teven Le Scao, Sylvain Gugger, Mariama Drame, Quentin Lhoest, and Alexander Rush. 2020. Transformers: State-of-the-art natural language processing. In *Proceedings of the 2020 Conference on Empirical Methods in Natural Language Processing: System Demonstrations*, pages 38–45, Online. Association for Computational Linguistics.

Nianwen Xue, Hwee Tou Ng, Sameer Pradhan, Rashmi Prasad, Christopher Bryant, and Attapol Rutherford. 2015. The CoNLL-2015 shared task on shallow discourse parsing. In *Proceedings of the Nineteenth Conference on Computational Natural Language Learning - Shared Task*, pages 1–16, Beijing, China. Association for Computational Linguistics.

Nianwen Xue, Hwee Tou Ng, Sameer Pradhan, Attapol Rutherford, Bonnie Webber, Chuan Wang, and Hongmin Wang. 2016. CoNLL 2016 shared task on multilingual shallow discourse parsing. In *Proceedings of the CoNLL-16 shared task*, pages 1–19, Berlin, Germany. Association for Computational Linguistics.

Amir Zeldes, Debopam Das, Erick Galani Maziero, Juliano Antonio, and Mikel Iruskieta. 2019. The DISRPT 2019 shared task on elementary discourse unit segmentation and connective detection. In *Proceedings of the Workshop on Discourse Relation Parsing and Treebanking 2019*, pages 97–104, Minneapolis, MN. Association for Computational Linguistics.

# A Appendix

## A.1 Distribution of Sense Label

The distribution of intra-sentential implicit sense labels is shown in Table 7. We can see that the sense labels are very imbalanced.

| Sense | Count | % |
|---|---|---|
| Comparison.Concession | 66 | 1.28% |
| Comp.Concession+S.A. | 4 | 0.08% |
| Comparison.Contrast | 112 | 2.17% |
| Comparison.Similarity | 7 | 0.14% |
| Contingency.Cause | 1366 | 26.49% |
| Contingency.Cause+Belief | 66 | 1.28% |
| Cont.Cause+SpeechAct | 1 | 0.02% |
| Contingency.Condition | 222 | 4.30% |
| Cont.Condition+SpeechAct | 1 | 0.02% |
| Cont.Negative-condition | 1 | 0.02% |
| Contingency.Purpose | 1323 | 25.65% |
| Expansion.Conjunction | 667 | 12.93% |
| Expansion.Disjunction | 17 | 0.33% |
| Expansion.Equivalence | 35 | 0.68% |
| Expansion.Instantiation | 86 | 1.67% |
| Expansion.Level-of-detail | 565 | 10.96% |
| Expansion.Manner | 183 | 3.55% |
| Expansion.Substitution | 82 | 1.59% |
| Temporal.Asynchronous | 178 | 3.45% |
| Temporal.Synchronous | 175 | 3.39% |

Table 7: The distribution of Level-2 labels for intra-sentential implicit relations in our dataset. Comp is short for Comparison, Cont is short for Contingency, and S.A. is short for SpeechAct.

## A.2 Additional Results for Argument Identification

In this section, we provide the results of the sequence tagging objective for all models variants as well as the results of argument order prediction. All results are reported on the test set. Table 8 shows results for our baseline LSTM model using GloVe word embeddings. Table 9 then shows results for the model when GloVe word embedding are replacrd with BERT embeddings. There is a large increase in Recall, with no drop in Precision except for `O` labels. Table 10 shows results when parse tree features are added to the model. Here, there is an increase in Recall for *Arg1*, and while Recall for **Arg2** decreases somewhat, it is accompanied by an increase in Precision. Then, we experiment with the vanilla BERT model and fine-tuning it on our dataset. The results are provided in Table 11. We can again observe a slight increase in performance, showcasing the power of BERT, even without the parse tree features. Finally, the last model we implement is BERT taking additional parse tree features fine-tuned on our dataset. The results are shown in Table 12. We can see that this is the best performing model for argument identification, proving that both BERT and parse tree features can improve performance.

| Label | Precision | Recall | $F_1$ |
|---|---|---|---|
| `B-Arg1` | 46.50 | 35.62 | 40.43 |
| `B-Arg2` | 54.07 | 46.76 | 50.15 |
| `I-Arg1` | 54.46 | 46.51 | 50.17 |
| `I-Arg2` | 48.64 | 60.03 | 53.74 |
| `O` | 95.38 | 95.24 | 95.31 |

Table 8: Results of the baseline LSTM model on test set using GloVe word embedding.

| Label | Precision | Recall | $F_1$ |
|---|---|---|---|
| `B-Arg1` | 48.10 | 52.35 | 50.14 |
| `B-Arg2` | 60.88 | 69.11 | 64.73 |
| `I-Arg1` | 63.34 | 65.59 | 64.45 |
| `I-Arg2` | 67.42 | 70.53 | 68.94 |
| `O` | 88.84 | 96.47 | 92.50 |

Table 9: Results of the LSTM model on test set using BERT word embedding.

| Label | Precision | Recall | $F_1$ |
|---|---|---|---|
| `B-Arg1` | 50.29 | 56.77 | 53.33 |
| `B-Arg2` | 63.57 | 61.13 | 62.33 |
| `I-Arg1` | 59.68 | 69.55 | 64.24 |
| `I-Arg2` | 73.08 | 66.74 | 69.77 |
| `O` | 88.86 | 96.51 | 92.53 |

Table 10: Results of the LSTM model on test set using BERT word embedding and parse tree feature.

## A.3 Additional Results for Sense Classification

In this section, we provide the full breakdown of performance of our sense classifier on each sense label. The results are provided in Table 13. Note that we only included senses existing in the test set. We provide a confusion matrix in Figure 3. In addition, we also provide results using 10-fold cross-validation in Table 14. We also provide the full comparison for sense classification results using

| Label | Precision | Recall | $F_1$ |
|---|---|---|---|
| B-Arg1 | 56.33 | 56.86 | 56.59 |
| B-Arg2 | 65.71 | 64.60 | 65.15 |
| I-Arg1 | 70.57 | 64.10 | 67.18 |
| I-Arg2 | 73.90 | 65.96 | 69.70 |
| O | 88.72 | 97.68 | 92.98 |

Table 11: Results on test set using fine-tuning BERT model without parse tree features.

| Label | Precision | Recall | $F_1$ |
|---|---|---|---|
| B-Arg1 | 52.65 | 58.74 | 55.53 |
| B-Arg2 | 61.27 | 66.10 | 63.60 |
| I-Arg1 | 63.52 | 70.54 | 66.85 |
| I-Arg2 | 69.32 | 71.93 | 70.60 |
| O | 89.10 | 96.46 | 92.64 |

Table 12: Results on test set using fine-tuning BERT model with parse tree features.

predicted arguments versus using gold arguments in Table 15. We can observe that for most senses, results using predicted arguments have slight inferior performance than those using gold arguments. For cases where results using predicted arguments are better, they are all under-represented senses in the dataset.

| Sense | Precision | Recall | $F_1$ |
|---|---|---|---|
| Comparison.Concession | 10.0 | 7.14 | 8.33 |
| Comparison.Contrast | 40.74 | 84.62 | 55.0 |
| Contingency.Cause | 79.43 | 76.45 | 77.91 |
| Contingency.Cause+Belief | 15.0 | 50.0 | 23.08 |
| Contingency.Condition | 68.52 | 84.09 | 75.51 |
| Contingency.Purpose | 93.09 | 92.71 | 92.90 |
| Expansion.Conjunction | 88.79 | 76.30 | 82.07 |
| Expansion.Disjunction | 0.00 | 0.00 | 0.00 |
| Expansion.Equivalence | 0.00 | 0.00 | 0.00 |
| Expansion.Instantiation | 64.71 | 73.33 | 68.75 |
| Expansion.Level-of-detail | 60.95 | 53.78 | 57.14 |
| Expansion.Manner | 48.28 | 68.29 | 56.57 |
| Expansion.Substitution | 53.33 | 72.73 | 61.54 |
| Temporal.Asynchronous | 72.97 | 65.85 | 69.23 |
| Temporal.Synchronous | 66.67 | 76.92 | 71.43 |
| Micro Average | 75.19 | 75.19 | 75.19 |
| Weighted Average | 75.98 | 75.19 | 75.19 |

Table 13: Full results on test set for sense classification. We only included senses existing in the test set.

| Sense | Precision | Recall | $F_1$ |
|---|---|---|---|
| Comparison.Concession | $21.75 \pm 21.91$ | $17.62 \pm 19.07$ | $17.15 \pm 15.73$ |
| Comparison.Contrast | $45.79 \pm 16.14$ | $47.23 \pm 12.42$ | $44.93 \pm 12.39$ |
| Contingency.Cause | $76.50 \pm 4.22$ | $74.60 \pm 4.89$ | $75.31 \pm 2.14$ |
| Contingency.Cause+Belief | $11.44 \pm 8.82$ | $21.78 \pm 17.88$ | $14.62 \pm 11.41$ |
| Contingency.Condition | $73.29 \pm 9.99$ | $77.34 \pm 8.69$ | $74.28 \pm 3.60$ |
| Contingency.Purpose | $86.78 \pm 2.05$ | $90.49 \pm 2.66$ | $88.56 \pm 1.57$ |
| Expansion.Conjunction | $73.99 \pm 8.05$ | $70.33 \pm 5.55$ | $71.82 \pm 5.03$ |
| Expansion.Disjunction | $0.00 \pm 0.00$ | $0.00 \pm 0.00$ | $0.00 \pm 0.00$ |
| Expansion.Equivalence | $24.83 \pm 31.10$ | $20.67 \pm 21.33$ | $20.67 \pm 21.33$ |
| Expansion.Instantiation | $25.97 \pm 14.89$ | $39.10 \pm 24.73$ | $29.11 \pm 13.85$ |
| Expansion.Level-of-detail | $57.79 \pm 4.70$ | $48.23 \pm 3.12$ | $52.37 \pm 2.06$ |
| Expansion.Manner | $44.10 \pm 12.40$ | $47.07 \pm 9.91$ | $44.18 \pm 7.96$ |
| Expansion.Substitution | $68.01 \pm 22.64$ | $66.02 \pm 15.04$ | $65.23 \pm 17.92$ |
| Temporal.Asynchronous | $57.88 \pm 13.06$ | $51.39 \pm 13.06$ | $52.81 \pm 9.81$ |
| Temporal.Synchronous | $56.99 \pm 13.29$ | $53.73 \pm 17.83$ | $53.84 \pm 13.07$ |
| Micro Average | $69.54 \pm 1.30$ | $69.54 \pm 1.30$ | $69.54 \pm 1.30$ |
| Weighted Average | $70.86 \pm 1.45$ | $69.54 \pm 1.30$ | $69.65 \pm 1.36$ |

Table 14: Full results on cross-validation for sense classification.

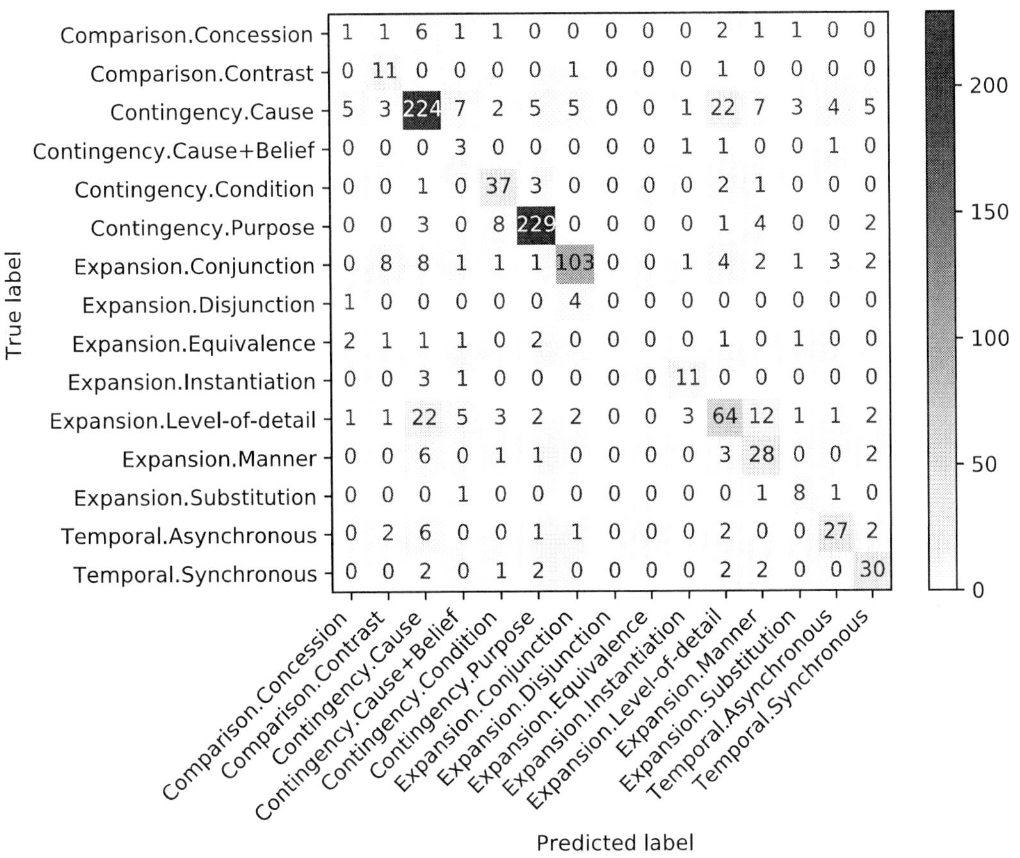


Figure 3: Confusion matrix of our sense classifier on the test set.

| Sense | Predicted arguments | | | Gold arguments | | |
|---|---|---|---|---|---|---|
| | Precision | Recall | $F_1$ | Precision | Recall | $F_1$ |
| Comparison.Concession | 11.11 | 8.33 | 9.52 | 10.0 | 8.33 | 9.09 |
| Comparison.Contrast | 34.62 | 75.0 | 47.37 | 40.74 | 91.67 | 56.41 |
| Contingency.Cause | 75.93 | 73.21 | 74.55 | 79.25 | 75.00 | 77.06 |
| Contingency.Cause+Belief | 17.65 | 60.0 | 27.27 | 11.11 | 40.0 | 17.39 |
| Contingency.Condition | 66.04 | 85.37 | 74.47 | 62.96 | 82.93 | 71.58 |
| Contingency.Purpose | 85.90 | 88.64 | 87.25 | 87.01 | 91.36 | 89.14 |
| Expansion.Conjunction | 74.55 | 68.33 | 71.30 | 83.00 | 69.17 | 75.45 |
| Expansion.Disjunction | 0.00 | 0.00 | 0.00 | 0.00 | 0.00 | 0.00 |
| Expansion.Equivalence | 0.00 | 0.00 | 0.00 | 0.00 | 0.00 | 0.00 |
| Expansion.Instantiation | 44.44 | 33.33 | 38.10 | 58.33 | 58.33 | 58.33 |
| Expansion.Level-of-detail | 53.41 | 43.52 | 47.96 | 57.30 | 47.22 | 51.78 |
| Expansion.Manner | 40.00 | 55.56 | 46.51 | 42.31 | 61.11 | 50.0 |
| Expansion.Substitution | 57.14 | 72.73 | 64.0 | 50.0 | 72.73 | 59.26 |
| Temporal.Asynchronous | 62.86 | 56.41 | 59.46 | 66.67 | 56.41 | 61.11 |
| Temporal.Synchronous | 65.0 | 68.42 | 66.67 | 63.41 | 68.42 | 65.82 |
| Micro Average | 69.30 | 69.30 | 69.30 | 71.52 | 71.52 | 71.52 |
| Weighted Average | 69.35 | 69.30 | 68.95 | 72.27 | 71.52 | 71.39 |

Table 15: Comparison of full results on test set for sense classification using predicted arguments versus using gold arguments.

# Improving Multi-Party Dialogue Discourse Parsing via Domain Integration

**Zhengyuan Liu, Nancy F. Chen**
Institute for Infocomm Research, A*STAR, Singapore
{liu_zhengyuan,nfychen}@i2r.a-star.edu.sg

## Abstract

While multi-party conversations are often less structured than monologues and documents, they are implicitly organized by semantic level correlations across the interactive turns, and dialogue discourse analysis can be applied to predict the dependency structure and relations between the elementary discourse units, and provide feature-rich structural information for downstream tasks. However, the existing corpora with dialogue discourse annotation are collected from specific domains with limited sample sizes, rendering the performance of data-driven approaches poor on incoming dialogues without any domain adaptation. In this paper, we first introduce a Transformer-based parser, and assess its cross-domain performance. We next adopt three methods to gain domain integration from both data and language modeling perspectives to improve the generalization capability. Empirical results show that the neural parser can benefit from our proposed methods, and performs better on cross-domain dialogue samples.

## 1 Introduction

Text-level discourse parsing is to convert a piece of text into a structured format, by identifying the links and relations between Elementary Discourse Units (EDUs). Incorporating discourse information is proved beneficial for various natural language processing tasks such as machine comprehension (Narasimhan and Barzilay, 2015) and summarization (Xu et al., 2020). Since discourse parsing is involved in capturing and comprehending various semantic and pragmatic phenomena as well as understanding the structural discourse properties, it is quite challenging for machines to conduct automatic processing. There are a series of studies that provide theories and data for developing computational solutions, such as the Penn Discourse Treebank (PDTB) (Prasad et al., 2008) with sentence-level annotation, and the Rhetorical Structure Theory (RST) (Carlson et al., 2002) with document-level annotation. In RST treebanks, each processed passage is in a hierarchical constituency-based tree structure, and adjacent EDUs are merged to form larger spans[1] recursively (Li et al., 2014a).

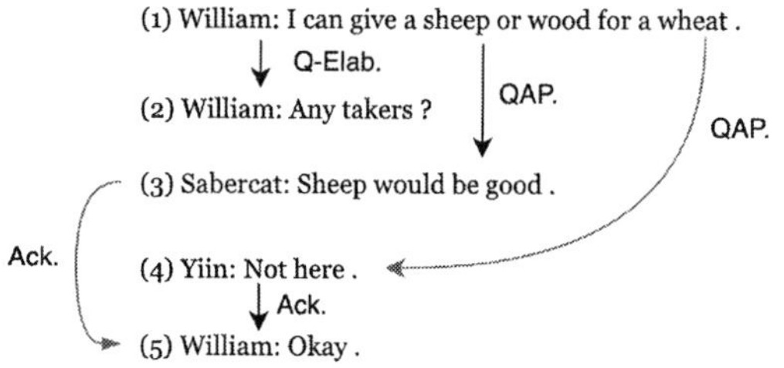


Figure 1: A multi-party dialogue example (Shi and Huang, 2019) with discourse link and relation annotation in the STAC Corpus (Asher et al., 2016). "Ack." is short for relation "Acknowledgement", "QAP." for "Question-Answer-Pair", and "Q-Elab." for "Question-Elaboration". The links in red form a non-projective structure (McDonald et al., 2005).

Recently, the Segmented Discourse Representation Theory (SDRT) is proposed for multi-party dialogue discourse parsing (Asher and Lascarides, 2005; Asher et al., 2016), which is different from RST whose annotations are on documents. Additionally, SDRT-based annotations contain non-projective links. For example, as shown in Figure 1, a discourse structure will become non-projective when it is impossible to draw the relations on the same side without crossing (McDonald et al., 2005). In this case, the constituency-based structure is not applicable. As a result, the SDRT proposed to transform dialogue discourse trees to a dependency-based structure, where EDUs are directly linked to their precedents without forming upper-level spans.

Since manual parsing is labor-intensive and time-consuming, automatic discourse analysis under the

[1]The merged spans are named as complex discourse units (CDUs) in which multiple EDUs and/or CDUs are grouped together to form a single argument to a discourse relation (Asher et al., 2016)



*Proceedings of the 2nd Workshop on Computational Approaches to Discourse*, pages 122–127
November 10–11, 2021. ©2021 Association for Computational Linguistics

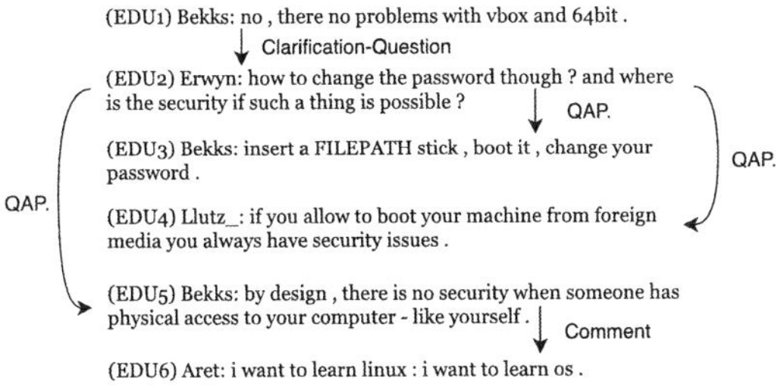


Figure 2: A multi-party dialogue example with its discourse annotation from the Molweni (Li et al., 2020).

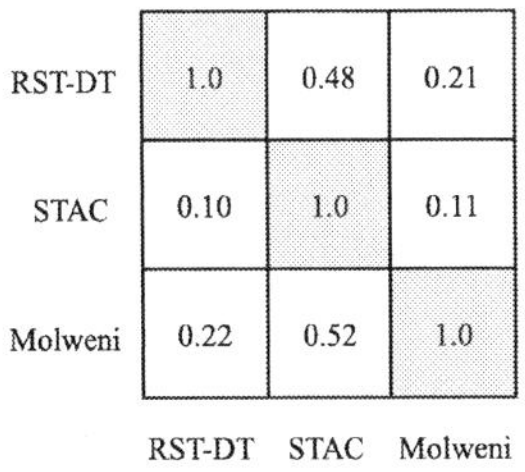


Figure 3: Word level vocabulary overlap of three text-level discourse treebanks. The vocabulary sizes of RST-DT, STAC, and Molweni are 17824, 3642, and 18936, respectively.

| | RST-DT | STAC | Molweni |
|---|---|---|---|
| Training Sample Size | 347 | 1091 | 9000 |
| Test Sample Size | 38 | 100 | 500 |
| Average EDU Number | 56.03 | 10.95 | 8.82 |
| Average Word Number | 531.8 | 46.7 | 96.1 |
| Annotation Scheme | RST | SDRT | SDRT |
| Relation Number | 18 | 17 | 17 |
| Data Domain | News | Game | Ubuntu |
| Conversational Data | No | Yes | Yes |

Table 1: Data statistics of training samples from three text-level discourse parsing treebanks.

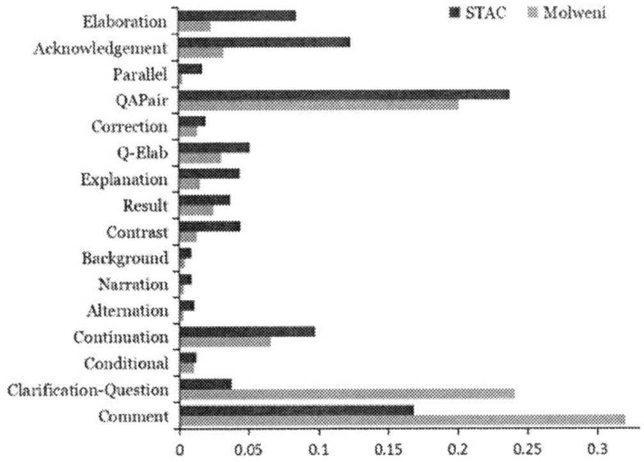


Figure 4: Discourse relation distributions of STAC and Molweni. X axis denotes the label frequency.

SDRT theory raises research interest (Badene et al., 2019). Previous models show reasonable results on benchmark treebanks (Shi and Huang, 2019), and utilizing structural information benefits follow-up applications such as dialogue summarization (Feng et al., 2020). However, domain generality is less studied yet important in practical use cases. Existing treebanks only contain limited training data (as shown in Table 1) and limited domain coverage. An SDRT parser trained on strategic game conversations (Asher et al., 2016) may not perform well on technical discussions (Li et al., 2020), and the sub-optimal parsing could further affect downstream task performance. Moreover, due to the annotation complexity, the labeled samples from various domains are not readily available for transfer learning (Yu et al., 2019).

In this paper, we evaluate and improve the cross-domain generality of neural dialogue discourse parsing: (1) we conduct a statistical analysis on existing dialogue discourse treebanks, and figure out the possible factors resulting in the gap across multiple domains from a data perspective; (2) we introduce a Transformer-based neural model for the dependency-based discourse parsing; (3) we propose three methods for better sharing the effective features across dialogue domains: utilizing prior language knowledge, cross-domain pre-training, and vocabulary refinement. Experimental results on STAC (Asher et al., 2016) and Molweni (Li et al., 2020) show that the parsing performance of single-domain training drops significantly on the out-of-domain samples, and it can be improved by our proposed methods.

## 2 Corpora Analysis

In this section, we conduct a statistical analysis of three text-level discourse treebanks for data-related factors that potentially affect model generality.

**RST Discourse Treebank** (RST-DT) (Carlson et al., 2002) is the first corpus for text-level document parsing, and contains articles from the Wall Street Journal (WSJ). While it is not in the dialogue domain, we include it for an extensive comparison.

**STAC** (Asher et al., 2016) is the first corpus for multi-party dialogue discourse parsing, and built on 1.2k strategic conversations where participants take discussion during playing an online game.

**Molweni** (Li et al., 2020) follows the same annotation scheme as STAC, and the data (12k samples) are collected from an online forum, where people discuss technical topics about the Ubuntu system.

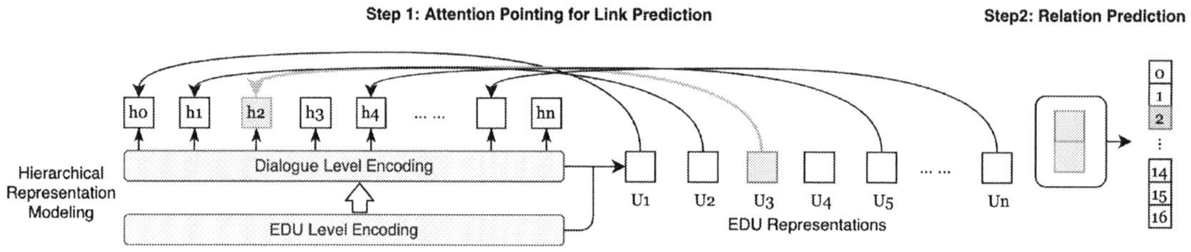


Figure 5: Overview of the dependency-based discourse parsing framework.

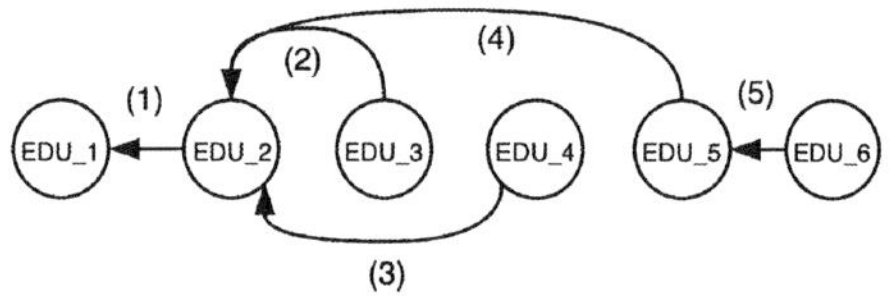


Figure 6: Illustration of parsing process on the dialogue example shown in Figure 2. Numbers in brackets denote the order of link prediction, which is in a sequential manner. This produces a dependency structure.

The data statistics are summarized in Table 1. (1) Compared with Molweni, the RST-DT and STAC have much smaller sample sizes. (2) Samples from RST-DT have a larger EDU number than STAC and Molweni, resulting in deeper parsed tree structures. The tree depth is one of the major factors that affect parsing complexity. (3) Interestingly, while the word number of Molweni is two times larger than that of STAC, no significant difference in their average EDU numbers, resulting in a similar parsing complexity from a depth perspective. (4) The lexical distributions of STAC and Molweni are significantly different sharing a small portion of common vocabulary (Figure 3), as they focus on different conversation scenarios (*Game* vs. *Ubuntu*). (5) Despite the domain distinction between STAC and Molweni, their relation distributions are similar, except that frequencies of the relation (*Clarification-Question* and *Comment*) are quite different, probably because the online technical forums contain more question-clarification and comments (Figure 4). While STAC and Molweni are annotated under the same SDRT theory, their lexical features and relation distributions are different, which we speculate will influence the domain generality.

## 3 Dialogue Discourse Parsing

### 3.1 Task Definition

Given a dialogue that has been segmented into a sequence of EDUs $\{u_0, u_1, ..., u_n\}$ where $n$ is the EDU number, the discourse parser is applied to predict links and the corresponding relation types between the EDUs. The predicted structure constitutes a dependency tree, which is a special type of Directed Acyclic Graph (DAG). As in previous work (Shi and Huang, 2019), each EDU is only linked to one of their precedent EDUs, and there are no backward links. As shown in Figure 6, the parsing process can be conducted by a sequential scan of the EDUs. For one EDU $u_i$, the model predicts a dependency link by estimating a probability distribution as $P(u_j|u_i, U_i^{pair})$ where $0 \leq j < i$ and $U_i^{pair} = \{(u_l, u_k, r_{l,k})|0 \leq l < k < i\}$ is the set of already predicted pairs before the current step $i$. The model then determines the relation type based on the predicted link $P(r_{i,j}|u_i, u_j)$ where $j < i$ and $r_{i,j}$ is in the range of $[0, C]$ ($C$ is the number of relation types). Following Li et al. (2014b), we add a *root* node as $u_0$, and if one EDU is not linked from any preceding nodes, it is pointed to $u_0$.

### 3.2 Transformer-Based Discourse Parser

In this paper, based on the sequential parsing process (Shi and Huang, 2019), we introduce a Transformer-based model for dialogue discourse parsing (as shown in Figure 5), which is comprised of the following components:

**Hierarchical Encoder.** The encoder computes EDU global representations in a hierarchical manner. A Transformer encoder (Vaswani et al., 2017) is used for token-level encoding.[2]

$$H_{token} = \text{TransformerEnc}([t_0, t_1, ..., t_m]) \quad (1)$$

where $t$ denotes token, and $m$ denotes token number. For the $i$-th EDU, its local representation $h^i_{edu}$ is obtained by averaging[3] its corresponding tokens hidden states. Then the local EDU representations

[2] Due to space limitation, refer to (Vaswani et al., 2017) for more details of the Transformer architecture.

[3] We also adopt *first-and-last* sum and *only-first* sum for EDU representation, and the averaging performs best.

are fed to a bi-directional GRU component (Chung et al., 2014) for dialogue-level encoding, and we get final representations $H'$ with both local and global information.

$$h'_i = [\text{GRU}^{Forward}_{h^i_{edu}}; \text{GRU}^{Backward}_{h^i_{edu}}] \quad (2)$$

**Link Prediction.** An attentive pointer network (Vinyals et al., 2015) is used for the link prediction. For the $i$-th EDU, we compute a list of attentive scores with a linear layer between the current node and each candidate $h'_i$ where $j < i$. Then scores are normalized by softmax function to a distribution over the previous EDUs, and we obtain the linked EDU with the largest pointing probability.

$$s_{i,j} = \text{Linear}([h'_i; h'_j]) \quad (3)$$

$$a_{i,j} = \frac{\exp(s_{i,j})}{\sum_{j=0}^{i} \exp(s_{i,j})} \quad (4)$$

**Relation Classification.** Given one linked pair is $h'_i$ and $h'_j$, we concatenate and feed them to a relation classifier (a linear component):

$$r_{i,j} = \text{Linear}([h'_i; h'_j]) \quad (5)$$

then the output is a probability over the 17 predefined discourse relations. For link and relation prediction, the negative log-likelihood is adopted for the loss function.

## 4 Cross-Domain Integration

Based on the corpora analysis in Section 2, to improve the domain-level generality, we investigate three methods to encourage the neural model to utilize the shared linguistic features from different dialogue domains.

**Utilizing Language Backbone.** Large-scale pre-trained language models provide feature-rich contextualized representations (Devlin et al., 2019). In previous work, utilizing prior knowledge can boost the performance in parsing tasks, and also shows some but still limited generalization capability at domain and language level (Liu et al., 2020). Here, we select the *'RoBERTa-base'* model (Liu et al., 2019) as the language backbone.

**Cross-Domain Pre-training.** Following Gururangan et al. (2020), we conduct the masked language modeling pre-training with the joint data of STAC and Molweni. This can fuse dialogue-related linguistic features to the language backbone, which is not pre-trained on human conversations. Moreover,

| Train on Joint Data | Link | Link+Rel. |
|---|---|---|
| Deep Sequential Parser (Shi and Huang, 2019) | | |
| Test on STAC | 72.8 | 54.8 |
| Test on Molweni | 77.4 | 54.3 |
| Our Proposed Parser w/ language backbone | | |
| Test on STAC | **75.5** | **57.2** |
| Test on Molweni | **80.2** | **56.9** |

Table 2: F1 scores of link and relation prediction with models trained on the joint data (**STAC+Molweni**).

| Train on STAC | Link | Link+Rel. |
|---|---|---|
| Deep Sequential Parser (Shi and Huang, 2019) | | |
| Test on STAC | 73.1 | 55.7 |
| Test on Molweni | 58.6 | 26.2 |
| Our Transformer-Based Parser | | |
| Test on STAC | 73.4 | 55.5 |
| Test on Molweni | 57.8 | 26.4 |
| + Utilizing Language Backbone | | |
| Test on STAC | 75.3 [2.5% ↑] | 56.9 [2.5% ↑] |
| Test on Molweni | 60.7 [5.0% ↑] | 31.5 [19.3% ↑] |
| + Cross-Domain Pre-training | | |
| Test on STAC | 75.1 [2.3% ↑] | 57.1 [2.8% ↑] |
| Test on Molweni | 62.1 [7.4% ↑] | 32.6 [23.4% ↑] |
| + Cross-Domain Vocabulary Refinement | | |
| Test on STAC | 75.3 [2.3% ↑] | 57.1 [2.8% ↑] |
| Test on Molweni | 63.2 [9.3% ↑] | 33.1 [25.3% ↑] |

Table 3: Micro-F1 scores of link and relation prediction with models trained on **STAC**. Values in brackets denote relative increase over the base model.

pre-training with multiple data resources can increase the domain coverage, and this step (parsing annotation is not required) can be conducted before the task-specified learning.

**Cross-Domain Vocabulary Refinement.** STIn Section 2, we observe that the vocabulary overlap between STAC and Molweni is limited (see Figure 3). Dialogues in Molweni contain a certain amount of technical-related words, whereas STAC contains more game-related words. As the model may overfit corpus-specified lexical features, a vocabulary refinement is adopted by filtering out words that are in lower frequency (< 20 occurrence) and not shared by the two datasets.

## 5 Experimental Result and Analysis

### 5.1 Configuration

The proposed models were implemented using PyTorch (Paszke et al., 2019) and Hugging Face[4]. Learning rate was set at 2e-5, and the AdamW (Loshchilov and Hutter, 2019) optimizer was ap-

[4]https://github.com/huggingface/transformers

| Train on Molweni | Link | Link+Rel. |
|---|---|---|
| Deep Sequential Parser (Shi and Huang, 2019) | | |
| Test on STAC | 42.5 | 18.3 |
| Test on Molweni | 77.9 | 54.4 |
| Our Transformer-Based Parser | | |
| Test on STAC | 42.3 | 18.0 |
| Test on Molweni | 75.9 | 52.5 |
| + Utilizing Language Backbone | | |
| Test on STAC | 48.3 [14.2% ↑] | 26.6 [47.7% ↑] |
| Test on Molweni | 79.7 [5.1% ↑] | 55.9 [6.4% ↑] |
| + Cross-Domain Pre-training | | |
| Test on STAC | 48.8 [15.3% ↑] | 28.4 [57.7% ↑] |
| Test on Molweni | 79.6 [5.0% ↑] | 55.7 [6.1% ↑] |
| + Cross-Domain Vocabulary Refinement | | |
| Test on STAC | 50.5 [19.4% ↑] | 28.9 [60.6% ↑] |
| Test on Molweni | 79.5 [5.0% ↑] | 55.7 [6.1% ↑] |

Table 4: Micro-F1 scores of link and relation prediction with models trained on **Molweni**. Values in brackets denote relative increase over the base model.

plied. We trained each model for 20 epochs, and selected the best checkpoints based on evaluation scores. Input dialogue sequences were processed with the sub-word tokenization scheme used in *'RoBERTa-base'* (Liu et al., 2019).

At the inference stage, we adopted the micro-averaged F1 score as the evaluation metric. Results of different settings are shown in Table 2-4. *"Link"* denotes link prediction, and *"Link+Rel."* stands for a prediction that the dependency link and relation type are correct at the same time.

### 5.2 Joint Domain Evaluation

To compare performance between single-domain and joint-domain training, we obtain the upper bound parsing results on the merged data of two dialogue discourse treebanks (STAC and Molweni). As shown in Table 2, models trained on merged data achieve favorable results on both corpora, and perform slightly better than single-domain training. Moreover, our Transformer-based model with the language backbone outperforms the previous state-of-the-art baseline.

### 5.3 Cross-Domain Evaluation

To evaluate the effectiveness of the proposed domain integration methods, we conduct single-corpus training and cross-corpus evaluation (each treebank represents one dialogue domain).

For single-corpus training on STAC, as shown in Table 3, the cross-domain performance on Molweni data of all models drops significantly, especially the relation prediction. Utilizing language backbone brings substantial improvement. This shows that linguistic features can be shared by samples from different treebanks under the SDRT theory. Adopting cross-domain pre-training and vocabulary refinement further improve the performance, and do not affect the original domain. Combining three methods provides the parser a relative 25.3% improvement on the link+relation F1.

For single-corpus training on Molweni, as shown in Table 4, baseline models obtain low link+relation F1 scores (around 18.0) on the STAC corpus. Noteworthy, the performance decrease of *STAC(train)->Molweni(test)* is smaller than that of *Molweni(train)->STAC(test)*, we speculate that this may stem from a larger linguistic diversity in STAC data. The scores are significantly elevated by adopting language backbone, cross-domain pre-training, and vocabulary refinement, achieving a relative 60.6% improvement on link+relation F1.

## 6 Conclusion

In this paper, we investigated the domain-level generality of dialogue discourse parsing. Since existing corpora are collected from different conversation scenarios, models with single-domain training cannot perform well in other domains. The statistical analysis and experimental results suggest that domain adaptation or integration is necessary when neural parsers are applied in practical use cases, and utilizing prior language knowledge and adopting cross-domain pre-training can improve their generality.

## Acknowledgments

This research was supported by funding from the Institute for Infocomm Research (I2R) under A*STAR ARES, Singapore. We thank Ai Ti Aw for the insightful discussions. We also thank the anonymous reviewers for their precious feedback to help improve and extend this piece of work.

## References

Nicholas Asher, Julie Hunter, Mathieu Morey, Benamara Farah, and Stergos Afantenos. 2016. Discourse structure and dialogue acts in multiparty dialogue: the stac corpus. In *Proceedings of the Tenth International Conference on Language Resources and Evaluation (LREC'16)*, pages 2721–2727.

Nicholas Asher and A. Lascarides. 2005. Logics of conversation. In *Studies in natural language processing*. Cambridge University Press.

Sonia Badene, Kate Thompson, Jean-Pierre Lorré, and Nicholas Asher. 2019. Weak supervision for learning discourse structure. In *Proceedings of the 2019 Conference on Empirical Methods in Natural Language Processing and the 9th International Joint Conference on Natural Language Processing (EMNLP-IJCNLP)*, pages 2296–2305.

Lynn Carlson, Mary Ellen Okurowski, and Daniel Marcu. 2002. *RST discourse treebank*. Linguistic Data Consortium, University of Pennsylvania.

Junyoung Chung, Caglar Gulcehre, Kyunghyun Cho, and Yoshua Bengio. 2014. Empirical evaluation of gated recurrent neural networks on sequence modeling. In *NIPS 2014 Workshop on Deep Learning, December 2014*.

Jacob Devlin, Ming-Wei Chang, Kenton Lee, and Kristina Toutanova. 2019. BERT: Pre-training of deep bidirectional transformers for language understanding. In *Proceedings of NAACL2019*, pages 4171–4186, Minneapolis, Minnesota. Association for Computational Linguistics.

Xiachong Feng, Xiaocheng Feng, Bing Qin, Xinwei Geng, and Ting Liu. 2020. Dialogue discourse-aware graph convolutional networks for abstractive meeting summarization. *arXiv preprint arXiv:2012.03502*.

Suchin Gururangan, Ana Marasović, Swabha Swayamdipta, Kyle Lo, Iz Beltagy, Doug Downey, and Noah A. Smith. 2020. Don't stop pretraining: Adapt language models to domains and tasks. In *Proceedings of ACL*.

Jiaqi Li, Ming Liu, Min-Yen Kan, Zihao Zheng, Zekun Wang, Wenqiang Lei, Ting Liu, and Bing Qin. 2020. Molweni: A challenge multiparty dialogues-based machine reading comprehension dataset with discourse structure. In *Proceedings of the 28th International Conference on Computational Linguistics*, pages 2642–2652.

Jiwei Li, Rumeng Li, and Eduard Hovy. 2014a. Recursive deep models for discourse parsing. In *Proceedings of the 2014 Conference on Empirical Methods in Natural Language Processing (EMNLP)*, pages 2061–2069.

Sujian Li, Liang Wang, Ziqiang Cao, and Wenjie Li. 2014b. Text-level discourse dependency parsing. In *Proceedings of the 52nd Annual Meeting of the Association for Computational Linguistics*, pages 25–35.

Yinhan Liu, Myle Ott, Naman Goyal, Jingfei Du, Mandar Joshi, Danqi Chen, Omer Levy, Mike Lewis, Luke Zettlemoyer, and Veselin Stoyanov. 2019. Roberta: A robustly optimized bert pretraining approach. *arXiv preprint arXiv:1907.11692*.

Zhengyuan Liu, Ke Shi, and Nancy Chen. 2020. Multilingual neural RST discourse parsing. In *Proceedings of the 28th International Conference on Computational Linguistics*, pages 6730–6738, Barcelona, Spain (Online). International Committee on Computational Linguistics.

Ilya Loshchilov and Frank Hutter. 2019. Decoupled weight decay regularization. *The International Conference on Learning Representations (ICLR2019)*.

Ryan McDonald, Fernando Pereira, Kiril Ribarov, and Jan Hajic. 2005. Non-projective dependency parsing using spanning tree algorithms. In *Proceedings of human language technology conference and conference on empirical methods in natural language processing*, pages 523–530.

Karthik Narasimhan and Regina Barzilay. 2015. Machine comprehension with discourse relations. In *Proceedings of the 53rd Annual Meeting of the Association for Computational Linguistics and the 7th International Joint Conference on Natural Language Processing*, pages 1253–1262, Beijing, China. Association for Computational Linguistics.

Adam Paszke, Sam Gross, Francisco Massa, Adam Lerer, James Bradbury, Gregory Chanan, Trevor Killeen, Zeming Lin, Natalia Gimelshein, Luca Antiga, et al. 2019. Pytorch: An imperative style, high-performance deep learning library. In *Proceedings of NeurIPS2019*, pages 8026–8037.

Rashmi Prasad, Nikhil Dinesh, Alan Lee, Eleni Miltsakaki, Livio Robaldo, Aravind K Joshi, and Bonnie L Webber. 2008. The penn discourse treebank 2.0. In *LREC*. Citeseer.

Zhouxing Shi and Minlie Huang. 2019. A deep sequential model for discourse parsing on multi-party dialogues. In *Proceedings of the AAAI Conference on Artificial Intelligence*, volume 33, pages 7007–7014.

Ashish Vaswani, Noam Shazeer, Niki Parmar, Jakob Uszkoreit, Llion Jones, Aidan N Gomez, Łukasz Kaiser, and Illia Polosukhin. 2017. Attention is all you need. In *Proceedings of NeurIPS2017*, pages 5998–6008.

Oriol Vinyals, Meire Fortunato, and Navdeep Jaitly. 2015. Pointer networks. In *Advances in Neural Information Processing Systems*, volume 28. Curran Associates, Inc.

Jiacheng Xu, Zhe Gan, Yu Cheng, and Jingjing Liu. 2020. Discourse-aware neural extractive text summarization. In *Proceedings of the 58th Annual Meeting of the Association for Computational Linguistics*, pages 5021–5031, Online. Association for Computational Linguistics.

Chaohui Yu, Jindong Wang, Yiqiang Chen, and Meiyu Huang. 2019. Transfer learning with dynamic adversarial adaptation network. In *2019 IEEE International Conference on Data Mining (ICDM)*, pages 778–786. IEEE.

# discopy: A Neural System for Shallow Discourse Parsing

**René Knaebel**
Applied Computational Linguistics
Department of Linguistics
University of Potsdam
Germany
rene.knaebel@uni-potsdam.de

## Abstract

This paper demonstrates `discopy`, a novel framework that makes it easy to design components for end-to-end shallow discourse parsing. For the purpose of demonstration, we implement recent neural approaches and integrate contextualized word embeddings to predict explicit and non-explicit discourse relations. Our proposed neural feature-free system performs competitively to systems presented at the latest Shared Task on Shallow Discourse Parsing. Finally, a web front end is shown that simplifies the inspection of annotated documents. The source code, documentation, and pretrained models are publicly accessible.

## 1 Introduction

Whenever people compose text, they (consciously or not) make sure that related sentences are cohesive and coherent within a common section. By using models to analyze discourse, we identify relations within a text that consist of phrases and a certain sense. These discourse relations and their understanding are important for other tasks in the NLP community such as abstractive summarization (Gerani et al., 2014), text simplification (Zhong et al., 2020), and argumentation mining (Hewett et al., 2019). The Penn Discourse Treebank (PDTB) (Prasad et al., 2008), for example, describes discourse as a set of individual relations. The following two (artificial) examples demonstrate the main types of relations annotated in their corpus:

1. While **it is raining outside**, *I clean the dishes*. (Temporal.Synchronous)

2. *Yesterday I walked through the rain*, **today I am sick**. (Contingency.Cause)

Relations consist of two *arguments* (Arg1 in italics and Arg2 in bold) and a *sense* (e.g. Temporal.Synchronous[1]) is assigned. The first example is called an *explicit* relation, because the relation is signaled by a phrase called *connective* (Conn is underlined). The second example refers to the group of *implicit* relations because of the absence of a connective that signals the relation. Additionally, if adjacent sentences have an *entity-based* relation, they are marked as EntRel.

The area of *shallow discourse parsing* (SDP) aims to build models finding aforementioned discourse structures. Started through the development of PDTB, shallow discourse parsing gained more awareness by two shared Tasks (Xue et al., 2015, 2016). Successful systems at the last competition were those of Wang and Lan (2016); Qin et al. (2016); Schenk et al. (2016); Oepen et al. (2016); Stepanov and Riccardi (2016).

This work introduces an end-to-end neural system that implements recently researched components for these tasks. Our goal is to design components that all rely on the same contextualized word embeddings as input and, thus, it avoids the necessity to train huge neural networks. We compare our results with state-of-the-art shallow discourse parsers that took part at the CoNLL Shared Task in 2016 (Xue et al., 2016) which is to our knowledge the last time full systems were published. The contributions of this paper are as follows:

1. We introduce a simple modular and easily extendable framework for shallow discourse parsing. We also provide pretrained systems by recent advances in word representations that demonstrate competitive performance compared to existing systems.

2. We provide a first version of a web front end to visualize parser outputs and, optionally, to connect a parser via REST API.

[1] Senses are ordered in a hierarchy of up to three levels. Temporal refers to the first level and Synchronous to the second, respectively.



*Proceedings of the 2nd Workshop on Computational Approaches to Discourse*, pages 128–133
November 10–11, 2021. 

## 2 System Architecture

In our framework `discopy`, we design a clean and modular parser pipeline principle. Each component has to implement a specified interface that assumes to process a well defined document structure. Starting with a document without annotated discourse relations, each component further adds its predictions while the document is passed through the pipeline, for example one component identifies connectives and their sense and, based on this prediction, another component extracts arguments around these connectives to complete the explicit relations. This parser architecture makes the definition of a custom pipeline easy and components remain interchangeable. Together with the framework, we provide multiple components for an end-to-end neural shallow discourse parser. The simple pipeline interface (exemplified in Listing 2) with methods such as *fit*, *parse*, and *eval*, ensures pleasant user experience. The system combines recent research on various subtasks with advances in contextualized word embeddings. We make the framework and pre-trained components available under `https://github.com/rknaebel/discopy`. In the following, we briefly summarize the components implemented in our system.

```
# load pdtb documents with contextualized embeddings
docs_train = load_bert_conll_dataset(...)
docs_val = load_bert_conll_dataset(...)
# definition of the parser pipeline by list of
    components
parser = ParserPipeline([
    # add connective and its sense
    ConnectiveSenseClassifier(...),
    # use connective to add explicit arguments
    ConnectiveArgumentExtractor(...),
    # extract adjacent sentences without explicit
      relation
    ImplicitArgumentExtractor(),
    # attach implicit sense
    ArgumentSenseClassifier(...),
])
# fit custom pipeline on annotated documents
parser.fit(docs_train, docs_val)
# extract discourse relations
parses = parser.parse(docs_val)
```

Listing 1: Discopy pipeline source code example.

**Contextualized Word Embeddings.** We start by generating contextualized embeddings for each document. These embeddings come from a chosen BERT architecture that is provided by the Hugging Face `transformers` library (Wolf et al., 2020). Pre-tokenized sentences are processed again by a specific BERT tokenizer which results in a possibly higher number of sub-tokens as the input sequence. For each input token, we select and concatenate the last four hidden layers that correspond to the first sub-token, following the principle demonstrated by Devlin et al. (2019) that performed best using the BERT architecture as a feature extractor. Each component in our discourse parser uses the same input embeddings. This has the advantage, to only produce the computation-intense embeddings once in the beginning.

**Connective Sense Classifier.** The first component in the pipeline refers to the problem of connective disambiguation and explicit sense classification. This component is based on the work of Knaebel and Stede (2020) of which we use the jointly trained model to keep the number of components as small as possible. The component first extracts connective candidates based on a pattern-matching approach. Then, these candidates are classified as having a sentential meaning or a connective meaning which is indicated by a predicted sense class. The idea of using the same features for both tasks originates from Pitler and Nenkova (2009).

**Explicit Connective Argument Extractor.** The component that is responsible to extract explicit arguments creates a window surrounding the previously predicted connective and searches for corresponding arguments (`Arg1` and `Arg2`) within this span. We extend the connective argument extractor of Knaebel et al. (2019) and replace GloVe embeddings (Pennington et al., 2014) by our contextualized embeddings.

**Implicit Sense Classifier.** Implicit relations are annotated on adjacent sentences within the same paragraph that do not contain any other explicit relation. For the implicit sense classifier, we choose a simple approach and collect all implicit candidate sentence pairs. We follow previous work by Rutherford et al. (2017) which has been recently chosen as a baseline in work by Liang et al. (2020). There, embeddings for both arguments are collected and processed by a recurrent neural network. Then, both intermediate representations are combined using a maximum pooling layer and given to a fully connected layer to predict the implicit sense. We adopt this approach by using our contextualized embeddings, and we add a labels for entity-based relations (EntRel) as well as a for the absence of any relation (NoRel) to the final set of predictions.

## 3 Visualization

In conjunction with our system, we provide a prototypical web-based front end with several views that simplifies the inspection of parser results. It can be used to visualize annotated documents, parse docu-

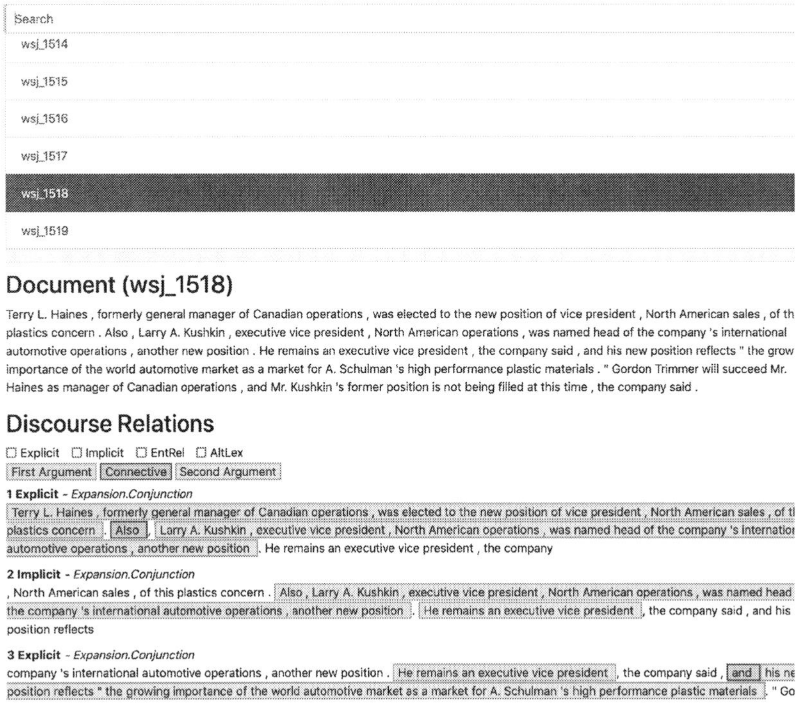


Figure 1: Web-based front end overview. A selected document is shown with its discourse relations in the bottom.

ments, and inspect them interactively. Further, the visual inspection makes it easier to identify weaknesses of a developed parser, e.g. inaccurate connective identification or misplaced argument spans. The system is built on top of a simple Python web service powered by FastAPI[2] and it is designed using a reactive JavaScript library called VueJS[3]. Both sides communicate via RESTful interface with each other.

Figure 1 demonstrates the view of a selected document. At the top, there is a simple search bar for easily accessing documents. Directly below, the document's text is shown together with a list of its discourse relations at the bottom of the view. Then, each discourse relation is listed with its corresponding relation type (e.g. Explicit, Implicit, EntRel, AltLex), as well as its sense. Different parts of a relation, first and second arguments as well as the connective, are highlighted by colors. Additionally, some context tokens are given before and after the relation if possible.

## 4 Experiments

The **connective sense classifier** takes the connective candidate and one surrounding context tokens as input. The two hidden layers both have dimensions 256. A dropout layer follows after each hidden layer with a 0.3 drop rate. Both **argument extractors** use two bi-directional recurrent layers with a hidden size of 256 in each direction, a dropout rate of 0.2 before and after the fully connected layer having a dimension of 128. The **explicit extractor** is trained on explicit examples with a window size of 100. The **implicit sense classifier** accepts two arguments with at most 35 tokens each. The same bi-directional recurrent layer with hidden size 128 processes both arguments. The drop rate of the dropout layer that follows after concatenation is 0.25, and the size of the hidden dimension afterward is 128. All models are trained with AMSGrad Adam (Reddi et al., 2018) and a 0.001 learning rate.

## 5 Results and Discussion

For our evaluation, we use the same experimental design as proposed at the CoNLL Shared Task 2016 (Xue et al., 2016). We have trained multiple pipelines with varying language models used to compute the input embeddings. The model names in our experiment tables follow the naming of the word embedding model[4]. As comparison systems, we choose the overall best performing submissions

[2] `fastapi.tiangolo.com`
[3] `vuejs.org`
[4] Model names follow `huggingface.co/models`

| Model | Explicits | | | | | Implicits | | | |
|---|---|---|---|---|---|---|---|---|---|
| | $F1_{parser}$ | $F1_{conn}$ | $F1_{A1}$ | $F1_{A2}$ | $F1_{A12}$ | $F1_{parser}$ | $F1_{A1}$ | $F1_{A2}$ | $F1_{A12}$ |
| **Standard WSJ Test (Section 23)** | | | | | | | | | |
| ecnucs | 40.31 | 93.96 | 51.39 | 76.43 | 44.31 | 22.38 | 64.66 | 66.86 | 50.83 |
| oslopots | 39.38 | 94.43 | **51.99** | 72.57 | 43.93 | 18.02 | **69.92** | **71.45** | **53.47** |
| bert-base | **62.75** | 95.64 | 51.24 | **78.30** | **51.79** | 25.80 | 45.57 | 46.82 | 39.87 |
| bert-large | 58.44 | 95.00 | 46.67 | 73.56 | 46.56 | 34.01 | 45.40 | 46.64 | 39.68 |
| roberta-base | 60.57 | 96.18 | 48.69 | 76.64 | 49.89 | 33.31 | 45.45 | 46.70 | 39.71 |
| roberta-large | 56.34 | 96.08 | 45.52 | 73.32 | 45.41 | 35.12 | 45.45 | 46.70 | 39.75 |
| albert-base | 60.57 | **96.87** | 47.57 | 76.38 | 48.54 | **40.71** | 45.69 | 46.94 | 39.99 |
| albert-large | 59.30 | 95.18 | 44.65 | 74.30 | 46.47 | 33.16 | 45.57 | 46.75 | 39.75 |
| **Wikipedia Blind Test** | | | | | | | | | |
| ecnucs | 33.94 | 91.34 | 51.05 | 74.20 | 42.84 | 19.54 | 61.05 | 75.83 | 51.15 |
| oslopots | 34.45 | 91.79 | 52.43 | 75.20 | 43.95 | 21.89 | **64.60** | **76.40** | **52.02** |
| bert-base | 57.80 | 93.88 | **56.22** | 74.58 | 53.06 | 23.20 | 44.58 | 55.30 | 41.42 |
| bert-large | 56.89 | 93.32 | 49.72 | 71.61 | 50.46 | 32.44 | 44.61 | 55.28 | 41.46 |
| roberta-base | **59.77** | 93.95 | 54.14 | **77.40** | **56.00** | 36.60 | 44.51 | 55.21 | 41.35 |
| roberta-large | 50.94 | 93.72 | 46.14 | 68.76 | 45.60 | 36.17 | 44.42 | 55.13 | 41.26 |
| albert-base | 55.77 | **94.70** | 50.46 | 74.77 | 49.91 | **39.33** | 44.90 | 55.61 | 41.74 |
| albert-large | 51.93 | 93.73 | 45.70 | 74.01 | 44.98 | 32.66 | 44.73 | 55.44 | 41.58 |

Table 1: Experimental results (**strict** F1 scores) for Section 23 of WSJ and the blind data set proposed for CoNLL Shared Task.

for each test set (`ecnucs` (Wang and Lan, 2016) and `oslopots` (Oepen et al., 2016)). Similar to the Shared Task, we compare two different thresholds: **strict** refers to an exact match of relations while **partial** counts relations as correct if their overlap is at least 70 %. Performances are measured on Section 23 of the PDTB as well as PDTB-like annotated Wikipedia data prepared for the Shared Task.

In Table 1, strict results of the studied models are summarized. In the table's left part pointing to explicit relations, neural models outperform traditional models in most categories except for `Arg1` identification, but still results are pretty close. Especially the `bert-base` model has an overall high performance. Interestingly, `albert-base` performs quite good, even though it has the smallest number of trained parameters. Also, it seems not beneficial in our experimental design to use a *large* version of a model. A reason for that might be the higher number of input values per token leading the model to an unstable training. The performance for implicit relations (arguments and overall) is noticeably weak as we used I fairly simple method for recognizing arguments following Lin et al. (2014). Thereby, the overall implicit results are lowered as relations were not counted as correct during evaluation. The partial scores in Table 2 were expected to be higher compared to their strict counter parts.

## 6 Conclusions

In this work, we demonstrated a framework for shallow discourse parsing and integrated a web-based graphical user interface to study parser outputs. We presented an exemplary pipeline built from neural components that are based on recent models. We extend previous approaches to incorporate precomputed contextualized word embeddings. Our pipeline system performs competitively to former discourse parsers and partially outperforms them, while not using any linguistic features.

In the future, we plan to integrate more recent neural architectures into the system to improve overall scores. Further, we want to improve the graphical interface to seamlessly integrate the visualization directly into the text such as done with brat[5] for dependency parses. Thus, it will be easier to compare multiple relations in their context. Overlapping arguments are a major problem, why we decided to list relations separately. Building on that a view would be useful for comparing discourse relations across documents, e.g. comparing predictions and gold annotations or multiple parser outputs.

## 7 Acknowledgments

This research was funded by the Deutsche Forschungsgemeinschaft (DFG, German Research Foundation), project 455911521.

[5]`brat.nlplab.org`

| Model | Explicits | | | | Implicits | | | |
|---|---|---|---|---|---|---|---|---|
| | $F1_{parser}$ | $F1_{A1}$ | $F1_{A2}$ | $F1_{A12}$ | $F1_{parser}$ | $F1_{A1}$ | $F1_{A2}$ | $F1_{A12}$ |
| **Standard WSJ Test (Section 23)** | | | | | | | | |
| ecnucs | 69.21 | **72.16** | 88.62 | 74.89 | 28.60 | 82.78 | 85.65 | **86.55** |
| oslopots | 65.96 | 70.75 | 86.90 | 71.27 | 24.36 | **84.74** | **86.47** | 85.85 |
| bert-base | 77.59 | 68.47 | **88.68** | 77.53 | 37.96 | 57.59 | 58.42 | 60.44 |
| bert-large | 76.11 | 65.78 | 85.67 | 75.33 | 42.74 | 57.39 | 58.15 | 60.21 |
| roberta-base | 76.19 | 69.21 | 87.12 | **78.17** | 40.97 | 57.28 | 58.25 | 60.19 |
| roberta-large | 73.04 | 64.30 | 86.21 | 74.18 | 43.74 | 57.26 | 58.23 | 60.18 |
| albert-base | 77.99 | 68.50 | **88.67** | 77.99 | **47.37** | 57.58 | 58.55 | 60.57 |
| albert-large | **79.19** | 67.45 | 85.65 | 77.52 | 42.37 | 57.41 | 58.31 | 60.32 |
| **Wikipedia Blind Test** | | | | | | | | |
| ecnucs | 57.25 | 70.19 | 79.67 | 71.69 | 26.90 | 79.53 | 84.11 | 82.73 |
| oslopots | 56.66 | 71.96 | 81.73 | 71.74 | 33.23 | **84.47** | **88.98** | **86.31** |
| bert-base | 74.49 | **73.47** | **83.86** | 79.22 | 35.96 | 57.45 | 60.05 | 60.61 |
| bert-large | 72.48 | 68.65 | 78.29 | 76.81 | 40.97 | 57.42 | 60.00 | 60.45 |
| roberta-base | 73.49 | 72.93 | 83.72 | **80.74** | 45.49 | 57.35 | 59.94 | 60.39 |
| roberta-large | 71.15 | 66.79 | 77.56 | 75.40 | 45.87 | 57.27 | 59.75 | 60.43 |
| albert-base | **75.06** | 71.66 | 83.36 | 80.62 | **48.67** | 57.76 | 60.24 | 60.80 |
| albert-large | 74.49 | 68.64 | 81.18 | 77.60 | 41.57 | 57.69 | 60.17 | 60.62 |

Table 2: Experimental results (**partial** F1 scores with 0.7 overlap) for Section 23 of WSJ and the blind data set proposed for CoNLL Shared Task.

## References


Jacob Devlin, Ming-Wei Chang, Kenton Lee, and Kristina Toutanova. 2019. BERT: Pre-training of deep bidirectional transformers for language understanding. In *Proceedings of the 2019 Conference of the North American Chapter of the Association for Computational Linguistics: Human Language Technologies, Volume 1 (Long and Short Papers)*, pages 4171–4186, Minneapolis, Minnesota. Association for Computational Linguistics.

Shima Gerani, Yashar Mehdad, Giuseppe Carenini, Raymond T. Ng, and Bita Nejat. 2014. Abstractive summarization of product reviews using discourse structure. In *Proceedings of the 2014 Conference on Empirical Methods in Natural Language Processing (EMNLP)*, pages 1602–1613, Doha, Qatar. Association for Computational Linguistics.

Freya Hewett, Roshan Prakash Rane, Nina Harlacher, and Manfred Stede. 2019. The utility of discourse parsing features for predicting argumentation structure. In *Proceedings of the 6th Workshop on Argument Mining*, pages 98–103, Florence, Italy. Association for Computational Linguistics.

René Knaebel and Manfred Stede. 2020. Contextualized embeddings for connective disambiguation in shallow discourse parsing. In *Proceedings of the First Workshop on Computational Approaches to Discourse*, pages 65–75, Online. Association for Computational Linguistics.

René Knaebel, Manfred Stede, and Sebastian Stober. 2019. Window-based neural tagging for shallow discourse argument labeling. In *Proceedings of the 23rd Conference on Computational Natural Language Learning (CoNLL)*, pages 768–777, Hong Kong, China. Association for Computational Linguistics.

Li Liang, Zheng Zhao, and Bonnie Webber. 2020. Extending implicit discourse relation recognition to the PDTB-3. In *Proceedings of the First Workshop on Computational Approaches to Discourse*, pages 135–147, Online. Association for Computational Linguistics.

Ziheng Lin, Hwee Tou Ng, and Min-Yen Kan. 2014. A pdtb-styled end-to-end discourse parser. *Natural Language Engineering*, 20:151–184.

Stephan Oepen, Jonathon Read, Tatjana Scheffler, Uladzimir Sidarenka, Manfred Stede, Erik Velldal, and Lilja Øvrelid. 2016. OPT: Oslo–Potsdam–Teesside. pipelining rules, rankers, and classifier ensembles for shallow discourse parsing. In *Proceedings of the CoNLL-16 shared task*, pages 20–26, Berlin, Germany. Association for Computational Linguistics.

Jeffrey Pennington, Richard Socher, and Christopher Manning. 2014. GloVe: Global vectors for word representation. In *Proceedings of the 2014 Conference on Empirical Methods in Natural Language Processing (EMNLP)*, pages 1532–1543, Doha, Qatar. Association for Computational Linguistics.

Emily Pitler and Ani Nenkova. 2009. Using syntax to disambiguate explicit discourse connectives in text. In *Proceedings of the ACL-IJCNLP 2009 Conference Short Papers*, pages 13–16, Suntec, Singapore. Association for Computational Linguistics.

Rashmi Prasad, Nikhil Dinesh, Alan Lee, Eleni Miltsakaki, Livio Robaldo, Aravind Joshi, and Bonnie Webber. 2008. The penn discourse treebank 2.0. In *In Proceedings of LREC*.

Lianhui Qin, Zhisong Zhang, and Hai Zhao. 2016. Shallow discourse parsing using convolutional neural network. In *Proceedings of the CoNLL-16 shared task*, pages 70–77, Berlin, Germany. Association for Computational Linguistics.

Sashank J. Reddi, Satyen Kale, and Sanjiv Kumar. 2018. On the convergence of adam and beyond. In *6th International Conference on Learning Representations, ICLR 2018, Vancouver, BC, Canada, April 30 - May 3, 2018, Conference Track Proceedings*. OpenReview.net.

Attapol Rutherford, Vera Demberg, and Nianwen Xue. 2017. A systematic study of neural discourse models for implicit discourse relation. In *Proceedings of the 15th Conference of the European Chapter of the Association for Computational Linguistics: Volume 1, Long Papers*, pages 281–291, Valencia, Spain. Association for Computational Linguistics.

Niko Schenk, Christian Chiarcos, Kathrin Donandt, Samuel Rönnqvist, Evgeny Stepanov, and Giuseppe Riccardi. 2016. Do we really need all those rich linguistic features? a neural network-based approach to implicit sense labeling. In *Proceedings of the CoNLL-16 shared task*, pages 41–49, Berlin, Germany. Association for Computational Linguistics.

Evgeny Stepanov and Giuseppe Riccardi. 2016. UniTN end-to-end discourse parser for CoNLL 2016 shared task. In *Proceedings of the CoNLL-16 shared task*, pages 85–91, Berlin, Germany. Association for Computational Linguistics.

Jianxiang Wang and Man Lan. 2016. Two end-to-end shallow discourse parsers for English and Chinese in CoNLL-2016 shared task. In *Proceedings of the CoNLL-16 shared task*, pages 33–40, Berlin, Germany. Association for Computational Linguistics.

Thomas Wolf, Lysandre Debut, Victor Sanh, Julien Chaumond, Clement Delangue, Anthony Moi, Pierric Cistac, Tim Rault, Remi Louf, Morgan Funtowicz, Joe Davison, Sam Shleifer, Patrick von Platen, Clara Ma, Yacine Jernite, Julien Plu, Canwen Xu, Teven Le Scao, Sylvain Gugger, Mariama Drame, Quentin Lhoest, and Alexander Rush. 2020. Transformers: State-of-the-art natural language processing. In *Proceedings of the 2020 Conference on Empirical Methods in Natural Language Processing: System Demonstrations*, pages 38–45, Online. Association for Computational Linguistics.

Nianwen Xue, Hwee Tou Ng, Sameer Pradhan, Rashmi Prasad, Christopher Bryant, and Attapol Rutherford. 2015. The CoNLL-2015 shared task on shallow discourse parsing. In *Proceedings of the Nineteenth Conference on Computational Natural Language Learning - Shared Task*, pages 1–16, Beijing, China. Association for Computational Linguistics.

Nianwen Xue, Hwee Tou Ng, Sameer Pradhan, Attapol Rutherford, Bonnie Webber, Chuan Wang, and Hongmin Wang. 2016. CoNLL 2016 shared task on multilingual shallow discourse parsing. In *Proceedings of the CoNLL-16 shared task*, pages 1–19, Berlin, Germany. Association for Computational Linguistics.

Yang Zhong, Chao Jiang, Wei Xu, and Junyi Jessy Li. 2020. Discourse level factors for sentence deletion in text simplification. In *AAAI*.

# Tracing variation in discourse connectives in translation and interpreting through neural semantic spaces

**Ekaterina Lapshinova-Koltunski** **Heike Przybyl** **Yuri Bizzoni**
Saarland University, University Campus A.2.2, DE-66123 Saarbrücken
e.lapshinova@mx.uni-saarland.de
heike.przybyl@uni-saarland.de
yuri.bizzoni@uni-saarland.de

## Abstract

In the present paper, we explore lexical contexts of discourse markers in translation and interpreting on the basis of word embeddings. Our special interest is on contextual variation of the same discourse markers in (written) translation vs. (simultaneous) interpreting. To explore this variation at the lexical level, we use a data-driven approach: we compare bilingual neural word embeddings trained on source-to-translation and source-to-interpreting aligned corpora. Our results show more variation of semantically related items in translation spaces vs. interpreting ones and a more consistent use of fewer connectives in interpreting. We also observe different trends with regard to the discourse relation types.

## 1 Introduction

This paper presents an explorative study of discourse connectives in cross-linguistically mediated communication. We compare written translation with spoken simultaneous interpreting in the domain of European Parliament discourse. We start from the perspective of *translationese*, an observation that translations share specific linguistic features distinguishing them from non-translated language. Although interpreting has recently received increased attention in computational approaches, there are not so many studies of *interpretese*.

In this work, we are aiming to understand the differences between translated and interpreted texts in terms of discourse connectives. Przybyl et al. (forthcoming) show that translations and interpreting transcripts differ significantly in the use of these linguistic units. For instance, there is a difference in the preference for the choice of connectives triggering the same relation. Specifically, the relation of contrast/concession is preferably expressed with the connective *however* in translation, whereas the use of *but* is characteristic of interpreting. This indicates that in marking logical relations, interpreters tend to prefer more general items over more specific ones. This is in line with the existing observations about differences between speech and writing (Crible and Cuenca, 2017): there are fewer but more polyfunctional discourse markers in speech than in writing.

To explore the differences between translated and interpreted texts, we follow the data-driven approach as in (Bizzoni and Teich, 2019) and use neural word embeddings (Word2Vec) to compare the bilingual semantic spaces from bilingual word embeddings built on aligned corpora. The resulting semantic spaces model the lexical choices of a specific translation. We train two bilingual distributional models on two comparable, aligned corpora (translation and interpreting) and compare the resulting semantic spaces to detect differences in the lexical patterns of discourse connectives impacted by translation mode (written vs. spoken). As stated by Bizzoni and Teich (2019) the existing constraints of interpreting (high cognitive load, time pressure) have impact on lexical choices, which is reflected in interpreting if compared to translation.

## 2 Related Work

Translated texts share linguistic characteristics which distinguish them from non-translated texts – the phenomenon of translationese (see Gellerstam, 1986; Baker, 1993; Toury, 1995). These differences can be traced in the distribution of various language patterns, i.e. linguistic features mostly organised in terms of more abstract categories (sometimes called translation universals or translation features) such as *normalisation* and *shining-through* (Teich, 2003), *simplification* (Toury, 1995), *convergence* (Laviosa, 2002) and *explicitation* (Olohan and Baker, 2000). The latter is often related to discourse connectives. For instance, Gumul (2006, 184) stated that explicitation in interpreting is related to adding discourse markers among other means of cohesive explicitness. At the same time, Shlesinger (1995) observed a reduction of cohe-



*Proceedings of the 2nd Workshop on Computational Approaches to Discourse*, pages 134–142
November 10–11, 2021. ©2021 Association for Computational Linguistics

sive ties in interpreting if compared to the source language input (implicitation). Kajzer-Wietrzny (2012) showed that there are differences between translation and interpreting in the usage of linking adverbials (with translation being more explicit).

The phenomena of explicitation and implicitation may also depend on the type of relations discourse connectives trigger: cognitively simple relations are more often left implicit than relations that are cognitively more complex (see Hoek et al., 2017). This is also confirmed in a recent study by Blumenthal-Dramé (2021) who showed that causal links are more expected than concessive ones and the processing of concessive sentences benefits more from the explicit marking than the processing of causal sentences (also pointing to cross-lingual differences between English and German).

Although we are not pursuing creation of a multilingual lexicon, our work is related to those dealing with mapping of discourse connectives (Stede et al., 2019; Bourgonje et al., 2018, 2017; Laali and Kosseim, 2017, 2014). Numerous studies analysed discourse connectives from a cross-lingual point of view using aligned texts (see Hoek and Zufferey, 2015; Zufferey and Cartoni, 2014; Meyer and Webber, 2013; Cartoni et al., 2011; Meyer et al., 2011). In our exploratory study of the differences between translation and interpreting, we do not focus on the direct transfer of specific discourse connectives, but look into their bilingual lexical context. In this sense, our work relates to the study by Roth and Upadhyay (2019), who used cross-lingual embeddings and discourse connectives to analyse semantically related words in several languages.

We rely on the methodology proposed by Bizzoni and Teich (2019), which is related to other studies that attempt to use word embeddings for linguistic analysis, such as Dubossarsky et al. (2017); Fankhauser and Kupietz (2017); Bizzoni et al. (2019). Whereas Bizzoni and Teich (2019) analyse general variation in lexical choices in interpreting and translation, our focus is on discourse-related phenomena. Besides that, our work is related to those with a focus on domain-specific word embeddings (Zhang et al., 2019; Wang et al., 2018), those dealing with multilingual word embeddings for lexicon induction and mapping (Shi et al., 2019; Zhang et al., 2019; Artetxe et al., 2017, 2018) and those focusing on creating consistent spaces (Huang et al., 2018) in cross-lingual word analogy tasks (Ulčar et al., 2020; Brychcín et al., 2019).

## 3 Data and Methods

Our data includes officially published original speeches, as well as transcripts of the speeches delivered at the European Parliament (EP) aligned with their translations or interpretations, correspondingly. Both parallel subsets are parts of the Europarl-UdS (Karakanta et al., 2018) and EPIC-UdS (Przybyl et al., forthcoming) corpora, with English as source and German as target. Both corpora are strictly comparable in terms of register, as they contain European Parliament speeches. The spoken part (EPIC-UdS) are true transcripts of the spoken utterances by members of the EP and interpeters, including spoken language features such as false starts, filled pauses and unfinished sentences. The basis of written dataset (Europarl-UdS) is also a spoken event in the European Parliament, however modified to respect written language characteristics. Overall, we have 130,000 sentence pairs in the translated data and 3,397 sentence pairs for the interpreted data. Refer to Table 1 for an overview of the size in tokens.

| written | token | spoken | token |
|---|---|---|---|
| WR | 9,654,581 | SP | 66,226 |
| TR | 8,954,825 | SI | 57,622 |

Table 1: Dataset used for written (Europarl-UdS) and spoken (EPIC-UdS). WR=English written original, TR=translation into German, SP=English spoken original, SI=simultaneous interpreting into German.

This paper uses the approach described by Bizzoni and Teich (2019): neural word embeddings (Word2Vec) are used to compare source-to-translation and source-to-interpreting lexical choices. The sentence aligned corpus data is used to create reshuffled bilingual pseudo-sentences. Subsequently, a standard skipgram Word2Vec model is trained on these sentences to create translation and interpreting spaces. The main idea of this method is that words with a consistent translation in an aligned corpus will share similar contexts with their translation, and will result in close proximity in distributional spaces. This is a mechanism similar to that used in standard distributional semantics, where words having similar contexts are closer in space, but it is applied to bilingual aligned contexts instead of standard monolingual texts.

For example, if a source word $A$ is always translated with a target word $B$, and $B$ is only used to translate $A$, such words will appear only together and their bilingual context will be identical. As an effect, their distributional vectors will be extremely similar and the two words will be very close neighbours in a semantic space. The more a translation deviates from this type of systematicity, the less two words will result close in the semantic space.

For the words without consistent translation, different configurations in translation space exist. If a word is ambiguous, it can be close to the variants of its translations in the space, but the similarity would be lower (reflected in the cosine similarity score). If a word is very hard or even impossible to translate with one term, there will be no translations close to the word, which does not show a high similarity to its neighbours. While this method, being based on Word2Vec, is sensitive to frequency effects, Bizzoni and Teich (2019) show that it is robust enough to obtain meaningful results from corpora few thousands sentences long (see Bizzoni and Teich, 2019, for more details and examples).

Our list of connectives is restricted to 14 items that appear to be most frequent in both written and spoken data at hand.[1] The connectives can be grouped according to their senses defined in PDTB-3 (Webber et al., 2019, p. 17) as temporal (*finally, first, firstly, secondly*), contingency (*as, because, if, so, why*), comparison (*but, however, yet*) and expansion (*also, that*). Some of them are ambiguous and may trigger different relations, e.g. the connective *as* is ambiguous and may express all the four meaning relations, although preference is given for temporal and contingency (Webber et al., 2019, p. 56). The connective *finally* is ambiguous between temporal meaning and the meaning of expansion, whereas the connective *if* is conditional, but may also express comparison.

The resulting semantic spaces of connectives are analyse in the following way: 10 nearest neighbours of the 14 discourse connectives are analysed for semantic relation to the connective – if an item expresses the same discourse function, i.e. source or target language synonym (e.g. *however – but – zwar*), can be used for paraphrasing the function (e.g. *why – for this reason, finally – to sum up*) or items that express other logical relations via discourse connective (e.g. *that – ob*), we consider them as semantically related.

We have a number of assumptions about the resulting semantic spaces. First of all, following the findings by Bizzoni and Teich (2019), we expect that the connectives translated consistently with the same target language equivalent will be very close to each other in the resulting semantic space. Besides that, we know that interpreters tend to use fewer connectives than translators. So we expect less variation in interpreting than translation, and consequently, fewer but closer semantic neighbours in interpreting than in translation. At the same time, as there should be more implicitation in interpreting than in translation, we expect more target language equivalents in the semantic spaces of translation than interpreting. Furthermore, we expect variation in the resulting semantic spaces with regard to the discourse relation a connective expresses.

## 4 Analysis and Observations

We qualitatively analyse the differences between resulting translation and interpreting spaces (TR and SI spaces in the following). For the sake of space, we will report on the most remarkable cases only. The whole list of spaces for both translation and interpreting is given in the Appendix.

**Overall observations** The TR spaces display far greater semantic proximity with synonyms or other semantically related items than the SI spaces. The interpreting space for 5 out of 14 discourse connectives under analysis (*also, but, however, so, yet*) shows no related item within the 10 nearest neighbours. The maximum amount of semantically related items in the list of 10 nearest neighbours in the interpreting space is 3, whereas up to 10 out of 10 nearest neighbours in the translation space are semantically linked to the connective studied.

**Content of TR and SI spaces** Translation spaces of some connectives (*but, however, yet, finally*) display many near synonyms in English or equivalents in German, however linked with lower cosine similarity score. By contrast, their interpreting spaces contain either few or no semantically related items. One of such examples is the discourse connective *but*, that we illustrate in Table 2.

Notably, this discourse connective is frequent in both translated and interpreted texts of our data, being even more frequent in interpreting than in

[1] We excluded some of the frequent connectives due to their high ambiguity (*and, or*). We also considered two discourse particles *well* and *now*, but excluded them from the current analysis, as they are more typical of spoken language, i.e. interpreting.

| TR space | SI space |
|---|---|
| however .86; whilst .7; while .7; yet .66; nevertheless .62; though .57; although .53; nonetheless .48; zwar .48; (bilden .41) | (ausschluss .57); (vorrecht .56); (kein .54); (forum .5); (exercising .5); (aktualisiert .5); (abtreibungsrecht .49); (wahrheitsfindung .49); (scheint .48); (institutionelle .47) |

Table 2: Translation and interpreting spaces for *but* and 10 nearest neighbours with cosine similarity; semantically unrelated items in brackets.

translation if compared to the other two discourse connectives of comparison under analysis (*however* and *yet*). However, the SI space does not contain any semantically related English words or German equivalents, while the TR space does so (e.g. the synonym *however* or the translation equivalent *zwar*). We assume that no matching equivalents within the nearest neighbours in interpreting confirms the general implicitation trend as discussed in the literature about interpreting: due to the time pressure and high cognitive load, interpreters tend to omit discourse connectives used in the source.

**Scores in TR and SI spaces** In general, very few semantically related items occur in the interpreting space. However, if there is a synonym or translation equivalent in the SI cluster, cosine similarity is generally higher in the interpreting space than for equivalent items in the translation space, as seen in Table 3 for the connectives *if, as* and *secondly*.

| | TR space | SI space |
|---|---|---|
| if | when .73; unless .66; though .51 | wenn .87; dann .72; |
| as | (angesehen .53) | wie 0.57 |
| secondly | zweitens .76 | zweitens .82 |

Table 3: Translation and interpreting spaces for *if, as* and *secondly* and the nearest neighbours with cosine similarity; semantically unrelated items in brackets.

This can be explained by the general tendency of interpreting to frequently use a smaller repository of discourse connectives. This reduced variation in interpreting leads to stronger clusters within the semantic space. For instance, *if* is consistently interpreted with the target language equivalent *wenn* and is frequently used in proximity to *dann*. Cosine similarity scores for *wenn* in the SI space with .87 is higher than the highest nearest neighbour cosine similarity score in the TR space (see Table 3). If interpreters add connectives in the German target and the English sources do not contain their triggers (see Defrancq, Bart, 2016), the systematicity of the translation is reduced and the connectives' similarity to their triggers is lower; thus, they might not appear at all in the semantic clusters we analyse.

**Connective ambiguity** Connectives *so* and *that* seem not to cluster well with semantically related words in either translation or interpreting space. This can be explained by their multiple functions: they not only serve as discourse connective, but also as other discourse elements, e.g. *that* can be used as demonstrative reference, whereas *so* can express clausal substitution or also be used as a modifying adverb or an intensifier. With the word embedding approach applied on the raw data (not annotated for true discourse connectives), we cannot distinguish between these functions.

**Observations on discourse senses** We also observe variation in the patterns for various types of discourse relations. For instance, connectives triggering the relation of comparison (*but, however* and *yet*), temporal connectives (*finally, first, firstly* and *secondly*) and the conditional *if* have almost always equivalents in the translation spaces. This confirms the dependency of the implicitation/explicitation process on the type of relation, as shown by Hoek et al. (2017) and Blumenthal-Dramé (2021), see Section 2 above. Cognitively more complex relations (concession, which is grouped within comparison and condition) cannot be easily left out, and have therefore almost always equivalents in translation spaces. At the same time, cognitively simple relations (expansion and contingency) do not necessarily do so. However, this observation is true for translation only and does not apply for the interpreting data. An exception is the conditional *if*. It clusters with its equivalents in both translation and interpreting space, however showing semantically related connectives in English in the translation space only (*when, unless*), see Table 3 and the whole spaces in the Appendix.

## 5 Conclusion and Future Work

We used neural semantic spaces to observe differences between discourse connectives in translation and interpreting. Generally, we observe similar trends reported by Bizzoni and Teich (2019) for the lexical differences between interpreting and translation. Our results are in line with implication and explicitation trends in translation. They confirm the assumption that interpreting shows more implicitation than translation. It was also interesting to see that cognitive complexity of relations also has impact on the resulting semantic spaces in translation, but has a different effect on the interpreting spaces.

In future, we plan to further investigate these differences using a wider range of connectives expressing different discourse relations. We would also like to systematically compare our results with the original aligned corpus, to provide a convincing qualitative test of the trends we have observed through our semantic spaces.

Also, Word2Vec represents one of the most efficient methods to produce a word's compact distributional profile, but it is not the only one. It could be interesting to compare the results of Word2Vec with other state of the art, non-contextualized[2] word embeddings when applied to the same corpus.

Moreover, our results also confirm the tendency of interpreting to show less variation in terms of the range of discourse connectives. Here, we would like to extend our work and include more discourse connectives. Finally, we plan to experiment with disambiguated data (include the cases of discourse relations only).

## Acknowledgement

This work is based on research funded by the Deutsche Forschungsgemeinschaft (DFG, German Research Foundation) - SFB 1102 / Project-ID 232722074, project B7 - Modelling Human Translation with a Noisy Channel.

## References

Mikel Artetxe, Gorka Labaka, and Eneko Agirre. 2017. Learning bilingual word embeddings with (almost) no bilingual data. In *Proceedings of the 55th Annual Meeting of the Association for Computational Linguistics (Volume 1: Long Papers)*, pages 451–462, Vancouver, Canada. Association for Computational Linguistics.

Mikel Artetxe, Gorka Labaka, and Eneko Agirre. 2018. A robust self-learning method for fully unsupervised cross-lingual mappings of word embeddings. In *Proceedings of the 56th Annual Meeting of the Association for Computational Linguistics (Volume 1: Long Papers)*, pages 789–798, Melbourne, Australia. Association for Computational Linguistics.

Mona Baker. 1993. Corpus linguistics and translation studies: Implications and applications. In G. Francis Baker M. and E. Tognini-Bonelli, editors, *Text and Technology: in Honour of John Sinclair*, pages 233–250. Benjamins, Amsterdam.

Yuri Bizzoni, Stefania Degaetano-Ortlieb, Katrin Menzel, Pauline Krielke, and Elke Teich. 2019. Grammar and meaning: Analysing the topology of diachronic word embeddings. In *Proceedings of the 1st International Workshop on Computational Approaches to Historical Language Change*, pages 175–185, Florence, Italy. Association for Computational Linguistics.

Yuri Bizzoni and Elke Teich. 2019. Analyzing variation in translation through neural semantic spaces. *Special topic: Neural Networks for Building and Using Comparable Corpora, Recent Advances in Natural Language Processing (RANLP), Varna, Bulgaria.*

Alice Blumenthal-Dramé. 2021. The online processing of causal and concessive relations: Comparing native speakers of english and german. *Discourse Processes*, 0(0):1–20.

Peter Bourgonje, Yulia Grishina, and Manfred Stede. 2017. Toward a bilingual lexical database on connectives: Exploiting a German/Italian parallel corpus. In *Proceedings of the Fourth Italian Conference on Computational Linguistics*, Rome, Italy.

Peter Bourgonje, Jet Hoek, Jacqueline Evers-Vermeul, Gisela Redeker, Ted Sanders, and Manfred Stede. 2018. Constructing a lexicon of dutch discourse connectives. *Computational Linguistics in the Netherlands Journal*, 8:163–175.

Tomáš Brychcín, Stephen Taylor, and Lukáš Svoboda. 2019. Cross-lingual word analogies using linear transformations between semantic spaces. *Expert Systems with Applications*, 135:287–295.

Bruno Cartoni, Sandrine Zufferey, Thomas Meyer, and Andrei Popescu-Belis. 2011. How comparable are parallel corpora? measuring the distribution of general vocabulary and connectives. In *Proceedings of the 4th Workshop on Building and Using Comparable Corpora: Comparable Corpora and the Web*, pages 78–86, Portland, Oregon. Association for Computational Linguistics.

Ludivine Crible and Maria Josep Cuenca. 2017. Discourse markers in speech: Characteristics and challenges for corpus annotation. *Dialogue and Discourse*, 8:149–166.

[2]Recent contextualized embeddings such as those produced by BERT and similar Transformers aim at capturing the a word's sense in context. Embeddings of this sort function like nuanced token vectors that change with every instance of a type. While this feature makes them excellent tools to build representations of larger semantic units, they could be a weakness for our experiment, since we aim at modelling the distributional profile of a word in a corpus.

Defrancq, Bart. 2016. Well, interpreters... a corpus-based study of a pragmatic particle used by simultaneous interpreters. In Corpas Pastor, Gloria and Seghiri Dominguez, Miriam, editor, *Corpus-based approaches to translation and interpreting : from theory to applications*, volume 106 of *Studien zur romanischen Sprachwissenschaft und interkulturellen Kommunikation*, pages 105–128. Peter Lang.

Haim Dubossarsky, Daphna Weinshall, and Eitan Grossman. 2017. Outta control: Laws of semantic change and inherent biases in word representation models. In *Proceedings of the 2017 Conference on Empirical Methods in Natural Language Processing*, pages 1136–1145, Copenhagen, Denmark. Association for Computational Linguistics.

Peter Fankhauser and Marc Kupietz. 2017. Visualizinglanguage change in a corpus of contemporary German. In *Proceedings of the 9th International Corpus Linguistics Conference*, University of Birmingham.

Martin Gellerstam. 1986. Translationese in Swedish novels translated from English. In L. Wollin and H. Lindquist, editors, *Translation Studies in Scandinavia*, pages 88–95. CWK Gleerup, Lund.

Ewa Gumul. 2006. Explicitation in simultaneous interpreting: A strategy or a by-product of language mediation? *Across Languages and Cultures. A Multidisciplinary Journal for Translation and Interpreting Studies*, 7:171–190.

Jet Hoek and Sandrine Zufferey. 2015. Factors influencing the implicitation of discourse relations across languages. In *Proceedings of the 11th Joint ACL-ISO Workshop on Interoperable Semantic Annotation (ISA-11)*, London, UK. Association for Computational Linguistics.

Jet Hoek, Sandrine Zufferey, Jacqueline Evers-Vermeul, and Ted J.M. Sanders. 2017. Cognitive complexity and the linguistic marking of coherence relations: A parallel corpus study. *Journal of Pragmatics*, 121:113–131.

Lifu Huang, Kyunghyun Cho, Boliang Zhang, Heng Ji, and Kevin Knight. 2018. Multi-lingual common semantic space construction via cluster-consistent word embedding. In *Proceedings of the 2018 Conference on Empirical Methods in Natural Language Processing*, pages 250–260, Brussels, Belgium. Association for Computational Linguistics.

Marta Kajzer-Wietrzny. 2012. *Interpreting universals and interpreting style*. Ph.D. thesis, Uniwersytet im. Adama Mickiewicza, Poznan, Poland. Unpublished PhD thesis.

Alina Karakanta, Mihaela Vela, and Elke Teich. 2018. Europarl-UdS: Preserving metadata from parliamentary debates. In *Proceedings of the 11th International Conference on Language Resources and Evaluation (LREC 2018)*. European Language Resources Association (ELRA).

Majid Laali and Leila Kosseim. 2014. Inducing discourse connectives from parallel texts. In *Proceedings of COLING 2014, the 25th International Conference on Computational Linguistics: Technical Papers*, pages 610–619, Dublin, Ireland. Dublin City University and Association for Computational Linguistics.

Majid Laali and Leila Kosseim. 2017. Automatic mapping of French discourse connectives to PDTB discourse relations. In *Proceedings of the 18th Annual SIGdial Meeting on Discourse and Dialogue*, pages 1–6, Saarbrücken, Germany. Association for Computational Linguistics.

Sara Laviosa. 2002. *Corpus-based Translation Studies, Theory, Findings, Application*. Rodopi, Amsterdam.

Thomas Meyer, Andrei Popescu-Belis, Sandrine Zufferey, and Bruno Cartoni. 2011. Multilingual annotation and disambiguation of discourse connectives for machine translation. In *Proceedings of the SIGDIAL 2011 Conference*, pages 194–203, Portland, Oregon. Association for Computational Linguistics.

Thomas Meyer and Bonnie Webber. 2013. Implicitation of discourse connectives in (machine) translation. In *Proceedings of the Workshop on Discourse in Machine Translation*, pages 19–26, Sofia, Bulgaria. Association for Computational Linguistics.

Maeve Olohan and Mona Baker. 2000. Reporting that in translated English: Evidence for subconscious processes of explicitation? *Across Languages and Cultures*, 1:141–158.

Heike Przybyl, Alina Karakanta, Katrin Menzel, and Elke Teich. forthcoming. Exploring linguistic variation in mediated discourse: translation vs. interpreting. In Marta Kajzer-Wietrzny, Silvia Bernardini, Adriano Ferraresi, and Ilmari Ivaska, editors, *Empirical investigations into the forms of mediated discourse at the European Parliament*, Translation and Multilingual Natural Language Processing. Language Science Press, Berlin.

Michael Roth and Shyam Upadhyay. 2019. Combining discourse markers and cross-lingual embeddings for synonym–antonym classification. In *Proceedings of the 2019 Conference of the North American Chapter of the Association for Computational Linguistics: Human Language Technologies, Volume 1 (Long and Short Papers)*, pages 3899–3905, Minneapolis, Minnesota. Association for Computational Linguistics.

Weijia Shi, Muhao Chen, Yingtao Tian, and Kai-Wei Chang. 2019. Learning bilingual word embeddings using lexical definitions. In *Proceedings of the 4th Workshop on Representation Learning for NLP (RepL4NLP-2019)*, pages 142–147, Florence, Italy. Association for Computational Linguistics.

Miriam Shlesinger. 1995. Shifts in cohesion in simultaneous interpreting. *The Translator*, 1:193–214.

Manfred Stede, Amália Mendes, and Tatjana Scheffler. 2019. Connective-lex: A web-based multilingual lexical resource for connectives. *Discours. Revue de linguistique, psycholinguistique et informatique*, 24.

Elke Teich. 2003. *Cross-Linguistic Variation in System and Text. A Methodology for the Investigation of Translations and Comparable Texts*. Mouton de Gruyter, Berlin.

Gideon Toury. 1995. *Descriptive Translation Studies – and Beyond*. John Benjamins, Amsterdam.

Matej Ulčar, Kristiina Vaik, Jessica Lindström, Milda Dailidėnaitė, and Marko Robnik-Šikonja. 2020. Multilingual culture-independent word analogy datasets. In *Proceedings of the 12th Language Resources and Evaluation Conference*, pages 4074–4080, Marseille, France. European Language Resources Association.

Yanshan Wang, Sijia Liu, Naveed Afzal, Majid Rastegar-Mojarad, Liwei Wang, Feichen Shen, Paul Kingsbury, and Hongfang Liu. 2018. A comparison of word embeddings for the biomedical natural language processing. *Journal of Biomedical Informatics*, 87:12–20.

Bonnie Webber, Rashmi Prasad, Alan Lee, and Aravind Joshi. 2019. *The Penn Discourse Treebank 3.0 Annotation Manual*.

Yijia Zhang, Qingyu Chen, Zhihao Yang, Hongfei Lin, and Zhiyong Lu. 2019. BioWordVec, improving biomedical word embeddings with subword information and MeSH. *Scintific Data*, 6.

Sandrine Zufferey and Bruno Cartoni. 2014. A multifactorial analysis of explicitation in translation. *Target*, 26(3):361–384.

# A Appendix

| | TR space | SI space |
|---|---|---|
| **temporal** | | |
| finally | abschließend .67; conclusion .59; lastly .55; (reiterate .53); schluss .5; (bemerken .49); abschluss .45; schließlich .42; conclude .42; (hervorheben .41) | sum .71; (unterbrechen .7); (lehrt .69); (gollnisch .69); (karte .68); (teach .68); (fish .66); (gollnish .66); (subject .65); (heben .65) |
| first | zweiten .61; second .58; firstly .57; ersten .51; zweite .49; mal .48; erstmals .46; zunächst .45; erste .44; (reading .43) | zunächst .76; (verbesserte .74); (französichen .74); (november .73); ersten .73; (mandats .72); erste .72; (wahl .71); (ehre .71); (vortragen .7) |
| firstly | erstens .75; secondly .72; zweitens .66; thirdly .6; first .57; drittens .56; (pfeiler .51); zunächst 0,50; (pillar .50); second .48 | (achtzehn .87); endlich .83; (eighteen .83); (ausreichende .82); (gefallen .82); (umweltausschusses .81); (gordon .8); (mitkollaborateure .8); (erfasst .8); (mcavan 0,8) |
| secondly | zweitens .76; erstens .75; firstly .72; drittens .68; thirdly .67; fourthly .55; second .55; zweite .45; (pillar .44); viertens .44 | zweitens .82; (procurement .77); (smes .74); (calculations .72); (roughly .72); (berechnungen .7); (fernen .7); (billionen .7); (fünfhundertachtzig .7); (edf .7) |
| **contingency** | | |
| as | (angesehen .53); (erstes .52); (bezeichnen .52); (bezeichnet .51); (betrachtet .48); (than .48); (how .47); (erweisen .45); (gut .45); (insofern .45) | wie .57; (beginnt .57); (begins .56); (wirklichen .56); (arbeitsdokument .55); european .53); presently .53; (getreten .52); (far .52); (worse .52) |
| because | since .38; (geschweige .37); (owing .28); as .24; (moreira .24); (louth .24); (kleinlich .23); (timed .23); (improper .23); (vilify .23) | (dumping .62); (rückstände .6); (hoher .6); (güte .59); (ninety .57); denn .56; attributed .54; weil .53; (awful .53); (food .52) |
| if | when .73; unless .66; though .51; whenever .49, albeit .48; (ansieht .47); (durchkommt .47); (bedenkt .46); dann .44; whether .42 | wenn .87; dann .72; (überhaupt .7); (nachzukommen .65); (cannot .64); (ohne .64); (prioritäten .64); (fährt .64); (without .62); (properly .62) |
| so | (genannten .4); (genannte .4); (möglich .39); (called .38); (schnell .37); therefore .36; why .35; (weitermachen .32); (getan .28); (quickly .28) | (oben .57); (schuhe .56); (represent .56); (unfortunate .56); (fight .55); (outer .55); (gut .55); (darzustellen .55); (vertrete .54); (sought .53) |
| why | reason .61; warum .59; weshalb .59; grund .54; explain .53; gründe .53; wieso .52; reasons .40; deshalb .39; therefore .38 | (mainstream .56); (legislativpaket .56); (umfasst .56); (backed .55); (letztes .54); deshalb .53; (started .52); (weaken .51); (doubled .51); (gebeten .5) |
| **comparison** | | |
| but | however .86; whilst .7; while .7; yet .66; nevertheless .62; though .57; although .53; nonetheless .48; zwar .48; (bilden .41) | (ausschluss .57); (vorrecht .56); (kein .54); (forum .5); (exercising .5); (aktualisiert .5); (abtreibungsrecht .49); (wahrheitsfindung .49); (scheint .48); (institutionelle .47) |
| | | *continued on next page* |

*continued from previous page*

| | TR space | SI space |
|---|---|---|
| however | but .86; nevertheless .73; yet .71; whilst .68; while .67; though .55; nonetheless .54; zwar .50; although .49; (coin .45) | (zweitausendzwölf .77); (informationssystem .77); (spiele .75); (achtunddreißig .74), (uk .73); (abtreibungsrecht .73); (paragraph .73); (characters .73); (zauberstab .72); (lewis .72) |
| yet | however .71; but .66; nevertheless .6; while .55; whilst .51; though .45; zwar .44; although .44, nonetheless .41; (stretches .39) | (destroy .64); (wussten .64); (produzierte .63); (pork .63); (kontrollierte .62); (zwang .61); (vernichten .61); (industrial .61); (throw .61); (wissenschaftler .60) |
| **expansion** | | |
| also | furthermore .72; addition .66; similarly .64; equally .6; (indeed .57); moreover .57; sowohl .56; including .53; likewise .48; too .46 | (sicherheit .54); (maßnahmen .51); (denk .51); (therapeuten .49); (gesundheitswesen .49); (repeal .49); (security .48); (fidschi .48); (interessen .48); (hum .48) |
| that | which .37; what .32; (tatsache .29); (assertion .29); (firmly .28); whatever .28; (richtig .27); (this .27); (klar .26); (sicherzustellen .26) | (verordnung .55); (daran .54); (fair .52); (veränderung .52); (study .52); (transparent .51); (incidentally .51); (offenheit .51); (spüren .51); (ob .5) |

Table 4: Translation and interpreting spaces containing their 10 nearest neighbours with cosine similarity; semantically unrelated items in brackets.

# Capturing document context inside sentence-level neural machine translation models with self-training

**Elman Mansimov**
New York University
mansimov@cs.nyu.edu

**Gábor Melis**
DeepMind
melisgl@google.com

**Lei Yu**
DeepMind
leiyu@google.com

## Abstract

Neural machine translation (NMT) has arguably achieved human level parity when trained and evaluated at the sentence-level. Document-level neural machine translation has received less attention and lags behind its sentence-level counterpart. The majority of the proposed document-level approaches investigate ways of conditioning the model on several source or target sentences to capture document context. These approaches require training a specialized NMT model from scratch on parallel document-level corpora. We propose an approach that doesn't require training a specialized model on parallel document-level corpora and is applied to a trained sentence-level NMT model at decoding time. We process the document from left to right multiple times and self-train the sentence-level model on pairs of source sentences and generated translations. Our approach reinforces the choices made by the model, thus making it more likely that the same choices will be made in other sentences in the document. We evaluate our approach on three document-level datasets: NIST Chinese-English, WMT19 Chinese-English and OpenSubtitles English-Russian. We demonstrate that our approach has higher BLEU score and higher human preference than the baseline. Qualitative analysis of our approach shows that choices made by model are consistent across the document.

## 1 Introduction

Neural machine translation (NMT) (Sutskever et al., 2014; Kalchbrenner and Blunsom, 2013; Bahdanau et al., 2014) has achieved great success, arguably reaching the levels of human parity (Hassan et al., 2018) on Chinese to English news translation that led to its popularity and adoption in academia and industry. These models are predominantly trained and evaluated on sentence-level parallel corpora. Document-level machine translation that requires capturing the context to accurately translate sentences has been recently gaining more popularity and was selected as one of the main tasks in the premier machine translation conference WMT19 (Barrault et al., 2019) and WMT20 (Barrault et al., 2020).

A straightforward solution to translate documents by translating sentences in isolation leads to inconsistent but syntactically valid text. The inconsistency is the result of the model not being able to resolve ambiguity with consistent choices across the document. For example, the recent NMT system that achieved human parity (Hassan et al., 2018) inconsistently used three different names "Twitter Move Car", "WeChat mobile", "WeChat move" when referring to the same entity (Sennrich, 2018).

To tackle this issue, the majority of the previous approaches (Jean et al., 2017; Wang et al., 2017; Kuang et al., 2017; Tiedemann and Scherrer, 2017; Maruf and Haffari, 2018; Agrawal et al., 2018; Zhang et al., 2018; Xiong et al., 2018; Miculicich et al., 2018; Voita et al., 2019a,b; Jean et al., 2019; Junczys-Dowmunt, 2019) proposed context-conditional NMT models trained on document-level data. However, none of the previous approaches are able to exploit trained NMT models on sentence-level parallel corpora and require training specialized context-conditional NMT models for document-level machine translation.

We propose a way of incorporating context into a trained sentence-level neural machine translation model at decoding time. We process each document monotonically from left to right one sentence at a time and self-train the sentence-level NMT model on its own generated translation. This procedure reinforces choices made by the model and hence increases the chance of making the same choices in the remaining sentences in the document. Our approach does not require training a separate context-conditional model on parallel document-



*Proceedings of the 2nd Workshop on Computational Approaches to Discourse*, pages 143–153
November 10–11, 2021. 

**Algorithm 1:** Document-level NMT with self-training at decoding time

**Input:** Document $\boldsymbol{D} = (X_1, ..., X_n)$, pretrained sentence-level NMT model $f(\theta)$, learning rate $\alpha$, decay prior $\lambda$ and number of passes over document $P$
**Output:** Translated sentences $(Y_1, ..., Y_n)$
Backup original values of parameters $\tilde{\theta} \leftarrow \theta$
**for** $p = 1$ **to** $P$ {*multi-pass document*} **do**
  **for** $i = 1$ **to** $n$ **do**
    Translate sentence $X_i$ using sentence-level model $f(\theta)$ into target sentence $Y_i$.
    Calculate cross-entropy loss $L(X_i, Y_i)$ using $Y_i$ as target.
    **for** $j = 1$ **to** $m$ **do**
      $\theta \leftarrow \theta - \alpha \nabla_\theta L(X_i, Y_i) + \lambda(\tilde{\theta} - \theta)$
    **end for**
  **end for**
**end for**

level data and allows us to capture context in documents using a trained sentence-level model.

We make the key contribution in the paper by introducing the document-level neural machine translation approach that does not require training a context-conditional model on document data and does not require separate document-level language model to rank the outputs of the NMT model according to consistency of translated document. We show how to adapt a trained sentence-level neural machine translation model to capture context in the document during decoding. We evaluate and demonstrate improvements of our proposed approach measured by BLEU score and preferences of human annotators on several document-level machine translation tasks including NIST Chinese-English, WMT19 Chinese-English and OpenSubtitles English-Russian datasets. We qualitatively analyze the decoded sentences produced using our approach and show that they indeed capture the context.

## 2 Proposed Approach

We translate a document $\boldsymbol{D}$ consisting of $n$ source sentences $X_1, X_2, ..., X_n$ into the target language, given a well-trained sentence-level neural machine translation model $f_\theta$. The sentence-level model parametrizes a conditional distribution $p(Y|X) = \prod_{i=1}^{T} p(y_t|Y_{<t}, X)$ of each target word $y_t$ given the preceding words $Y_{<t}$ and the source sentence $X$. Decoding is done by approximately finding $\arg\max_Y p(Y|X)$ using greedy decoding or beam-search. $f$ is typically a recurrent neural network with attention (Bahdanau et al., 2014) or a Transformer model (Vaswani et al., 2017) with parameters $\theta$.

### 2.1 Self-training

We start by translating a first source sentence $X_1$ in the document $\boldsymbol{D}$ into the target sentence $Y_1$. We then self-train the model on the sentence pair $(X_1, Y_1)$, which maximizes the log probabilities of each word in the generated sentence $Y_1$ given source sentence $X_1$. The self-training procedure runs gradient descent steps for a fixed number of steps with a weight decay. Weight decay keeps the updated values of weights closer to original values. We repeat the same update process for the remaining sentences in the document. The detailed implementation of self-training procedure during decoding is shown in Algorithm 1.

### 2.2 Multi-pass self-training

Since the document is processed in the left-to-right, monotonic order, our self-training procedure does not incorporate the choices of the model yet to be made on unprocessed sentences. In order to leverage global information from the full document and to further reinforce the choices made by the model across all generated sentences, we propose multi-pass document decoding with self-training. Specifically, we process the document multiple times monotonically from left to right while continuing self-training of the model. Multi-pass self-training only requires adding additional parameter $P$ to self-training Algorithm 1. This parameter specifies the number of passes over the entire document.

### 2.3 Oracle self-training to upper bound performance

Since generated sentences are likely to contain some errors, our self-training procedure can reinforce those errors and thus potentially hurt the performance of the model on unprocessed sentences in the document. In order to isolate the effect of imperfect translations and estimate the upper bound of performance, we evaluate our self-training procedure with ground-truth translations as targets, which we call *oracle self-training*. Running oracle self-training makes it similar to the dynamic evaluation approach introduced in language modeling (Mikolov, 2012; Graves, 2013; Krause et al.,

2018), where input text to the language model is the target used to train the neural language model during evaluation. Oracle self-training is also related to domain adaptation in machine translation (Axelrod et al., 2011; Freitag and Al-Onaizan, 2016; Chu and Wang, 2018). Unlike domain adaptation in MT, oracle self-training only runs adaptation within a single document and does not rely on the entire in-domain document-level test data. We do not use the oracle in multi-pass self-training since this would make it equivalent to memorizing the correct translation for each sentence in the document and regenerating it again.

## 3 Related Work

Although there have been some attempts at tackling document-level neural machine translation (for example see proceedings of discourse in machine translation workshop (Popescu-Belis et al., 2019)), it has largely received less attention compared to sentence-level neural machine translation. Prior document-level NMT approaches (Jean et al., 2017; Wang et al., 2017; Kuang et al., 2017; Tiedemann and Scherrer, 2017; Maruf and Haffari, 2018; Agrawal et al., 2018; Zhang et al., 2018; Miculicich et al., 2018) proposed different ways of conditioning NMT models on several source sentences in the document. Perhaps closest of those document NMT approaches to our work is the approach by Kuang et al. (2017), where they train a NMT model with a separate non-parametric cache (Kuhn and Mori, 1990) that incorporates topic information about the document. Recent approaches (Jean et al., 2019; Junczys-Dowmunt, 2019; Voita et al., 2019a) use only partially available parallel document data or monolingual document data. These approaches proposed to fill in missing context in the documents with random or generated sentences. Another line of document-level NMT work (Xiong et al., 2018; Voita et al., 2019b) proposed a two-pass document decoding model inspired by the deliberation network (Xia et al., 2017) in order to incorporate target side document context. A parallel line of work (Garcia et al., 2017, 2019; Yu et al., 2019) introduced document-level approaches that do not require training the context-conditional NMT model by introducing a separate language model to enforce the consistency in the outputs of sentence-level NMT model. Garcia et al. (2019) used a simple $n$-gram based semantic space language model (Hardmeier et al., 2012) to re-rank the outputs of the sentence-level NMT model inside the beam-search algorithm to enforce document-level consistency. Yu et al. (2019) proposed a novel beam search method that incorporates document context inside noisy channel model (Shannon, 1948; Yu et al., 2017; Yee et al., 2019) that uses a powerful GPT2 language model (Radford et al., 2019). Similar to our work, their approach doesn't require training context-conditional models on parallel document corpora, but relies on separate target-to-source NMT model and unconditional language model to re-rank hypotheses of the source-to-target NMT model.

Closest to our work is the *dynamic evaluation* approach proposed by Mikolov (2012) and further extended by Graves (2013); Krause et al. (2018), where a neural language model is trained at evaluation time. However unlike language modeling where inputs are ground-truth targets used both during training and evaluation, in machine translation ground-truth translation are not available at decoding time in practical settings. The general idea of storing memories in the weights of the neural network rather than storing memories as copies of neural network activations, that is behind our approach and dynamic evaluation, goes back to 1970s and 1980s work on associative memory models (Willshaw et al., 1969; Kohonen, 1972; Anderson and Hinton, 1981; Hopfield, 1982) and to more recent work on fast weights (Ba et al., 2016).

Our work belongs to the broad category of self-training or pseudo-labelling approaches (Scudder, 1965; Lee, 2013) proposed to annotate the unlabeled data to train supervised classifiers. Self-training has been successfully applied to NLP tasks such as word-sense disambiguation (Yarowsky, 1995) and parsing (McClosky et al., 2006; Reichart and Rappoport, 2007; Huang and Harper, 2009). Self-training has also been used to label monolingual data to improve the performance of sentence-level statistical and neural machine translation models (Ueffing, 2006; Zhang and Zong, 2016). Recently, He et al. (2019) proposed noisy version of self-training and showed improvement over classical self-training on machine translation and text summarization tasks. Backtranslation (Sennrich et al., 2016a) is another popular pseudo-labelling technique that utilizes target-side monolingual data to improve performance of NMT models.

| Method | Model | MT06 | MT03 | MT04 | MT05 | MT08 |
|---|---|---|---|---|---|---|
| (Wang et al., 2017) | RNNSearch | 37.76 | - | - | 36.89 | 27.57 |
| (Kuang et al., 2017) | RNNSearch | - | - | 38.40 | 32.90 | 31.86 |
| (Kuang et al., 2017) | Transformer | 48.14 | 48.05 | 47.91 | 48.53 | 38.38 |
| (Zhang et al., 2018) | Doc Transformer | 49.69 | 50.21 | 49.73 | 49.46 | 39.69 |
| Ours (Non-BT) | Transformer | 48.90 | 48.55 | 49.55 | 48.04 | 40.89 |
| | Transformer + self-train | 49.17 | 49.46 | 50.12 | 48.67 | 41.18 |
| Ours (BT) | Transformer | 51.29 | 51.69 | 52.48 | 53.00 | 42.72 |
| | Transformer + self-train | 52.30 | 53.36 | 52.83 | 53.67 | 43.68 |

Table 1: Results on NIST evaluation sets. The first four rows show the performance of the previous document-level NMT models from (Wang et al., 2017; Kuang et al., 2017; Zhang et al., 2018). The last four rows show performance of our baseline sentence-level Transformer models with and without self-training. BT: backtranslation.

| | Model | MT06 | MT03 | MT04 | MT05 | MT08 | $\Delta_{\text{BLEU}}$ |
|---|---|---|---|---|---|---|---|
| Non-BT | Baseline | 48.90 | 48.55 | 49.55 | 48.04 | 40.89 | - |
| | ST | 49.26 | 48.91 | 49.81 | 48.27 | 41.10 | +0.28 |
| | Multi-pass ST | 49.17 | 49.46 | 50.12 | 48.67 | 41.18 | +0.53 |
| | Oracle ST | 49.82 | 49.59 | 49.93 | 48.58 | 42.30 | +0.86 |
| BT | Baseline | 51.29 | 51.69 | 52.48 | 53.00 | 42.72 | - |
| | ST | 52.19 | 52.45 | 52.63 | 53.01 | 43.25 | +0.47 |
| | Multi-pass ST | 52.30 | 53.36 | 52.83 | 53.67 | 43.68 | +0.93 |
| | Oracle ST | 53.11 | 53.90 | 53.05 | 53.81 | 45.45 | +1.63 |

Table 2: Ablation study on NIST evaluation sets measuring the effect on multiple passes of decoding and the oracle on self-training procedure. BT: backtranslation. ST: self-training.

## 4 Experiments

### 4.1 Datasets

We use the NIST Chinese-English (Zh-En), the WMT19 Chinese-English (Zh-En) and the OpenSubtitles English-Russian (En-Ru) datasets in our experiments.

The NIST training set consists of 1.5M sentence pairs from LDC-distributed news. We use MT06 set as validation set. We use MT03, MT04, MT05 and MT08 sets as held out test sets. The MT06 validation set consists of 1649 sentences with 21 sentences per document. MT03, MT04, MT05 and MT08 consist of 919, 1788, 1082 and 1357 sentences with 9, 9, 11 and 13 sentences on average per document respectively. We follow previous work (Zhang et al., 2018) when preprocessing NIST dataset. We preprocess the NIST dataset with punctuation normalization, tokenization, and lowercasing. Sentences are encoded using byte-pair encoding (Sennrich et al., 2016b) with source and target vocabularies of roughly 32K tokens. We use the case-insensitive `multi-bleu.perl` script with 4 reference files to evaluate the model.

The WMT19 dataset includes the UN corpus, CWMT, and news commentary. We filter the training data by removing duplicate sentences and sentences longer than 250 words. The training dataset consits of 18M sentence pairs. We use newsdev2017 as a validation set and use newstest2017, newstest2018 and newstest2019 as held out test sets. newsdev2017, newstest2017, newstest2018 and newstest2019 consist of total of 2002, 2001, 3981 and 2000 sentences with average of 14, 12, 15 and 12 sentences per document respectively. We similarly follow previous work (Xia et al., 2019) when preprocessing the dataset. Chinese sentences are preprocessed by segmenting and normalizing punctuation. English sentences are preprocessed by tokenizing and true casing. We learn a byte-pair encoding (Sennrich et al., 2016b) with source and target vocabularies of roughly 32K tokens. We use sacreBLEU (Post, 2018) for evaluation.

The OpenSubtitles English-Russian dataset, consisting of movie and TV subtitles, was prepared by (Voita et al., 2019b).[1] The training dataset consists of 6M parallel sentence pairs. We use the context aware sets provided by the authors consisting of 10000 documents both in validation and test sets. Due to the way the dataset is processed, each document only contains 4 sentences. The dataset is preprocessed by tokenizing and lower casing. We

[1] `https://github.com/lena-voita/good-translation-wrong-in-context`

use byte-pair encoding (Sennrich et al., 2016b) to prepare source and target vocabularies of roughly 32K tokens. We use `multi-bleu.perl` script for evaluation.

### 4.2 Hyperparameters

We train a Transformer (Vaswani et al., 2017) on all datasets. Following previous (Zhang et al., 2018; Voita et al., 2019b; Xia et al., 2019) work we use the Transformer base configuration (`transformer_base`) on the NIST Zh-En and the OpenSubtitles En-Ru datasets and use the Transformer big configuration (`transformer_big`) on the WMT19 Zh-En dataset. Transformer base consists of 6 layers, 512 hidden units and 8 attention heads. Transformer big consists of 6 layers, 1024 hidden units and 16 attention heads. We use a dropout rate (Srivastava et al., 2014) of 0.1 and label smoothing to regularize our models. We train our models with the Adam optimizer (Kingma and Ba, 2014) using the same warm-up learning rate schedule as in (Vaswani et al., 2017). During decoding we use beam search with beam size 4 and length penalty 0.6. We additionally train backtranslated models (Sennrich et al., 2016a) on the NIST Zh-En and the OpenSubtitles En-Ru datasets. We use the publicly available English gigaword dataset (Graff et al., 2003) to create synthetic parallel data for the NIST Zh-En dataset and use synthetic parallel data provided by (Voita et al., 2019a) for the OpenSubtitles En-Ru dataset. When training backtranslated models, we oversample the original parallel data to make the ratio of synthetic data to original data equal to 1 (Edunov et al., 2018). We tune the number of update steps, learning rate, decay rate, and number of passes over the document of our self-training approach with a random search on a validation set. We use the range of $(5 \times 10^{-5}, 5 \times 10^{-1})$ for learning rate, range of $(0.001, 0.999)$ for decay rate, number of update steps $(2, 4, 8)$ and number of passes over the document $(2, 4)$ for random search. We found that best performing models required a small number of update steps (either 2 or 4) with a relatively large learning rate ($\sim 0.005 - 0.01$) and small decay rate ($\sim 0.2 - 0.5$). We use 3 random seeds to train each model in our experiments and report the average results. We use the Tensor2Tensor library (Vaswani et al., 2018) to train baseline models and to implement our method.

## 5 Results

We present translation quality results measured by BLEU on NIST dataset on Table 1. The self-training procedure improves the results of our sentence-level baseline by the average of 0.53 BLEU for non-backtranslated model and by 0.93 BLEU for backtranslated model for all evaluation sets. Our baseline sentence-level Transformer model trained without backtranslation outperforms previous document-level models by Wang et al. (2017) and Kuang et al. (2017) and is comparable to the document-level model proposed by Zhang et al. (2018). Backtranslation further improves the results of our sentence-level model leading to higher BLEU score compared to the Document Transformer (Zhang et al., 2018).

In Table 2, we show a detailed study of effects of multi-pass self-training and oracle self-training on BLEU scores on NIST evaluation sets. First, multiple decoding passes over the document give an additional average improvement of $0.25 - 0.45$ BLEU points compared to the single decoding pass over the document. Using oracle self-training procedure gives an average of 0.86 and 1.63 BLEU improvement over our non-backtranslated and backtranslated sentence-level baseline models respectively. Compared to using generated translations by the model, oracle self-training gives an improvement of 0.3 and 0.7 BLEU points for non-backtranslated and backtranslated models respectively.

The results on the WMT19 evaluation sets are presented on Table 3. Compared to the NIST dataset our self-training procedure shows an improvement of 0.1 BLEU over a sentence-level baseline model. Oracle self-training outperforms sentence-level baselines by a significant margin of 2.5 BLEU. We hypothesize that such a large gap between performance of oracle and non-oracle self-training is due to the more challenging nature of the WMT dataset which is reflected in the worse performance of sentence-level baseline on WMT compared to NIST. We investigate this claim by measuring the relationship between BLEU achieved by self-training and the relative quality of the sentence-level model on the NIST dataset. Figure 1 shows that the BLEU difference between self-training and sentence-level models monotonically increases as the quality of the sentence-level model gets better on the NIST dataset. This implies that we can expect a larger improvement from applying self-training as we improve the sentence-level model

| Method | Architecture | Model | Valid17 | Test17 | Test18 | Test19 | $\Delta_{\text{BLEU}}$ |
|---|---|---|---|---|---|---|---|
| (Xia et al., 2019) | Transformer Big | - | - | 24.2 | 24.5 | - | - |
| Ours | Transformer Big | Baseline | 22.5 | 23.4 | 24.1 | 25.4 | - |
| | | ST | 22.6 | 23.4 | 24.1 | 25.5 | +0.0 |
| | | Multi-pass ST | 22.6 | 23.5 | 24.2 | 25.6 | +0.1 |
| | | Oracle ST | 24.3 | 25.7 | 25.6 | 29.8 | +2.5 |

Table 3: Results on WMT'19 Chinese-English evaluation sets. The first row shows the performance of the Transformer Big model by (Xia et al., 2019). All models were trained without additional monolingual data and without pretraining. ST: self-training.

| | Model | Valid | Test | $\Delta_{\text{BLEU}}$ |
|---|---|---|---|---|
| Non-BT | Baseline | 31.38 | 31.38 | - |
| | ST | 31.41 | 31.39 | +0.02 |
| | Multi-pass ST | 31.44 | 31.43 | +0.06 |
| | Oracle ST | 31.65 | 31.66 | +0.28 |
| BT | Baseline | 32.22 | 32.21 | - |
| | ST | 32.24 | 32.23 | +0.02 |
| | Multi-pass ST | 32.25 | 32.26 | +0.04 |
| | Oracle ST | 32.56 | 32.54 | +0.34 |

Table 4: Results on OpenSubtitles English-Russian evaluation sets. ST: self-training.

on the WMT dataset. Preliminary experiments on training back-translated models didn't improve results on the WMT dataset. We leave further investigation of ways to improve the sentence-level model on the WMT dataset for future work.

The results on OpenSubtitles evaluation sets are in Table 4. Our self-training and oracle self-training approaches give the performance improvement of 0.1 and 0.3 BLEU respectively. We hypothesize that the small improvement of self-training is due to relatively small number of sentences in the documents in the OpenSubtitles dataset. We validate this claim by varying the number of sentences in the document used for self-training on NIST dataset. Figure 2 shows that the self-training approach achieves higher BLEU improvement as we increase the number of sentences in documents used for self-training.

## 6 Human Evaluation

We conduct a human evaluation study on the NIST Zh-En and the OpenSubtitles En-Ru datasets. For both datasets we sample 50 documents from the test set where translated documents generated by the self-training approach are not exact copies of the translated documents generated by the sentence-level baseline model. For the NIST Zh-En dataset we present reference documents, translated documents generated by the sentence-level baseline, and translated documents generated by self-training approach to 4 native English speakers. For the OpenSubtitles En-Ru dataset we follow a similar setup, where we present reference documents, translated documents generated by sentence-level baseline, and translated documents generated by self-training approach to 4 native Russian speakers. All translated documents are presented in random order with no indication of which approach was used to generate them. We highlight the differences between translated documents when presenting them to human evaluators. The human evaluators are asked to pick one of two translations as their preferred option for each document. We ask the human evaluators to consider fluency, idiomaticity and correctness of the translation relative to the reference when entering their preferred choices.

We follow the setup of Yu et al. (2019) when performing human evaluation. We collect a total of 200 annotations for 50 documents from all 4 human evaluators and show results in Table 5. For both datasets, human evaluators prefer translated documents generated by the self-training approach to translated documents generated by the sentence-level model. For NIST Zh-En, 122 out of 200 annotations indicate a preference towards translations generated by self-training approach. For OpenSubtitles En-Ru, 118 out of 200 annotations similarly show a preference towards translations generated by our self-training approach. This is a statistically significant preference $p < 0.05$ according to two-sided Binomial test. When aggregated for each document by majority vote, for NIST Zh-En, translations generated by the self-training approach are considered better in 25 documents, worse in 12 documents, and the same in 13 documents. For OpenSubtitles En-Ru, translations generated by self-training approach are considered better in 23 documents, worse in 15 documents, and the same in 12 documents. The agreement between annotators for NIST Zh-En and OpenSub-

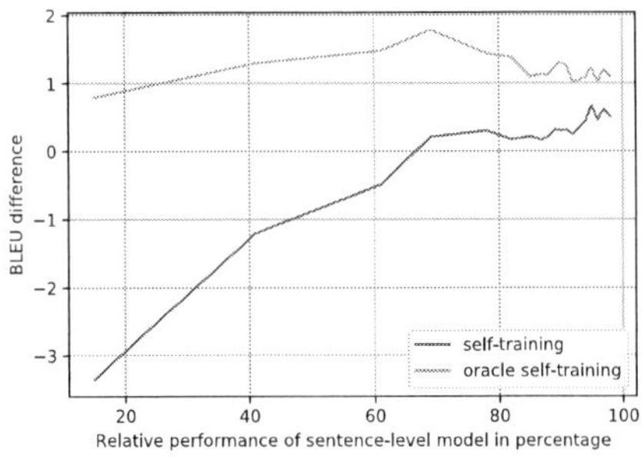


Figure 1: Relationship between relative performance of the sentence-level model and BLEU difference of self-training on the NIST dataset.

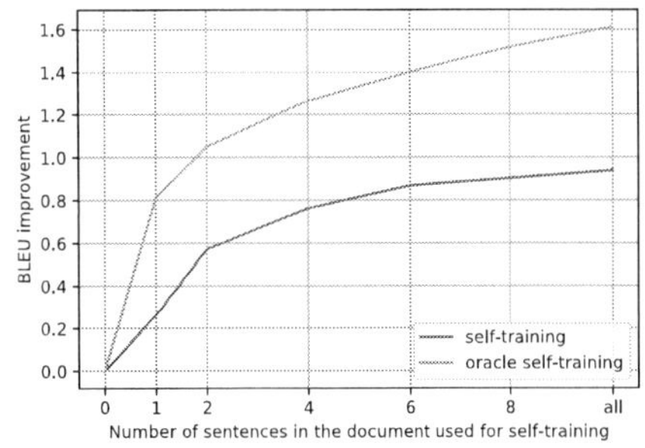


Figure 2: Relationship between number of sentences and BLEU improvement of self-training on the NIST dataset.

| Dataset | Total | Self-train | Baseline |
|---|---|---|---|
| NIST Zh-En | 200 | 122 | 78 |
| OpenSubtitles En-Ru | 200 | 118 | 82 |

Table 5: Human evaluation results on the NIST Zh-En and the OpenSubtitles En-Ru datasets. "Total" denotes total number of annotations collected from humans. "Self-train" denotes number of times evaluators preferred documents by the self-training approach. "Baseline" denotes number of times evaluators preferred documents by sentence-level baseline.

titles En-Ru is $\kappa = 0.293$ and $\kappa = 0.320$ according to Fleiss' kappa (Fleiss, 1971). For both datasets, the inter-annotator agreement rate is considered fair. The agreement rate is similar to the inter-annotator agreement found in the previous WMT human evaluation studies (Bojar et al., 2014).

## 7 Qualitative Results

In Table 6, we show four reference document pairs together with translated documents generated by the baseline sentence-level model and by our self-training approach. We emphasize the underlined words in all documents.

In the first two examples we emphasize the gender of the person marked on verbs and adjectives in translated Russian sentences. In the first example, the baseline sentence-level model inconsistenly produces different gender markings on the underlined verb сказал (masculine told) and underlined adjective сильной (feminine strong). The self-training approach correctly generates a translation with consistent male gender markings on both the underlined verb сказал and the underlined adjective сильным. Similarly, in the second example, the baseline model inconsistenly produces different gender markings on the underlined verbs приглашена (feminine invited) and поругался (masculine fought). Self-training consistently generates female gender markings on both the underlined verbs приглашена (feminine invited) and поссорилась (feminine fought).

In the third example, we emphasize the underlined named entity in reference and generated translations. The baseline sentence-level model inconsistently generates the names "doyle" and "du" when referring to the same entity across two sentences in the same document. The self-training approach consistently uses the name "doyle" across two sentences when referring to the same entity. In the fourth example, we emphasize the plurality of the underlined words. The baseline model inconsistenly generates both singular and plural forms when referring to same noun in consecutive sentences. Self-training generates the noun "pilots" in correct plural form in both sentences.

## 8 Conclusion

In this paper, we propose a way of incorporating the document context inside a trained sentence-level neural machine translation model using self-training. We process documents from left to right multiple times and self-train the sentence-level NMT model on the pair of source sentence and generated target sentence. This reinforces the choices made by the NMT model thus making it more likely that the choices will be repeated in the rest of the document.

We demonstrate the feasibility of our approach on three machine translation datasets: NIST Zh-En, WMT19 Zh-En and OpenSubtitles En-Ru. We show that self-training improves sentence-level

| | |
|---|---|
| **Ref** | мы с эйприл развелись . как я и сказал ... игра в ожидание . будь сильным . и всё получится . |
| **Baseline** | мы с эйприл развелись . ну , как я уже сказал ... игра ожидания . будь сильной . ты справишься . |
| **Ours** | мы с эйприл развелись . ну , как я уже сказал ... игра ожидания . будь сильным . ты справишься . |
| **Ref** | сёрен устраивает вечеринку по поводу своего дня рождения в субботу , а я не знаю , пойду ли я .<br>почему бы тебе не пойти ? просто всё пошло не так . - и я поссорился с кнудом . |
| **Baseline** | в субботу день рождения сёрена и я не знаю , приглашена ли я .<br>почему тебя не пригласили ? все просто пошло не так . - и я поругался с кнудом . |
| **Ours** | в субботу день рождения сёрена и я не знаю , приглашена ли я .<br>почему тебя не пригласили ? все просто пошло не так . - и я поссорилась с кнудом . |
| **Ref** | we are actively seeking a local partner to set up a joint fund company , " duchateau said .<br>duchateau said that the chinese market still has ample potentials . |
| **Baseline** | we are actively looking for a local partner to establish a joint venture fund company , " doyle said .<br>du said that there is still a lot of room for the chinese market . |
| **Ours** | we are actively looking for a local partner to establish a joint venture fund company , " doyle said .<br>doyle said that there is still great room for the chinese market . |
| **Ref** | in may this year , 13 pilots with china eastern airlines wuhan company<br>in succession handed in their resignations , which were rejected by the company .<br>soon afterwards , the pilots applied one after another at the beginning of june<br>to the labor dispute arbitration commission of hubei province for labor arbitration ,<br>requesting for a ruling that their labor relationship with china eastern airlines wuhan company be terminated . |
| **Baseline** | in may this year , 13 pilots of china eastern 's wuhan company<br>submitted their resignations one after another , but the company refused .<br>the pilot then applied for labor arbitration with the hubei province<br>labor dispute arbitration committee in early june , requesting the ruling<br>to terminate the labor relationship with the wuhan company of china eastern airlines . |
| **Ours** | in may this year , 13 pilots of china eastern 's wuhan company<br>submitted their resignations one after another , but the company refused .<br>subsequently , in early june , the pilots successively applied for labor arbitration<br>with the hubei province labor dispute arbitration committee ,<br>requesting that the labor relationship with china eastern airlines be terminated . |

Table 6: Four reference documents together with translations generated by the baseline sentence-level model and by our self-training approach. First two documents are taken from the OpenSubtitles English-Russian and second two documents are taken from the NIST Chinese-English dataset.

baselines by up to 0.93 BLEU. We also conduct a human evaluation study and show a strong preference of the annotators to the translated documents generated by our self-training approach. Our analysis demonstrates that self-training achieves higher improvement on longer documents and using better sentence-level models.

In this work, we only use self-training on source-to-target NMT models in order to capture the target side document context. One extension could investigate the application of self-training on both target-to-source and source-to-target sentence-level models to incorporate both source and target document context into generated translations. Overall, we hope that our work would motivate novel approaches of making trained sentence-level models better suited for document translation at decoding time.

## 9 Acknowledgements

We would like to thank Phil Blunsom, Kris Cao, Kyunghyun Cho, Chris Dyer, Wojciech Stokowiec and members of the Language team for helpful suggestions.

## References

Ruchit Agrawal, Marco Turchi, and Matteo Negri. 2018. Contextual handling in neural machine translation: Look behind, ahead and on both sides.

James A Anderson and Geoffrey E Hinton. 1981. Models of information processing in the brain. *Parallel models of associative memory.*

A. Axelrod, X. He, and Jianfeng Gao. 2011. Domain adaptation via pseudo in-domain data selection. In *EMNLP*.

Jimmy Ba, Geoffrey E. Hinton, Volodymyr Mnih,

Joel Z. Leibo, and Catalin Ionescu. 2016. Using fast weights to attend to the recent past. In *NIPS*.

Dzmitry Bahdanau, Kyunghyun Cho, and Yoshua Bengio. 2014. Neural machine translation by jointly learning to align and translate. *arXiv preprint arXiv:1409.0473*.

Loïc Barrault, Magdalena Biesialska, Ondřej Bojar, Marta R. Costa-jussà, Christian Federmann, Yvette Graham, Roman Grundkiewicz, Barry Haddow, Matthias Huck, Eric Joanis, Tom Kocmi, Philipp Koehn, Chi-kiu Lo, Nikola Ljubešić, Christof Monz, Makoto Morishita, Masaaki Nagata, Toshiaki Nakazawa, Santanu Pal, Matt Post, and Marcos Zampieri. 2020. Findings of the 2020 conference on machine translation (WMT20). In *Proceedings of the Fifth Conference on Machine Translation*, pages 1–55, Online. Association for Computational Linguistics.

Loïc Barrault, Ondřej Bojar, Marta R. Costa-jussà, Christian Federmann, Mark Fishel, Yvette Graham, Barry Haddow, Matthias Huck, Philipp Koehn, Shervin Malmasi, Christof Monz, Mathias Müller, Santanu Pal, Matt Post, and Marcos Zampieri. 2019. Findings of the 2019 conference on machine translation (WMT19). In *ACL*.

Ondrej Bojar, C. Buck, C. Federmann, B. Haddow, Philipp Koehn, Johannes Leveling, Christof Monz, Pavel Pecina, Matt Post, Herve Saint-Amand, Radu Soricut, Lucia Specia, and A. Tamchyna. 2014. Findings of the 2014 workshop on statistical machine translation. In *WMT@ACL*.

Chenhui Chu and Rui Wang. 2018. A survey of domain adaptation for neural machine translation. In *Proceedings of the 27th International Conference on Computational Linguistics*, pages 1304–1319, Santa Fe, New Mexico, USA. Association for Computational Linguistics.

Sergey Edunov, Myle Ott, Michael Auli, and David Grangier. 2018. Understanding back-translation at scale. In *EMNLP*.

Joseph L. Fleiss. 1971. Measuring nominal scale agreement among many raters. *Psychological Bulletin*.

Markus Freitag and Y. Al-Onaizan. 2016. Fast domain adaptation for neural machine translation. *ArXiv*, abs/1612.06897.

Eva Martínez Garcia, C. Creus, and C. España-Bonet. 2019. Context-aware neural machine translation decoding. In *DiscoMT@EMNLP*.

Eva Martínez Garcia, C. Creus, C. España-Bonet, and Lluís Màrquez i Villodre. 2017. Using word embeddings to enforce document-level lexical consistency in machine translation. *The Prague Bulletin of Mathematical Linguistics*, 108:85 – 96.

David Graff, Junbo Kong, Ke Chen, and Kazuaki Maeda. 2003. English gigaword. *Linguistic Data Consortium, Philadelphia*, 4(1):34.

Alex Graves. 2013. Generating sequences with recurrent neural networks. *arXiv preprint arXiv:1308.0850*.

Christian Hardmeier, Joakim Nivre, and J. Tiedemann. 2012. Document-wide decoding for phrase-based statistical machine translation. In *EMNLP-CoNLL*.

Hany Hassan, Anthony Aue, Chang Chen, Vishal Chowdhary, Jonathan Clark, Christian Federmann, Xuedong Huang, Marcin Junczys-Dowmunt, William Lewis, Mu Li, Shujie Liu, Tie-Yan Liu, Renqian Luo, Arul Menezes, Tao Qin, Frank Seide, Xu Tan, Fei Tian, Lijun Wu, Shuangzhi Wu, Yingce Xia, Dongdong Zhang, Zhirui Zhang, and Ming Zhou. 2018. Achieving human parity on automatic chinese to english news translation. *arXiv preprint arXiv:1803.05567*.

Junxian He, Jiatao Gu, Jiajun Shen, and Marc'Aurelio Ranzato. 2019. Revisiting self-training for neural sequence generation. *arXiv preprint arXiv:1909.13788*.

J J Hopfield. 1982. Neural networks and physical systems with emergent collective computational abilities. *Proceedings of the National Academy of Sciences*.

Zhongqiang Huang and Mary Harper. 2009. Self-training pcfg grammars with latent annotations across languages. In *EMNLP*.

Sebastien Jean, Ankur Bapna, and Orhan Firat. 2019. Fill in the blanks: Imputing missing sentences for larger-context neural machine translation. *arXiv preprint arXiv:1910.14075*.

Sebastien Jean, Stanislas Lauly, Orhan Firat, and Kyunghyun Cho. 2017. Does neural machine translation benefit from larger context? *arXiv preprint arXiv:1704.05135*.

Marcin Junczys-Dowmunt. 2019. Microsoft translator at wmt 2019: Towards large-scale document-level neural machine translation. In *WMT*.

Nal Kalchbrenner and Phil Blunsom. 2013. Recurrent continuous translation models. In *EMNLP*.

Diederik P Kingma and Jimmy Ba. 2014. Adam: A method for stochastic optimization. *arXiv preprint arXiv:1412.6980*.

Teuvo Kohonen. 1972. Correlation matrix memories. *IEEE Transactions on Computers*.

Ben Krause, Emmanuel Kahembwe, Iain Murray, and Steve Renals. 2018. Dynamic evaluation of neural sequence models. In *ICML*.

Shaohui Kuang, Deyi Xiong, Weihua Luo, and Guodong Zhou. 2017. Modeling coherence for neural machine translation with dynamic and topic caches. *arXiv preprint arXiv:1711.11221*.

Roland Kuhn and Renato De Mori. 1990. A cache-based natural language model for speech recognition. In *PAMI*.

Dong-Hyun Lee. 2013. Pseudo-label : The simple and efficient semi-supervised learning method for deep neural networks. *ICML 2013 Workshop : Challenges in Representation Learning (WREPL)*.

Sameen Maruf and Gholamreza Haffari. 2018. Document context neural machine translation with memory networks. In *ACL*.

David McClosky, Eugene Charniak, and Mark Johnson. 2006. Effective self-training for parsing. In *ACL*.

Lesly Miculicich, Dhananjay Ram, Nikolaos Pappas, and James Henderson. 2018. Document-level neural machine translation with hierarchical attention networks. In *EMNLP*.

Tomas Mikolov. 2012. *Statistical language models based on neural networks*. Ph.D. thesis, Brno University of Technology.

Andrei Popescu-Belis, Sharid Loáiciga, Christian Hardmeier, and Deyi Xiong. 2019. *Proceedings of the Fourth Workshop on Discourse in Machine Translation (DiscoMT 2019)*. https://www.aclweb.org/anthology/D19-65.pdf.

Matt Post. 2018. A call for clarity in reporting BLEU scores. In *WMT*.

A. Radford, Jeffrey Wu, R. Child, David Luan, Dario Amodei, and Ilya Sutskever. 2019. Language models are unsupervised multitask learners.

Roi Reichart and Rai Rappoport. 2007. Self-training for enhancement and domain adaptation of statistical parsers trained on small datasets. In *ACL*.

H. Scudder. 1965. Probability of error of some adaptive pattern-recognition machines. *IEEE Trans. Inf. Theor.*

Rico Sennrich. 2018. *Why the Time Is Ripe for Discourse in Machine Translation*. http://homepages.inf.ed.ac.uk/rsennric/wnmt2018.pdf.

Rico Sennrich, Barry Haddow, and Alexandra Birch. 2016a. Improving neural machine translation models with monolingual data. In *ACL*.

Rico Sennrich, Barry Haddow, and Alexandra Birch. 2016b. Neural machine translation of rare words with subword units. In *ACL*.

Claude E. Shannon. 1948. A mathematical theory of communication. *Bell Syst. Tech. J.*

Nitish Srivastava, Geoffrey Hinton, Alex Krizhevsky, Ilya Sutskever, and Ruslan Salakhutdinov. 2014. Dropout: A simple way to prevent neural networks from overfitting.

Ilya Sutskever, Oriol Vinyals, and Quoc V Le. 2014. Sequence to sequence learning with neural networks. In *NIPS*.

Jörg Tiedemann and Yves Scherrer. 2017. Neural machine translation with extended context. In *Proceedings of the Third Workshop on Discourse in Machine Translation*.

Nicola Ueffing. 2006. Using monolingual source-language data to improve mt performance. In *IWSLT*.

Ashish Vaswani, Samy Bengio, Eugene Brevdo, Francois Chollet, Aidan N. Gomez, Stephan Gouws, Llion Jones, Łukasz Kaiser, Nal Kalchbrenner, Niki Parmar, Ryan Sepassi, Noam Shazeer, and Jakob Uszkoreit. 2018. Tensor2tensor for neural machine translation. *CoRR*, abs/1803.07416.

Ashish Vaswani, Noam Shazeer, Niki Parmar, Jakob Uszkoreit, Llion Jones, Aidan N Gomez, Łukasz Kaiser, and Illia Polosukhin. 2017. Attention is all you need. In *NIPS*.

Elena Voita, Rico Sennrich, and Ivan Titov. 2019a. Context-aware monolingual repair for neural machine translation. In *EMNLP*.

Elena Voita, Rico Sennrich, and Ivan Titov. 2019b. When a good translation is wrong in context: Context-aware machine translation improves on deixis, ellipsis, and lexical cohesion. In *ACL*.

Longyue Wang, Zhaopeng Tu, Andy Way, and Qun Liu. 2017. Exploiting cross-sentence context for neural machine translation. In *EMNLP*.

David J Willshaw, O Peter Buneman, and Hugh Christopher Longuet-Higgins. 1969. Non-holographic associative memory. *Nature*.

Yingce Xia, Xu Tan, Fei Tian, Fei Gao, Di He, Weicong Chen, Yang Fan, Linyuan Gong, Yichong Leng, Renqian Luo, Yiren Wang, Lijun Wu, Jinhua Zhu, Tao Qin, and Tie-Yan Liu. 2019. Microsoft research asia's systems for WMT19. In *WMT*.

Yingce Xia, Fei Tian, Lijun Wu, Jianxin Lin, Tao Qin, Nenghai Yu, and Tie-Yan Liu. 2017. Deliberation networks: Sequence generation beyond one-pass decoding. In *NIPS*.

Hao Xiong, Zhongjun He, Hua Wu, and Haifeng Wang. 2018. Modeling coherence for discourse neural machine translation. *arXiv preprint arXiv:1811.05683*.

David Yarowsky. 1995. Unsupervised word sense disambiguation rivaling supervised methods. In *ACL*.

Kyra Yee, Nathan Ng, Yann N. Dauphin, and Michael Auli. 2019. Simple and effective noisy channel modeling for neural machine translation. In *EMNLP*.

L. Yu, Laurent Sartran, Wojciech Stokowiec, Wang Ling, Lingpeng Kong, P. Blunsom, and Chris Dyer. 2019. Better document-level machine translation with bayes' rule. *Transactions of the Association for Computational Linguistics*, 8:346–360.

Lei Yu, Phil Blunsom, Chris Dyer, Edward Grefenstette, and Tomas Kocisky. 2017. The neural noisy channel. In *ICLR*.

Jiacheng Zhang, Huanbo Luan, Maosong Sun, Feifei Zhai, Jingfang Xu, Min Zhang, and Yang Liu. 2018. Improving the transformer translation model with document-level context. In *EMNLP*.

Jiajun Zhang and Chengqing Zong. 2016. Exploiting source-side monolingual data in neural machine translation. In *EMNLP*.

# DMRST: A Joint Framework for Document-Level Multilingual RST Discourse Segmentation and Parsing

**Zhengyuan Liu[†]*, Ke Shi[†], Nancy F. Chen[†]***
Institute for Infocomm Research, A*STAR, Singapore
{liu_zhengyuan,shi_ke,nfychen}@i2r.a-star.edu.sg

## Abstract

Text discourse parsing weighs importantly in understanding information flow and argumentative structure in natural language, making it beneficial for downstream tasks. While previous work significantly improves the performance of RST discourse parsing, they are not readily applicable to practical use cases: (1) EDU segmentation is not integrated into most existing tree parsing frameworks, thus it is not straightforward to apply such models on newly-coming data. (2) Most parsers cannot be used in multilingual scenarios, because they are developed only in English. (3) Parsers trained from single-domain treebanks do not generalize well on out-of-domain inputs. In this work, we propose a document-level multilingual RST discourse parsing framework, which conducts EDU segmentation and discourse tree parsing jointly. Moreover, we propose a cross-translation augmentation strategy to enable the framework to support multilingual parsing and improve its domain generality. Experimental results show that our model achieves state-of-the-art performance on document-level multilingual RST parsing in all sub-tasks.

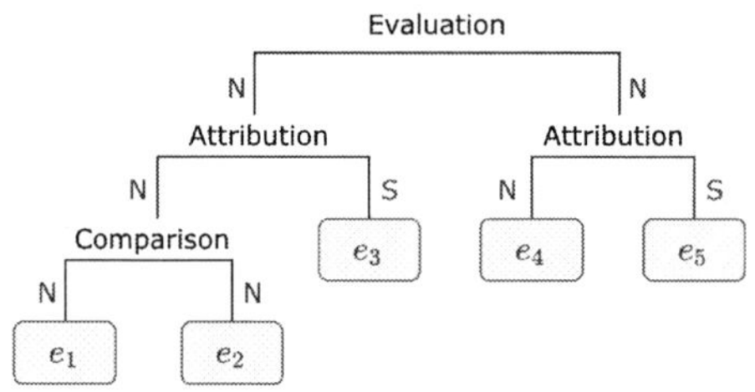


$e_1$[ The European Community's consumer price index rose a provisional 0.6% in September from August ] $e_2$[ and was up 5.3% from September 1988, ] $e_3$[ according to Eurostat, the EC's statistical agency. ] $e_4$[ The month-to-month rise in the index was the largest since April, ] $e_5$[ Eurostat said. ]

Figure 1: One constituency tree with RST discourse annotation. $e_i$, $N$ and $S$ denote elementary discourse units, nucleus, and satellite, respectively. Nuclearity and discourse relations are labeled on each span pair.

## 1 Introduction

Rhetorical Structure Theory (RST) (Mann and Thompson, 1988) is one of the predominant theories for discourse analysis, where a document is represented by a constituency tree with discourse-related annotation. As illustrated in Figure 1, the paragraph is split to segments named Elementary Discourse Units (EDUs), as the leaf nodes of the tree, and they are further connected by rhetorical relations (*e.g., Elaboration, Attribution*) to form larger text spans until the entire document is included. The spans are further categorized to *Nucleus* (the core part) or *Satellite* (the subordinate part) based on their relative importance in the rhetorical relations. Thus, document-level RST discourse parsing consists of four sub-tasks: EDU segmentation, tree structure construction, nuclearity determination, and relation classification. Since discourse parsing provides structural information of the narrative flow, downstream natural language processing applications, such as reading comprehension (Gao et al., 2020), sentiment analysis (Bhatia et al., 2015), and text summarization (Liu and Chen, 2019), can benefit from incorporating semantic-related information.

RST discourse parsing has been an active research area, especially since neural approaches and large-scale pre-trained language models were introduced. On the test set of the English RST benchmark (Carlson et al., 2002), the performance of automatic parsing is approaching that of human annotators. However, compared with other off-the-shelf text processing applications like machine translation, RST parsers are still not readily applicable to massive and diverse samples due to the following challenges: (1) Most parsers take EDU segmentation as a pre-requisite data preparation step, and only conduct evaluations on samples with

[†]Equal Contribution. *Corresponding Author.



*Proceedings of the 2nd Workshop on Computational Approaches to Discourse*, pages 154–164
November 10–11, 2021. ©2021 Association for Computational Linguistics

gold EDU segmentation. Thus it is not straightforward to utilize them to parse raw documents. (2) Parsers are primarily optimized and evaluated in English, and are not applicable on multilingual scenarios/tasks. Human annotation under the RST scheme is labor-intensive and requires specialized linguistic knowledge, resulting in a shortage of training data especially in low resource languages. (3) Data sparsity also leads to limited generalization capabilities in terms of topic domain and language variety, as the monolingual discourse treebanks usually concentrate on a specific domain. For instance, the English RST corpus is comprised of Wall Street Journal news articles, thus its parser might not perform well on scientific articles.

In this paper, to tackle the aforementioned challenges, we propose a joint framework for document-level multilingual RST discourse analysis. To achieve parsing from scratch, we enhance a top-down discourse parsing model with joint learning of EDU segmentation. Since the well-annotated RST treebanks in different languages share the same underlying linguistic theory, data-driven approaches can benefit from joint learning on multilingual RST resources (Braud et al., 2017a). Inspired by the success of mixed multilingual training (Liu et al., 2020), we further propose a cross-translation data augmentation strategy to improve RST parsing in both language and domain coverage.

We conduct extensive experiments on RST treebanks from six languages: English, Spanish, Basque, German, Dutch, and Portuguese. Experimental results show that our framework achieves state-of-the-art performance in different languages and on all sub-tasks. We further investigate the model's zero-shot generalization capability, by assessing its performance via language-level cross validation. Additionally, the proposed framework can be readily extended to other languages with existing treebanks. The pre-trained model is built as an off-the-shelf application, and can be applied in an end-to-end manner.

## 2 Related Work

**RST Discourse Parsing** Discourse structures describe the organization of documents/sentences in terms of rhetorical/discourse relations. The Rhetorical Structure Theory (RST) (Mann and Thompson, 1988) and the Penn Discourse TreeBank (PDTB) (Prasad et al., 2008) are the two most prominent theories of discourse analysis, where they are at document level and sentence level respectively. The structure-aware document analysis has shown to be useful for downstream natural language processing tasks, such as sentiment analysis (Bhatia et al., 2015) and reading comprehension (Gao et al., 2020). Many studies focused on developing automatic computational solutions for discourse parsing. Statistical approaches utilized various linguistic characteristics such as $N$-gram and lexical features, syntactic and organizational features (Sagae, 2009; Hernault et al., 2010; Li et al., 2014; Heilman and Sagae, 2015), and had obtained substantial improvement on the English RST-DT benchmark (Carlson et al., 2002). Neural networks have been making inroads into discourse analysis frameworks, such as attention-based hierarchical encoding (Li et al., 2016) and integrating neural-based syntactic features into a transition-based parser (Yu et al., 2018). Lin et al. (2019) explored encoder-decoder neural architectures on sentence-level discourse analysis, with a top-down parsing procedure. Recently, pre-trained language models were introduced to document-level discourse parsing, and boosted the overall performance (Shi et al., 2020).

**Multilingual Parsing** Aside from the English treebank, datasets in other languages have also been introduced and studied, such as German (Stede and Neumann, 2014), Dutch (Redeker et al., 2012), and Basque (Iruskieta et al., 2013). The main challenge of multilingual discourse parsing is the sparsity of annotated data. Braud et al. (2017a) conducted a harmonization of discourse treebanks across annotations in different languages, and Iruskieta and Braud (2019) used multilingual word embeddings to train systems on under-resourced languages. Recently, Liu et al. (2020) proposed a multilingual RST parser by utilizing cross-lingual language model and EDU segment-level translation, obtaining substantial performance gains.

**EDU Segmentation** EDU segmentation identifies the minimal text spans to be linked by discourse relations. It is the first step in building discourse parsers, and often studied as a separated task in discourse analysis. Existing segmenters on the English discourse corpus achieve sentence-level results with 95% F1 scores (Li et al., 2018), while document-level segmentation is more challenging. Muller et al. (2019) proposed a discourse segmenter that supports multiple languages and schemes. Recently, taking segmentation as a se-

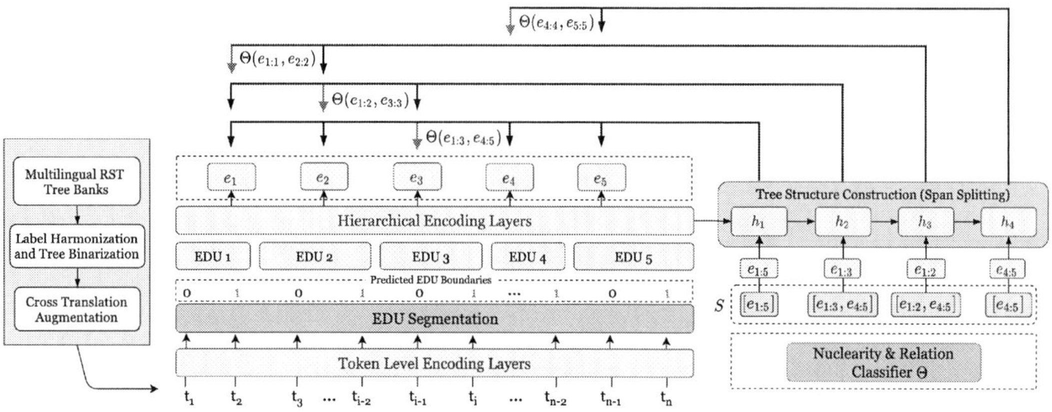


Figure 2: The architecture of the proposed joint document-level neural parser. A segmenter is first utilized to predict the EDU breaks, and a hierarchical encoder is used to generate the EDU representations. Then, the pointer-network-based decoder and the relation classifier predict the tree structure, nuclearity, and rhetorical relations. $t$, $e$ and $h$ denote input tokens, encoded EDU representations, and decoded hidden states. The stack $S$ is maintained by the decoder to track top-down depth-first span splitting. With each splitting pointer $k$, sub-spans $e_{i:k}$ and $e_{k+1:j}$ are fed to a classifier $\Phi$ for nuclearity and relation determination.

quence labeling task was shown to be effective in reaching strong segmentation results. Fusing syntactic features to language models was also introduced (Desai et al., 2020). In this work, to the best of our knowledge, we are the first to build a joint framework for document-level multilingual RST discourse analysis that supports parsing from scratch, and can be potentially extended to any language by text-level transformation.

## 3 Methodology

In this section, we elaborate on the proposed joint multilingual RST discourse parsing framework. We first integrate EDU segmentation into a top-down Transformer-based neural parser, and show how to leverage dynamic loss weights to control the balance of each sub-task. We then propose cross-translation augmentation to improve the multilingual and domain generalization capability.

### 3.1 Transformer-based Neural Parser

The neural model consists of an EDU segmenter, a hierarchical encoder, a span splitting decoder for tree construction, and a classifier for nuclearity/relation determination.

#### 3.1.1 EDU Segmentation

The EDU segmentation aims to split a document into continuous units and is usually formulated to detect the span breaks. In this work, we conduct it as a sequence labeling task (Muller et al., 2019; Devlin et al., 2019). Given a document containing $n$ tokens, an embedding layer is employed to generate the token-level representations $T = \{t_1, ..., t_n\}$, in particular, a pre-trained language backbone is used to leverage the resourceful prior knowledge. Instead of detecting the beginning of each EDU as in previous work (Muller et al., 2019), here we propose to predict both EDU boundaries via token-level classification. In detail, a linear layer is used to predict the type of each token in one EDU span, i.e., at the begin/intermediate/end position.[1] For extensive comparison, we also implement another segmenter by using a pointer mechanism (Vinyals et al., 2015). Results in Table 3 show that the token-level classification approach consistently produces better performance.

#### 3.1.2 Hierarchical Encoding

To obtain EDU representations with both local and global views, spans are hierarchically modeled from token and EDU-level to document-level. For the document containing $n$ tokens, the initial EDU-level representations are calculated by averaging the token embeddings $t_{i:j}$ of each EDU, where $i, j$ are its boundary indices. Then they are fed into a Bidirectional-GRU (Cho et al., 2014) to capture context-aware representations at the document level. Boundary information has been shown to be effective in previous discourse parsing studies (Shi et al., 2020), thus we also incorporate boundary embeddings from both ends of each EDU to

[1]For the EDU that only contains one token, its begin and end position are the same.

implicitly exploit the syntactic features such as part-of-speech (POS) and sentential information. Then, the ensemble representations are fed to a linear layer, and we obtain the final contextualized EDU representations $E = \{e_1, ..., e_m\}$, where $m$ is the total number of EDUs.

#### 3.1.3 Tree Structure Construction

The constituency parsing process is to analyze the input by breaking down it into sub-spans also known as constituents. In previous studies (Lin et al., 2019; Shi et al., 2020), with a generic constituency-based decoding framework, the discourse parsing results of depth-first and breadth-first manner are similar. Here the decoder builds the tree structure in a top-down depth-first manner. Starting from splitting a span with the entire document, a pointer network iteratively decides the delimitation point to divide a span into two sub-spans, until it reaches the leaf nodes with only one EDU. As the parsing example illustrated in Figure 2, a stack $S$ is maintained to ensure the parsing is conducted under the top-down depth-first manner, and it is initialized with the span containing all EDUs $e_{1:m}$. At each decoding step, the span $e_{i:j}$ at the head of $S$ is popped to the pointer network to decide the split point $k$ based on the attention mechanism (Bahdanau et al., 2015).

$$s_{t,u} = \sigma(h_t, e_u) \textbf{ for } u = i...j \tag{1}$$

$$a_t = \text{softmax}(s_t) = \frac{\exp(s_{t,u})}{\sum_{u=i}^{j} \exp(s_{t,u})} \tag{2}$$

where $\sigma(x, y)$ is the dot product used as the attention scoring function. The span $e_{i:j}$ is split into two sub-spans $e_{i:k}$ and $e_{k+1:j}$. The sub-spans that need further processing are pushed to the top of the stack $S$ to maintain depth-first manner. The decoder iteratively parses the spans until $S$ is empty.

#### 3.1.4 Nuclearity and Relation Classification

At each decoding step, a bi-affine classifier is employed to predict the nuclearity and rhetorical relations of two sub-spans $e_{i:k}$ and $e_{k+1:j}$ split by the pointer network. More specifically, the nuclearity labels *Nucleus* (N) and *Satellite* (S) are attached together with rhetorical relation labels (e.g., *NS-Evaluation*, *NN-Background*). In particular, the EDU representations are first fed to a dense layer with Exponential Linear Unit (ELU) activation for latent feature transformation, and then a bi-affine layer (Dozat and Manning, 2017) with softmax activation is adopted to predict the nuclearity and rhetorical relations.

### 3.2 Dynamic Weighted Loss

The training objective of our framework is to minimize the sum of the loss $\mathcal{L}_e$ of document-level EDU segmentation, the loss $\mathcal{L}_s$ of parsing the correct tree structure, and the loss $\mathcal{L}_l$ of predicting the corresponding nuclearity and relation labels:

$$\mathcal{L}_e(\theta_e) = -\sum_{n=1}^{N} \log P_{\theta_e}(y_n|X) \tag{3}$$

$$\mathcal{L}_s(\theta_s) = -\sum_{t=1}^{T} \log P_{\theta_s}(y_t|y_1, ..., y_{t-1}, X) \tag{4}$$

$$\mathcal{L}_l(\theta_l) = -\sum_{m=1}^{M}\sum_{r=1}^{R} \log P_{\theta_l}(y_m = r|X) \tag{5}$$

$$\mathcal{L}_{total}(\theta) = \lambda_1\mathcal{L}_e(\theta_e) + \lambda_2\mathcal{L}_s(\theta_s) + \lambda_3\mathcal{L}_l(\theta_l) \tag{6}$$

where $X$ is the given document, $\theta_e$, $\theta_s$ and $\theta_l$ are the parameters of the EDU segmenter, the tree structure decoder, and the nuclearity-relation classifier, respectively. $N$ and $T$ are the total token number and span number. $y_1, ..., y_{t-1}$ denote the sub-trees that have been generated in the previous steps. $M$ is the number of spans with at least two EDUs, and $R$ is the total number of pre-defined nuclearity-relation labels.

To find the balance of training multiple objectives, we adopt the adaptive weighting (Liu et al., 2019) to dynamically control the weights of multiple tasks. Specifically, each task $k$ is weighted by $\lambda_k$, where $\lambda_k$ is calculated as:

$$w_k(i-1) = \frac{\mathcal{L}_k(i-1)}{\mathcal{L}_k(i-2)} \tag{7}$$

$$\lambda_k(i) = \frac{K \cdot \exp(w_k(i-1)/Temp)}{\sum_j \exp(w_j(i-1)/Temp)} \tag{8}$$

where $i$ is the training iterations, $K$ is the task number, and $Temp$ represents the temperature value that smooths the loss from re-weighting. In our experimental settings, adopting dynamic weighted loss brought about relative 2.5% improvement on all sub-tasks.

### 3.3 Cross Translation Augmentation

Data augmentation is an effective approach to tackle the drawbacks of low resource training by creating additional data from existing samples. For

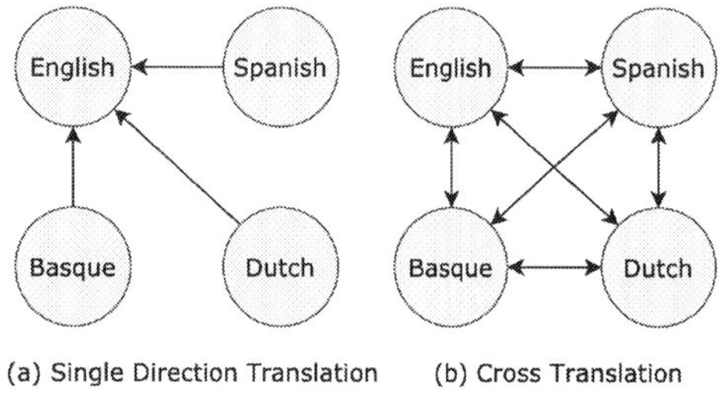


Figure 3: Overview of single direction translation (a) and cross-translation strategy (b). Here we take 4 languages as an example. Arrows denote the translate directions.

| |
|---|
| **English (Source Text)**<br>$e_1$[ The European Community's consumer price index rose a provisional 0.6% in September from August ] $e_2$[ and was up 5.3% from September 1988, ] $e_3$[ according to Eurostat, the EC's statistical agency. ] $e_4$[ The month-to-month rise in the index was the largest since April, ] $e_5$[ Eurostat said. ] |
| **Dutch (Translated Text)**<br>$e_1$[ De consumentenprijsindex van de Europese Gemeenschap is in september met een voorlopige 0,6% gestegen ten opzichte van augustus ] $e_2$[ en steeg met 5,3% ten opzichte van september 1988, ] $e_3$[ volgens Eurostat, het statistiekbureau van de EC. ] $e_4$[ De maand-op-maand stijging van de index was de grootste sinds april, ] $e_5$[ aldus Eurostat. ] |
| **Spanish (Translated Text)**<br>$e_1$[ O índice de preços ao consumidor da Comunidade Europeia subiu 0.6 % provisório em setembro ante agosto ] $e_2$[ e aumentou 5.3 % em relação a setembro de 1988, ] $e_3$[ de acordo com o Eurostat, a agência de estatísticas da CE. ] $e_4$[ A alta mensal do índice foi a maior desde abril, ] $e_5$[ Eurostat disse. ] |

Table 1: One example of EDU segment-level translation. The three text samples share the same discourse tree structure, nuclearity, and relation annotation.

instance, back translation, a popular data augmentation method, is widely applied to tasks like machine translation (Edunov et al., 2018). Since the well-annotated RST treebanks in different languages share the same underlying linguistic theory, data-driven approaches can benefit from joint learning on multilingual RST resources. In previous work, Liu et al. (2020) uniformed the multilingual task to a monolingual one by translating all discourse tree samples at the EDU level to English.

In this paper, we propose a cross-translation data augmentation strategy.[2] The method with single direction translation converts all samples to one language in both the training and the inference stage (see Figure 3(a)). This approach cannot exploit the capability of multilingual language backbones. It also increases the test time due to additional computation for translation. In contrast, cross-translation

| Treebank Lang. | Train No. | Dev No. | Test No. |
|---|---|---|---|
| English (En) | | | |
| - English RST-DT | 309 | 38 | 38 |
| - English GUM-DT | 78 | 18 | 18 |
| Portuguese (Pt) | 256 | 38 | 38 |
| Spanish (Es) | 203 | 32 | 32 |
| German (De) | 142 | 17 | 17 |
| Dutch (Nl) | 56 | 12 | 12 |
| Basque (Eu) | 84 | 28 | 28 |

Table 2: The collected RST discourse treebanks from 6 languages. We use the split of train, developmental and test set, as well as the data pre-processing following (Braud et al., 2017a).

will convert samples from one language to other languages, to produce multilingual training data (see Figure 3(b)). Thus the model is able to process multilingual input during inference. As shown in Table 1, adopting segment-level translation retains the original EDU segmentation as the source text, thus the converted sample in a target language will share the same discourse tree structure and nuclearity/relation labels. We postulate that this text-level transformation will bridge the gaps among different languages. Moreover, since different RST treebanks use articles from different domains (Liu et al., 2020), we speculate that adopting cross-translation can also increase domain coverage in the monolingual space, and further improve the model's overall generalization ability.

## 4 Experimental Results

In this section, we elaborate on experiment settings of the multilingual RST segmentation and parsing task, compare our proposed framework with previous models, and conduct result analysis.

### 4.1 Multilingual Dataset

We constructed a multilingual data collection by merging RST treebanks from 6 languages: English (En) (Carlson et al., 2002), Brazilian Portuguese (Pt)[3] (Cardoso et al., 2011; Pardo and Nunes, 2004; Collovini et al., 2007; Pardo and Seno, 2005), Spanish (Es) (Da Cunha et al., 2011), German (De) (Stede and Neumann, 2014), Dutch (Nl) (Redeker et al., 2012), and Basque (Eu) (Iruskieta et al., 2013), and their details are shown in Table

[2]The neural machine translation engine from Google is used: https://cloud.google.com/translate.

[3]The Portuguese RST dataset consists of 140 samples from CST-News (Cardoso et al., 2011), 100 samples from CorpusTCC (Pardo and Nunes, 2004), 50 samples from Summ-it (Collovini et al., 2007), and 40 samples from Rhetalho (Pardo and Seno, 2005).

| | English (En) | Portuguese (Pt) | Spanish (Es) | German (De) | Dutch (Nl) | Basque (Eu) |
|---|---|---|---|---|---|---|
| Braud et al. (2017b) | 89.5 | 82.2 | 79.3 | 85.1 | 82.6 | - |
| Muller et al. (2019) | 93.7 | 91.3 | 88.2 | 94.1 | 90.7 | 85.8 |
| Pointer-Net Segmenter | 91.8 | 92.5 | 93.6 | 93.4 | 94.9 | 87.3 |
| Boundary CLS Segmenter (Ours) | **96.5** | **92.8** | **93.7** | **95.1** | **95.5** | **88.7** |

Table 3: Document-level multilingual EDU Segmentation performance on 6 languages. Micro F1 scores are reported as in (Muller et al., 2019).

| | English (En) | | | Portuguese (Pt) | | | Spanish (Es) | | |
|---|---|---|---|---|---|---|---|---|---|
| Model | Sp. | Nu. | Rel. | Sp. | Nu. | Rel. | Sp. | Nu. | Rel. |
| Yu et al. (2018) | 85.5 | 73.1 | 60.2 | - | - | - | - | - | - |
| Iruskieta and Braud (2019) | 80.9 | 65.5 | 52.1 | 79.7 | 62.8 | 47.8 | 85.4 | 65.0 | 45.8 |
| Cross Rep. (Liu et al., 2020) | 87.5 | 74.7 | 63.0 | 86.3 | 71.7 | 60.0 | 86.2 | 71.1 | 54.4 |
| Segment Trans. (Liu et al., 2020) | 87.8 | 75.4 | 63.5 | 86.5 | 72.0 | 60.3 | 87.9 | 71.4 | 56.1 |
| DMRST w/o Cross Trans. | 87.9 | 75.3 | 64.0 | 86.5 | 73.3 | 61.5 | 88.2 | 73.7 | 60.3 |
| DMRST (Our Framework) | **88.2** | **76.2** | **64.7** | **87.0** | **74.3** | **62.1** | **88.7** | **75.7** | **63.4** |
| | German (De) | | | Dutch (Nl) | | | Basque (Eu) | | |
| Model | Sp. | Nu. | Rel. | Sp. | Nu. | Rel. | Sp. | Nu. | Rel. |
| Cross Rep. (Liu et al., 2020) | 83.6 | 62.2 | 45.1 | 85.9 | 64.5 | 49.4 | 85.1 | 65.8 | 47.7 |
| Segment Trans. (Liu et al., 2020) | 82.3 | 58.9 | 41.0 | 84.6 | 62.7 | 47.2 | 84.4 | 65.5 | 47.3 |
| DMRST w/o Cross Trans. | 83.1 | 62.2 | 45.9 | 85.5 | 64.4 | 50.6 | 80.2 | 59.8 | 42.1 |
| DMRST (Our Framework) | **84.3** | **64.1** | **47.3** | **85.6** | **66.3** | **52.3** | **85.1** | **67.2** | **48.3** |

Table 4: Document-level multilingual RST parsing comparison of baseline models and our framework. *Sp.*, *Nu.*, and *Rel.* denote span splitting, nuclearity determination, and relation classification, respectively. Micro F1 scores of RST Parseval (Marcu, 2000) are reported. Here gold EDU segmentation is used for baseline comparison.

2. We conducted label harmonization (Braud et al., 2017a) to uniform rhetorical definitions among different treebanks. The discourse trees were transformed into a binary format. Unlinked EUDs were removed. Following previous work, we reorganized the discourse relations to 18 categories, and attached the nuclearity labels (i.e., *Nucleus-Satellite* (NS), *Satellite-Nucleus* (SN), and *Nucleus-Nucleus* (NN)) to the relation labels (e.g., *Elaboration*, *Attribution*). For each language, we randomly extracted a set of samples for validation. The original training size was 1.1k, and became 6.7k with cross-translation augmentation. The sub-word tokenizer of the *'XLM-RoBERTa-base'* (Conneau et al., 2020) is used for input pre-processing.

## 4.2 Evaluation Metrics

For EDU segmentation evaluation, micro-averaged F1 score of token-level segment break classification as in (Muller et al., 2019) was used. For tree parsing evaluation, we applied the standard micro-averaged F1 scores on *Span* (**Sp.**), *Nuclearity-Satellite* (**Nu.**), and *Rhetorical Relation* (**Rel.**), where *Span* describes the accuracy of tree structure construction, *Nuclearity-Satellite* and *Rhetorical Relation* assesses the ability to categorize the nuclearity and the discourse relations, respectively. We also adopted *Full* to evaluate the overall performance considering both *Nuclearity-Satellite* and *Relation* together with *Span* as in (Morey et al., 2017). Following previous studies, we adopted the same 18 relations defined in (Carlson and Marcu, 2001). We reported the tree parsing scores in two metrics: the Original Parseval (Morey et al., 2017) and the RST Parseval (Marcu, 2000) for ease of comparison with previous studies.

## 4.3 Training Configuration

The proposed framework was implemented with PyTorch (Paszke et al., 2019) and Hugging Face (Wolf et al., 2019). We used *'XLM-RoBERTa-base'* (Conneau et al., 2020) as the language backbone, and fine-tuned its last 8 layers during training. Documents were processed with the sub-word tokenization scheme. The dropout rate of the language backbone was set to 0.2 and that of the rest layers was 0.5. AdamW (Kingma and Ba, 2015) optimization algorithm was used, with the initial learning rate of 2e-5 and a linear scheduler (decay ratio=0.9). Batch size was set to 12. We trained each model for 15 epochs, and selected the best checkpoints on the validation set for evaluation. For each round of evaluation, we repeated the training 5 times with different random seeds and averaged their scores. The

| Model | English (En) Sp. | Nu. | Rel. | Seg. | Portuguese (Pt) Sp. | Nu. | Rel. | Seg. | Spanish (Es) Sp. | Nu. | Rel. | Seg. |
|---|---|---|---|---|---|---|---|---|---|---|---|---|
| Original Parseval (Morey et al., 2017) | | | | | | | | | | | | |
| DMRST (Gold Seg.) | 76.7 | 66.2 | 56.5 | 100.0 | 72.5 | 61.8 | 53.1 | 100.0 | 79.2 | 70.3 | 57.1 | 100.0 |
| DMRST (Predicted Seg.) | **70.4** | **60.6** | **51.6** | **96.5** | **62.5** | **51.6** | **44.7** | **92.8** | **71.2** | **60.1** | **50.9** | **93.7** |
| w/o Cross Trans. (Predicted Seg.) | 70.3 | 60.4 | 51.3 | 96.4 | 65.3 | 53.6 | 46.3 | 93.7 | 70.2 | 59.3 | 51.1 | 93.7 |
| RST Parseval (Marcu, 2000) | | | | | | | | | | | | |
| DMRST (Gold Seg.) | 88.2 | 76.2 | 64.7 | 100.0 | 87.0 | 74.3 | 62.1 | 100.0 | 88.7 | 75.7 | 63.4 | 100.0 |
| DMRST (Predicted Seg.) | **83.2** | **71.1** | **60.5** | **96.5** | **77.8** | **64.9** | **53.2** | **92.8** | **79.5** | **67.4** | **56.7** | **93.7** |
| w/o Cross Trans. (Predicted Seg.) | 83.0 | 70.8 | 60.7 | 96.4 | 78.4 | 65.3 | 54.7 | 93.7 | 79.4 | 66.9 | 56.5 | 93.7 |

| Model | German (De) Sp. | Nu. | Rel. | Seg. | Dutch (Nl) Sp. | Nu. | Rel. | Seg. | Basque (Eu) Sp. | Nu. | Rel. | Seg. |
|---|---|---|---|---|---|---|---|---|---|---|---|---|
| Original Parseval (Morey et al., 2017) | | | | | | | | | | | | |
| DMRST (Gold Seg.) | 68.6 | 45.9 | 37.1 | 100.0 | 71.2 | 54.1 | 43.1 | 100.0 | 66.6 | 48.3 | 34.7 | 100.0 |
| DMRST (Predicted Seg.) | **58.1** | **40.1** | **32.3** | **95.1** | **62.3** | **46.6** | **39.4** | **95.5** | **53.3** | **39.1** | **31.2** | **88.7** |
| w/o Cross Trans. (Predicted Seg.) | 56.3 | 39.6 | 31.2 | 94.6 | 63.1 | 44.9 | 37.8 | 95.5 | 44.4 | 31.1 | 23.3 | 87.8 |
| RST Parseval (Marcu, 2000) | | | | | | | | | | | | |
| DMRST (Gold Seg.) | 84.3 | 64.1 | 47.3 | 100.0 | 85.6 | 66.3 | 52.3 | 100.0 | 85.1 | 67.2 | 48.3 | 100.0 |
| DMRST (Predicted Seg.) | **76.4** | **57.8** | **41.8** | **95.1** | **80.2** | **62.3** | **49.4** | **95.5** | **71.2** | **52.7** | **37.2** | **88.7** |
| w/o Cross Trans. (Predicted Seg.) | 75.4 | 57.0 | 41.1 | 94.6 | 80.1 | 61.9 | 48.3 | 95.5 | 66.0 | 47.5 | 33.0 | 87.8 |

Table 5: Multilingual parsing performance comparison of using gold and predicted EDU segmentation. *Sp.*, *Nu.*, *Rel.* and *Seg.* denote span splitting, nuclearity classification, relation determination, and segmentation, respectively. Micro F1 scores of RST Parseval (Marcu, 2000) and Original Parseval (Morey et al., 2017) are reported. Scores from the proposed framework are in bold for better readability.

total trainable parameter size was 91M, where 56M parameters were from fine-tuning *'XLM-RoBERTa-base'*. All experiments were run on a single Tesla A100 GPU with 40GB memory.

### 4.4 EDU Segmentation Results

EDU segmentation is the first step of discourse analysis from scratch, and its accuracy is important for the follow-up parsing steps. Thus in this section, we evaluate the performance of our boundary detection segmenter, and compare it with state-of-the-art document-level multilingual EDU segmenters (Braud et al., 2017b; Muller et al., 2019). Additionally, we implemented our model with a pointer mechanism (Vinyals et al., 2015; Li et al., 2018) as a control study.

From the results shown in Table 3, our segmenter outperforms baselines significantly in all languages. This potentially results from adopting the stronger contextualized language backbone (Conneau et al., 2020). Moreover, conducting EDU segmentation in a sequence labeling manner is more computationally efficient, and achieves higher scores than the pointer-based approach, which is consistent with the observation from a recent sentence-level study (Desai et al., 2020).

### 4.5 Multilingual Parsing Results

We compare the proposed framework with several strong RST parsing baselines: Yu et al. (2018) proposed a transition-based neural parser, obtaining competitive results in English. Iruskieta and Braud (2019) introduced a multilingual parser for 3 languages (English, Portuguese, and Spanish). Liu et al. (2020) proposed a multilingual parser that utilized cross-lingual representation (**Cross Rep.**), and adopted segment-level translation (**Segment Trans.**), and produced state-of-the-art results on 6 languages. Aside from the proposed model (**DMRST**), we added an ablation study on the cross-translation strategy (**DMRST w/o Cross Trans.**). In this section, we use the gold EDU segmentation during the inference stage for a fair comparison to the baselines.

| Model | Sp. | Nu. | Rel. | Full |
|---|---|---|---|---|
| (Zhang et al., 2020) | 62.3 | 50.1 | 40.7 | 39.6 |
| (Nguyen et al., 2021) | 68.4 | 59.1 | 47.8 | 46.6 |
| DMRST (only EN) | 69.8 | 59.4 | 49.4 | 48.6 |
| DMRST (Multilingual) | **70.4** | **60.6** | **51.6** | **50.1** |

Table 6: Performance comparison on the English RST treebank with predicted EDU segmentation.

From the results shown in Table 4: (1) Adopting multilingual pre-trained language backbone significantly boosts the RST parsing performance. (2) The multilingual model obtains further improvement with the cross-translation augmentation in all sub-tasks and languages. (3) All sub-tasks are improved substantially compared to previous mul-

| Model | Sp. | English (En) Nu. | Rel. | Seg. | Sp. | Portuguese (Pt) Nu. | Rel. | Seg. | Sp. | Spanish (Es) Nu. | Rel. | Seg. |
|---|---|---|---|---|---|---|---|---|---|---|---|---|
| Original Parseval (Morey et al., 2017) | | | | | | | | | | | | |
| DMRST w/o Cross Trans. | 36.9 | 26.2 | 17.8 | 78.4 | 39.2 | 29.5 | 23.1 | 80.9 | 40.0 | 33.0 | 26.4 | 76.6 |
| DMRST (Our Framework) | **43.9** | **30.8** | **23.3** | **82.7** | **44.7** | **35.8** | **28.9** | **83.7** | **48.1** | **36.8** | **29.5** | **82.2** |
| RST Parseval (Marcu, 2000) | | | | | | | | | | | | |
| DMRST w/o Cross Trans. | 57.8 | 40.7 | 27.0 | 78.4 | 60.4 | 44.4 | 31.8 | 80.9 | 58.1 | 42.8 | 28.3 | 76.6 |
| DMRST (Our Framework) | **63.4** | **46.5** | **30.2** | **82.7** | **64.5** | **50.0** | **37.7** | **83.7** | **65.2** | **49.3** | **34.3** | **82.2** |
| Model | Sp. | German (De) Nu. | Rel. | Seg. | Sp. | Dutch (Nl) Nu. | Rel. | Seg. | Sp. | Basque (Eu) Nu. | Rel. | Seg. |
| Original Parseval (Morey et al., 2017) | | | | | | | | | | | | |
| DMRST w/o Cross Trans. | 43.8 | 29.3 | 21.7 | 87.6 | 51.8 | 35.3 | 27.2 | 89.0 | 30.7 | 17.7 | 8.5 | 80.5 |
| DMRST (Our Framework) | **49.0** | **30.7** | **22.8** | **88.2** | **56.5** | **36.0** | **27.1** | **91.0** | **41.0** | **30.1** | **21.3** | **79.1** |
| RST Parseval (Marcu, 2000) | | | | | | | | | | | | |
| DMRST w/o Cross Trans. | 66.1 | 45.4 | 30.1 | 87.6 | 70.6 | 50.6 | 36.4 | 89.0 | 55.5 | 32.5 | 16.8 | 80.5 |
| DMRST (Our Framework) | **68.9** | **46.2** | **30.3** | **88.2** | **73.9** | **52.3** | **36.1** | **91.0** | **60.3** | **43.3** | **28.3** | **79.1** |

Table 7: Zero-shot performance comparison of models w/ and w/o cross-translation strategy. *Sp.*, *Nu.*, *Rel.* and *Seg.* denote span splitting, nuclearity classification, relation determination, and segmentation, respectively. Micro F1 scores of RST Parseval (Marcu, 2000) and Original Parseval (Morey et al., 2017) are reported.

tilingual baselines (Braud et al., 2017a; Liu et al., 2020). Moreover, our model also outperforms the state-of-the-art English RST parsers (see Table 6), demonstrating that fusing multilingual resources is beneficial for monolingual tasks.

### 4.6 Parsing from Scratch

In most previous work on RST parsing, EDU segmentation is regarded as a separate data preprocessing step, and the test samples with gold segmentation are used for evaluation. However, in practical cases, gold EDU segmentation is unavailable. Thus in this section, we assess the proposed framework with the predicted segmentation, simulating the real-world scenario. We compare our model **DMRST** to the model without cross-translation augmentation (**DMRST w/o Cross Trans.**). Aside from the common metric RST Parseval (Marcu, 2000) used in many prior studies, we also report test results on the Original Parseval (Morey et al., 2017).

From the results shown in Table 5, we observe that: (1) EDU segmentation performance of the two models are similar. This is likely because using lexical and syntactic information is sufficient to obtain a reasonable result. (2) For both metrics, our framework achieves overall better performance in all sub-tasks and languages, especially in the lower resource languages like Basque and Dutch. (3) Since the tree structure and nuclearity/relation classification are calculated on the EDU segments, their accuracy are affected significantly by the incorrect segment predictions. For instance, when gold segmentation is provided, *DMRST* outperforms *DMRST w/o Cross Trans.* at all fronts. However, the former produces slightly lower scores than the latter in Portuguese, due to its suboptimal segmentation accuracy (92.8 vs. 93.7). This also emphasizes the importance of EDU segmentation in a successful end-to-end RST parsing system.

## 5 Analysis on Zero-Shot Generalization

Incorporating discourse information is beneficial to various downstream NLP tasks, but only a small number of languages possess RST treebanks. Such treebanks have limited annotated samples, and it is difficult to extend their sample size due to annotation complexity. To examine if our proposed multilingual framework can be adopted to languages without any monolingual annotated sample (e.g., Italian, Polish), we conducted a zero-shot analysis via language-level cross validation.

In each round, we select one language as the target language, and RST treebanks from the remaining 5 languages are used to train the multilingual parser. We then evaluate it on the test set from the target language. For example, we assume that a small set of Portuguese articles is to be parsed, and we only have training samples from the other 5 languages (i.e., En, Es, De, Nl, and Eu). Then zero-shot inference is conducted on Portuguese. As shown in Table 7, compared with full training (see Table 5), all the zero-shot evaluation scores drop significantly, especially on English, since the

English corpus is the most resourceful and well-annotated RST treebank. Aside from English, the other 5 languages result in acceptable performance for zero-shot inference. With the cross-translation augmentation, the proposed multilingual discourse parser achieves higher scores, this is because (1) the text transformation helps language-level generalization, and (2) the mixed data have a larger domain coverage. For example, combining samples from Basque (science articles) with English (finance news) makes model perform better on Portuguese (science and news articles). This also suggests that the multilingual parser can be extended to other languages via cross-translation augmentation from existing treebanks of 6 languages.

## 6 Conclusions

In this work, we proposed a joint framework for document-level multilingual RST discourse parsing, which supports EDU segmentation as well as discourse tree parsing. Experimental results showed that the proposed framework achieves state-of-the-art performance on document-level multilingual discourse parsing on six languages in all aspects. We also demonstrated its inference capability when limited training data is available, and it can be readily extended to other languages.

## Acknowledgments

This research was supported by funding from the Institute for Infocomm Research (I2R) under A*STAR ARES, Singapore. We thank Ai Ti Aw for the insightful discussions and Chloé Braud for sharing linguistic resources. We also thank the anonymous reviewers for their precious feedback to help improve and extend this piece of work.

## References

Dzmitry Bahdanau, Kyunghyun Cho, and Yoshua Bengio. 2015. Neural machine translation by jointly learning to align and translate. In *3rd International Conference on Learning Representations, ICLR 2015, San Diego, CA, USA, May 7-9, 2015, Conference Track Proceedings*.

Parminder Bhatia, Yangfeng Ji, and Jacob Eisenstein. 2015. Better document-level sentiment analysis from RST discourse parsing. In *Proceedings of the 2015 Conference on Empirical Methods in Natural Language Processing*, pages 2212–2218, Lisbon, Portugal. Association for Computational Linguistics.

Chloé Braud, Maximin Coavoux, and Anders Søgaard. 2017a. Cross-lingual RST discourse parsing. In *Proceedings of the 15th Conference of the European Chapter of the Association for Computational Linguistics: Volume 1, Long Papers*, pages 292–304, Valencia, Spain. Association for Computational Linguistics.

Chloé Braud, Ophélie Lacroix, and Anders Søgaard. 2017b. Cross-lingual and cross-domain discourse segmentation of entire documents. In *Proceedings of the 55th Annual Meeting of the Association for Computational Linguistics (Volume 2: Short Papers)*, pages 237–243, Vancouver, Canada. Association for Computational Linguistics.

Paula CF Cardoso, Erick G Maziero, Mara Luca Castro Jorge, Eloize MR Seno, Ariani Di Felippo, Lucia Helena Machado Rino, Maria das Gracas Volpe Nunes, and Thiago AS Pardo. 2011. Cstnews-a discourse-annotated corpus for single and multi-document summarization of news texts in Brazilian Portuguese. In *Proceedings of the 3rd RST Brazilian Meeting*, pages 88–105.

Lynn Carlson and Daniel Marcu. 2001. Discourse tagging reference manual. *ISI Technical Report ISI-TR-545*, 54:56.

Lynn Carlson, Mary Ellen Okurowski, and Daniel Marcu. 2002. *RST discourse treebank*. Linguistic Data Consortium, University of Pennsylvania.

Kyunghyun Cho, Bart van Merriënboer, Caglar Gulcehre, Dzmitry Bahdanau, Fethi Bougares, Holger Schwenk, and Yoshua Bengio. 2014. Learning phrase representations using RNN encoder–decoder for statistical machine translation. In *Proceedings of the 2014 Conference on Empirical Methods in Natural Language Processing (EMNLP)*, pages 1724–1734, Doha, Qatar. Association for Computational Linguistics.

Sandra Collovini, Thiago I Carbonel, Juliana Thiesen Fuchs, Jorge César Coelho, Lúcia Rino, and Renata Vieira. 2007. Summ-it: Um corpus anotado com informaç oes discursivas visandoa sumarizaç ao automática. *Proceedings of TIL*.

Alexis Conneau, Kartikay Khandelwal, Naman Goyal, Vishrav Chaudhary, Guillaume Wenzek, Francisco Guzmán, Edouard Grave, Myle Ott, Luke Zettlemoyer, and Veselin Stoyanov. 2020. Unsupervised cross-lingual representation learning at scale. In *Proceedings of the Association for Computational Linguistics*. Association for Computational Linguistics.

Iria Da Cunha, Juan-Manuel Torres-Moreno, and Gerardo Sierra. 2011. On the development of the RST Spanish treebank. In *Proceedings of the 5th Linguistic Annotation Workshop*, pages 1–10.

Takshak Desai, Parag Pravin Dakle, and Dan Moldovan. 2020. Joint learning of syntactic features helps discourse segmentation. In *Proceedings of The 12th Language Resources and Evaluation Conference*, pages 1073–1080.

Jacob Devlin, Ming-Wei Chang, Kenton Lee, and Kristina Toutanova. 2019. BERT: Pre-training of deep bidirectional transformers for language understanding. In *Proceedings of the 2019 Conference of the North American Chapter of the Association for Computational Linguistics: Human Language Technologies, Volume 1 (Long and Short Papers)*, pages 4171–4186, Minneapolis, Minnesota. Association for Computational Linguistics.

Timothy Dozat and Christopher D. Manning. 2017. Deep biaffine attention for neural dependency parsing. In *5th International Conference on Learning Representations, ICLR 2017, Toulon, France, April 24-26, 2017, Conference Track Proceedings*.

Sergey Edunov, Myle Ott, Michael Auli, and David Grangier. 2018. Understanding back-translation at scale. In *Proceedings of the 2018 Conference on Empirical Methods in Natural Language Processing*, pages 489–500.

Yifan Gao, Chien-Sheng Wu, Jingjing Li, Shafiq Joty, Steven CH Hoi, Caiming Xiong, Irwin King, and Michael R Lyu. 2020. Discern: Discourse-aware entailment reasoning network for conversational machine reading. In *Proceedings of the 2020 Conference on Empirical Methods in Natural Language Processing*.

Michael Heilman and Kenji Sagae. 2015. Fast rhetorical structure theory discourse parsing. *arXiv preprint arXiv:1505.02425*.

Hugo Hernault, Helmut Prendinger, Mitsuru Ishizuka, et al. 2010. Hilda: A discourse parser using support vector machine classification. *Dialogue & Discourse*, 1(3).

Mikel Iruskieta, Marıa J Aranzabe, Arantza Diaz de Ilarraza, Itziar Gonzalez, Mikel Lersundi, and Oier Lopez de Lacalle. 2013. The RST Basque treebank: an online search interface to check rhetorical relations. In *4th workshop RST and discourse studies*, pages 40–49.

Mikel Iruskieta and Chloé Braud. 2019. EusDisParser: improving an under-resourced discourse parser with cross-lingual data. In *Proceedings of the Workshop on Discourse Relation Parsing and Treebanking 2019*, pages 62–71, Minneapolis, MN. Association for Computational Linguistics.

Diederik P Kingma and Jimmy Ba. 2015. Adam: A method for stochastic optimization. In *Proceedings of the 3rd International Conference for Learning Representations*.

Jing Li, Aixin Sun, and Shafiq Joty. 2018. Segbot: A generic neural text segmentation model with pointer network. In *Proceedings of the 27th International Joint Conference on Artificial Intelligence and the 23rd European Conference on Artificial Intelligence*, IJCAI-ECAI-2018, Stockholm, Sweden.

Qi Li, Tianshi Li, and Baobao Chang. 2016. Discourse parsing with attention-based hierarchical neural networks. In *Proceedings of the 2016 Conference on Empirical Methods in Natural Language Processing*, pages 362–371.

Sujian Li, Liang Wang, Ziqiang Cao, and Wenjie Li. 2014. Text-level discourse dependency parsing. In *Proceedings of the 52nd Annual Meeting of the Association for Computational Linguistics (Volume 1: Long Papers)*, pages 25–35.

Xiang Lin, Shafiq Joty, Prathyusha Jwalapuram, and M Saiful Bari. 2019. A unified linear-time framework for sentence-level discourse parsing. In *Proceedings of the 57th Annual Meeting of the Association for Computational Linguistics*, pages 4190–4200, Florence, Italy. Association for Computational Linguistics.

Shikun Liu, Edward Johns, and Andrew J Davison. 2019. End-to-end multi-task learning with attention. In *Proceedings of the IEEE Conference on Computer Vision and Pattern Recognition*, pages 1871–1880.

Zhengyuan Liu and Nancy Chen. 2019. Exploiting discourse-level segmentation for extractive summarization. In *Proceedings of the 2nd Workshop on New Frontiers in Summarization*, pages 116–121, Hong Kong, China. Association for Computational Linguistics.

Zhengyuan Liu, Ke Shi, and Nancy Chen. 2020. Multilingual neural RST discourse parsing. In *Proceedings of the 28th International Conference on Computational Linguistics*, pages 6730–6738, Barcelona, Spain (Online). International Committee on Computational Linguistics.

William C Mann and Sandra A Thompson. 1988. Rhetorical structure theory: Toward a functional theory of text organization. *Text-interdisciplinary Journal for the Study of Discourse*, 8(3):243–281.

Daniel Marcu. 2000. The rhetorical parsing of unrestricted texts: A surface-based approach. *Computational linguistics*, 26(3):395–448.

Mathieu Morey, Philippe Muller, and Nicholas Asher. 2017. How much progress have we made on RST discourse parsing? a replication study of recent results on the RST-DT. In *Proceedings of the 2017 Conference on Empirical Methods in Natural Language Processing*, pages 1319–1324, Copenhagen, Denmark. Association for Computational Linguistics.

Philippe Muller, Chloé Braud, and Mathieu Morey. 2019. ToNy: Contextual embeddings for accurate multilingual discourse segmentation of full documents. In *Proceedings of the Workshop on Discourse Relation Parsing and Treebanking 2019*, pages 115–124, Minneapolis, MN. Association for Computational Linguistics.

Thanh-Tung Nguyen, Xuan-Phi Nguyen, Shafiq Joty, and Xiaoli Li. 2021. RST parsing from scratch. In *Proceedings of the 2021 Conference of the North American Chapter of the Association for Computational Linguistics: Human Language Technologies*, pages 1613–1625, Online. Association for Computational Linguistics.

Thiago Alexandre Salgueiro Pardo and Eloize Rossi Marques Seno. 2005. Rhetalho: um corpus de referência anotado retoricamente. *Anais do V Encontro de Corpora*, pages 24–25.

Thiago AS Pardo and Maria das Graças Volpe Nunes. 2004. Relações retóricas e seus marcadores superficiais: Análise de um corpus de textos científicos em português do brasil. *Relatório Técnico NILC*.

Adam Paszke, Sam Gross, Francisco Massa, Adam Lerer, James Bradbury, Gregory Chanan, Trevor Killeen, Zeming Lin, Natalia Gimelshein, Luca Antiga, et al. 2019. Pytorch: An imperative style, high-performance deep learning library. In *Advances in Neural Information Processing Systems*, pages 8024–8035.

Rashmi Prasad, Nikhil Dinesh, Alan Lee, Eleni Miltsakaki, Livio Robaldo, Aravind Joshi, and Bonnie Webber. 2008. The Penn Discourse TreeBank 2.0. In *Proceedings of the Sixth International Conference on Language Resources and Evaluation (LREC'08)*, Marrakech, Morocco. European Language Resources Association (ELRA).

Gisela Redeker, Ildikó Berzlánovich, Nynke Van Der Vliet, Gosse Bouma, and Markus Egg. 2012. Multi-layer discourse annotation of a Dutch text corpus. *age*, 1:2.

Kenji Sagae. 2009. Analysis of discourse structure with syntactic dependencies and data-driven shift-reduce parsing. In *Proceedings of the 11th International Conference on Parsing Technologies*, pages 81–84. Association for Computational Linguistics.

Ke Shi, Zhengyuan Liu, and Nancy F Chen. 2020. An end-to-end document-level neural discourse parser exploiting multi-granularity representations. *arXiv preprint arXiv:2012.11169*.

Manfred Stede and Arne Neumann. 2014. Potsdam commentary corpus 2.0: Annotation for discourse research. In *LREC*, pages 925–929.

Oriol Vinyals, Meire Fortunato, and Navdeep Jaitly. 2015. Pointer networks. In *Advances in neural information processing systems*, pages 2692–2700.

Thomas Wolf, Lysandre Debut, Victor Sanh, Julien Chaumond, Clement Delangue, Anthony Moi, Pierric Cistac, Tim Rault, R'emi Louf, Morgan Funtowicz, and Jamie Brew. 2019. Huggingface's transformers: State-of-the-art natural language processing. *ArXiv*, abs/1910.03771.

Nan Yu, Meishan Zhang, and Guohong Fu. 2018. Transition-based neural RST parsing with implicit syntax features. In *Proceedings of the 27th International Conference on Computational Linguistics*, pages 559–570.

Longyin Zhang, Yuqing Xing, Fang Kong, Peifeng Li, and Guodong Zhou. 2020. A top-down neural architecture towards text-level parsing of discourse rhetorical structure. In *Proceedings of the 58th Annual Meeting of the Association for Computational Linguistics*, pages 6386–6395, Online. Association for Computational Linguistics.

# Visualizing Cross-Lingual Discourse Relations in Multilingual TED Corpora

Zae Myung Kim[1,3], Vassilina Nikoulina[1], Dongyeop Kang[2], Didier Schwab[3], Laurent Besacier[1]
[1]NAVER LABS Europe
[2]University of Minnesota
[3]Univ. Grenoble Alpes, CNRS, LIG
{zae-myung.kim,vassilina.nikoulina,laurent.besacier}@naverlabs.com
dongyeop@umn.edu
didier.schwab@univ-grenoble-alpes.fr

## Abstract

This paper presents an interactive data dashboard that provides users with an overview of the preservation of discourse relations among 28 language pairs. We display a graph network depicting the cross-lingual discourse relations between a pair of languages for multilingual TED talks and provide a search function to look for sentences with specific keywords or relation types, facilitating ease of analysis on the cross-lingual discourse relations.

## 1 Introduction

Discourse relations in texts describe how two discourse segments–which can be phrases, sentences, or even paragraphs–are connected logically to each other. For example, given the following two sentences, *"I have cooked some pasta."* and *"I am hungry."*, we may infer that the latter is a `cause` for the former, in which case, the discourse relation between them can be classified as an `implicit causation`.[1] Now, when we translate these sentences into another language, the grammar and pragmatics of that language may prefer a certain discourse relation over the others that may not be the same as that of the original language. For example, in the case of Korean, which is an agglutinative language, the heavy usage of Korean postpositions (particles) dictates that the `causal` relation in the above example is revealed `explicitly` (regardless of the usage of explicit discourse connectives).

Such a cross-lingual discourse analysis can provide some insights for improving the quality of (machine) translation (Meyer and Webber, 2013; Meyer and Poláková, 2013; Guzmán et al., 2014; Iruskieta et al., 2015; Chen et al., 2020). This paper presents an interactive system that visualizes the cross-lingual discourse relations using two human-annotated multilingual discourse datasets (Zeyrek et al., 2019; Long et al., 2020) derived from TED talks following the Penn Discourse Treebank (PDTB) (Prasad et al., 2008) framework. Our interactive data dashboard provides users with an overview of relation preservation among all language pairs. We also display a graph network depicting the cross-lingual discourse relations between a pair of languages for a given TED talk, and provide a search function to find sentences with specific query or relation types. We believe that, with this visualization tool, users can easily browse through the multilingual talks and discover which parts of the talks share similar discourse relations, and where they diverge.

## 2 Preprocessing Datasets

We abbreviate the two discourse-annotated datasets, Zeyrek et al. (2019) and Long et al. (2020), as `TED-Mult` and `TED-ZH`, respectively. `TED-Mult` involves seven languages (English, German, Lithuanian, Polish, Portuguese, Russian, and Turkish); and `TED-ZH`, two languages (English and Chinese). Thus, our analysis is conducted across the 28 possible language pairs.

In order to facilitate cross-lingual analysis, we first performed sentence level alignment using a sentence segmentation tool[2] based on conditional random fields and a set of heuristic rules. We note that the reason for using this particular tool is that it guarantees the reconstruction of original texts when segmented sentences are joined together; and that it supports custom regex-based rules to add to allowlist or denylist if need be.

Once the TED talk scripts for all eight languages were segmented into sentence level, we cross-lingually matched the English sentences with sentences from other languages by the following procedure:

1. Using a multilingual Sentence-BERT model

[1]It is *implicit* because these sentences are not connected with an explicit discourse marker such as *"Because"*.

[2]`https://github.com/zaemyung/sentsplit`



*Proceedings of the 2nd Workshop on Computational Approaches to Discourse*, pages 165–170
November 10–11, 2021. 

| | Sentences | Annotations | | Relation Types | | | | | Level-1 Senses | | | | |
|---|---|---|---|---|---|---|---|---|---|---|---|---|---|
| | | Intra. | Inter. | Exp. | Imp. | AltLex | EntRel | NoRel | Temp. | Cont. | Comp. | Exp. | Other |
| Chinese | 173 | 217 | 163 | 135 | 122 | 46 | 46 | 27 | 40 | 88 | 49 | 126 | 0 |
| English | 397 | 314 | 365 | 299 | 202 | 48 | 81 | 49 | 44 | 133 | 73 | 288 | 10 |
| German | 408 | 186 | 379 | 242 | 216 | 18 | 59 | 30 | 31 | 119 | 57 | 260 | 9 |
| Lithuanian | 403 | 385 | 370 | 379 | 246 | 18 | 79 | 33 | 46 | 167 | 82 | 339 | 9 |
| Polish | 430 | 198 | 380 | 217 | 200 | 5 | 104 | 52 | 43 | 108 | 82 | 183 | 6 |
| Portuguese | 386 | 271 | 358 | 272 | 256 | 30 | 38 | 33 | 54 | 139 | 71 | 287 | 7 |
| Russian | 408 | 179 | 386 | 237 | 221 | 20 | 57 | 30 | 30 | 111 | 56 | 269 | 12 |
| Turkish | 424 | 332 | 408 | 336 | 213 | 67 | 72 | 52 | 41 | 162 | 75 | 330 | 7 |

Table 1: Table of corpora statistics for `TED-Mult` and `TED-ZH`.

(Reimers and Gurevych, 2019, 2020), fixed-size sentence embeddings were computed for all sentences of the eight languages.

2. In addition, non-English sentences were machine-translated into English, and their English sentence embeddings were computed using a monolingual English Sentence-BERT model.
3. For each TED talk, cosine similarity scores were computed between English and non-English sentences using the multilingual sentences embeddings, and also the monolingual sentence embeddings, separately.
4. Similarly, chrF scores (Popović, 2015) were computed between the English and the machine-translated (English) sentences.
5. We note that all of these scores were calculated for a fixed-size window of sentences as the cross-lingual sentences should be within a close range to each other.
6. Each type of scores was computed in both direction, i.e., `English` to `Lang.X` and `Lang.X` to `English`, and only their intersection of matched groups was kept.
7. Finally, the three types of scores were filtered by empirically defined thresholds and majority voting was used to pick the final matching groups of cross-lingual sentences for `Lang.X:English` pair for each TED document.

When aligning two non-English documents (`Lang.X:Lang.Y`), we used the alignments with the English (`Lang.X:English` and `Lang.Y:English`) as a pivot to cross-lingually match them.

To ensure the quality of the resulting alignments, we checked and revised each of them manually. We note that the manual correction was seldom required.

In total, we used seven cross-lingual talks from `TED-Mult` and four talks from `TED-ZH`, which are aligned with other languages. Overall, there are about 400 sentences per language, and Table 1 shows more details on the corpora statistics.

| Level-1 | Level-2 | Level-3 |
|---|---|---|
| Temporal | Synchronous | - |
| | Asynchronous | Precedence<br>Succession |
| Contingency | Cause | Reason<br>Result<br>Neg. Result |
| | Cause+Belief | Reason+Belief<br>Result+Belief |
| | Cause+Speech Act | Reason+Speech Act<br>Result+Speech Act |
| | Condition | Arg1-as-Cond<br>Arg2-as-Cond |
| | Condition+Speech Act | - |
| | Negative-Condition | Arg1-as-Neg. Cond<br>Arg2-as-Neg. Cond |
| | Negative-Condition+ Speech Act | - |
| | Purpose | Arg1-as-Goal<br>Arg2-as-Goal |
| Comparison | Concession | Arg1-as-Denier<br>Arg2-as-Denier |
| | Concession+Speech Act | Arg2-as-Denier+Speech Act |
| | Contrast | - |
| | Similarity | - |
| Expansion | Conjunction | - |
| | Disjunction | - |
| | Equivalence | - |
| | Exception | Arg1-as-Excpt<br>Arg2-as-Excpt |
| | Instantiation | Arg1-as-Instance<br>Arg2-as-Instance |
| | Level-of-Detail | Arg1-as-Detail<br>Arg2-as-Detail |
| | Manner | Arg1-as-Manner<br>Arg2-as-Manner |
| | Substitution | Arg1-as-Subst<br>Arg2-as-Subst |

Table 2: Table of PDTB-3's hierarchical senses. In this paper, we consider up to the level-2 senses.

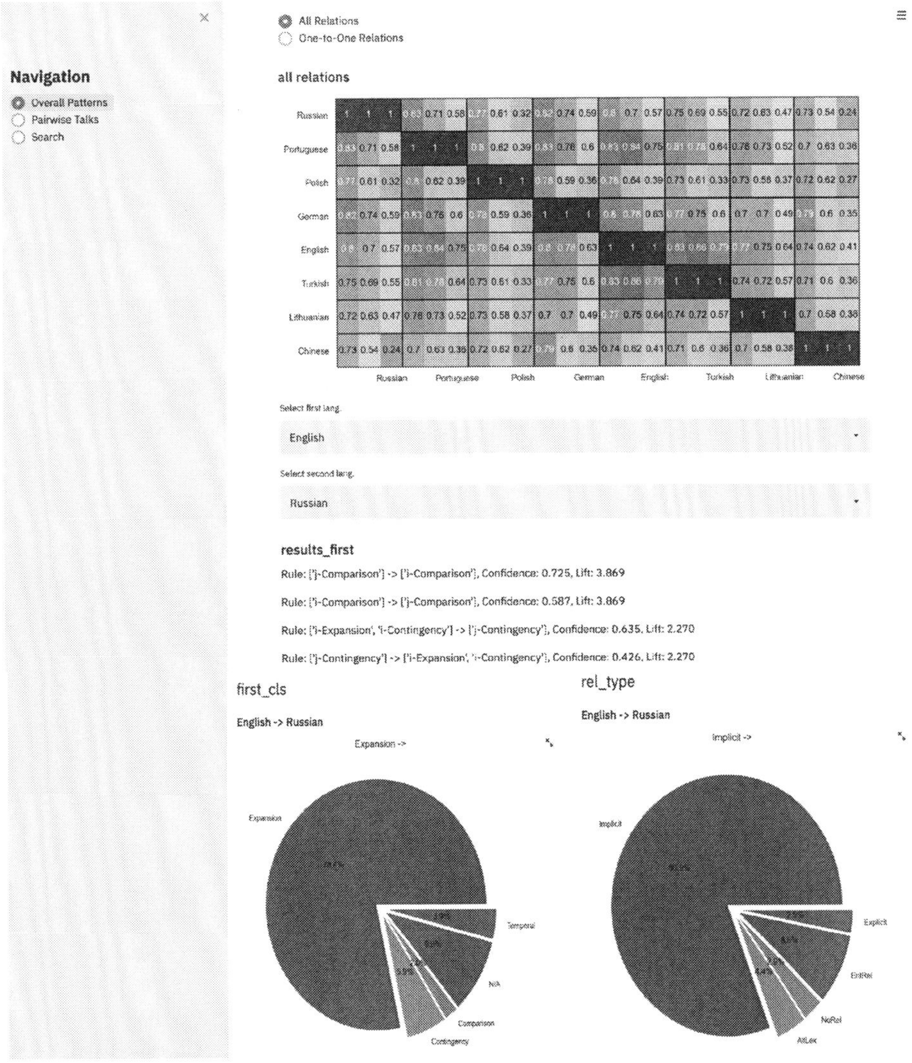


Figure 1: A screenshot showing the *"Overall Patterns"* of discourse relations among language pairs.

## 3 System Description

Our system is implemented using *Streamlit*[3] which is an open-source web application framework in Python. The aligned dataset with codes[4] and the demo system[5] are available online.

The system is organized into three sections, *"Overall Patterns"*, *"Pairwise Talks"*, and *"Search"*, where each section can be accessed via a navigation panel on the left-hand side.

### 3.1 Overall Patterns

In PDTB-3 framework, a discourse relation is represented by four components: relation type, level-1, 2, and 3 senses. As shown in Table 2, each subsequent sense level contains more fine-grained classes for the previous level, and we consider up to level-2 senses in our system.

The overall pattern in the preservation of cross-lingual discourse relations is depicted in a heatmap shown in Figure 1. We compute how many relations are exactly matched across the language pairs, considering relation type and levels of senses. For each language pair, from left to right, each cell denotes the accuracy of matching (1) relation type (implicit or explicit); (2) level-1 senses; and (3) level-1 and 2 senses jointly. The accuracy of rela-

[3] `https://streamlit.io/`

[4] `https://github.com/zaemyung/Visualizing-Cross-Lingual-Discourse-Relations`

[5] `https://share.streamlit.io/zaemyung/visualizing-cross-lingual-discourse-relations/main/main.py`

Figure 2: A screenshot showing the cross-lingual relation network graph of *"Pairwise Talks"*.

tions for cross-lingual alignments is computed as: $\frac{2*|I \cap J|}{|I|+|J|}$, where $I$ and $J$ are the set of corresponding relations for each alignment pair.

We observe that the relation type and level-1 senses are quite well matched across the language pairs, averaging 77% and 68%, respectively. The accuracy scores drop when we compare more fine-grained level-2 senses (48%).[6]

We note that, while the scores for Figure 1, were computed considering both the intra- and inter-sentential relations, it is possible to conduct the computation separately as well.

Below the heatmap, we have the top-scoring rules mined from association rule mining (Agrawal et al., 1993) where the algorithm is applied to a collection of language-specific occurrences of relations for a given language pair. While most of the rules learned are "identity" (same discourse relation preserved across language pairs), there are some interesting non-identical rules as well. For example, it is often observed that with high confidence (0.59), level-1 sense `Contingency` for Russian co-occurs with level-1 sense `Expansion` for English.[7]

At the end of the page, we present pie charts that illustrate the proportion of each relation type and level-1 and -2 senses of a source language being transferred to that of a target language, showing more fine-grained information than the heatmap. For example, in Figure 1, the left pie chart for the level-1 senses (`fist_cls`) depicts that the English's `Expansion` sense is mostly preserved (78.4%) in the corresponding Russian sentences. Similarly, the right pie chart shows that the English's `Implicit` relation type is kept the same in the Russian sentences 80.9% of the time across all talks.

These analyses on overall patterns can show how and where the discourse relations are preserved or diverged cross-lingually. From observations, we speculate about some of the causes for the divergence to be as follows: (1) The grammar and pragmatics of one language may favor the usage of one discourse relation over the other. (2) In some cases, especially when a discourse relation is `Implicit`, more than one relation could be possible. For

[6]We note that the avg. F1 score of matching Rhetorical Structure Theory (RST) relations across English, Spanish and Basque is 55% (Iruskieta et al., 2015).

[7]Both *confidence* and *lift* are two useful concepts in association rule mining that select interesting rules from the set of all possible rules. Given a rule, $A \rightarrow B$, the former (ranging from 0 to 1) computes the probability of seeing the consequent in a transaction given that it also contains the antecedent; the latter (ranging from 0 to $\infty$), measures how much more often the antecedent and consequent of the rule occur jointly than if they were statistically independent ($lift = 1.0$).

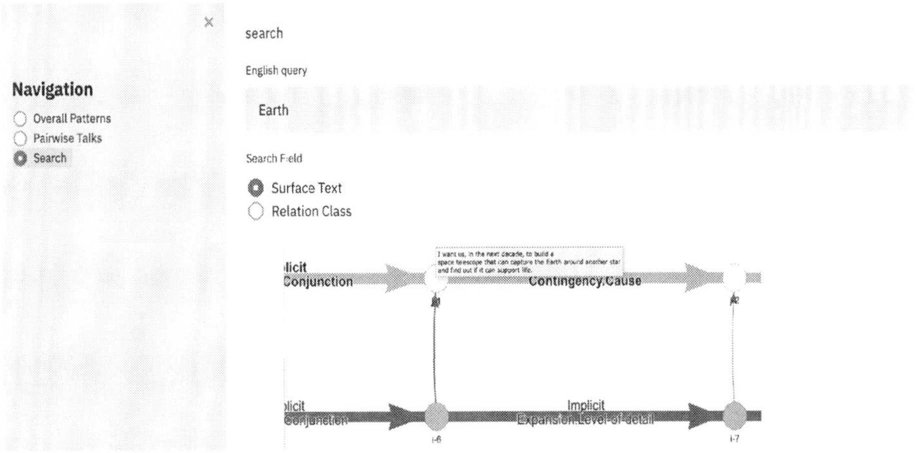


Figure 3: A screenshot showing the results of *"Search"* function where a sentence containing a specific English query is returned along its immediate neighboring sentences.

example, we often observed cases where the `Implicit.Expansion.Conjunction` and `Implicit.Comparison.Concession` relations were quite similar to each other.[8]

## 3.2 Pairwise Talks

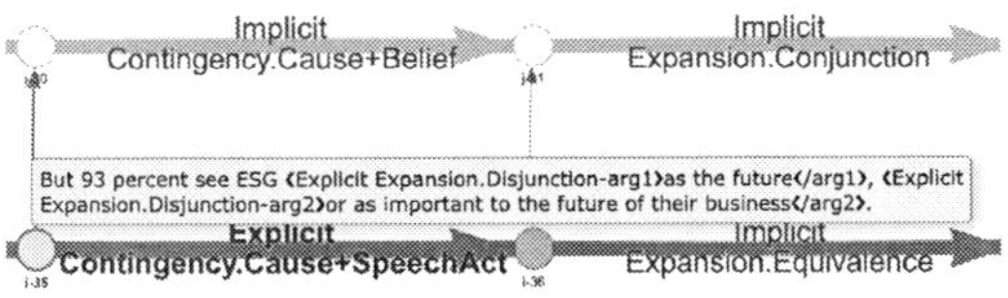


Figure 4: A screenshot showing an intra-sentential relation within a node.

For each TED talk and a pair of source and target languages, an interactive graph network is rendered to show cross-lingual discourse relations (Figure 2). A node in the graph represents a sentence, while an edge depicts inter-sentential discourse relation between two nodes. In the graph of the screenshot, the orange graph represents the discourse graph for the first five sentences in the Russian document, while the blue one shows that of the English counterpart. The vertical line between the two discourse graphs indicates cross-lingual sentence alignment. We note that the context window of the generated graph can be adjusted by the *Lower index* and *Upper index* sliders, in the case of really long TED talks where, otherwise, the resulting graph would be too large to render efficiently.

With this graph representation, we can easily view which nodes share similar cross-lingual discourse relations. For example, in the screenshot, we observe that the second relation between the second and third sentences is `Implicit.Expansion.Conjunction` for Russian and `Implicit.Expansion.Level-of-detail` for English. In this case, for both languages, the relation types and level-1 senses are `Implicit` and `Expansion`, respectively, while the level-2 senses are different (`Conjunction` versus `Level-of-detail`). In addition, by clicking on the node, we can observe any intra-sentential discourse relation present in the node by tagged spans in texts as illustrated in Figure 4.

## 3.3 Search

Users can look for a set of sentences that contain specific keywords or certain discourse relations on the *"Search"* page as displayed in Figure 3. Currently, the search is based on an English keyword, and it retrieves all the other multilingual sentences that are cross-lingually aligned with the English ones containing the keyword. The results include both the previous and the subsequent neighboring sentences to show the context around the query sentence.

# 4 Conclusion

We presented an interactive system that visualizes the cross-lingual discourse relations among multilingual TED talks, along with other related statistics. As future work, we plan to integrate an online multilingual discourse parser and a multilingual machine translation model into the system so that users can translate and analyze any given document and its translation on the fly.

[8]These kinds of issues were resolved via majority voting or discussion when creating the annotated datasets by their respective authors.

## References


Rakesh Agrawal, Tomasz Imieliński, and Arun Swami. 1993. Mining association rules between sets of items in large databases. In *Proceedings of the 1993 ACM SIGMOD international conference on Management of data*, pages 207–216.

Junxuan Chen, Xiang Li, Jiarui Zhang, Chulun Zhou, Jianwei Cui, Bin Wang, and Jinsong Su. 2020. Modeling discourse structure for document-level neural machine translation. In *Proceedings of the First Workshop on Automatic Simultaneous Translation*, pages 30–36, Seattle, Washington. Association for Computational Linguistics.

Francisco Guzmán, Shafiq Joty, Lluís Màrquez, and Preslav Nakov. 2014. Using discourse structure improves machine translation evaluation. In *Proceedings of the 52nd Annual Meeting of the Association for Computational Linguistics (Volume 1: Long Papers)*, pages 687–698, Baltimore, Maryland. Association for Computational Linguistics.

Mikel Iruskieta, Iria Da Cunha, and Maite Taboada. 2015. A qualitative comparison method for rhetorical structures: identifying different discourse structures in multilingual corpora. *Language resources and evaluation*, 49(2):263–309.

Wanqiu Long, Xinyi Cai, James Reid, Bonnie Webber, and Deyi Xiong. 2020. Shallow discourse annotation for Chinese TED talks. In *Proceedings of the 12th Language Resources and Evaluation Conference*, pages 1025–1032, Marseille, France. European Language Resources Association.

Thomas Meyer and Lucie Poláková. 2013. Machine translation with many manually labeled discourse connectives. In *Proceedings of the Workshop on Discourse in Machine Translation*, pages 43–50, Sofia, Bulgaria. Association for Computational Linguistics.

Thomas Meyer and Bonnie Webber. 2013. Implicitation of discourse connectives in (machine) translation. In *Proceedings of the Workshop on Discourse in Machine Translation*, pages 19–26, Sofia, Bulgaria. Association for Computational Linguistics.

Maja Popović. 2015. chrF: character n-gram F-score for automatic MT evaluation. In *Proceedings of the Tenth Workshop on Statistical Machine Translation*, pages 392–395, Lisbon, Portugal. Association for Computational Linguistics.

Rashmi Prasad, Nikhil Dinesh, Alan Lee, Eleni Miltsakaki, Livio Robaldo, Aravind Joshi, and Bonnie Webber. 2008. The Penn Discourse TreeBank 2.0. In *Proceedings of the Sixth International Conference on Language Resources and Evaluation (LREC'08)*, Marrakech, Morocco. European Language Resources Association (ELRA).

Nils Reimers and Iryna Gurevych. 2019. Sentence-bert: Sentence embeddings using siamese bert-networks. In *Proceedings of the 2019 Conference on Empirical Methods in Natural Language Processing*. Association for Computational Linguistics.

Nils Reimers and Iryna Gurevych. 2020. Making monolingual sentence embeddings multilingual using knowledge distillation. In *Proceedings of the 2020 Conference on Empirical Methods in Natural Language Processing*. Association for Computational Linguistics.

Deniz Zeyrek, Amália Mendes, Yulia Grishina, Murathan Kurfalı, Samuel Gibbon, and Maciej Ogrodniczuk. 2019. Ted multilingual discourse bank (ted-mdb): A parallel corpus annotated in the pdtb style. *Language Resources and Evaluation*, pages 1–27.

**Association for Computational Linguistics**
209 N. Eighth Street
Stroudsburg, Pennsylvania 18360

ISBN 978-1-7138-9184-0

CURRAN ASSOCIATES INC.
proceedings.com